girls

Feminine Adolescence

in Popular Culture

& Cultural Theory

girls

Catherine Driscoll

Columbia University Press   New York

Columbia University Press
New York
Publishers Since 1893
New York   Chichester, West Sussex
Copyright © 2002 Columbia University Press
All rights reserved

Library of Congress Cataloging-in-Publication Data
Driscoll, Catherine.
    Girls : feminine adolescence in popular culture and
cultural theory / Catherine Driscoll.
       p. cm.
    Includes bibliographical references and index.
    ISBN 0–231–11912–7 (cloth) — ISBN 0–231–11913–5
(pbk.)
    1. Teenage girls. 2. Teenage girls—Public opinion.
3. Girls in popular culture. 4. Girls in literature. I. Title.
    HQ798 .D75 2002
    305.235—dc21
2001047331

Printed in the United States of America
Designed by Lisa Hamm
c 10 9 8 7 6 5 4 3 2 1
p 10 9 8 7 6 5 4 3 2 1

Contents

Acknowledgments

PARTS OF THIS BOOK have previously appeared, though in very different forms, as: "Becoming Bride" in *UTS Review* (1998); "Cybergurls, Riot Grrls, Spice Girls: Girl Culture, Revenge and Global Capitalism," in *Australian Feminist Studies* (1999); "Girl Culture; or, Why Study the Spice Girls" in Hosking and Schwerdt, eds., *eXtensions* (Wakefield Press, 1999); and *In Visible Bodies*, an occasional paper published by the Women's Studies Centre at Monash University (1996). The book also draws on material published as "The Little Girl" in *Antithesis* (1997) and reprinted in Genosko, ed., *Deleuze and Guattari: Critical Assessments* (Routledge, 2001); "The Woman in Process: Deleuze, Kristeva and Feminism," in Buchanan and Colebrook, eds., *Deleuze and Feminist Theory* (University of Edinburgh Press, 2000); and "Who Needs a Boyfriend?: The Homoerotic Virgin in Adolescent Women's Magazines," in English and van Toorn, eds., *Speaking Positions* (Victoria University of Technology, 1996).

For permission to reprint images in this book I am grateful to Tobi Vail and Kill Rock Stars (Bikini Kill), Jamie Hewlett, House and Moorhouse Productions, Tracey Moffatt (and Roslyn Oxley Galleries), Oxford University Press, FilmFour Inc., the Italian Ministry for Cultural Artefacts and

Activities, Kodansha Ltd., Mariana Hardwick, and Fox Television. This book would have taken far longer to complete without grants from the Faculty of Humanities and Social Sciences at Adelaide University, and the Australian Research Council.

This book is indebted to many people. I warmly appreciate the generosity of my colleagues at Adelaide University. The entire staff of the Department of English helped this book appear with their encouragement and support. Particular thanks for making it happen in this form (though yes, its problems are all mine) go to my research assistant, Daniel Marshall, and the editors at Columbia University Press, including Jennifer Barager, Jennifer Crewe, and Susan Heath.

For important guidance and support I want to thank David Bennett, Meaghan Morris, Ken Ruthven, and Joan Wallach Scott. I am also deeply grateful for many important and stimulating friendships—thanks to Ian Buchanan, Marion Campbell, Judith Fielsen, Ros Harris, Doug Henwood, Belinda Johnston, Heather Kerr, Oona Leary, Susan Magarey, Lyn McRedden, Lesley McDowell, Mark Mitchell, Sara Murphy, Deborah Staines, Patrick West, and Craig Williams. I owe special gratitude to Karen Gai Dean, for years of being there with new perspectives.

Nothing in this book escapes a debt to my family in its many forms. Thanks to Bill Driscoll, Judith Driscoll, Rowan Driscoll, Neville Wylde Sheather, and the rest of the Sheather family, Norman Talbot, and Ruth Talbot-Stokes. To my son, Sean, deepest thanks and admiration. And, finally, this book is dedicated with love and gratitude to my grandmother Ada Florence Sheather, who knows things about girls.

List of Illustrations

girls

Introduction:
Toward a Genealogy of Girlhood

An "age" does not pre-exist the statements which express it, nor the visibilities which fill it.

—Gilles Deleuze, *Foucault*

MY GRANDMOTHER tells me "You're not a little girl any more." This is *menarche*. She asks me if I know what it is and I nod (quickly), but what I mostly know is that "it" is embarrassing and inconvenient. I'm not sure how I feel about not being a little girl any more; possibly I am happy about that. But if I am not sure exactly how different I became today it is clear that I am still a girl in some important ways—as in "There's plenty of time for that kind of thing later." "That kind of thing" includes: "boys," though I see boys every day; staying up late or going out at night; makeup and jewelry; and getting my own way about things like clothes, hairstyles and underwear, music, friends, subject choices, and my bedroom—just the kind of things that *the book* tells me "girls" (as distinct from little girls) are especially interested in. In fact it seems in *the book* that being interested in or needing these things is part of what defines me as a girl.

The book is one my grandmother gives me to read about puberty, sex, childbirth, and masturbation (in that order), and it tells me that I am now a young woman. It tells me to be proud of that in the rather ominous context of warnings about the physical and emotional distresses of being a girl-becoming-a-woman, as well as the difficulty of successfully getting through girlhood as the right kind of woman. The point at which I will stop being a girl is even less clear to me, but I know it has to happen. Girls should grow up.

In my mid-thirties I am not a girl any longer, in most senses of the word. And yet I might still be called a girl and use the word "girl" about myself, especially among women around my own age. Moreover, I remain socially connected to, interested in, and sometimes still strongly identify with "girl" things, "girl" behaviors, and experience of girlhood. This connection remains because girlhood seems something I have experienced, even if it is only my own experience rather than access to any essential girlhood, and even if it doesn't seem truly to have been completed. I'm still not sure when I stopped being a girl, if I did.

It seems self-evident that girls are female children, or young women. But this self-evident understanding raises a number of questions. When speaking to or of girls as female children or as young women, do these two understandings actually mean the same thing, and how are they defined? When we call an older woman a "girl," are we really evoking characteristics of childhood or youth? And what does it mean for girls that girlhood is a stage to be passed through on the way to something else—mostly to "being a woman." While it seems every woman has been a girl and every female child is one, it is not clear what this means given, for example, the differences between my own and my grandmother's ideas of what a girl is, or given the necessity and importance of mediation between us of what girlhood means.

Girls, young women, and feminine adolescents were highly visible in twentieth-century Western cultures—mostly as a marker of immature and malleable identity, and as a publicly preeminent image of desirability. This book considers the significance of girls to the period often called late modernity (the period of mass commodity production) that spans the late-nineteenth to early-twenty-first centuries, extending some decades either side of my grandmother's girlhood and my own. The modern in this sense means modernity as opposed to the classical period, modernity being understood as the period of Western history that focuses on "the person" as the knowing center of the world, the period usually thought to begin with the eighteenth-century philosophies referred to as the Enlightenment. Across the broad span of modernity, girls and young women seem to have become increasingly visible in public life and taken increasingly diverse public roles. Looking at the range of positions allocated to girls in the Westernized and globalized twentieth century, I want to consider how girls have functioned as an index of broad cultural changes and continuities.

Girls have been the object of many critical and popular studies that reflect their visibility in the late modern world. This book is designed to add to these existing studies a history of the category "feminine adolescence," an idea that generated new meanings for girlhood in the twentieth century. In part it is a history, a map of what girls have meant to late modernity, but it also focuses on how we understand girls, and for this reason I also want to focus on what is now called Cultural Studies, as the discourse most likely to consider girls' involvement in the production of the world that defines them. Before anything else, however, it will be useful to introduce some of the terms that underpin this book—including "genealogy," "feminism," and "cultural studies," as well as some that might seem more obvious, such as "adolescence" and "girls." In analyzing the emergence of the twentieth-century categories of feminine adolescence and girl culture, *Girls* also aims to produce an intersection of contemporary feminist, historical, and cultural studies practices in exploring how that history might be written. A history of feminine adolescence would traditionally follow the method of histories that survey the "discovery" of childhood, such as the influential work of Phillipe Ariés. When historical texts on girlhood cross over into female adolescence they tend to treat the idea of adolescence—and of a form of adolescence specific to girls—as a discovered fact. Somewhere in the nineteenth century, such texts suggest, people started to talk about how a girl becomes a woman in new scientific terms that made it possible to better understand what happened to girls when they became women. Adolescence, then, was always there, just waiting to be discovered or understood and have helpful books written about it. In relation to such histories this book takes up the work of French historian/theorist Michel Foucault to argue for the importance of a different kind of history of girlhood—a *genealogy*. This is a method of writing history (historiography) that Foucault called at one point a "history of the present," and some indication of the differences of genealogy from that story of discovery will be useful here.

A genealogy is a history that does not look for causes and points of origin so much as map how things and ideas are possible within a given context. It does not uncover previously hidden facts, in the sense of finding female adolescence in a particular period, nor does it focus on sequential narratives of change, in the sense of tracing the causal development of an idea such as female adolescence. By recognizing female adolescence as an idea that depends on and contributes to a range of particular but not inevitable knowledges, a genealogy of feminine adolescence focuses instead on how that idea works and what it has been used to say. A genealogy will not discover new knowledge about girls, and it will not discover new forms of girlhood, but it will discuss how knowledge about girls has shaped what it means to be a girl and how girls experience their own positions in the world in relation to diverse ways of talking about and understanding girls. It will recognize, then, the effects of particular forms of knowledge about girls—of how we know about girls.

Genealogies do not look for causes and points of origin so much as map how things and ideas (such as girls, female adolescence, girlhood, girl culture) are possible within a given context. Instead of asking what or who produced feminine adolescence, and why—a story that inevitably leaves feminine adolescence as the passive object and neutral product of larger and more important historical changes and voices—a genealogy asks how knowledges and their objects work in particular situations. This book looks at the constitution of feminine adolescence in a range of *discourses*—ways of speaking about and knowing the world—as well as in the more recognizable institutions, such as legal systems or schools, which are usually the objects of history. The sites and events identified in this discussion of feminine adolescence are connected by lines of questioning and analysis of effects rather than causal propositions. To take a well-known example, Sigmund Freud's studies of child sexuality are seen by Foucault as intervening in discourses on children's sex to state that it has not been discussed. Freud is not, then, the cause of a discourse on child sexuality. Rather he renames and redeploys a discourse on child sexuality. This moment can be discussed in terms of its effects without claiming that child sexuality originated in Freud's work. What we know about an object such as girls or child sexuality is equal to how we speak about it, and we cannot speak or think independently of available ways of knowing the world. This is the dilemma of history for Foucault: the enmeshing of things and knowledge.

I am not claiming that feminine adolescence has not been studied. Indeed, from its earliest appearances—and perhaps most strikingly when it has been used to contextualize by its difference childhood, womanhood, or masculine adolescence—feminine adolescence has been closely, even obsessively, observed and discussed. Feminine adolescence is in fact inseparable from processes of observing and discussing girls. This genealogy approaches critical, theoretical, public, and popular discourses to consider how they have constituted girls and feminine adolescence as the object of their knowledge. The specific sites and instances I will consider include legislation on age of consent and education, feminism, psychoanalysis, anthropology and sociology, girls' magazines, cinema, developmental and popular psychology, popular music, subculture theory, theoretical accounts of body image, and discourses on girl culture. These analyses are assembled as a map of the emergence of feminine adolescence and girl culture as new twentieth-century categories for understanding the relations between genders, sexes, and ages, and between individuals, groups, and the production and reproduction of culture. In assembling this map I will thus necessarily also engage with the twentieth-century history of cultural analysis.

A genealogy of feminine adolescence would trace the deployment or use of that idea in relation to concepts of childhood and womanhood as well as in relation to other discourses on the modern world. This necessitates analysis of a broad field of definitions and other representations of girls in popular culture, everyday life, the public sphere, and social or cultural theory, particularly at points where these fields intersect—such as discourses on puberty or girl deviance. It is important to avoid assuming that such representations inevitably followed from one another—that once puberty was discovered, for example, disorders produced by it would also be discovered. Thus I analyze how girls are articulated in specific sites rather than attempting to define what links girls across different contexts, and the instances selected here appear in distinct historical and cultural locations. This analysis emphasizes the expansion of explanatory discourses on girls in late modernity without imagining any uniformity to this expansion or to the increased public visibility of girls.

Girlhood is made up and girls are brought into existence in statements and knowledge about girls, and some of the most widely shared or commonsensical knowledge about girls and feminine adolescence provides some of the clearest examples of how girls are constructed by changing ways of speaking about girls. For example, while adolescence has often implied a development of increased maturity and (eventual) stabilization of identity, it is only since the nineteenth century that adolescence has become very strongly identified with puberty and with teenage years. This identification remains incomplete in the sense that someone who is called a girl or is visible as a girl is not necessarily any particular age or at any particular point of physiological development. Despite how obviously puberty seems to define a boundary between girlhood and womanhood and a field for female adolescence, adolescence is not a clear denotation of any age, body, behavior, or identity, because it has always meant the process of developing a self (though that has meant very different things in different sociohistorical contexts) rather than any definition of that self. However if adolescence has never concretely specified an age range, it has been gendered and sexed.[1] Adolescence has historically been applied predominantly to conceptions (both theoretical and popular) of developing manhood. In the context of increasing nineteenth-century interest in girlhood, discourses framing a female adolescence and new ideas about femininity enabled further twentieth-century innovations in theorizing feminine adolescence.

In this book I have utilized the term "feminine adolescence" as different from "female adolescence" (which is predominantly a discourse on puberty) and with a degree of independence from any specific age category. These decisions are discussed more fully in part 1 of this book, but it is crucial to begin by asking how feminine adolescence can be defined at all if it is not defined by puberty, chronological age, or specific behaviors or identities. The girls I call "adolescent" here are not necessarily teenagers and not exclusively young women either; rather, they are defined as in transition or in process relative to dominant ideas of Womanhood. Feminine adolescence is always retrospectively defined, always definitively prior to the Woman it is used to explain. Its history is also retrospectively constituted, so that it now seems that feminine adolescence must always have existed and that it would always have been how and where an individual's womanhood was established. Despite changes in understanding childhood and youth and the distinctions between them, adolescence continues to be conceived as a disruption of childhood and prior to a projected adulthood. Adolescence also functions as an explanation of the indispensable difficulty of becoming a subject, agent, or independent or self-aware person, as well as a periodization that constructs both childhood and adulthood as relative stabilities. Understanding this difficult adolescence as universal trauma is a twentieth-century Western idea that retrospectively constructs childhood as a period of stability, heightening both the crucial intensity of adolescence as transformative passage and the distance between childhood and maturity.

The dissemination of both "feminine adolescence" and "feminist" as categories for organizing knowledge about modern women, and as labels for the behavior of women, responded to changes already apparent in the mid to late nineteenth century. The adolescence of girls is not, as it is sometimes constructed, a clear break from Victorian discourses on girlhood but, rather, a way of mapping shifts across a range of discourses. By the 1920s and 1930s women were popularly represented as passing through a definitive adolescent stage and as intensely invested in the evaluation and interpretation of adolescence. The impact of both feminism and psychoanalysis on Western society is inseparable from their importance to this emergence, and these discourses will be of particular interest in the following discussion. Turn of the century theories of adolescence, such as those produced by Sigmund Freud and G. Stanley Hall, centered on developing a model of masculine adolescence but also referred to girls, or at least referred the idea of adolescence to an idea of femininity. Twentieth-century adolescence became increasingly characterized by feminized attributes such as difficulty, malleability, and pre-maturity, even when the adolescents were men—a conflation that contributes to the importance of thinking about feminine rather than female adolescence. This book rarely mentions boys, and then with reference to girls, but in duplicating (in reverse) the dominant mode of studying youth, I do want to acknowledge that the adolescence attributed to boys is intricately bound up with these new discourses on girlhood. Adolescence, including boys' adolescence, has been "feminized," and the specification of behaviors and experiences as feminine or adolescent is not reliant on any biological definition, despite the importance of girls' bodies to the delineation and experience of feminine adolescence.

While girls, therefore, are products and performances of the long history of Western discourses on gender, sex, age, and identity, adolescent girls are specific to late modernity and the dissemination of a concept of feminine adolescence. As adolescent—in their demonstration of the difficulty of becoming a subject—girls are very modern. The concept of adolescence is central to the development of the modern subject, and the difficult negotiations and performances of feminine adolescence are crucial data for modern theories of subjectivity, where they most often figure as a definitive failure of subjectification (of coming to be a coherent self-aware subject). Far from being transcultural even in this sense, girls have also been crucial markers of cultural specificity and social change.[2] While I have referred here to Western cultures (meaning cultures founded equally on European histories and on industrialized economies), this book will also consider what "Western" means with reference to a category or idea such as "girlhood," to which is attributed transcultural and even transhistorical significance. If in fact dominant modes of girlhood in the twentieth century, ways of thinking and talking about and of being girls, are specific to Western cultures, how does that translate into our conception of cultural production as it now operates on a global scale, a new understanding of cultural location that is especially dominant in the field of popular culture where girls are so visible? And what impact might this recognition have on categories, such as girl, previously held to be both culturally specific and transcultural facts of human society? Late modern adolescence is not only a physiological and psychosocial periodization, it is also a separation of certain behaviors, lifestyles, interests, and forms of cultural production, not only from childhood but from the subject's properly mature sphere of action. Even if it was possible to argue that puberty names actions of the body beyond the control of consciousness or culture, adolescence is an entirely cultural phenomenon. Moreover, the history of the emergence of feminine adolescence intersects with the emergence of new forms of cultural production.

It would be possible to write a book exclusively on girls in popular culture, as others have done. But I want this book to acknowledge that popular culture and theories about culture and society are complexly imbricated in one another—indeed even the category "popular culture" is a theory about culture. In juxtaposing these terms in this book, I also want to stress that critical theory and popular culture, apart from sharing historical contexts insofar as they are both products of late modernity, necessarily respond to one another. This seems obvious in one respect, as the authors of critical theory are presumed to have access to a whole range of cultural materials, including popular culture. But popular culture is also directly affected by developments in critical theory, for which process psychoanalysis and feminism provide important examples, and the dissemination of feminine adolescence has also taken effect in this way.

The discipline of feminist cultural studies might be especially productive for this history because it is equally interested in theories or reflections on culture and in the everyday life specific to late modernity. While even in cultural studies there is apparently still far more academic work available on the masculine experience of youth, increasing attention is being paid to girls within fields of cultural production, and to girl culture as a form of youth culture. I want to argue, however, that despite appearances popular culture in late modernity has always been equally if not more concerned with debating the forms and functions of feminine as compared to masculine adolescence. By focusing on girls and girl culture it will be possible not only to introduce the conceptual terrain of feminist cultural studies through a history of feminine adolescence but to do so through a useful set of case studies in that discipline. *Girls* is thus directed to an intersection between the dominant concerns of feminist theory and cultural studies. While it is not a primer for either feminist theory or cultural studies, this book introduces many of the terms, methods, and concerns of contemporary feminist and cultural studies because girls have been significant objects of and participants in the development of both fields.

The highly visible dissemination of feminine adolescence in popular discourses such as literature, psychology, cinema, fashion, and advertising demonstrates its significance to changing ideas about modernity. However, feminine adolescence has been excluded from theories of modern subjectivity despite being widely employed as both metaphor for modern life and crucial data source for developmental models of identity. Despite the exemplary modernity of girls, the Subject on which modern popular, public, and academic discourses center is never a girl, even for feminism. Feminist practices (including feminist theory) are still dominated by adult models of subjectivity presumed to be the endpoint of a naturalized process of developing individual identity that relegates a vast range of not only people but roles, behaviors, and practices to its immature past. As a future-directed politics, as a politics of transformation, girls and the widest range of representations of, discourses on, and sites of becoming a woman are crucial to feminism. Yet feminist discussions of girls rarely engage with feminine adolescence without constructing girls as opposed to, or otherwise defining, the mature, independent woman as feminist subject. The lack of feminist interest in girls on their own terms (and without presuming their necessary redundancy for feminist politics) helps shape a dominant feminist address to a woman-subject defined in relation to norms of independence, agency, and originality that while liberatory for some also works to restrict and homogenize the category of women. In this context, my discussion will also address now established debates over postfeminism, girls and feminism, and feminist generations, arguments elsewhere played out in more polemical texts that rarely consider the historical context of continuities and discontinuities between feminism and girls or girl culture.

Having described the project here as both genealogical and feminist, some consideration of this conjunction is necessary. Feminist engagement with Foucault's work and methods has often been troubled, because Foucault not only does not talk very much about women but is often seen to imply that sexual difference and gender are not necessarily definitive forces in people's lives or definitive categorizations of subjectivity. While I will consider this relation in more detail elsewhere, I want to suggest here the value for me of Foucault's genealogical method within feminist analysis. As it is concerned with the particular effects rather than the origin of discourses, genealogy, according to Foucault, attempts to render "historical knowledges . . . capable of opposition and of struggle against the coercion of a theoretical, unitary, formal and scientific discourse [about human beings]" (Foucault 1980:26). Genealogies question the political, legal, and ethical authoritativeness of scientific, historiographical, and other discourses on origin and offer opportunities to think differently about histories of how one becomes a woman and about the idea of girlhood. Australian critic Meaghan Morris has also described cultural studies as "an investigation of particular ways of using culture, of what is available *as* culture to people inhabiting particular social contexts, and of people's ways of *making* culture" (1997:43). This investigation intersects with feminism—necessarily interested in what Morris describes as "the historical and social constraints on interpretation and . . . the pressures that limit choices, constrain semiosis and shape experience—constraints and pressures that are produced by human institutions and that can, and sometimes should, be changed" (1997:50). The contradictions I will argue are inherent in girl culture also work to question what might constitute such change, and change continues to be the both the desire and the context of much girl culture.

Youth has been consistently important to cultural analysis because it presents a crucial point of cultural reproduction and cultural change. Youth names a field in which society reproduces itself and marks changes through the incorporation and exclusion of individuals and groups in relation to social systems that precede and contextualize them. Twentieth-century cultural analysis has especially focused on how the world has changed—or, by contrast, what parts of the world have not changed in the same way—and has also emphasized youth and adolescence as sites for speaking about such change (or lack of change). Many publications attest to the fascination of cultural studies and popular cultural analysis—such as media commentary and advice or guidance books—with youth culture, particularly as a scene of resistance to preceding cultural structures and ideals. But as Dick Hebdige has argued, what is mostly missing from the general emphasis on youth as transition from childhood to maturity is "any idea of historical specificity, any explanation of why these particular forms should occur at this particular time" (1979:73). Hebdige is specifically referring to the 1960s, now widely conceived as the preeminent watershed for defining youth culture.

The 1960s were in fact highly reflexive on earlier twentieth-century youth culture, but they remain important to contemporary commentary on popular and youth culture. This significance reflects more certainly the 1960s as a period in which the analytic field and object of youth culture was defined, producing a new emphasis on studies of youth as studies of cultural resistance, perhaps most influentially through the group known as the Birmingham School (formed in England in the 1960s).

The Birmingham School talked about new youth and new youth cultures, under which rubric they almost exclusively discussed boys or young men. This focus not only marginalizes girls within the new field of youth culture studies but consequently erases the significance of modern girls to earlier twentieth-century cultural analysis. In the first half of the twentieth century girls were repeatedly, and even obsessively, associated with the rise of mass culture and accompanying cultural changes, and this continued in the second half of the century despite the dominant association of youth studies and youth culture with young men. Youth as a struggle with hegemonic tendencies has seemed to be more easily identified in the cultural activities of young men, and feminist cultural studies thus inherits from cultural studies (as well as feminism) a tendency to represent and discuss girls as conformist rather than resistant or at least to study them almost exclusively with reference to that division. Influential texts on feminist cultural studies rarely focus on girls, feminine adolescence, or girl culture, or provide introductions to those concepts. This erased history of girls as indices of youth and late modernity reinforces the importance of a study of girl culture at the end of the twentieth century.

These working definitions and introductory remarks indicate the parameters of this book, and shape its tripartite structure. Part 1, "Becoming a Girl," expands on the genealogy of feminine adolescence while part 2, "Becoming a Woman," refers that genealogy to a consideration of how feminine adolescence works—how it has produced the processes of becoming women. Part 2 also examines the discourses that have helped constitute feminine adolescence through the observation, analysis, interpretation, and recording of girls, introducing and contextualizing what is now called feminist cultural studies through these discourses. Part 3, "Girl Culture," provides a set of case studies for feminist cultural studies that also surveys both discourses on girls and sites of cultural production especially associated with girls. The analysis of discourses on girls in part 2 thus assembles a set of tools and terms that can be applied to the analysis of girl culture in part 3.

Although the book thus moves away from an easily recognizable historiography, it continues to be interested in a genealogy, analyzing representations of and ideas about girls in popular culture and critical theory in different historical and cultural locations. The emphasis here on anglophone cultures—particularly the United States, the United Kingdom, and Australia—reflects my own position and knowledges but also acknowledges the influence of anglophone culture on late modern constructions of youth and femininity across different Western (and Westernized) nations, as well as the ways in which it is expanding into recently globalized popular culture. My selection of Japan as primary non-anglophone point of reference in my final chapter similarly reflects my own knowledge and experience and does not at all short-circuit the focus of this book on what we know as Western culture and late modernity, given their influence in twentieth-century Japan. While I will consider some of the limitations of that perspective on girls I also want to disclaim the project of looking at girls as a generality and instead see this book as a map of how girls function as a set of statements about late modern culture. Within this specific context I want to account for relations between the increasing public visibility of girls and the expansion of discourses on feminine adolescence, as well as to consider ways in which girls are involved in the production of theories about and representations of girls, feminine adolescence, and girl culture.

Part 1
Becoming a Girl

one

The Girl of the Period

I almost wish I hadn't gone down that rabbit-hole—and yet—and yet—it's rather curious, you know, this sort of life! I do wonder what *can* have happened to me!

—Lewis Carroll, *Alice's Adventures in Wonderland*

THIS FIRST CHAPTER considers the idea of the girl as an historically specific term and as a set of culturally specific histories. Although the first sections of this chapter consider changes to dominant readings of young women in Shakespeare and references to classical girlhood, this is not an attempt to trace a history of all Western girlhood. In fact I am primarily interested in nineteenth- and twentieth-century constructions of these earlier representations of girls, and their contexts and significance. The examples selected here produce girls as a universal and yet culturally specific category; they are deployed retrospectively in late modernity as grounds for understanding feminine adolescence, which I will argue is itself specific to the late nineteenth and twentieth centuries.

The second part of this chapter considers girls as an index of cultural continuity and cultural crisis through a series of public re-definitions of Victorian girlhood that helped constitute what we now understand to be feminine adolescence. New and changing public discourses on femininity and development enabled a range of still recognizable roles for girlhood in dominant discourses on culture, gender, and the self. The girl's role as a marker of cultural identity—the English or the American girl; the traditional or the

1.2
John Everett Millais,
Cherry Ripe (1879)
(Printed in The Graphic
[1880]; reprinted in
Graphic Magazine *[1919])*

modern girl—also installs her as representative of the coherence of an historical period and as indicative of cultural differences and of transitions between periods.

Renaissance Girls: The Girl as Retrospective
Gender and Youth in the Renaissance

This first section considers the perhaps surprising importance of Renaissance girlhood as a marker of what and who girls are in late modernity. It does not comprehensively survey historical materials on girls in the Renaissance, nor does it survey representations of girlhood at the time, but instead focuses on the most significant figure for late modern discussion of Renaissance girl-hood, the playwright William Shakespeare. Sustained acclaim of Shake-speare's work in the nineteenth and twentieth centuries has often presented it as an account of human psychology and development. This reputation has helped maintain the significance of the Renaissance in both popular and the-oretical discourses on the essentially human. Young male characters have perhaps been most significant to this positioning of Shakespeare, especially the figure of Hamlet, who has been taken up by such noted analysts of self, sex, age, and society as G. W. F. Hegel, Sigmund Freud, Virginia Woolf, and Jacques Lacan. Indeed, Hamlet has figured as a template for understanding psychological development even when positioned as a pathological rather than a developing subject. The affirmation of Shakespeare as accurately por-traying developmental psychology and other processes of character forma-tion has been less uniformly applied to his girl characters. This not only re-flects a sidelining of girls in psychological models but positions girls as not developing in the same essentially human way.

Among preserved representations of youth from the early modern period of Western history Shakespeare's plays have a representative status and a de-gree of popular recognition exceptional for Western cultural production. The canonical position of Shakespeare as an index of Western culture can suggest, among other things, the retrospective construction of modern girls via available representations of girls in the past. The early modern period is often designated as marking the birth of the human-centered world and of a recognizable concept of the human subject—designations apparent in the term "Renaissance." The Renaissance is therefore a significant moment to look for constructions of both adolescence and gender as pivotal elements of this human subjectivity. Here I want to use Shakespeare's *Hamlet* (1601) and *Romeo and Juliet* (c. 1597) to consider a history of configuring girls and girl-hood in relation to the modern, and modern understandings of identity.

If girls are young or physically immature women, then in some senses there have clearly been girls all across human history—at least for as long as females have been identified as socially differentiated from males and children have been distinguished from adults. But just as there have not al-ways been women in the way we currently understand that term, or a dis-tinction, let alone a comparable distinction, between children and adults, there weren't always girls in the sense that we now mean the word, or in the sense that being a girl is now experienced. Contemporary discourses on girlhood—our ideas about what girls are and should be—include what we recognize as girlhood in earlier or other cultures. This is clearly positioned by our own cultural contexts, but even if we acknowledge that our Western or late modern understandings of girlhood are not homogenous across the range of different cultures constituting these fields it still often seems that girlhood itself is a natural stage of a woman's life. The next chapter considers the category of feminine adolescence as specific to late modernity, but in this chapter I want to consider how we see feminine adolescence in earlier periods, what kind of developmental stage the idea of girlhood provides, and what makes girlhood necessary for Western cultures. I want to contend not only that we see our ideas about girlhood in earlier texts but also that we must see girlhood there in order for girlhood to be the crucial and natural developmental stage it is now required to be.

The Renaissance is important to contemporary constructions of youth and sex/gender in part because it situates some important developments in the conception of childhood. The French historian Phillipe Ariés has famously argued that childhood as a separate identity and way of life did not exist before the eighteenth century. According to Ariés, prior to the 1700s there were babies and then there were people—although their social position would be shaped by various contexts, including age, and they also might be perceived as in training for different kinds of roles. A new idea of the child was gradually disseminated in public discourses on the individual and the family throughout the Renaissance and the Enlightenment. This childhood required new processes of education to produce an adult, as exemplified in the influential model produced by the French philosopher Jean-Jacques Rousseau's polemic on education in *Emile* (1762). Rousseau's model of training in human values was subsequently modified by newly "scientific" understandings of childhood and the maturing body developed in the nineteenth century, and elaborations on adolescence are generally tied in this way to changes in social sciences. Ilana Ben-Amos specifically links Ariés's thesis to the expansion of anthropological and sociological discourses:

> Ariés's conception of an early and abrupt transition to adult life in the medieval past had some affinity with anthropological descriptions of the transition to adulthood in tribal societies, but it also accentuated and brought into sharper focus ideas current among sociologists, especially regarding the invisibility of the young and lack of marked differences between youths and adults in the pre-industrial past. (Ben-Amos 4)

Historians of the early modern period have subsequently questioned this abrupt transition thesis, which minimizes the importance and duration of "youth":

> They have applied, or tacitly assumed, a model in which emphasis is placed on the longevity and extension of that stage in the life cycle. They all stress that in early modern English society full participation in adult life was retarded, and legal, social and economic rights and obligations were accorded to the young only many years after they had reached puberty. (Ben-Amos 5)

This alternate view equally demonstrates the influence of late modern adolescence, although the label "prolonged youth" often accorded to this thesis does not describe adolescence or its functions.[1] Both sides of this debate apply late modern understandings of adolescence, and models of development and maturity, to Renaissance texts.

One of the key texts engaged by Ben-Amos is Lawrence Stone's well-known study, *The Family, Sex, and Marriage.* Stone's focus is on changes to emotional or personal relations in these fields, although his material in fact represents discourses on or representations of these personal and emotional relations rather than attempts to reveal those experiences. These changes, which Stone describes as "from distance, deference and patriarchy" to "affective individualism" (22), rely on the "stratified diffusion of new ideas and practices" (23) of gender relations. Stone implies that this diffusion moved from legal (and canonical) changes—many of which, such as education and marriage laws, centered on "youth"—out through early modern England. However, both Stone and Ben-Amos generally discuss adolescence as primarily concerning boys, identifying girls as a variation that can be sectioned of from the generality of adolescence.[2] Stone primarily discusses girls in his chapter on sexual practices, which is also where he directly discusses the idea of adolescence: "The idea that adolescence only became a social problem in the nineteenth century is sheer historical fantasy, and there was constant anxiety about the danger to the social and moral order of the huge numbers of unmarried apprentices in London at this period" (318). Ben-Amos also concedes that "adulscentia" was well known to early modern writers, although the term "youth" was generally preferred and " 'youth' itself was sometimes divided into distinct stages or sub-categories" (9).

Patricia Meyer Spacks notes that youth has often been "synonymous with *puberty*" and that writers such as Samuel Johnson defined adolescence as prior to puberty. Of this terminological confusion she claims that "adolescence presented practical problems precisely because no one had a clear concept of it. Parents, teachers, clergymen apparently expected the young to behave either like children or like adults. In their teen-age years, the young behaved, instead, like adolescents" (90). Certainly, as Spacks points out and historians of early modern youth insist, the difficulty of youth and its passions have been stressed for centuries. While this is still not equal to the concept of adolescence as practiced in the twentieth century, a number of additional qualifications to the discovery of adolescence in the past will be noted in this chapter, beginning with this kind of retrospectivity. Youth as a modern category has always been retrospectively understood—compared to a past constructed as less disruptive and difficult. As new theories of youth are disseminated in popular or more specialized forums they must account for changed understandings of youth. The throwaway line "youth today" depends on this—youth today is worthy of comment as a summary of some discontinuity with the past. This relation to the past is also underscored by youth as a relation to family and society that is responsible for the passage of culture between generations.

Juliet and Ophelia

The girls in Shakespeare's plays represent both social continuity and social change; they are symbols of society rather than examples of it. In comparison, the girls and daughters of the novel tend to focus on character development in relation to multiple social norms. For example, the distinctions between Jane, Elizabeth, Lydia, and Mary Bennett in Jane Austen's *Pride and Prejudice* (1813) are possible moral positions in relation to a world that was changing more rapidly than the foreground dramas of Austen's fiction suggest. They also evidence the increasing specialization of the modern girl's role in relation to culture. While fashion and other distracting pleasures were sometimes moral issues in Shakespeare's plays, by Austen's time these are both closely linked to individualized developmental failings and qualities seen as increasingly specific to girls. No such developmental evaluation attends the virtuous if not always obedient daughters in *Hamlet* and *Romeo and Juliet*.

Both these plays draw on existing narratives and reorient them to an early modern British audience. *Romeo and Juliet* reworks a story appearing in several versions before Shakespeare's play. The long popularity of this drama of youthful love seems to support claims about the significance of adolescent turmoil during and before the early modern period. Certainly age is important to the play, or at least Juliet's age is strongly emphasized in the script as well as in commentary on the play. Shakespeare reduced Juliet's age from eighteen or sixteen in his source-texts to thirteen. While this heightens an emphasis in the earlier stories, where she was also considered too young to marry (see Franson), Shakespeare thus makes the question of whether Juliet is too young to marry less problematic. Nevertheless, this debate is often staged. Ann Cook claims that "twelve and fourteen are called the 'Ripe Age,' a contemporary term denoting physical maturity, which brings 'abilitie and fitnesse for procreation' " (20), implying that both contemporary conceptions of puberty and a recognizable age of consent were relevant to early modern Britain.[3] Although it referred chiefly to marriage rather than sex, there are continuities between the late modern age of consent and Renaissance legislation on the age of discretion, including that such laws seem to have technically applied to both men and women but been constructed primarily with reference to girls.[4] Noting recorded contexts for this drama over Juliet's age—such as minimum or usual marriage ages—cannot reconstruct for us the meanings of Juliet's age, or of her girlhood, to Renaissance audiences. While the feasibility of using literature to unpack an historical context has often been debated, contradictions between recorded laws, as well as the difficulty of interpreting their meaning, means that laws and other records may be equally problematic foundations for understanding an historical period and may equally rely on localized interests and intentions.

Some commentary emphasizes that women among the English aristocracy generally married at around twenty to twenty-one when the play was written.[5] Records are, of course, unevenly available for anyone except aristocrats, but it is possible that younger ages for marriage were more common among other groups and that the play's emphasis on Juliet's age contains a narrative about social divisions now not readily available to us. This is supported by and makes explicable Capulet's change of heart after Tybalt's death, when producing an heir might be more important than Juliet's usefulness for negotiating alliances. Both the nurse's jokes about her own virginity and Juliet's mother's pleading Paris's cause—"I was your mother much upon these years That you are now a maid" (I.iii.73–4)—emphasize that thirteen does not seem young to the women in Juliet's household. Perhaps, as many critics have argued, this reflects a representation of Italians as overly passionate or an assumption that in warmer countries people matured faster than in England. However, while Juliet is clearly young, the play does not position her as a child in the late modern sense. Shakespearian characterization emphasizes age as one among a range of variants that shape social roles, but maturity is not primarily determined by age. Rather, it is articulated through forms of cultural (but not institutional) education for both male and female characters: love, virginity, and marriageability particularly supplement this education for the girl characters as does independence for the young men. These themes also shape our selection of which Shakespearean characters we will, as modern readers, identify as girls rather than women.

While there is an extensive range of criticism and commentary dealing with humanity, identity, and gender in Shakespeare, very little of it recognizes the importance of girls and daughters to Shakespeare's plays. Shakespeare's androgynous girl-boys and pivotal bridal figures raise a range of questions about the role of the daughter in cultural reproduction that are not adequately addressed by reference to the reproduction of Woman or even of the family or patriarchy. Discussion of Shakespeare's girls often notes the practice of employing boys to act their parts, which somewhat problematizes these references, but this does not sufficiently address the significance to Shakespearian texts of the transitional social positions that centuries later seem proper to feminine adolescence. Shakespeare's young women are emblems of the future, whether as pastoral promise, social disintegration, or something more ambiguous. Social order, the plays make clear, requires order among young women, while the collapse of patriarchal systems exposes the ambivalence of figures such as Cordelia (rejected and mourned in *King Lear*) or Ophelia (chaste and lascivious) or Juliet (manipulative and innocent).[6] Cook notes that

> Shakespeare's late romances repeatedly employ the figure of the child bride. Marina is fourteen, Perdita is sixteen, and Miranda almost fifteen. As with Juliet, their ages are all clearly specified. The reasons for the reappearance of the very young heroine lie partly in the sources and partly in

the peculiar nature of this kind of drama. For one thing, the cyclical, familial context of the plays is more manageable with immature offspring
than with a second generation of fully grown adults. (33)

Identifying this pattern does not answer why girls' ages are significant and
boys' irrelevant (or obvious or uninterrogated) in Shakespearian drama.
While Juliet's age is repeatedly stressed, Romeo's age is never stated. Although Hamlet seems young in his thirties, writers on *Romeo and Juliet* have
generally thought Romeo much younger than that, more because he evokes
so many of the qualities now recognized as adolescent than because characters refer to him as a youth. As Katherine Dalsimer phrases this, "his phase
of development is recognisable, his adolescence has begun" (83).

Criticism frequently implies that the historical context of Shakespeare's
plays is not greatly relevant to appreciating them. Dalsimer representatively claims that "the emotional power with which the story continues to engage audiences makes clear its resonance with psychological realities not
limited by the particularities of the time and place in which it was written"
(78). Shakespeare's dramatization of youth and its conflicts has been seen
as proof of his genius in representing eternal human truths. But it is also
arguable that, rather than the truth of Shakespeare's youths appealing
across the ages and in different contexts, people are repeatedly taught to
understand the relevance of Shakespeare's youths. If our idea of youth has
been shaped by Shakespeare, it is not surprising the plays should fit it.
Romeo and Juliet was a remarkably popular play in the twentieth century,
and the idea that the appeal of this play is about youth has been underscored by its twentieth-century association with educational institutions.
While the play opposes the youthfulness of Romeo and Juliet and their
love to an older generation, it is debatable whether this is more important
than the opposition between the lovers and Romeo's peers. It is even more
uncertain that the play acclaims youth, or the youthful love it is often held
to represent so excellently. *Romeo and Juliet* seems to play on the impetu-
ousness of youth regardless of nationality or other social context while still
framing this behavior as foreign. While repetitions of the play on stages,
screens, and in schools work to foreground similarities and to articulate
(and translate) differences between the Renaissance and the late modern,
the play always did this kind of work. Yet *Romeo and Juliet* does not claim
any transcultural significance for youth, because it does not talk about

Verona as another culture at all but, rather, as the name for a romantic foreign place from an English point of view.

Some difficulty we now identify as adolescent is apparent in *Romeo and Juliet*, where Romeo mopes over an unrequited love, his friends pick fights with neighboring gangs, and Juliet is described as "greensickness carrion." For Dalsimer, Juliet's narrative centers on the classically modern desire for separation from the parents, who resist that separation. But Romeo's and Juliet's parents are in fact enthusiastic about the imminent separation of their children from the family home, and they do not stand in the way of their child's love—as in other Shakespearian plays, such as *The Merchant of Venice*—because they do not know about it. The substantive question when trying to align this narrative with contemporary models of adolescence is whether Juliet's psychological development is an issue either in her desire to marry Romeo (and not Paris) or her parents' desire that she marry Paris. Dalsimer interprets the play as "a translation into action of the central inner experience of adolescence" (77), which is, she argues, separation from the parents through sexual love. But the familiarity of Dalsimer's account of *Romeo and Juliet* attests less to the eternal verities apparent in the play than the degree to which this psychoanalytic account has permeated Western public discourse and popular culture.[7]

Since the nineteenth century in particular, Shakespeare has been employed to explicate human psychology, principally on the grounds of the continued acclaim granted his work (which these interpretations of course themselves perpetuate). *Hamlet* in particular has often been used to exemplify the modern self. It would be hard to ascertain whether psychoanalysis established this template by interpretation of Hamlet or whether *Hamlet* has helped shape this modern construction of the subject. Freud himself sees *Hamlet* as "an emblem of 'the secular advance of repression in the emotional life of mankind' " (quoted in Rose 124). Psychoanalytic interpretation of Hamlet is certainly not the only way the play has been read, but Jacques Lacan's exemplary claim that "the play is the drama of an individual subjectivity" (1977a:12) permeates *Hamlet* criticism.[8] Significantly, in Lacan's account Ophelia "becomes one of the innermost elements in Hamlet's drama, the drama of Hamlet as the man who has lost the way of his desire" (1977a:12)—in other words she is relegated to "that piece of bait named Ophelia" (1977a:11).[9] For psychoanalytic readings—and for all those readings more implicitly framed by psychoanalysis—both Hamlet and Ophelia locate narratives of separation from family entwined with increased social knowledge, as well as madness, but these narratives are differentiated according to what we would call gender.

Ophelia, like Juliet, has become an icon of feminine adolescence repeatedly invoked as emblematic of girlhood difficulties and passions. Mary Pipher's highly successful *Reviving Ophelia* is exemplary. In arguing that "something dramatic happens to girls in early adolescence . . . [t]hey crash and burn in a social and developmental Bermuda Triangle" (19), Pipher refers to fairy tales where girls "eat poisoned apples or prick their fingers with poisoned needles and fall asleep for a hundred years" (19), and to Ophelia: "As a girl, Ophelia is happy and free, but with adolescence she loses herself" (20). Despite the inadequacy of this reading of *Hamlet*, where Ophelia doesn't have any such clear developmental psychology, Pipher is interested in Ophelia as part of a twentieth-century iconography of girls drowning in sex, love, and femininity.[10] Both Bridget Lyons and Kaara Peterson emphasize the way in which the play presents Ophelia as an image. Lyons argues that

> when Polonius arranges Ophelia's meeting with Hamlet in the third act of the play, he assigns gestures to her and provides her with a prop, deliberately fashioning her into an image intended to convey an easily readable meaning. . . . Ophelia is not coached in what to say to Hamlet. Rather, she is supposed to communicate an impression by her visual appearance alone, and it is this which will trigger Hamlet's response. (60)[11]

Like most citations of Ophelia, these discussions of her as image focus on her death. The fact that Ophelia dies offstage further stresses a displacement of Ophelia emphasized by repeated reinterpretations of her and re-narrations of her tragedy. The queen's description of Ophelia's death constitutes a striking visual tableau (Lyons 71), but one that suggests "mythical and symbolic meanings more appropriate to pastoral comedy than to the realistic world of political intrigue and sexual danger in which she actually finds herself" (72). As Peterson notes, this scene "has been augmented by a substantial catalogue of representations of a primarily visual nature," and the centrality of this scene and of visually inserting Ophelia in this and other scenes in productions of *Hamlet* is less required by the play than an indication that "we have been trained to 'read' [Gertrude's] speech as a visual experience" (8). Visualizations of Ophelia avoid the fact that the play itself rarely foregrounds Ophelia in person—they thus "regularly take as their subject a literary fragment from Hamlet reporting Ophelia's death, a fragment in which it is doubly impossible for Ophelia's body to be present" (7). This Shakespearean tradition appears in filmic productions and in stage and visual art, indicating the significance of visual culture to the modern dissemination of feminine adolescence.

The filmic redeployment of Shakespeare is now an important element of the continual redirection and negotiation of Shakespeare's images of youth and girlhood. The popular interpretations of *Romeo and Juliet* by Franco Zefirelli (1968) and Baz Luhrmann (1996) provide good examples. Luhrmann accentuates the play's divisions between older and younger generations by including dramatic contemporary images of youth culture. While Zefirelli's film, "by framing Romeo apart from the other men in the play both visually and aurally" (Applebaum 265n), foregrounds a distinction between his manliness and the violence of most other men in the play, Luhrmann separates the narratives of Romeo and his friends and Romeo and Juliet by diverse tactics of mise-en-scène from the opening credits of the film.[12] Luhrmann thus articulates in *Romeo and Juliet* a representation of "youth culture" as well as youth psychology. Luhrmann's film may never have been possible without Wise and Robbins's film of *West Side Story* (1961), but it remains clear that some young men at least occupy identifiably exclusive spaces in Shakespeare's play. Is this a youth culture? Ben-Amos notes that historians of the period have identified

> a sense of the separate identity of young people . . . an identity which has been defined in terms of the separate values, associations and life styles of the young. Historians have pointed to youth riots, the receptivity of the young to novel or radical ideas, their recreations, festivities, popular literature and sexual mores, as expressions of their distinct position and culture. . . . But just how significant were these age-related differences, and was there such a marked split between "youth" and "adult" cultures?" (183–4)

Ben-Amos acknowledges some distinctive traits and a significant degree of visibility among young people in early modern England but argues that "most youths had few values that truly distinguished them from adults, and they had few, if any, institutions which were wholly theirs, separating them from society at large. That is, few, if any, of the features we tend to associate with a cohesive subculture can be attributed to them" (205).

It is impossible to read *Romeo and Juliet* or *Hamlet* unmediated by changing conceptions of youth, and the extent of popular and critical reference to

Shakespeare's plays about young people can provide a partial map of how ideas about youth became possible or prominent. These plays have in fact received a great deal more attention following the increased discussion of youth and adolescence since the mid-nineteenth century. It is also relevant that developmental psychology, including psychoanalysis, has influenced critical readings of Shakespeare's plays and pedagogical practices and stage productions. This mode of interpretation is dominated by the presumption that development is centered on the masculine term in a binary structure where the girl is object rather than subject of desire and law. Although I will return to Shakespeare and youth culture much later in this book through the popularity of Luhrmann's film, I want here to take up this exclusion of the girl from what is understood as "subjectivity" and her relegation to the known about rather than knowing. I will do so through a typically influential statement by Lacan: "This is the sense in which Hamlet's drama has the precise metaphysical resonance of the question of the modern hero. Indeed, something has changed since classical antiquity in the relationship of the hero to his fate . . . the thing that distinguishes Hamlet from Oedipus is that Hamlet *knows*" (1977a:19).

Classical Girls: The Girl as Universal
The Girl as Emblem of Nature and Culture

What Hamlet knows, for Lacan, is not about the girl—though this knowledge comprehends her—but about the dominant Law or Order that mediates social relations through symbolic terms such as "Mother" and "Father," and the human destiny of failure in relation to this Law. Lacan takes as exemplary of this Law Freud's interpretation of the Oedipus complex drawn from Sophocles' ancient tragedies. In this section I want to discuss what the girl means within this mesh of classical texts and how that girl has been used to represent a range of ambivalent positions in relation to knowledge, identity, and agency for late modernity.

During the early twentieth century girls were increasingly understood by reference to Freud's developmental theories, within which the oedipal has been particularly influential. Freud used the narrative of Oedipus and his family as an explanatory model for masculine subjectivity, for which it appeared ideal in conflating the masculine roles in the nuclear family into one central conflicted figure: Oedipus as Son-Father-Husband. In turn, this model positions the girl as a set of questions about subjectivity. Reference to classical girlhood in psychoanalysis and late modern philosophy provides exemplary instances of the retrospective construction of girlhood, the centrality of girls to modern critical theory, and some of the assumptions deployed in thinking about the girl as a universal psychological pattern. Classical representations of girlhood seem to provide ideal material for discussing what is universal about girlhood because, unlike the Renaissance, it is definitively prior to the modern, and even perceived as a source of the sophisticated human mediation of nature that the concept and pattern of "adolescence" articulates.

Aristotle described youth as a character type with its own field of interests and passions:

> Young men have strong passions, and tend to gratify them indiscriminately. Of the bodily desires, it is the sexual by which they are most swayed and in which they show absence of self-control. . . . They are fonder of their friends, intimates, and companions than older men are, because they like spending their days in the company of others, and have not yet come to value either their friends or anything else by their usefulness to themselves. All their mistakes are in the direction of doing things excessively and vehemently. (xii)

Much of what Aristotle has to say about youth seems tenable within late modern discourses on masculine adolescence. However, Aristotle's assertion that "all the valuable qualities that youth and age divide between them are united in the prime of life," located "from thirty to five-and-thirty" and for "the mind about forty-nine" (xii) sits uneasily with the late modern centrality of youth. Nevertheless, the classical classification of life into stages influenced the range of increasingly scientific accounts of adolescence in late modernity, a scientificity that is not confined to descriptions of the body but also encompasses social and cultural mechanisms.

Among other critics, Eve Cantarella details the significance of ancient Greek myths and rituals surrounding transition to adulthood:

> The rite of passage (specifically, in this case, the passage from the pre-pubertal to the pubertal age) signifies the death of the adolescent and the birth of an adult: in the case of male initiation, a man capable of fighting, and, in the case of female initiation, a woman capable of marrying and having children. (61)

This pattern of analysis has passed into rite-of-passage narratives in anthropological studies of the primitive, and while such symbolic transitions are sometimes identified in late modern culture, they are usually perceived as hangovers from a preindustrial world. Adolescence in late modernity is instead often presumed to be a more complex cover for this kind of transformation. Cantarella particularly focuses on girl-to-woman transformation in classical narratives and images, seeing in a complex imagery of swing and noose (and other mobile suspensions) reference to Persephonic myths crucial to understanding girlhood in classical times. The Persephone cycle of rape/capture, disappearance and mourning, and renewed fertility through ritual separation has been a key reference for figures of girlhood in Western mythologies. But what the capture and rescue of Persephone narrates, like various princesses in numerous towers, is a process we are now inclined to understand as adolescence (Frances Oppel even describes Persephone as a teenager [82]). Despite relevant materials gleaned from historical writings and written and visual arts, the Persephone cycle is not a recognized component of late modern adolescence to the same degree as the Sophoclean tragedies. Persephone's archetypal role as daughter is, however, important to Carl Jung's analytic psychology for defining women's relation to both time and the Mother with reference to the better-known Greek tragedies. This symbolic structure has continued influence through references to mythology as diverse as the impact of classicism on high modernism[13] and the reappearance of Jungian archetypes in new age psychology—in fact wherever the premodern is a useful concept for late modernity but especially whenever this engages with ambivalent sex/gender roles.[14]

Appropriations of classical girlhood as specifying what is innate or natural to girls have not been about the body as much as they have narrated dominant and residual cultural norms. Insofar as she can be conceived as adolescent, the classical girl acts across a space between child and woman, both already ambivalent positions in relation to dominant models of subjectivity. The girl marks the ambivalence of boundaries around crucial territories such as the State, the Mother, and the Law.

Antigone

That she is an ambivalent boundary is the focal point of modern appropriations of the girl as metaphor—G. W. F. Hegel, Jacques Derrida, and Lacan respond to an already dominant model of the girl's ambivalent relationship to the propriety/property of the Subject and the State when they take up the figure of Antigone, Oedipus' daughter, from what would apparently be the background of the oedipal cycle. Hegel positions Antigone as not yet owned by another but unable to *own* herself. As sister, then, she is an exemplary ethical figure because she is entirely distinct from the Mother (aligned with "First Nature"): "The feminine element . . . in the form of the sister, premonizes and foreshadows most completely the nature of ethical life" (476). It is inasmuch as she does not desire (the Subject) that the girl can maintain an ethical relation (to him), and as not mother and not wife she is independent from those strictly delineated territorializations of women that fix their dependent relations to men. Despite critiques of Hegel's interpretation, feminists have been attracted to Antigone and similar figures as daughters rather than sons of an archetypal family, and as an engagement with women's relations to the formation of the Subject under law.

Freud's deployment of the cycle of classical narratives surrounding the figure of Oedipus claims to be a familial rather than a political narrative, and Freud's interpretation elevates the psychological over the social despite reconsidering the shaping of the psyche by social forces. This kind of transhistorical narrative about desire, agency, and familial relations reinforces the assumption that feminine adolescence was always there, just waiting to be discovered or understood. But *Antigone*, even less than *Romeo and Juliet* or *Hamlet*, is not a narrative about psychological development, nor about the positioning of a body on a developmental ladder. Freud's use of the oedipal cycle does not attempt to recapture an historical period, but it does attempt to capture the truth of the present by reference to the classical as manifesting the human unmediated by modernity. Historically specific social elements are important to Freud in other contexts, and his reference to a classical world might be intended as inspirational allegory, but it manifests a narrative external to any history smaller than Western humanity. Freud's reference to the psychological verities of the Oedipus cycle does not produce a conventional historical narrative. No series of events displays the development of the familial relations he associates with Oedipus; rather, they are external to the particular situation of Oedipus as they are to any of Freud's patients. And yet Freud is not proposing a continuity between classical and late modern subjectivity but deploying the classical as a metaphysical origin for his teleological narrative of development.

Andrea Nye criticizes Luce Irigaray's reading of Plato's *Symposium*—a reading that is critical of dominant psychoanalytic readings of the classical world—for an ahistorical imposition of contemporary notions of sexual difference onto classical literature. Any similar criticisms of Freud have been made more quietly. Nye's criticism specifically interrogates the feminist connotations of any assumption that classical women should be relevant to twentieth-century women. Yet the emphases of Irigaray's reading of *Antigone*, focused on distinctions between genealogies and faiths, do belong to the play. Moreover, as classical scholar Ruth Padel argues, "Greek consciousness accepted underlying analogies between a tutelary god's occupation of human territory . . . [and] male 'self-possession' or mental control, and male economic and sexual possession of women" (13). A fundamental debate on self-possession is thus played out on the girl's body in *Antigone*, as Irigaray suggests.

What is foreign to the classical oedipal cycle, however, is the Oedipus complex as Freud describes it—sex as destiny, and virginity as a fated pause before heterosexuality. The basic oedipal narrative for Freud is the son's desire for the mother, which manifests as jealousy and resentment of the father (and other competitors), a drama that needs to be overcome in order to find a viable place in the social world. Crucially, although the oedipal drama is thus centered on a son it also applied to daughters (see chapter 4). While some feminists have criticized this as phallocentric or at least patriarchal, others have found it a valid description of the dilemma facing girls in a world where men hold the central if not the exclusive access to the position of ubject. Critics of Freud have employed his classical reference in order to debate the theories on their own terms. Jung's specific narrative for girls' psychological development, titled the "Electra complex," was initially designed as a complement to Freud's analysis, but Freud quickly detected within it an anti-oedipal narrative and expelled it from psychoanalysis proper. The Electra complex was never a story about development in relation to desire.

It remains unclear what place Antigone takes in the Freudian understanding of the oedipal family, but in fact she has been more influential in the field of philosophy, particularly ethical philosophy, and feminism's responses to those fields.[15] Antigone has been important to debates over Freud's classical allusions, but her story has a prior importance as an instance of ethical ambiguity and debates over self-possession and social responsibility. *Antigone* is the final text in a group of plays negotiating personal and political responsibility, and can be used to map ways in which the idea of the girl relates to womanhood, maturity, and citizenship, as well as other discourses on the modern world. As a story about women and politics, *Antigone* gained greater visibility through late modern debates about those relations. Gerhard Joseph claims that

> Creon's determination not to be bested by an irrational "girl" (l. 561), Ismene's conventional acceptance of woman's inferior status (ll. 61–2), and Antigone's pride in herself as self-sufficient being throughout the play have made the *Antigone* a natural counter for both sides in late nineteenth- and early twentieth-century discussions of the Woman Question. (27)

On the subject of Antigone, then, I want to turn to Hegel as a supplement to Freud's understanding of the oedipal family. Hegel's questions about whether Antigone should follow her responsibility to her family or to her *polis* in fact presume that she has both. But he articulates Antigone's ethical position as distinct from womanhood and the process by which "womankind—the everlasting irony (in the life) of the community—changes by intrigue the universal end of government into a private end" (Hegel 288). Seyla Benhabib translates Hegel's philosophy in this instance as containing an indirect discourse on women's rights. When Hegel argues that "the natural determinacies of both sexes acquire though its reasonableness *intellectual* as well as *ethical* significance" (trans. Benhabib 134), this deploys a classical frame of reference to define some social positions as innately proper to girls. Benhabib stresses that in the revolutionary context in which Hegel wrote his attitude to women's rights was not only conformist but reactionary and conservative: "Hegel saw the future, and he did not like it" (Benhabib 140).

Roslyn Diprose shows Hegel arguing that women's ethical subjectivity, her possible ethical action

> is grounded in her constitution of self in relation to her brother: a relation to a man based on mutual recognition rather than sexual desire, a relation where the woman is no longer a daughter and not yet a wife . . . woman, as a result of this relation, will be devoted to the universalization of a body as a sign not of herself, but of her brother. (166)

It is crucial, however, that Antigone be a girl rather than a woman because, as Lisa Walsh suggests, the determinant relations of women to husband and children suggest an "erotically tinged corporality [that] . . . renders them incompatible with the universal purity of ethical action" (99). It is thus left to the girl to found for Hegelian philosophy and its antecedents a heroism that can mark the expected and necessary failure of subject-formation and citizenship. Only with direct reference to a late modern understanding of girls as not quite individual can the girl can be seen as neither brother/citizen (conscious ethical action) nor the mother/*oikos* (unconscious immanence). As writers such as Irigaray, Kelly Oliver, and Roslyn Diprose have noted, Hegel's prioritization of Antigone's relation to her dead brother, Polynices, occurs at the expense of her relation to her living sister Ismene.[16] But Ismene is not at issue for the interpretations of the play—such as Hegel's and Lacan's—that focus on heterosexual desire as the inevitable frame for a girl's ethical position (her relations to others). Hegel finds no desire at all in Antigone, although as Oliver notes this requires an "assertion of the universality of the incest taboo," which is "an odd stance considering the family in question" (72).

On the other hand, Antigone's independent ethical action is denied to her even as she acts because she is not the citizen/brother. Referring to the place of Antigone in the psychoanalytic use of the oedipal triangle, Julia Kristeva locates in the oedipal formation of self-hood an "Other," that must be jettisoned in order to speak or take a place in terms of the law, a process she refers to as "abjection" (see Kristeva 1982). Tina Chanter sees Antigone as manifesting just this distasteful excess, and Oliver and Benhabib also argue that she is consumed and rejected in the process of reinstating the law.[17] Antigone is consigned to a paradoxically unconscious action that has no place in either foundational term of the dialectic that produces the modern subject—nature/unconsciousness and society/consciousness. But neither in Hegel nor in Freud does Antigone's excess place her in the position of actively *transcending* that dichotomy. The woman's place in the oedipal story will thus be assigned to the mother, placed within this opposition and superseded in the dialectical process of history. The law Antigone recognizes is read by Hegel as "divine law" (see Hegel 1977), and it cannot recognize or validate her as it recognizes only god/s. Chanter argues that, rather than being subject to or of the law she recognizes, Antigone situates a process of "decorating" or "beautifying" the law of which she becomes the object (76).

Hegel believes that the human law posited by Creon has "rightfully supplanted divine law" (Walsh 100), and this higher level of ethical consciousness operates by excluding Antigone:

> If Antigone's greatness derives precisely from the fact that she represents the ties of the "hearth and blood" over and against the *polis*, notwithstanding her grandeur, the dialectic will sweep Antigone in its onward historical march, precisely because the law of the city is public as opposed to private, rational as opposed to corporal, promulgated as opposed to intuited, human as opposed to divine. (Benhabib 142)

Antigone references a law that is not alien to her society, and she acts according to an ostensibly patriarchal model of personal responsibilities and rights. Yet she rejects the demands of the Father's law, framed as societal, for a bond of blood that runs counter to that law. Irigaray claims these laws of blood "relate to cultural obligations towards the blood of the *mother*" (1993:199). This bond is also a form of resistance consistent with other perspectives articulated in the play: through her fidelity to a patriarchal system Antigone has a reason for her desire. The issue at stake in debates over whether Antigone qualifies as an ethical agent is whether the knowledge and experience to which she has access sufficiently informs her choice. Ironically, any experience proper to Antigone would disqualify her from the kind of knowledge of the universal that would enable her to act ethically. Other models of ethics that posit relations to the self rather than responsibility to a community would not compromise Antigone in the same way, but they are not established as proper for girls in late modernity—the context of Hegel's as well as Freud's reading.

Although we might attempt to trace appearances of girlhood in earlier historical periods, and even to delineate a kind of adolescent process or space that was considered proper to girls in those periods, we do so substantially because the late modern period has naturalized feminine adolescence as an explanation for all girls and, teleologically, draws on selected instances of these past girls in order to naturalize that position. These repeated references to classical girlhood place the late modern girl as an innately problematic relation to the Law. In popular culture girls are closely attached to the mechanisms of the family and the state and are responsible for dignifying those institutions with their pleasure; and in critical theory the girl has been tied in late modernity to the grounds for reproducing the Law or

Order that Lacan and others see as the deep structure of modern life.[18] Antigone's reason is not adequate to the Law, and it is in this respect that she is programmatic for modernity.

Victorian Girls: Girl as Cultural Crisis
Discursive Formation

The Victorian period, encompassing the Western nineteenth century, situates the emergence of public discourses that produced a recognizable figure of feminine adolescence. This renovation of the girl and her connotations is what Foucault calls a *discursive formation*—a "systematic dispersion of statements" (Foucault quoted in Tolson 117) across various fields. In newspapers, legislation, and parliamentary debate, literary and visual representations, official reports, changes to established institutions and constitution of new ones, and social commentary in various forms, we can locate multiple "surfaces of emergence" (see Tolson 117) for a new modern girl who forms a crucial precursor for the twentieth-century category of feminine adolescence. In the mid to late Victorian period these sites evidence a simultaneous construction of new girls and a recapturing of girls from the past within which our readings of Hegel and Freud can be usefully situated.

Deborah Gorham claims that "the period between childhood and adulthood . . . by the end of the nineteenth century was beginning to be generally known as adolescence" (356), and John Gillis and Carol Dyhouse concur that adolescence "was first 'discovered' in the nineteenth century" (see Dyhouse 115). However, the relation between Victorian girlhood and twentieth-century conceptions of feminine adolescence is not straightforward. In the background of publications on Victorian girlhood there are ongoing debates in which ideas about historical change and cultural identity as well as the meaning of girlhood are at issue. The experience of girlhood in the nineteenth century was clearly diverse—striated by differences such as class, race, occupation, and location. The girls of the British Empire, for example, were invested with a representative status in cultural forms produced for British girls and girls in the British colonies. They were emblems of the continuity of Britishness in the private realm, the natural continuity of the empire in individual persons and families, and reinforced a home culture in the face of the colonial experience. As girls took on this role for the colonial center, the idea of the native girl also represented her culture—materializing an image of those cultures, their capacity to be inculcated into British/Christian cultures, and the seductive threat of interracial desire. And yet Victorian girlhood is often presented as a relatively homogenous category, in part because of the dramatic appearance of new discourses on childhood and gender in the period.

Any claims to recover the history of girlhood are compromised by the fact that, as both Sally Mitchell and Dyhouse note, "virtually all of our information [on Victorian girlhood] comes from adults, who may well be unreliable or at least selective in what they observe or recall" (1994:252). However, representations of childhood and adolescence always work by retrospective observation, not only because of the greater opportunities for adult expression but because experience outside mediated representation of that experience is inaccessible. Girls themselves are influenced by equally selective categories for understanding girlhood. Victorian discussion of how girls became women claimed to account for those processes by more rigorous, objective, and thus more modern means, and this is apparent in girls' as well as adult and scientific or official representations. Dorothy Margaret Stuart's *The Girl Through the Ages* (1933) concludes her study by presenting the late Victorian era as

a new world, peopled by parents and children with new points of view . . . time-hallowed standards were to be abandoned; time-honoured relationships were to be readgusted [sic]; traditions that had persisted for nearly two-thousand years were to fade out. Here, then, while yet the old ways were remembered and the old things endured, let us end this history. (258)[19]

The abandonment of standards was a vibrant refrain of the late Victorian period, countered and complemented by narratives of human progress, and girls figured prominently on both rhetorical sides.

Eliza Lynn Linton's famous 1868 tirade against the moral decay of young women, "The Girl of the Period," specifically accuses girls of both abandoning, and being unfit for, woman's noble destiny in motherhood. The modern girl condemned by Linton was invested in pleasure and unseemly self-assertion, while the "ideal Victorian Girl" was, as Gorham points out, "innocent, gentle and self-sacrificing" (4). As Christina Boufis suggests, "the reactions to Linton's essay demonstrate that regulating the modern girl and controlling her presentation and representation is part of a larger struggle in England for national self-definition" (99). Linton's essay belongs to the context of the 1867 Reform Act, which broadened enfranchisement and escalated the campaign for women's suffrage (presented to parliament in 1866 by John Stuart Mill). Boufis's essay aligns Linton with purity reform movements, which overlapped with the suffrage movements both in questioning the content and implications of majority and in a concern for the production of proper subjects of the nation-state. Feminism often garnered support from purity reform, within which "by virtue of the moral influence with which both women and children were credited, their very otherness lent them an oppositional power over the public sphere from which they were supposed to be excluded" (Nelson and Vallone 5). Woman suffrage also questioned what a woman was or functioned as and how she should be formed, doubling the significance of girls and how they were socially defined and positioned.

The girl of the period was also the disturbingly active "hoyden," denoting "a deplorable degree of roughness, and puerile imitation of the off-hand manners of young men" in which Gorham discerns "an expression of antagonism towards the nascent women's movement" (56). In a review of Linton's essay, Henry James—himself responsible for influential representations of Victorian girls including *Daisy Miller* (1878) and *Portrait of a Lady* (1881)—emphasizes the American girl's active independence and crucially urban context:

> Accustomed to walk alone in the streets of a great city, and to be looked at by all sorts of people, she has acquired an unshrinking directness of gaze. She is the least bit *hard.* If she is more than this—if she is painted and touzled [sic] and wantonly *chiffonée*—she is simply an exception, and the sisterhood of "modern women" are in no way responsible for her. (quoted in Helsinger et al. 122)

James's suggestive caveat evinces an anxiety over the modern girl becoming some new form of woman associated with feminism, and these interactions situate a late modern entanglement of law, feminism, and girls in Western Europe and the most privileged strata of European colonies.[20]

Technologies of the Self

While girls were invested with influence over family members, future children, and men they associated with, the first effects of a girl's influence were on herself. The expansion of middle-class girls' education meant the establishment of a broader period of transition between childhood and adulthood. Age of consent legislation and new labor laws, both reliant on a border articulated by new ideas about puberty, allowed a further space between maturity and adult activities.[21] Changes to compulsory education for girls and other legislation concerning the proper development of girls signal the centrality of the girl to public discourses on how society and culture are reproduced. New laws about sex, age, work, education, and property did not articulate a separate cultural space for adolescence, but such a space was provided by discourses on self-production and self-possession in popular culture framed as guidance for late Victorian girls.[22] While I will also discuss the aforementioned legislation, this section focuses on the dissemination of cultural forms that articulate a need for, and provide, personal and social training for these new girls.

Compulsory education was extensively debated in England in the 1860s and 1870s, predominantly as a measure to improve the lot of working-class men, spawning organizations such as the National Education League. But the education of middle-class girls also expanded rapidly at this time. Schooling for middle-class girls apparently also shaped what working-class girls were compared to, and perhaps aspired to, under the aegis of a recognized class hierarchy. Sally Mitchell goes so far as to wonder whether it might "be argued that schools were responsible for creating girlhood" (1995:74). The reforms associated with girls' education were explicitly referenced to the maintenance of social standards as well as personal discipline among girls—although this may have been a pragmatic choice for some feminist reformers. But the new Victorian girls' schools were not only a modernizing form of guidance and observation but also a new way of being a person. Thus gymnastics, for example, along with domestic sciences including management of money, were implemented in girls' school or college curriculums. New peer groups also coalesced in these formations, and newly recognized types, such as the schoolgirl and the sporting girl, produced new communities, values, and ways of living.

Victorians were troubled by how to define girlhood. Despite if not because of the uncertainty of what it described, Mitchell argues,

the word [girl] became enormously popular in the last quarter of the nineteenth century. Young lady and young person—like lady and woman—

had class referents; *girl* is inclusive. It takes in workgirl, servant girl, factory girl, college girl or girl graduate, shop-girl, bachelor girl, girl journalist, and office girl. It includes schoolgirl as well, but she is not a child. (1995:25)

Such girls participated in new and changing cultural forms for girls. Mitchell traces this girls' culture in "books, magazines, clothing styles, clubs, sports, schools and memoirs" (1995:3), and advice manuals, this last being "perhaps more significant as markers of culture and imaginative life than as actual agents of instruction: through them as well as through fiction the daughter at home in a provincial town with a daily routine virtually indistinguishable from her mother's at the same age could be, in her mind, a new girl" (1995:9–10).

I have called these texts dedicated to the better understanding and regulation of girls "guidance manuals." Compulsory schooling for girls made the guidance manual genre tenable because it refers to a literate audience (en masse rather than as informed specialists). The girl of these guidance manuals was primarily responsible for the condition of her self, even if that imperative was often phrased as a duty to others. This is signified in the magazines' titles—the girl's own, the girl's realm, the girl's friend: her magazine, her culture, her self.

Victorian girls' magazines helped construct audiences for the young housewife materials that dominated women's magazines in the next century, but no more than they helped constitute the idea of feminine adolescence. Mitchell claims "girls were consciously aware of their own culture and recognized its discord with adult expectations. They perhaps suspected that they could be (new) girls for only a few brief years before they grew up to be (traditional) women" (1995:3). While Mitchell employs letters, diaries, and memoirs to support this recognition of "discord," it is unclear what evidence she uses to support her suspicion about the brevity of girlhood opportunities. However, the simultaneous concentration and multiplication of separate spheres for girls is one of the dominant effects of girl culture. Like many other writers, I'm going to use *The Girl's Own Paper* as an example.[23] Generally supporting claims that the definition of girlhood was a public and popular issue in the late the nineteenth century, *The Girl's Own* of 1889–90 includes Sophia F. Caulfield's series "Some Types of Girlhood; or, Our Juvenile Spinsters." Caulfield frames the problem of defining girls as an issue of concern to her readers, for whom presentation and articulation of self—taste, appearance, behavior, personality, character, potential, and intellect—cohere into an explicitly manipulable girls' identity.

Across three installments Caulfield considers muscular, aesthetic, society, scholastic or scientific, medical, devotee, missionary, church, literary, musical, artistic, colorless or commonplace girls and housewives—the first and the last being given the most attention. These are all specified as aspects of the "educated classes," underscoring the redefinition of the girl by the Education Act, which, while it was no longer news, had now pervasively redefined modern girlhood. "Girl" is placed in the *Paper* as a point between child and woman, beginning here with an invocation of the "childlike simplicity and blooming healthfulness" of girls in the past, which rested on forms of knowledge that the guidance manual is now required to replace: "It needs but to read the 'Answers to Correspondents' in this paper to see . . . how little their own self-respect has done to substitute the guiding and restraining influence of their mothers" (Sophia Caulfield 4). Although Victorian magazines tend not to include the corresponding girl's voice, advice in response to letters was one of several important conventions for girls' magazines cohering at this time. They name experiences and desires they are required to guide, and this consultation is framed as a matter of public concern. But letters from girls to *The Girls' Own Paper* also mostly fall outside the categories of advice endorsed by its preselected headings, and by far the majority have to be listed under "MISCELLANEOUS." Guidance manuals are always in this way at least dialogic, allowing a speaking position to the practices they censure or want to modify as well as to those they extol or invent. Thus the regular fashion spreads under the title "Dress: In Season and in Reason" imply that it might not be so reasonable, and the exclusion of actual letters from advice pages nevertheless cryptically includes what they might have said.

I want to discuss these conventions as what Michel Foucault calls "Technologies of the Self." Foucault describes technologies of the self as permitting "individuals to effect by their own means or with the help of others a certain number of operations on their own bodies and souls, thoughts, conduct, and way of being, so as to transform themselves in order to attain a certain state of happiness, purity wisdom, perfection, or immortality" (1988:18)—but always within a preexisting set of discourses on the self. Thus, for example, the self-interrogation demanded by evangelism is continuous with rather than opposed to beauty culture or reflections on a girl's own career. The final installment of "Types of Girlhood" makes this clear:

A Little amalgamation of a few of these distinctive types might produce a charming woman. Study each portrait, and improve your own individuality, taking a lovely tint from one and a graceful line from another. But beware of skin-deep appearances. . . . God speed your upward course. (246)

Making the care of the self a public duty gives the girl as self an important public role. Dedication to self-improvement and the right to self-articulation could fantastically transcend as well as underscore class identities in a sweeping conception of "the girl" that remains relevant more than a century later.

Such technologies of the self manifest in "training and modification of individuals, not only in the obvious sense of acquiring certain skills but also in the sense of acquiring certain attitudes" (Foucault 1988:18). Even the illustrations in these magazines detail instructions about modes of self-care and desirable behaviors or preferences attached to the girl as narrative or pictorial tableau. Through detailed elaboration of techniques for being a girl, Victorian guidance manuals seem to oppose the public discourses on girls that claimed that the desires and identities of girlhood were self-evident, stressing self-discipline rather than required obedience. Education reformer Emily Shirreff articulated this as follows: "The willing submission to the rule felt to be lawful and wise is the germ of self-government" (quoted in Pederson 203). The phrase "felt to be" demands that girls' self-reflection endorse what is to be obeyed, and reformers by default replaced obligation and instruction with an internalized order that recollects Foucault's theories about disciplinization in late modernity (see chapter 8). Invested with some of the privileges of citizenship, including education and employment, these new girls belonged to the movement toward suffrage, and these exercises of power are the fertile if also captive space of selfhood.[24]

Foucault's studies of prisons, medicine, and madness describe the diverse and specific practices and effects of power, identifying subject-positions constituted in relation to these regimes of power. For Foucault, technologies of the self began with the imperative to speak about the self, exemplarily through an imperative to speak about sex. In the introduction to the *History of Sexuality* (1976) Foucault credits the invention of interiorized sexual identity to the Victorian period and its diverse sciences of disciplined sexualization of the self (which often claimed sex was not discussed). He claims these imperatives to speak about sex produced sex as the (secret) significance of sexual identity. Foucault suggests that prior ethical systems organized around the care of the self were substantially replaced by this machinery of sexuality, and this claim may be significant for debates over the sexualization of a Victorian girlhood that appears to engage with, rather than take the place of, what Foucault later called the care of the self. Guidance manuals generically represented the end of girlhood in marriage and maternity but also stressed a detailed and ongoing care of the self that forestalls the closure of girlhood. Mitchell places a great deal of importance on the Victorian girl being unsexed, claiming that "terms such as college girl, girl graduate, working girl, or bachelor girl unsex" the middle-class counterpart of the working girl because "a 'girl' is not husband-hunting. The ascription of immaturity and liminality gives her permission to behave in ways that might not be appropriate for a woman" (1994:245). But this *un*sexing attributed intrinsic sex to girls in claiming its erasure or absence. The sexuality of Victorian girlhood was projected into their future but then reflected onto their past. It was an anticipation of having spoken about sex.[25]

Alice

Guidance manuals as technologies of the self occur in many other forms than advice books and magazines. This section considers new laws about sexual consent and new technologies for representing girls as they intersect in Lewis Carroll's *Alice Adventures in Wonderland* and *Through the Looking-Glass*. Alice (see fig. 1.1) is not only a highly influential image of Victorian girlhood but also enables questions about relations between girlhood and feminine adolescence, in part through Carroll's investment, as Rev. Charles Lutwidge Dodgson, in both age of consent debates and photography, as well as the production of stories for girls. It is worth asking whether Alice fits the narratives of psychological development with which she would now be associated. Is her ever changing body indicative of new discourses on puberty, adolescence, and gender production? Psychoanalytic readings sourced in these new Victorian discourses find many monstrous mothers in Alice, including not only queens and nurses but the rabbit hole, the pool of tears, and the house that Alice outgrows. But figures of feminine adolescence are also vital to these texts and often trapped by these maternal metaphors in houses, wells, lessons, and discourses on self-restraint. Alice falls into the *Wonderland* of adolescence and her momentum in *Through the Looking-*

Glass places her as a queen in a girl's body. Reading Alice as pubescent might also draw on Dodgson's concern about a border between child and woman he describes as "where the stream and river meet" (quoted in Green 66). The transformations and displacements of both books evoke this border, and if Alice always remains a child this is nevertheless fraught with unstable definitions and attributes. Alice undertakes all possible transformations, but on the other side of these dreams and mirrors still the ways aren't her ways.[26]

Carroll extols innocence and gentleness as explicitly as instructional texts on girls of the period. But Alice is as self-interested as she is generous and is not unambiguously a good girl (i.e., loving, courteous, or trustful). More than "simple and loving" (Carroll 163–4), the little girl in Carroll is marked by curiosity and delight. I could have selected texts on Victorian girls by women for this discussion, or even fictions by girls about girls, but these selections would not have been less concerned with the disciplined formation of a paradoxical girl-subject. Moreover, like *Romeo and Juliet*, Alice has been insistently returned to the field of popular culture, adapted to the stage, film, animation, and children's narratives across the course of the twentieth century. And like *Antigone* Alice has also continually appeared in theoretical texts—from literary formalism to poststructuralist philosophy—implicitly elaborating the significance of the girl to late modernity. Selecting Alice allows me to consider how Victorian discourses on the girl participate in both the arrival of girl culture and the modernization of representation and public policy.

As Lindsay Smith records, Dodgson/Carroll's texts, photography, and correspondence engage with concerns about identity, development, and sex that informed the emergence of feminine adolescence. Dodgson took photographs of little girls in various states of fancy dress, décolletage, and undress. Smith argues that Carroll specifically chose the subjects of his photography for their littleness: "*Please* don't grow any taller, if you can help it, till I've had time to photograph you again" (quoted in Smith 382). While photography is often related to Alice because of Dodgson's well-known interest in photographing little girls, Dodgson's interest in age of consent debates is just as relevant here. Carroll's desire to capture the littleness of girls could not operate outside social discourses on propriety and consent. By photographing the littlest of girls, Carroll avoided transgressing what he understood to be relevant sexual proprieties. While the little girl and woman were held to be discrete, the point at which one becomes the other remained slippery, constituting a period of ambiguity in which Carroll's photographic preferences are tolerated. Such littleness is not just a physical characteristic;it is also an incorporeal quality. Smith notes Dodgson's obsession with not only the littleness of girls but also the capture of their growth as signifier of maturity: "The problematic nature of a concept of adolescence is, as a result, displaced to height, and thereby linked to consent in such a way that height, rather than the more obvious signs of puberty, comes to stand in for markers of the psycho-sexual development of the subject" (371).

Carroll's anxiety about his girl-objects' growth is often represented by Carroll as the girl exceeding the frame of the photographs he might take (Smith 382–3). Carol Mavor also links the age of consent and photography as technologies for the capture and redefinition of children. Mavor discusses Carroll's photograph of Evelyn Hatch as a reclining nude, noting that "nudes . . . [often] imaged women, like children, as lacking the telltale marks of womanhood: full breasts and (especially) pubic hair" (165), and seeing in its arrangement an "attachment to the past" (and past iconography) that veiled "what would have otherwise been unacceptable" (165). In response to Mitchell's assertion that sex was not an issue in Victorian discourses on girlhood we might take up Mavor's recognition that "although their bodies have been cleansed of the markings of 'sex.' . . pose, transparent draperies, flowers, and so forth all connote the womanhood that is not there" (165). Mavor relates this "fetishization" of girl sexuality to the fifty thousand people who bought the 1880 *Graphic* Christmas annual with a colored print of John Everett Millais's painting *Cherry Ripe* (Mavor 162, see fig. 1.2). The scholarly debate over *Cherry Ripe* focuses on whether it is an image of girlhood as sexual object or a painterly homage to the English pastoral. These readings might in fact be complementary. *Cherry Ripe* suggests a nostalgia for a girlhood that never was, before it is a nostalgia for an England that never was, but it is an image that also captures relations between the two. Similarly the tension between Rousseau's image of the child as tabula rasa and discourses on original sin meant that girlhood took on different meanings as it was divested of innocence by entry into social institutions (especially knowledge institutions).

Mavor refers to a quite different signification of girlhood appearing around the same time in her citation of Thomas Richards's analysis of the "seaside girl" in Victorian advertising. These images of girls by the sea, according to Richards, "eulogized adolescence and signalled the formation of what we now call 'youth culture' " (Mavor 241).[27] However, both *Cherry Ripe* and the seaside girls interact with debates on sexual consent, which placed the girl as a marker of morality, civilization, and the adult. Mavor claims these debates

> only referred to those beings who were problematically sliding between the categories of girl and woman; male children were outside of "sex," a division set up both to mark women from girls and to mark female from the rest of society. As a result . . . the various age-of-consent amendments were only addressed to girls. They were about "sex," not about childhood. (169)[28]

Such laws constituted new meanings exchanged between legislators, public commentators, and new social scientists, and debated the concept of agency underpinning modern ideas of majority and citizenship.[29] Age of consent legislation referred to and defined girls (with a few significant exceptions); however, not only girlhood itself but such a concept of consent remains contradictory.[30] These unstable terms meet in constituting girlhood as the impossible inverse of majority and citizenship, and the various disciplines implied by age of consent discourse map a terrain on which girls are not subjects of the public sphere that identifies them by that discourse.

The establishment of age of consent laws did not reverse the uncertainty intrinsic to the boundary between girl and woman or around the ethical status of sexual activity involving girls. Crucial complications and qualifications were retained and produced in this legislation. After 1885 the age of (hetero)sexual consent was sixteen, though there was room for appeal on the grounds of seduction and ignorance between thirteen and sixteen. In Australia these changes to English laws directly impacted on parliamentary debate, with particular reference to the protection of young men from "seduction" as well as of girls from debauchery (see Barber 1977). These laws also concretely separate sex from marriage as involving apparently greater economic issues. They were always, then, class-specific narratives, often directly invoking the threat of girlhood in seduction by maids or nurses, in relation to which consent was not phrased in terms of the same modes of culpability and agency.[31] British social reform campaigns directed at sex were crucially influenced after 1885 by the prosecution of William Stead. Stead participated in a hyperbolic media campaign against street prostitution, associated with the mythical threat of a "white slave trade of virgins" smuggled through Europe to "the Orient" (see Walkowitz 1993). Stead was prosecuted for immorally exposing girls to both sex and prostitution in the course of his "investigation" for the *Pall Mall Gazette.* After a range of debates in the media and parliament the Criminal Law Amendment Act (also called the Stead Act) raised the age of consent from thirteen to sixteen in 1893.[32] While English common law concerning majority referred not to the young person's relationship to the state but to "the adults directly in authority over him or her" (Gorham 1978:362), this new legislation defined majority more concretely and at the same time articulated a less specific intermediary state between childhood and majority.

two

Feminine Adolescence

Youth, when properly understood, will seem to be not only the revealer of the past but of the future, for it is dimly prophetic of that best part of history which is not yet written because it has not yet transpired, of the best literature the only criterion of which is that it helps to an ever more complete maturity, and of better social organizations, which, like everything else, are those that best serve youth.

—G. Stanley Hall, *Adolescence*

THIS CHAPTER maps the emergence of feminine adolescence as an explanatory category in the twentieth century, and its relation to generic ideas about modern youth. It surveys changing definitions of adolescence in modernity, unpacking the invention of feminine adolescence as a public discourse and new twentieth-century discourses that foregrounded theories of feminine adolescence—including the institutionalization of the normal and the hysterical or deviant girl.

Girls in the sense we now use the word—encompassing no specific age group but rather an idea of mobility preceding the fixity of womanhood and implying an unfinished process of personal development—are produced at a nexus of late modern ways of being in and knowing the world. While chapter 1 considered the materialization of a space for feminine adolescence, this chapter will focus on the public arrival of feminine adolescence as an explanation of a difficult and indispensable progression to maturity, majority, or agency. I want to point in this chapter to some of the conditions that make a feminine process of adolescence possible and necessary for late modernity.

Adolescere: In Process/on Trial
Modernity and Maturity

Claiming that feminine adolescence emerged with late modernity does not propose it as a summary of late modernity or as merely analogous to everything else proper to late modernity. Instead, girls (feminine adolescence) exemplify some of the most pervasive and dramatic constitutive forces of late modernity. The modern period requires both the development of capitalist industrial production and a religious or philosophical turn toward the human. This modernity is usually dated from the eighteenth-century period now known as the Enlightenment in which these developments took on some forms recognizable to us, including a discourse on immaturity. Immanuel Kant's "What Is Enlightenment?" proposes an opposition between the "enlightenment"—the progress of the human world—and immaturity, articulating a process of enlightenment or maturation as the development of independence and identity. To be free in Kant's sense of "free public rationality" is to have some subjectivity outside of your social functions, your roles as a cog in the social machine (37), and also to use that subjectivity in a mature fashion. Across late modern philosophy—bridging even dominant philosophical oppositions such as that between Kant and Friedrich Nietzsche—girls have been figured as having little or no access to such a subjectivity, and not only because until relatively recently they were literally excluded from legal majority.

Maturity is a crucial force in structuring late modern life. Modern political rights and responsibilities are invested at majority—a fixed marker, although not the only marker, of entrance into the Enlightenment rhetoric of social contract. Late modern adolescence has been publicly and popularly figured as expressing a tension, a disjunction, between (physiological) maturity and (social) majority, a representation that naturalizes both maturity and majority. This model has not applied to girls in the same way as to boys, and feminine adolescence itself questions this relation between maturity and majority. If coming of legal age automatically qualifies the subject for majority then it does not in fact infer or require maturity. None of the rights and responsibilities invested in such a majority draw on any experience or process of the subject and they are not in any case chosen or endorsed by the subject attaining majority. If entrance into the social contract is, moreover, enforced by law—if not literally in the case of being forced to vote then by implication under the law's delineation of what is unacceptable—then maturity is not at issue in majority at all.[1] While majority does make a boy a (young) man, it does not complete an apprenticeship in experience but instead functions to distinguish law and agency under the law (the only place agency can be invested) from experience, puberty, and adolescence.

Adolescence has consistently been used to constitute a gendered field, but this usually becomes apparent only when girls are being discussed. As adolescence implies a physiological difference from what precedes and follows it, the question of sexual difference is easily seen as intrinsic to adolescence. However, as a description of personal and social development, adolescence is still usually distinguished from puberty as a name for physiological changes, and it is thus possible to detach adolescence from a binary construction of physiological difference. I have used the term "feminine" rather than female adolescence to avoid an incautious collapse of adolescence into puberty, particularly in relation to discourses on individual maturity. In *The Modern Girl*, Lesley Johnson questions "the relation of women to the cultural ideal of the self-determining, autonomous individual considered to be central to what is often referred to as the project of modernity" (3). The problem of woman or femininity has been widely identified as crucial to discourses on subjectivity in modernity, but this is no less true of discourses on youth. In "Modernity—An Incomplete Project" Jürgen Habermas notes that "modernity revolts against the normalizing functions of tradition; modernity lives on the experience of rebelling against all that is normative" (5). Habermas's essay rejects claims that the progress of the modern has superseded the Enlightenment understanding of the subject, culture, and society as organized according to a hierarchy of maturity. The Enlightenment enables a process of philosophy reflecting on its own present and inquiring as to what difference today introduces with respect to yesterday (Foucault 1980:34). The Enlightenment thus inflects preexisting concerns about youth with this investment in the modern and, at the same time, an emphasis on what we might call "critique." It also seems, given the references to youth that appear in Enlightenment and post-Enlightenment texts, that this process of modernization and critique was always accompanied by what Andreas Huyssen describes as a "decline in paternal authority" defining modern subjectivity (22). The subject of modernity is a problem defined as immaturity.

Exemplarily, Jean-Jacques Rousseau's *Emile* (1762), a treatise on education and the ideal citizen, produced an influential model of youth teleologically designed to produce the mature citizen proper to that social contract.

In this context Rousseau argues that if "women . . . seem in many respects never to be anything else" than children, "man in general is not made to remain always in childhood. He leaves it at the time prescribed by nature; and this moment of crisis, although rather short, has far-reaching influences" (211). The difficulty of becoming a subject, let alone a relatively independent person, has continued to be perceived as considerably greater for girls. But even Rousseau's naturalization of gender differences in childhood and youth allows, in its anxious cautions against the pitfalls on the way to becoming a man, for the failure of what he otherwise describes as destiny. The modern models of maturity that elevated the progress from child to man without especially focusing on the adolescent, such as those propounded by Rousseau and Kant, were significantly modified by understandings of physiology which followed the Enlightenment. The more rigid demarcation of childhood relied on and produced a more forceful account of biological maturation, culminating in both new attention to puberty and detailed analogies between physiology and cultural difference—for example those produced by anthropologists such as Bronislaw Malinowski or psychologists such as Havelock Ellis. These classificatory analyses remained influential definitions of adolescent processes in the early twentieth century, although they were partly eclipsed by other psychologies.

As a process of classification that infers a normative discourse on behavior as well as tracing biological development, adolescence is specific to modernity. But the role of adolescence as psychological crescendo, as psychosocial crucible for becoming a Subject, is specific to *late* modernity. As Michael Rutter argues,

> the term adolescence was rarely used prior to the eighteenth century and although the characteristics of puberty were well recognized, little psychological significance was attached to them. The reaching of adulthood was determined by the acquisition of independence, a point having no direct connection with physiological maturity. (5)

In the twentieth century new models of adolescence displaced some of the importance of the Victorian child. French historiographer Michel De Certeau, citing Philippe Ariés, claims that if

> the child was born as a social and cultural category in the sixteenth and seventeenth centuries, the young man could have appeared in the nine-

teenth century with the spread of secondary schools, the growing needs of technical training, the universalisation of military service, and the beginnings of the literary figure of the "adolescent" poet. In the nineteenth century the boy slowly withdraws [out] . . . of things. (1997:89)

The history of adolescence prior to late modernity was consistently reconstructed and reinterpreted to claim different elements of adolescence as transhistorical and transcultural attributes of human development. This modern deployment of supposedly archetypical elements especially drew on observation of distant cultures and on ancient pedagogical and biological theories.[2] However, adolescence is not a clear denotation of any age, body, behavior, or identity. Patricia Spacks notes John and Virginia Demos's argument that "adolescence constitutes an idea masquerading as a fact; they believe the idea to have originated in the late nineteenth century and to be 'on the whole an American discovery' " (6). Spacks's *The Adolescent Idea* locates the beginnings of adolescent "difficulty" in the dramas of displacement and alienation in Gothic novels (140) and the frustrations of central protagonists in realist novels (132). A history of literary examples could also be employed to map the emergence of public discourses on feminine adolescence. For example, it is pivotal to the concerns of public discourse on late modern girls and the ways they become women that nineteenth- and early-twentieth-century novels focusing on young women tended to newly balance the conventions of romance fiction and the realist novel of development. The bildungsroman generally focused on boys/men—not because there were no novels written about girls growing up but because a novel about girls' development tends to be romance fiction, a novel about how she grows up and into love, is made by love. Spacks notes that in the mid- to late-Victorian period adolescents begin to constitute "a version of the self" in literary texts (195) via a "clear, inclusive concept of adolescence" (226) not evident in earlier examples. While this development is contemporary with the emergence of modern girls, the dissemination of these new discourses is not specific to literature.

In the late nineteenth and early twentieth centuries adolescence gradually extended into an unspecific age category ending around twenty-one or twenty-five, contracting in subsequent years to specify the teenage years. Late modern adolescence differs in several senses from prior models, and the emergence of feminine adolescence is crucial to these differences. The characteristics of the twentieth-century teenager point to this influence. While "teen" was commonly used in the nineteenth century, the public and popular categorization of teenage attributes and behaviors belongs initially to the 1920s and 1930s, when new theories of puberty, adolescence, and femininity were being widely disseminated. In the 1950s and 1960s "teenager" became a more visible term than "adolescent" for marking the personal effects of social changes, a shift I will consider in the final section of this chapter. But from its earliest formations the teenager foregrounds questions of cultural conformity and frames adolescence as a dialectic of dependence and independence. "Teenager," unlike "pubescent" or "adolescent," equally if not especially implies girls and has even been represented as a feminized because contained and disempowered role. "Teenager" specifies no particular experience or process. She will cease to be a teenager at a certain chronological point, which will neither manifest her experience nor necessarily make her an adult. In the twentieth century, adolescence means something other than the teenage stage and implies both pubescence and experience.

While "youth" is generally perceived as having expanded in modernity with the extension of education and economic dependence, it is arguable that adolescence became more specialized and condensed:

> Adolescence is recognized and treated as a distinct stage of development because the coincidence of extended education and early sexual maturation have meant a prolonged phase of physical maturity associated with economic dependence; because many of the widely held psychological theories specify that adolescence *should* be different; because commercial interests demanded a youth culture; and because schools and colleges have ensured that large numbers of young people are kept together in an age-segregated group. (Rutter 7)

Adolescence is thus intrinsic to late modernity. Moreover, it connotes transitions between dependence and independence and between ignorance and knowledge linked to standards of education defined against models of immaturity. English cultural critic F. R. Leavis's *Mass Civilisation and Minority Culture* (1930) is an exemplary and influential text in this regard. Noting the absorption of the young in new cultural forms, Leavis stridently advocated a range of pedagogical practices to counter this tendency, stressing the importance of youth to the maintenance of culture and improvement of society. For Leavis, modern youth is in need of education to become fully developed cultural subjects.[3]

Adolescence defines the ideal coherence of the modern subject—individuality, agency, and adult (genital) sexuality—while not necessarily ensuring its achievement. When critics such as Kant or Leavis understand the modern subject as immature—as threatened by possible immaturity, as engaged with self-doubt—they understand it as adolescent. This alignment becomes more overt in late modern critical theory and popular culture after the impact of what Julia Kristeva calls Freud's "Copernican" realization that the subject was "split" or not "self-identical." Kristeva argues that this modern subjectivity locates no coherent Subject but rather a "*sujet-en-procès*," a subject in process (1984). The significance of adolescence to ideas about modernity and the modern subject interact at an everyday level with the material form of young people's lives. In her analysis of disenfranchised adolescents in 1980s United States, *Teenage Wasteland*, Donna Gaines notes that "Although nineteenth-century reformers and industrialists had very different agendas, their combined efforts ultimately transformed young people into a powerless age caste" (240). Gaines cites child labor laws, mandatory schooling, and the invention of "juvenile court," to claim that "through the notion of 'adolescence' as a preparatory stage for adulthood, young people of all classes were reduced to complete psychological and economic dependence on adults" (240). This presumed dependence, though it is not a description of any demographic and does not literally apply to a genre of young people, marks a space in which processes of identity-formation and social placement are monitored.

Defining Feminine Adolescence: After G. Stanley Hall

Adolescence had an established importance for twentieth-century social and psychological theories by the time Erik Erikson identified "the major crisis of adolescence" as an identity crisis, occurring "in that period of the life cycle when each youth must forge for himself some central perspective and direction, some working unity" (quoted in Friedan 69). Central among the texts that impelled the emergence of this significance is G. Stanley Hall's 1904 study, *Adolescence: Its Psychology and Its Relations to Physiology, Anthropology, Sociology, Sex, Crime, Religion, and Education.* Hall's text helped redefine adolescence for the twentieth century, although it draws on earlier observation and analysis to a degree that few commentators stress sufficiently (see Dyhouse 126). As the epigraph to this chapter attests, Hall venerates adolescence as fertile and regenerative and depicts modern society as dependent on the value of its adolescents, by which he generally means young men. Hall sees the turbulent self-definition of adolescence as a masculine sociopsychological process, but at the same time he speaks about girls as closer to adolescence.[4] The malleability and difficulty of the late modern adolescent's insistent self-reference are closely aligned to those "uncertainties" or "inadequacies" linked to women and girls in modernity. The "artist as a young man" is eulogized by Hall's assertion that gifted people are those that "conserve their youth," but the characteristics Hall thus advocates—"the plasticity and spontaneity of adolescence" (1:547)—are more often associated with girls. Hall emphasizes this analogy between women and adolescents: "woman at her best never outgrows adolescence as man does, but lingers in, magnifies and glorifies this culminating stage of life with its all-sided interests, its convertibility of emotions, its enthusiasm, and zest for all that is good, beautiful, true, and heroic" (2:624). Twentieth-century adolescence is thus characterized by feminized attributes such as changeability and malleability even when the adolescents are men, and Hall incorporates this feminization as a positive aspect of adolescence even while marginalizing and dismissing girls.

Adolescence is a retrospective construction of individual subjectification grounded in a dominant analogy between women and adolescents: "treated like women, judged like women, defended . . . like women" (Spacks 79).[5] The specification of behaviors and experiences as feminine or adolescent is not reliant on any biological definition despite the importance of girls' bodies to definitions of feminine adolescence. Late modern theories of adolescence have, moreover, been dominated by observation of girls in popular culture and in critical theory. Feminine adolescence or female youth have on the one hand been considered specific to the "other" gender/sex, and on the other hand as the most adolescent of adolescents. The adolescence of boys has been distinguished as either successful or flawed, but the problems of girls' adolescence increasingly came to be seen as entirely normal and without a certain endpoint. In her *Girls Growing Up in Late Victorian and Edwardian England,* Carol Dyhouse discusses Hall's definition of feminine adolescence as "a time of instability; a dangerous phase when she needed special protection from society" (122). Dyhouse contends that Hall directly contributed to an ongoing debate about girls' education:

Both at the time of publication and subsequently, the book aroused fury among feminists. M. Carey Thomas's reaction, as President of Bryn Mawr

College in the United States, has often been quoted. . . . She declared that although she had spent thirty years between 1874 and 1904 reading every book on women that she could obtain, in any language, she "had never chanced again upon a book that seemed to me to so degrade me in my womanhood as the seventh and seventeenth chapters on women and women's education of President Stanley Hall's *Adolescence*." (121)

This exchange over social and psychological norms through a study of adolescents is a benchmark for early-twentieth-century attitudes, and no more so than in its prioritization of gendered models of consciousness and identity.

Women, Hall asserted, "must be studied objectively and laboriously as we study children, and partly by men, because their sex of necessity must always remain objective and incommensurate with regard to women, and therefore more or less theoretical" (Hall quoted in Dyhouse 124). For Hall, as for Hegel, girls were dominated by "deep unconscious instincts," and a girl's self-knowledge was confined to "the reflected knowledge others have of her" (ibid.). This idea of self-knowledge is shaped by distinctions between self-observation and the establishment of identity being made by Sigmund Freud at around the same time. Hall's text, as its title insists, entwines physiology with the social in forming a psychological theory of adolescence, and this movement dominates the expanding psychologies of the time, including psychoanalysis. Both Hall and Freud produce, out of the nineteenth-century confusion over girlhood, structuralist accounts of adolescence troubled by rapid social changes and the increasing visibility of modern girls.

Hall's chief contribution to this transformation of adolescence is his role in entwining psychological, social, and biological aspects of adolescence— evident in his bringing Freud and Jung to lecture in America and in his representation of adolescence as characterized by "storm and stress" (Hall 1:xiii). The ideas about adolescence developing around Hall and Freud normalized adolescence as "the establishment of a sense of one's own identity as a unique person and the avoidance of role confusion" (Rutter 3). Hall's thesis that adolescence was not only a time of change and opportunity but—because it was so filled with change, opportunity, and adjustment—a period of Sturm und Drang does not certainly exclude women, as does the earlier model of adolescence as the period prior to manhood. Attributing stress to adolescence is not an invention of the twentieth century. Much earlier writing evidences concern that young people be properly molded and debates the special difficulties of youth. But as Michel Foucault recognizes in his volumes on the history of sexuality, apparently recognizable discourses of care or concern in the classical era are in fact distinguishable from the development of a psychologized narrative of individual development proper to modernity and specialized in the nineteenth century.

Dinah Mulock's 1864 essay, "In Her Teens," states that "the years between twelve and twenty are, to most, a season anything but pleasant; a crisis in which the whole heart and brain are full of tumult, when all life looks strange and bewildering—delirious with exquisite unrealities" (quoted in Spacks 31). The idea that youth constitutes a necessary crisis in the formation of the self was widely recognized in expanding public and popular cultures in the wake of Hall's work. Hall's influence extended into popular publishing such as Mary Moxcey's 1916 guidance manual *Girlhood and Character*, which presumes that

> the recognition of adolescence as a period of human life separate from childhood and from maturity has been a slow achievement of civilization. Its beginnings are seen in the puberty rites with which primitive peoples marked the passage of the individual from one status to the other. The most recent development of society's valuation of the "lengthened infancy" (that is, the longer teachableness) of the individual is the extension of recognized adolescence into the late teens and beyond them. (275)

In the twentieth century, the clubs and charitable concerns that had worked to publicize the Victorian management of children were redirected and substantially overtaken by privatizing discourses that established behavioral norms for adolescence as personal development. While knowledge about adolescents was debated in multiplying public forums, successful adolescence became a responsibility monitored through guided introspection, and these presumptions inflected extant discourses on the observation of the family.

Feminine adolescence emerged as a way of talking about girls as facing new obligations and new freedoms, and by the early twentieth century was figured as a natural and definitive phase in women's development—an expected struggle to become not just the right kind of woman but a woman at all. The definition of adolescence as developing independence was then accompanied by a definition of feminine adolescence as a problem with or even foreclosure on that development. Feminine adolescence cannot succeed as progression toward manhood, but neither does the girl become a woman. Girls do not become Woman because womanhood arrives at points of passage defined by relations to the Subject from which she is excluded. Feminine adolescence as growing-up is measured by the womanly roles of motherhood, feminine sexuality, and wifedom, which proscribe end points to that process. However, feminine adolescence is performed in transitional roles—including daughter, virgin, bride, model, girlfriend, schoolgirl, shopper, dieter, and so on—that do not necessarily lead to the mature concretization of Woman. Feminine adolescence is not merely a representation of girlhood, though it is represented; it is both a categorical definition of what will be thought normal and deviant among girls, and a lived experience of bodily change not separable from and not prior to transformed social identities. Exemplarily in the influential work of Hall and Freud, who both focused on adolescent girls while not centrally discussing them, feminine adolescence marks the materialization of women and does not exist. While masculine adolescence is a progress to Subjectivity, feminine adolescence ideally awaits moments of transformation from girl to Woman. The feminine adolescent has no past identity as herself and her future identity is divorced from what she presently is; her historical identity is thus not ordered in terms of duration.

The Problem Girl: Hysterics and Deviants

Freud and Girls

While chapter 4 considers in more detail how feminine adolescence works within theories and representations of the late modern subject, the second half of this chapter considers some crucial elements of feminine adolescence as a process of defining, if never achieving, subjectivity in our time. I have outlined some of the conditions that made the explanatory category "feminine adolescence" not only possible but also necessary and that guided the form feminine adolescence took in the twentieth century. These conditions include new discourses on puberty and majority, new legislative definitions of girlhood including labor laws and the age of consent, new educational structures and expectations, new disciplined understandings of relations between citizenship, sex, and age, new production and consumption practices, and new modes of knowing the subject and its more or less desirable relations to culture. These are changes to the meanings of whatever we could call sexual difference so dramatic as to be best perceived as having constituted not only new gender norms and roles, but new genders, including the girl. And the principle characteristic of this girl was her failure at a dominant model of individual subjectivity—this is not to say that young men actually achieved the coherence desired by that model but that the modern girl was positioned as delineating what was excluded from that movement toward maturity.

As Johnson argues, the autonomous individual is "a cultural ideal encountered in particular historical and social institutions" (17), and this girl is a figure of immaturity constituted by dependence on the agency of others. In dominant mass-cultural narratives as well as in theories of women's development, the putative independence of modern women has seemed to be a problem precisely because of her immaturity, and her immaturity is defined by her dependence. Moreover, from this state of immaturity, modern women could develop only by developing forms of dependence. Analyzing fiction in the turn-of-the-century *Ladies Home Journal,* Searles and Mickish suggest that its conservative themes of submission and dependence "may have helped readers interpret and cope with reality at a time when social change was prevalent and conceptions of women's roles and women's rights were in flux" (262). They note an increasing recognition of the possibility that women might be reluctant to fill traditional feminine roles but, as Hall's work exemplifies, these women were nonetheless excluded from any naturalization of this discontent in an adolescent narrative of storm and stress.

Instead, the difficulties with which girls negotiate adolescence have mostly been interpreted as the struggle for proper femininity, or the struggle to retain a sense of self in the face of expected femininity. Adolescence and femininity are thus seen as contradictory even though femininity is simultaneously presented as being formed in adolescence. Gilbert and Taylor representatively argue that the rebellion associated with the storm and stress theory of adolescence conflicts with many behavioral norms for girls (19) and that feminine adolescence constitutes a different kind of struggle: "Becoming feminine . . . represents the attempt to reconcile the irreconcilable; to seek coherence where there clearly is none; to find solutions to an endless stream of problems" (77–8). Feminine adolescence is not a transitional period but an assemblage of transitions, many of which are repeatable or reversible and all of which are culturally specific, subject to interpretation and regimes of power. These transitions include menarche and other instances of puberty, school and birthday milestones, first romance and first sex, engagement, marriage and childbirth, along with accompanying changes to employment, to legal status, or to family relations.[6] The kinds of authority, knowledge, and signs that girls ordinarily contest in such negotiations with proper femininity and adult womanhood might not resemble the classic images of deviant or rebellious youth, but then those images generically constitute expectations about the public lives of young men.

Rebellion and deviance are nevertheless at issue in public and privatized concern over feminine adolescence. The hysterical girl of turn of the century psychology is an important precursor to the deviant girl who appeared in much social psychology in the middle decades of the twentieth century. Psychoanalysis had a profound impact on new theories of deviance despite the methodological and other differences between therapeutic and social-analytic discourses. The role of psychoanalysis in popular discourses on the self, and the impact of Freudianism—infantile sexuality, the Oedipus complex, penis envy, castration anxiety, dream interpretation, and the unconscious—on cultural production and popular culture has not been sufficiently acknowledged. This impact includes significant influence on public culture and policy through education systems, for the most part, and the documents and strategies designed to meet (and often compensate for) the changing modern world, particularly the changing modern family. In these contexts, insights imported from psychoanalysis were often designed to address changes that were themselves equally influenced by psychoanalysis, including changed ideas about gender constitution and the effects of adolescence.

If nineteenth-century girls often experienced a newly significant period of transition between childhood and adult life, feminine adolescence emerged as a way of understanding, positioning, and disciplining that period of transition. Feminine adolescence has not only always been closely observed, it has also been substantially defined as a category of objects for observation by legal, educational, political, familial, artistic, sexual, and psychological discourses. Feminine adolescence remains inseparable from the processes of observing young women that helped define it, including psychoanalysis. The techniques of psychoanalysis not only produced analyses that helped define late modern girlhood, they also shaped the kinds of inquiry thought relevant to girls and therefore the kind of object that girls were thought to constitute. Freud's contributions to these new discourses were initially based on his observation of young women in nineteenth-century Europe. I will consider a range of psychoanalytic theories about girls in subsequent chapters, but it is significant here that young women were importantly constituted as a new form of deviant subject around Freud's analyses of the bourgeois family. Instead of narrating ego development, the girl is represented by psychoanalysis as recalcitrant femininity or fantasizing hysteria. Various strands of psychology have negotiated gender's inflection of adolescence, but the influence of psychoanalysis has been significantly enabled by feminist interest in Freud's work on sex or gender. This interest is particularly indebted to the fact that for Freud adolescence does not have a priority over gender in accounting for a girl's problems in the world.

After Freud, late modern psychology has generally viewed adolescence as what his student Helene Deutsch called "the period of the decisive last battle fought before maturity" (91). Within this dominant model the adolescent is still figured as a "he" and "his" adolescence is the norm that feminine adolescence varies in such a way as to materialize its exemplary difficulty. Freud's account of that variation has been highly influential. Freud's neurotic and hysterical girls are not only people who have failed to accomplish the repressions and cathexes necessary for maturity (thus remaining adolescent); they are simultaneously defending "against fully experiencing the events of adolescence" (Masson 122)—disavowing the adolescence they cannot pass. Girl hysterics, according to psychoanalysis, disavow adolescence because it insists on a sexuality they would deny and that expressly defines them. Insofar as (healthy) women are required by this model to (naturally) disavow sexuality, they are developmentally stranded in this denying-adolescence adolescence. In the same year as Hall published *Adolescence*, Freud published one of his most influential case studies—*A Fragment of an Analysis of a Case Study of Hysteria*, usually called "Dora" after its heroine/analysand. "Dora" is an exemplary intersection of nineteenth-century discourses on the family and new languages about adolescence, framing the girl as the object of a discourse that speaks about her in the process of outlining a subjectivity she cannot acquire.

The uncertainty of modern subjectivity articulated in psychoanalysis requires the observation that psychoanalysis supplied. Foucault's analysis of truth as an effect of power is highly important to understanding such forms of knowledge about girls. While Foucault's *History of Sexuality* does not directly address Freud, it traces Freud's antecedents and contexts and engages indirectly with many of his claims and subsequent variations on those claims. Foucault's observations about the entanglement of sex, truth, power, identity, and "scientific observation" seem especially directed to Freud but are applicable to other psychologists focusing on the exemplary instability of girls at the beginning of the twentieth century. Hall's work on adolescence is one example, as is Morton Prince's 1906 case study of the "dissociated personality" suffered under the name Christine Beauchamp.[7] Prince's definition of the self as "free from mental and physical stigmata" and as "the harmonious integration" of all aspects, requires a series of value judgments, such as whether the "fragment" named Sally is "immature" or the one named BIV is "cold"—"unnatural" attributes to be excluded from the acceptable girl personality (Prince 1913).[8] The proliferation of personalities outlined in Prince's study is dominated by "Sally," whose self-recognizing rebelliousness and "will" prove her existence for Prince (123, see Leys 93). While Prince identifies with Sally in the course of her treatment—which is also the course of Sally's "development'—she is condemned by "the law of psychology" (Prince 388–9) because of her immaturity. Leys describes Sally as "the untutored, irresponsible young girl whose love of adventure, play, and excitement and dislike of books and the passive, scholarly life declare her unmistakably to be the adolescent of Stanley Hall's recent, influential definition" (182–3). As Jacques Lacan argues that Dora only exists as the "subject" of Freud's treatment (1982b:64), Sally is the means to the end of Prince's theoretical innovations.

Unlike Prince's theory of "dissociation," psychoanalysis cannot be relegated to a set of past historical documents, having produced a range of still relevant discourses including many meanings for feminine adolescence. But an historical account of Freud's influence should also recognize changes in his work. The internal theoretical shifts emphasized by commentators such as Elizabeth Grosz and Jacqueline Rose are related to social changes not often otherwise credited with having an impact on Freud's work. Freud's famous lectures on "Female Sexuality" (1931) and "Femininity" (1933) are influenced by but fail to directly address the dramatic changes in "normal" women's behavior between Dora (1905) and the 1930s. Stephen Marcus concedes that Freud's distinction between the "normative responses" of adolescents and women might be an "assumption of his time and culture" (78), and Freud's understanding of Dora was subsequently annotated in the light of new theories and historical contexts.

Marianne Hirsch, noting that "Female *Künstlerromane* of the 1920s feature young and middle-aged women who renounce love and marriage in favor of creative work, who renounce connection in favor of self-affirmation" (96), connects this assertion ("Significantly, it is also in the 1920s") to Freud's "revising his developmental theory . . . to recognize the importance of the preoedipal bond between the girl and her mother, a bond that underlies and, in some ways, outweighs the formative power of the Oedipus complex" (98). While in "Dora" a conflict between the mother as normative model and natural bond was already apparent, this new emphasis on relations between women responds to the new visibility of women in a variety of social situations. After the institutionalization of adolescence as a public lifestyle and public problem, Erik Erikson, an influential figure in American ego psychology, could stress that Dora's "femininity" conflicted with the aims of modern adolescence: "*identity* . . . must prove itself against sometimes confusing role demands. As a *woman*, Dora did not have a chance" (52). The patient—performing the desired and incoherent body of one becoming a woman—is only one possible performance of feminine adolescence, but it remains a significant one, modified by later forms of diagnosis, including sociological and criminological discourses on deviance.

Flappers, Gangs, and the Teenager

Youth as a modern category has always been understood in comparison to a past constructed as less disruptive and difficult—a discourse dependent on historical periods. The dominant retrospective view of youth at the beginning of the twenty-first century focuses on the adolescence of the currently dominant demographic strata (centering on the 1960s). This structurally resembles the ways in which the flaming youth of the 1920s were silhouetted against the familial harmony of pre–World War I America, or 1950s teenagers were compared to the calm development of previous decades. Although the attributes associated with the youth of the 1960s are not calm and harmonious, the retrospective definition of adolescence through an opposition between present-day youth and a more promising youth in the past is sustained.[9] While modern life changed for many different groups assimilated within adolescence or youth across the course of the twentieth century, I want to consider here some changing images of how modern girls behaved, focusing on the flapper of the 1920s, discourses on delinquent girls, and the exceptionally visible figure of the teenager.

Feminine adolescence in the 1920s and 1930s was experienced by a range of young women with occupations, educations, and other social positions that concretely differentiated their lives from those of most women in several preceding generations. These new women were represented in texts for and about them as urban and likely to be educated and to work, and they were understood as responding directly to ideas about the new potential of modern women. Dorothy Parker claimed in *Vogue* in 1919 that "the style in heroines has completely changed. In fact, the style in all women has changed. It is all directly due to the war" (39). World War I dramatically altered a wide range of influences on the ways women became women, which were in turn affected by other economic and political changes including the depression, the socialist revolution(s), suffrage campaigns, the expansion of higher education, and women's enfranchisement. Recognizing that such emancipation applied more to public images of women than to women, Miriam Hansen foregrounds

> the upheaval of gender relations during the war, such as the massive integration of women into the work force and their emergence as a primary target in the shift to a consumer economy; the partial breakdown of gender-specific divisions of labour and a blurring of traditional delimitations of public and private; the need to redefine notions of femininity in terms other than domesticity and motherhood; the image of the New Woman promoted along with a demonstrative liberalisation of sexual behaviour and lifestyles; the emergence of the companionate marriage. (259)

Most obviously of all, modern girls were visibly involved in more forms of paid employment. Girls' increased employment prior to World War I demonstrates that this is not dependent on the war and that concern over this employment was not exclusively about restoring prewar normality. Instead, modern girls were objects of concern as an index of the modern and of cultural change.

Discourses on rebellion, deviance, and delinquency arose around the figure of these new girls. While these terms are more usually associated with young men, girls as emblems of cultural continuity were important markers of what was substantial social change rather than transient discord. Discourses on youth deviance were well established by World War II, despite the tendency in studies of youth deviance to simplify that period in relation to later instances of youth culture, such as the rock-and-roll culture of the 1950s and the protest movements of the 1960s. Expanding anthropologies and psychologies of the 1930s observed girls' increased visibility, although often from a theoretical distance constructed by analysis in supposedly primitive cultures or by the therapeutic scene. Through and around the work of writers such as Freud, Hall, and Margaret Mead, studies of old and new social norms became studies of deviance, and studies of deviance became the usual way to observe and comment on social norms. The "normal" girl has consequently not been the subject of much discussion within social, cultural, or critical theory, except as the requisite complement in discourses on deviance. Moreover, girls' deviance was thought to take different forms reflecting the presumed difference of their adolescence, as the work of Freud and Mead exemplifies.

The pervasive equation between modern girls and mass production, which I will discuss at length in part 3, tied the new youth cultures that accompanied adolescence to theories about how popular culture forms identity categories. One significant instance of this association, which is not often enough considered in histories of youth culture, is the figure of the flapper. As Sally Mitchell suggests, "In the immediate prewar years, 'flapper' identified a new stage of life. It described girls who were interested in looks and fashions, boy-conscious, flirtatious, teasing—but cute, rather than fast" (1995:183). The coquetry Mitchell associates with flappers signals the sexualization she credits with expunging an authentic girl's culture. Thomas Richards recognizes the formation of the consumer in the same discourses on adolescence, noting that: "Hall's rendering of adolescence reads like an extended account of the modern consuming subject. As someone young enough not to work but old enough to consume, the adolescent lives in a state of pure leisure" (242–3). Richards sees this consumer as directly drawing on the iconic sexual ambiguity of Victorian girlhood while insisting that the adolescent consumer was advertised as a state of repeated self-indulgence particularly relevant to an ideal of womanhood as "prolonged girlhood" perfected in the "fashionably tyrannical" flapper type of the 1920s. By this time, "advertised adolescence had long been a permanent condition, the privileged domain of modern commodity culture" (244). Mitchell claims that flapper culture "was less open, less fluid, less promising" as a result of this ongoing commercialization of girl culture and that it "lacked the range and promise and daring agency" produced for Victorian girls (1995:188).[10] The qualities Mitchell sees as lacking in flapper culture are, however, exactly the attributes for which the flapper was particularly condemned.

In commentary on modernism and interwar Western cultures, the flapper appears in many countries and many different cultural scenes. She foregrounds the transnational distribution of popular culture, and closely links youth, femininity, and mass consumption.[11] The distribution of elements of flapper culture was perceived as a component of Americanization, extending the degree to which American girls were associated with a distinc-

tive development that in some ways presages conceptions of feminine adolescence.[12] The success of the flapper in diverse cultures suggests, in Western and Western-influenced societies, a widespread perception that a new
kind of girl had emerged, of which the flapper was both exemplary and an
exceptional instance. Sueann Caulfield's discussion of criminality and transgression among young women in 1920s Rio de Janeiro argues that modern
girls "presented problems of contradictory identities," that overturned oppositions coding different types of femininity, such as mother/daughter,
virgin/whore, boy/girl (171). These girls "did not step outside of culture to
construct alternative identities but mimicked performances they observed in
films, fashion magazines, and advertisements aimed at the New Woman
that they became" (Sueann Caulfield 172). The flapper signified a lifestyle,
connoting certain occupations and opinions as well as a range of leisure pur-
suits. Such cultural formations of the modern girl continue to be dependent on class and other cultural locations. As a lifestyle choice or as a model
for identity, the flapper was not unilaterally accessible. But the flapper was
neither necessarily wealthy nor necessarily young. She might be a factory
girl, *la bohème*, married or not. The flapper was an assemblage of normative
lines and attitudes, cultural consumptions and social positions, rather than
a specific role or identity. The significance of the flapper did not so much
shift across time—from a girl with few responsibilities and new pleasures to
a disruptive or bad girl at the center of various moral panics in the public
sphere—but was always a performance with different effects according to its
context.

New forms of analyzing youth emerged in this interwar period, as "the
disciplines of criminology, psychology and sociology . . . crystallized within delinquency and deviancy studies" (Valentine et al. 10). Within these
disciplines the need to explain youth behavior that did not fit the successful model of adult-in-training led to diverse theories constructing "the
'delinquent youth' as Other" (Griffin 99). Delinquents and youth gangs
were known social formations well before the institutionalization of sociology. Groups of young men offering varying degrees of threat recur in a
range of modern situations, but a group is only a gang when associated
with those public cultural exchanges of anxiety now often referred to as
moral panic (see Davis 2000). Like adolescence, the dissemination and
coverage of anxieties about how young people represent a culture escalated
with the social reform movements of the nineteenth century. The word
"gang" still did not automatically connote the delinquent social formations

that came to be associated with the term in the mid-twentieth century. A gang in this last sense is not only a threatening group but one comprised of individuals with particular psychological tendencies, usually character-ized as interrupted, arrested, or refused development. Gang members are suspended, in sociological analysis, between childish identification and adult individuation, as well as between feminized images of peer influence and masculinized images of social uprising. The sociological urban gang was associated directly with the stress and challenge of masculine adoles-cence and as such it did not tend to include girls as central subjects even when girls were present. Instead female delinquency and the delinquent girl were predominantly consigned to a different narrative of familial neg-lect and sexual deviance. Delinquent girls were understood to have been brought to delinquency by the effects of their sex, even when their delin-quency was not itself understood as sexual. This personalization of femi-nine deviance conforms to the psychology of girls posited by psychoanaly-sis—shaped by the same influences as those contextualizing Freud's analyses of feminine sexuality and group psychology when it does not di-rectly draw on Freud's work. Deviance, then, is not as readily applied to girls because of the problematic status of girls' agency.

For Mead, for example, despite her stress on the cultural negotiation of sex differentials, girls "be" and boys "do":

> Women's biological-career line has a natural climax structure that can be overlaid, muted, muffled, and publicly denied, but which remains as an essential element in both sexes' view of themselves. . . . This special fe-male climax-structure carries with it the possibility of a greater emphasis on states of *being* than does that of the male. A girl *is* a virgin. After the breaking of the hymen . . . she is *not* a virgin . . . stage after stage in women's life-histories thus stand, irrevocable, indisputable, accom-plished. This gives a natural basis for the little girl's emphasis on *being* rather than *doing*. The little boy learns that he must act like a boy, do things, prove that he is a boy, and prove it over and over again, while the little girl learns that she *is* a girl, and all she has to do is to refrain from acting like a boy. (1967:175)

Writing in the late 1920s Mead can already assume the normality of both the gang and the teenager in accounting for early adolescent Samoan girls:

Soberly they perform their household tasks, select a teacher from the older women of the family, learn to bear the suffix, meaning "little," dropped from the "little girl" which had formerly described them. But they never again amalgamate into such free-and-easy groups as the before-the-teen gang. (1963:58–9)

The gang thus figures as disruptive and enjoyable, marking a freedom from social necessity. This formulation also heralds the attribution of conformity to the teenager (relative to the gang) that would escalate in the decades following Mead's influential work. Still identifying the gang against the teen, Donna Gaines locates among her 1980s suburban subjects a narrative of futility and marginalization that is specific to this opposition as much as to any socioeconomic climate:

according to established adult reasoning if you didn't get absorbed into the legitimate, established routine of social activity, you'd be left to burn out on street corners, killing time, getting wasted. It was impossible for anyone to imagine any autonomous activity that non-conforming youth en masse might enjoy that would not be self-destructive, potentially criminal, or meaningless. (86)

Gaines explicates a class hierarchy tied to, but not equivalent to, a behavioral hierarchy, and these jointly position young men on a disciplinary ladder that she aligns with a dominant imaginary family.[13] Gaines does not focus on what roles girls might take in this family structure, or what positions might be assigned to them on this disciplinary ladder. But she does acknowledge the influence in this narrative of highly successful images of juvenile delinquency inherited from the public and popular culture of the 1950s (121). The most spectacularly successful of these were firmly gendered scenarios that narrated an unavoidable conflict between the teenager, the gang, the high school, and the nuclear family.

This popular understanding of the teenager had an enormous impact on the differentiation of adolescent experiences and desires for boys and for girls. Teenagers came to be clearly distinguished according to whether they were in or out of school, in or out of home, and in or out of normative gender models. New schooling practices in Western countries after World War II kept far larger numbers of teenagers in disciplined communities in the name of education, and for girls in particular cultivated new allegiances between femininity and school as well as femininity and new forms of domesticity. As the teenager was always placed within disciplinary structures such as families and schools, he or she always articulated tensions between containment and freedom and between conformity and agency; in these ways the teenager always resembled feminine adolescence. The teenager was also always directly associated with a range of mass-produced popular cultural products and leisure industries that attributed to school-age girls a crescendo of social achievements within a strictly delimited context.

Drawing on a longer tradition of girls' school stories, new forms of girls' fiction exemplify some of these changes. In line with the expansion of a fixed teen market, fiction series that had extended across the aging of their heroines (such as the Anne of Green Gables novels) "were replaced in the 1930s by Nancy Drew and her like, forever just older than the readers, with access to some of adulthood's possibilities but none of its constraints and responsibilities" (Mitchell 1995:101). The Nancy Drew series ran from the 1930s till the 1970s and entered television in 1980s, providing a singular perspective on how the popular figure of the teenage girl changed across this period in the United States. Both Sally Mitchell and Bobbie Anne Mason claim that Nancy doesn't change over the series, although it was in fact heavily revised in the mid-1960s to expunge racist and classist elements (Mason 133), and the television Nancy clearly voices opinions the 1930s Nancy would never hold.[14] Mason, however, sees Nancy as an eternal teenager:

> Cool Nancy Drew figures it is better to be locked in the timeless role of the girl sleuth—forever young, forever tops, above sex, above marriage—an inspiring symbol of freedom. But was she? . . . [Drew] always has it both ways—protected and free. She is an eternal girl, a stage which is a false ideal for women of our time. Nancy's adventures take place outside time and space. Her task is to restore a crumbling place to a past and perfect order. (Mason 75)

The teenage girls' role in such cultural continuity nevertheless changes with a culture's expectations and engages with threats to that continuity in order to deflect them. She thus locates points of fragility and tension in a dominant sex/gender system and may all too easily turn into a bad girl.

This vision of the teenage girl is an important component of late-twentieth-century girlhood, in which girls' disruptive potential was assigned jointly to

sexuality and the realm of popular culture, if continually shaped by changing political and economic relationships marking the simultaneous importance and irrelevance of girls. The numerous texts addressed to adolescents
on how to activate their independent selves in adolescence—at the same time
as they are learning to control themselves in adolescence—attest to the ambivalence of both teen rebellion and teen conformity. Adolescence continues
to be a disruption of childhood prior to an adulthood projected as more stable and important, even if, as Lawrence Grossberg claims, by the late twentieth century no one thought they could reach that maturity anyway (186).
In his essay "The Deconstruction of Youth" Grossberg calls for a genealogy
of youth culture—a map of how its particular forms are possible within a
given context:

> The issue is not whether the various discourses about youth and child-
> hood are referentially accurate, but that they are themselves part of the
> context in which youth is organised. The discourses and practices that in-
> terpenetrate and surround youth articulating its very existence—these are
> what need to be mapped out. (185)[15]

The Discourse on Adolescence: Guidance Manuals
Social Hygiene and Puberty Manuals

Guidance manuals belong to a model of modern subjectivity defined by
labor on, pleasure in, and responsibility for the self, a model that developed
in late modernity with particular reference to the exemplary self-involve-
ment of girls. Guidance manuals for being a girl elaborate on what will happen to "you" or "her" in puberty and what will be offered to and expected
of girls. Publication of these texts escalated between the end of the nineteenth century and the 1950s as they were attached to new public concerns
about "girls today" as well as new production and marketing techniques.
These manuals for girls and their parents, or others having responsibility for
girls' guidance, were continually revised to draw on expected (desires for)
knowledge, whether about the chemical and other physical forms of puberty or about the adolescent problem. Nevertheless a degree of continuity is
evident in this discourse on the difficulty of being a girl.

In 1933 *The Modern Hand Book For Girls* could offer strikingly similar advice on a wide range of issues to that articulated in 1879 by Dio Lewis's *Our*

Girls and includes a similar profusion of girl types to that enumerated by Sophia Caulfield. It seems to differ chiefly in greater reference to technology and mass consumption and a more direct address to girls themselves rather than their parents. Their presumed girl audiences seem to be interested in and anxious about many of the same things, and the significant differences between these texts center around received popular truths about the psychology of the normal girl, with which it was assumed the post-flapper girl might be somewhat familiar. The section on "Personality" in *Modern Hand Book* explains not only how to "manage yourself"—while the character of *Our Girls* had needed only guidance and management by others—but also how to "be popular" (Landers 4). *Modern Hand Book* implores girls to view their talents as adornments, as did *Our Girls*, but also "seeks to be suggestive, provocative to your own eager, active imagination, your own ingenuity and originality, to urge and encourage you to experiment and adventure" (Landers 1). *Hand Book* is a guide to style rather than goodness, then, but it also construct girls as being inherently difficult. Being a Victorian girl was not in itself a problem, except that the modern girl had more opportunities and thus more challenges. But the twentieth-century flood of guidance for girls invoked the girl as a problem in and of herself. Between the hoyden and the teenage girl a range of discourses on the regulation of girls appeared. Guidance manuals explicitly directed to the better training of girls, girlhood, and development became expected or required reading for educators and (predominantly middle-class) parents.

Modern accounts of girls' development aimed to detect and reveal an instability concealed within modern subjectivity. This focus continually defines modern girls as having, being, and representing the problem of modernity. In *Emile*, which foreshadows the more monologic form of guidance manual properly called an "advice handbook," Rousseau describes the development of the boy as an accumulation of knowledges that include regulation of his body and his relation to women. Sophie, Emile's bride, is also shaped by her socialization, but her education struggles with the natural inclinations of her body and soul to unruliness. The nineteenth-century social hygiene movements inherited this position, mostly addressing their treatises to boys against the evils of masturbation, venereal disease, general profligacy, and economic and personal disorder. These discourses were, up until the late nineteenth century, addressed to girls in more desperately veiled terms and mostly via their teachers and parents. But the late nineteenth century saw the introduction of advice to girls into the social hygiene movement. Girls' clubs and their accompanying pledges and creeds, as well as other popular and institutional educational texts, raised social hygiene themes for girls—focusing on protecting the purity of body (and soul) for (god and) the future of mankind.

Guidance manuals elaborately detail the proper techniques for being a girl. In *Our Girls* (dedicated "To My Girls" but principally addressing parents and teachers), Lewis proselytizes concerning the moral superiority of Woman and the future manifest in girls, while he simultaneously deplores the tendency of girls to silliness, childishness, and "frippery." Within his larger project, which advocates moderate education and careers for women as of benefit to humanity, Lewis's advice on such peripherals as styles of clothing and diet seems tangential. However, concern with exercise and other forms of bodily monitoring was crucial to the social hygiene movements, which required a scientific (repeatable, observable) discourse on the body directed to analysis of the body not for its own sake but for the greater good of society. This medicalization of girls' schooling and parenting manuals was continuous with both new discourses on feminine illness—what Foucault calls "hystericization" (1984a:146–7)—and the purity and suffrage movements.[16] The definition of the modern girl as a problem emphasized the need for her guidance and for the guidance of those charged with responsibility over her. While this difficulty produced a wide range of guidance discourses and industries for her better regulation, its necessity suggests that modern girls were not unequivocally shaped by macrosocial hegemonic requirements. Girls were even credited with some responsibility for the changes they were seen to reflect: thus the protosociology of the popular guidance manual for parents and teachers was designed to recognize as well as manage girls.[17]

The clubs that influenced girls' culture in the late nineteenth century were often explicitly designed to instruct and aid girls in avoiding the pitfalls inherent in the modern girl's life. The clubs helped guarantee the formation of a recognizable girls' culture because they were specific as to age and gender even when they included (however differently) girls from different social groups. Such specificity works to produce more coherent discourses on sex/gender difference in popular and public cultures, but in the twentieth century many of these clubs disappeared as no longer relevant to girls who shared their cultural interests and definitions by other means, including mass-produced magazines, fiction, fashions, and the cinema. Some, however, such as the Girls Friendly Society, persisted from Victorian origins through their sponsorship by institutions such as churches and schools. Others with more direct appeal to the changing cultural interests of girls, such as the Girl Guides, responded to demands for (and parental endorsement of) girl versions of active, adventurous boys' clubs and not only survived but expanded. Although they did not disappear, girls' clubs in the twentieth century predominantly shifted to more mass-mediated forms: magazine clubs, fan clubs, and other textually mediated collectives.

While girls are continually interrogated as to their progress toward womanhood, their grown-upness, there is no comparable monitoring of adolescence among boys. In recent decades the plethora of guidance manuals has produced even more specialized texts on how to raise and/or be quite specific kinds of girls: lesbian, feminist, ethnically specific, academic, or environmentalist manuals have appeared alongside the already established types of sporting, beautiful, and Christian-girl manuals. The continuity and diversity of guidance manuals for girls is evident in recent examples, including pop psychology such as Mary Pipher's *Reviving Ophelia: Saving the Selves of Adolescent Girls*, girl's own puberty manuals such as *Everygirl*, by Suzanne Abraham and Derek Llewellyn-Jones, and collages of girls' voices such as Maria Pallotta-Chiarolli's collection *Girls' Talk*.[18] I want to consider these 1990s versions of the guidance manual for their organization and definition of what is proper to feminine adolescence. Pipher describes early adolescence as "a time of physical and psychological change, self-absorption, preoccupation with peer approval and identity formation" (23–4), taking up the themes and concerns of earlier manuals. Pipher divides her case studies under headings drawn from existing public commentary on girls and frames them with her own analysis of how feminine adolescence threatens rather than stabilizes coherent selfhood for girls. Pipher's best-selling book thus thematically resembles many other guidance manuals, but it addresses a particular audience in feminist mothers of teenage girls.[19]

Abraham and Llewellyn-Jones's *Everygirl* follows the classic structure of the puberty manual: opening with puberty and menstruation, followed by discussion of bodily disciplines such as eating and sex, and finally psychology and behaviors with an emphasis on "problems" and "risk." It is also inflected by second-wave feminism, referencing feminist theories in some of its discourse on puberty, including in its glossary, which lists mainly hormones and sexual practices and their effects, such terms as "rape," "transsexual," and "gender role" (262–4). The book opens with an acknowledgment of the difficulty of defining girls: "To avoid these problems, in this book we call female children 'girls,' and once they have reached puberty we call them 'teenagers' or 'young women' " (7). However, the chapter on puberty notes the impossibility of assigning the beginning and end of puberty (35), while the book otherwise treats girls as a self-evident object. The introduction frames this book as directed to what "teenage women" want to know, and although how these desires were ascertained is not explained, this apparently consists of information on: bodily changes, bodily form, menstruation, sexual behaviors, contraception and pregnancy, eating and eating disorders, drugs and diseases (2). The writers note, however, that they omitted pregnancy as more properly about women (2), and they have supplemented this list with what they apparently saw as more appropriate concerns, including delinquency, parental conflict, independence, and the psychological attributes and problems of teenagers.

Girls' Talk is a collection of short pieces by girls discussing their experience of being girls (and a smaller selection of pieces by women on girlhood), compiled, arranged, and interspersed with comments by the editor. This process of collage is heavily indebted to the format of girls' magazines, and the intervening "talks" by Pallotta-Chiarolli are explicitly apologetic about interrupting what is presented as a conversation between girls as writers and readers. *Girls' Talk* covers a wide range of girls' interests and concerns, but the editorial frame of the book remains one of guidance predicated on the not-yet of feminine adolescence: "What happens after this book? You can make choices about your life" (viii). The book does not claim all girls have equal capacity to shape their lives with sufficient effort, but it still valorizes the elements of a girls' life apparently under her personal control: "all girls, obviously, do not have the same economic opportunities. But there are many parts of life (such as love, friendship and funky people) that have little to do with how much money you have" (viii). *Girls' Talk* aims to guide how girls might talk about their lives in the "Talk Tracks for Your Girls' Talk" sections. Girls' individual voices are often framed in the service of this guidance: "Rebekah Venn-Brown's experiences of family are a great example of what I've been trying to explain, so I think I'll just hand it over to her" (90). *Girls' Talk* also actively seeks to guide girls' relations to popular culture, a theme it shares with *Reviving Ophelia* and *Everygirl*. While *Girls' Talk* does not explain feminine adolescence by distinctions between normalcy and pathology, all three books preselect issues they consider relevant to girls and naturalize and foreground the difficulty of feminine adolescence in relation to these issues. These popular books presume a significant degree of continuity between girls in different cultural locations whilst recognizing some variations and conflicts between cultural norms for girls. Such a decontextualizing and dehistoricizing approach to girlhood is in fact an aspect of the guidance manual's contemporary appeal, naturalizing both the difficulty of girlhood and the techniques by which it can be surmounted in the process of becoming a woman.

Girls' Magazines

Diverse popular cultural forms and social institutions conducive to such guidance helped shape the market sectors that are now recognizable as girl culture. These have functioned in part to discipline the desires of girls recognized as having measurably more disposable income and have helped constitute girls as elements of not just the working but the employed populace; they have also helped distinguish a field that resembles an adolescent "class" (see chapter 4). Increased interest in guiding feminine adolescents thus reflected their greater importance as a labor force to be trained, a consumer group with expendable income to be cajoled, and a group that, simultaneous to these requirements, must remain available for their role in sexual reproduction. I have already considered girls' magazines as an index of Victorian girlhood, and I will return to them again in my discussion of girl culture, but I want to use this highly successful genre to outline in concluding this chapter some continuing conventions of feminine adolescence.

Girls' magazines are one of the few forms of popular culture for girls that emerged alongside feminine adolescence and has maintained its importance across that history. Girls' magazines have, moreover, provided a forum for girls' experiences of feminine adolescence and can be seen to both reflect and shape many of the changing interests and expectations of girls. Nineteenth-century girls' magazines gave way in the early twentieth century to new provision for young women in women's magazines, and few magazines remained that were exclusively addressed to young girls.[20] Late-nineteenth-century girls' magazines discharged the duty of raising good girls and presumed recognition of that duty in their readers. Girls' sections of women's magazines and the specifically adolescent girls' magazines that became more popular in the 1920s continued many of the prior girls' magazine formats, including their function as guidance manual, through provision for audience participation in relation to the expertise of the magazine. A 1929 advertisement for *Smart Set: The Young Woman's Magazine* is representative:

> Articles on fashions, make-up, business careers, charm, written in inimitable style by young women who know. And in addition—a wealth of delightful-snappy-clean fiction by America's best known story writers.
>
> And be sure not to miss Smart Set's nation-wide quest for the Typical American Girl.

Between the 1920s and 1940s, adolescent women's magazines became widely available as a distinct genre, with titles including *Seventeen, Flair, Charm, Glamour, Young Miss, Ingenue,* and *Teen.* Some of these were explicitly subsidiary to women's magazines—*Seventeen* was a daughter publication of *Ladies Home Journal* (Humphreys 185) and *Teen* of *Harper's Bazaar* (257)—and training a readership for women's magazines continues to be a function of girls' magazines.

Girls' magazines are defined by their audience and define this audience by a stylized address and an idealized projection of a sexualized body. Acknowledging the lived variations in this audience, the genre is initially defined by addressing its readers as girls rather than women. Girls' magazines also form an important text for the presentation of girls' voices and desires and present an interplay of choice and guidance that permeates much girls' culture. The shared characteristics of late-twentieth-century girls' magazines, which retain a remarkable degree of consistency among international publications (see chapter 9), focus on the feminine adolescent body, the girl group, taste-formation, youth culture, and girl sexuality. Twentieth-century discourses on the girl's sexualized identity clearly mediate and monitor the feminine adolescent's progress among her peer group in this genre. The body produced, consumed, and recorded in girls' magazines refers to what might be called her sexualized gender identity—the girl— delineating a simultaneous and equated development of gender identity and sexual identity.

Girls' magazines foreground both self-surveillance and self-production, most explicitly in the problem pages and other scenarios of guidance. This advice and information exchange sells its own necessity by emphasizing the unavoidable and all-important difficulty of unguided feminine adolescence and the untrained girl body. This is presented as a private relation between girl and guide which nevertheless always involves the girl as group rather than individual. Everything is shared, including that privacy. Cynthia White describes an early girls' magazine, *Peg's Paper* (1919–39), as "a determined effort to achieve clear identification with readers" (98), a project outlined in its editorial introduction:

> It is going to be your weekly pal girls. My name is Peg, and my one aim in life is to give you a really cheery paper like nothing you've ever read before. Not so very long ago, I was a mill-girl too. Because I've been a worker like you, I know what girls like, and I'm going to give you a paper you'll enjoy. . . . Look on me as a real friend and helper. I will try to advise you on any problem. (quoted in C. White 97–8)

This is "the surrogate sister" role of women's magazines (Ferguson 9) continued in Helen Gurley-Brown's claim that "*Cosmopolitan* is every girl's sophisticated older sister" (quoted in Ferguson 37). Historian Marjorie Ferguson claims that "male magazines" are by contrast interest oriented (2), a claim that Angela McRobbie supports: "there is no consistent attempt to link interests with age, nor is there a sense of natural or inevitable progression from one to another complementary to the life-cycle" (1991:83). Boys are invited to consume sport, pornographic, or other hobby magazines, but these are not distinguished from an audience of men and are at most markers of development rather than interrogations of maturity or competence.

In *Feminism and Youth Culture* McRobbie notes that the girls' magazine "introduces the girl to adolescence, outlining its landmarks and characteristics in detail and stressing the problematic features as well as the fun" (83), while also asserting "a class-less, race-less sameness, a kind of false unity which assumes a common experience of womanhood or girlhood" (83–4). As girls' magazines have mapped the category "feminine adolescent" and record changing perceptions of girls and their cultures during the twentieth century, they also suggest a range of questions regarding the fluctuating distinction of girls and their interests from adult women. The genre of girls' magazines is particularly shaped by a pedagogic approach to femininity— they not only recognize but foreground training in being a girl, as well as the tensions between living and knowing the body and between lived and ideal bodies. These magazines are thus guides on how to become the girl who becomes the desirable woman. It does not necessarily follow, however, that this becoming defines the girl as an object of heterosexual desire. Far from prescribing sexual activity, the girl's body is eroticized in a space of preparation for heterosexuality, in an aestheticized space of waiting that is nevertheless not at all passive. In the conventions of feminine adolescence, Woman remains the future while the reader remains adolescent—desiring to be the most ideal girl possible and in need of advice/products in order to enable that becoming.

McRobbie argues that after the 1970s, presumably following the feminist movements of the time, girls' magazines newly emphasized self-development at the expense of romance. After this shift, "practices and rituals of femininity which were once carried out in order to attract boys and to secure a future based on being a wife and mother are now done on behalf of the self" (1991:183), sidelining romance "*in favour of simple concentration on the potentially sophisticated and discerning young consumer*" (146). This shift may not be as dramatic as McRobbie suggests. Technologies of the self and commodifications of the self dominate the earliest girls' magazines, and romance—itself presented as a technology of the self in this genre—remains the only path to full happiness or maturity in the newer modes of girls' magazines.[21] Though girls' culture changes it evidences a dominant perception of feminine adolescence as both establishing new womanly identities and, in that establishment, erasing the community of girl identities that precedes it. This is an erasure of the girl's process toward identity and presumes her unavoidable failure to obtain and secure subjectivity *as a girl*. I am not claiming that girlhood really is erased in becoming women. But this is primarily the way girls' magazines talk about becoming a woman—as a transformation from which there is no return and little residue. It is a fundamental paradox of girl culture that this erasing transformation is accompanied by elaboration of the intricately pleasurable practices of becoming a girl.

three
Puberty

Even in the healthiest woman a worm, however harmless and unperceived, gnaws periodically at the roots of life.

—Havelock Ellis, *Man and Woman*

THIS CHAPTER will consider what constitutes female puberty within definitions of girlhood and feminine adolescence and for theories about identity production and corporeality. Theories of adolescence generally rely on the inseparable causal headings of physiological change and psychological development, and this chapter focuses on the physical changes thought to underlie adolescence and the idea of female puberty as both bodily change and psychosocial development. This chapter also unpacks some of the contradictions in twentieth-century representations of female puberty disseminated in medical, educational, and psychological theory, as well as in popular culture. Discipline, education, and self-production are all invoked in representations of female puberty, exemplarily in those guidance manuals designed to advise girls and to help adults cope with the dramatic reconstitution of girls in puberty, and these discourses construct a feminine puberty that helps identify certain effects as female physical development. Discussion of how the body is seen to intervene or persist in the social for feminist, anthropological, and psychoanalytic accounts of puberty is related here to popular cultural representations of

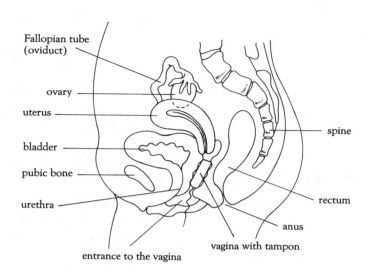

Fallopian tube
(oviduct)

ovary

uterus

bladder

pubic bone

urethra

spine

rectum

anus

vagina with tampon

entrance to the vagina

3.1 "Where the Tampon Lies in the Vagina," from *Everygirl* (1992)
(Reproduced with permission of Oxford University Press Australia from Everygirl *by Derek Llewellyn Jones and Suzanne Abrahams © Oxford University Press, 1992, www.oup.com.ua)*

puberty for and among girls, and this chapter concludes by considering the Barbie doll as an influential manifestation of the functions and contradictions of feminine puberty.

The Body's Intervention in the Social
Body Drama

Female puberty is the operation of the feminine in discourses on puberty (for which the puberty of girls is always relative to the puberty of boys), and this chapter focuses on how this feminine puberty is placed in dominant Western discourses on adolescence. Puberty claims to describe a physiological process that is supplemented by experience (rather than the other way around) in dominant models of how the mature subject is constituted. This apparent fact of puberty underpins the placement of majority somewhere around the end of the teenage years (eighteen or twenty-one in most Western societies). However, this fact is not actually referenced in coming of age, nor are girls finishing puberty or attaining legal majority understood to have finished all necessary development in popular and public discourses on adolescence, youth, and subjectivity. Neither puberty nor majority make a girl a woman, and it is becoming a woman, rather than majority or the unlocatable end of puberty that constitutes the end of feminine adolescence.

The representation of adolescence as identity formation and identity crisis relies on the physiological trauma and psychological crisis of puberty, and ideas about puberty have in turn helped define distinctions between child and adult. Puberty both defines the boundaries of adolescence and asserts its importance. Only since the nineteenth century has adolescence been strongly identified with the physical development and increasing physical maturity assigned to puberty, and any identification between adolescence and puberty remains incomplete insofar as being called adolescent or being visible as a girl is not contingent on a particular point of physiological development. Both puberty and adolescence have codified the body since classical times, but not in the same ways. Following the Enlightenment displacement of the "determination of social life by metaphysical legitimations of power . . . by the determination through the laws of nature" (Huyssen 69), puberty became a far more pivotal mode of constructing subjectivity. In conjunction with emerging ideas about childhood and adolescence, puberty became a scene of transformation rather than merely functioning to release and engage preexisting physical attributes. The post-Enlightenment age of "modern technology and its legitimatory apparatuses" (Huyssen 69) required the new observation and knowledge of the body that puberty articulates, and closely linked this to the social development of the Subject by suggesting the simultaneity of puberty and adolescence. Modern models of puberty as a strictly delimited range of physical changes tend to be precise about the age range in which puberty should operate, vague as to how it can be identified, and specific about categorizing bodies as to sex/gender:

Up to the nubile age children of the two sexes have nothing apparent to distinguish them: the same visage, the same figure, the same complexion, the same voice. Everything is equal: girls are children, boys are children; the same name suffices for beings so much alike. Males whose ulterior sexual development is prevented maintain this similarity their whole lives; they are always big children. And women, since they never lose this same similarity, seem in many respects never to be anything else. (Rousseau 211)

Puberty's significance to and distinction from the social development of the subject in adolescence thus forms an important precursor for the emergence of feminine adolescence, and puberty's emphasis on sexual maturation reflects the degree to which it has explained the difference of female development.

Modern models of puberty are not confined to the arrival of physical change and its effects—that was in fact how the classical version of puberty operated. In modernity puberty centers on the emergence of the adult subject and remains attached to the social and cultural implications of that subjectivity. It is, moreover, affected by specific locations and practices—including class positions and cultural norms—as new twentieth-century medical, anthropological, and therapeutic discourses attest. Discourses on puberty have in fact relied on the identification of both cultural specificity and the relations between culture and nature, which is why the popular dissemination of anthropology helped expand the significance attributed to puberty. Anthropological studies of puberty extended this body into the field of culture, adding new effects to the appearance of puberty, and the identification of puberty as a cross-cultural phenomenon, supplemented by the identification of puberty in past historical periods, provided a foundation for statements about essential human development. The characteristics identified by such studies of puberty are not all otherwise assigned to biological determination. Chief among them is the idea that puberty is a process of physical disruption and then stabilization that extends into the social. While early modern claims that the humors of youth were disruptive did not necessarily infer that life after puberty becomes more stable, late modern puberty marks a crescendo of bodily disruption that should ideally be resolved in the course of puberty. This understanding of puberty justifies less mutable understandings of the adult body, ideally confining personal upheaval to a space and time that is thus justifiably subject to intensive management and training.

Physiology has constituted and relied on ideas of sexual difference, as evidenced by its early precursors in the texts of Galen and Aristotle. The sexing of puberty has emphasized schemas of activity and passivity, with concomitant implications of health and disability. Developmental discourses on puberty in the twentieth century more or less overtly reinforced such assumptions rather than questioning them. In 1923 the London Board of Education's *Report of the Consultative Committee on the Differentiation of the Curriculum for Boys and Girls Respectively in Secondary Schools* emphasized these "physiological and emotional differences between the sexes":

> Adolescent girls, the Report suggested, had less energy than adolescent boys. This was partly because their blood was lower in specific gravity, carrying less haemoglobin than did boys' blood after puberty. Further, menstruation posed problems: "the periodic disturbances to which girls and women are constitutionally subject, condemn many of them to a recurring if temporary diminution of general mental efficiency." The calcium metabolism in females was believed to become unstable with the onset of puberty: a deficiency in calcium, it was mooted, might be considered at least partly responsible for the "greater nervous excitability of the female sex." (quoted in Dyhouse 133–4)

In a model of adolescence understood as linear sequence, puberty forms the biologically determined crux asserting this dichotomous structure, an apparently logical causality that neglects the extent to which it was ideas about puberty that defined the child as constitutionally different from an adult. While I question Sally Mitchell's claims about the "sexualizing and consequent regendering" of young women in the early twentieth century as what "turned the girl into the adolescent" (1995:182), a process of "sexualizing" and "regendering" is at stake in the new force attributed to puberty.

The examination of puberty by medical and psychological specialists defined the process of feminine adolescence as essentially unseen and positioned the new visibility of girls in the public spheres as to some extent only superficial because their fundamental girlness, and both its difficulties and possible diagnosis, was not visible there. But the increasing examination of girls across different institutions and practices made puberty itself much more visible. New observation of puberty placed it as both knowable and at the limit of the knowable—as materializing the unrepresentability of the body. Freud closes his lecture "Femininity" with a reference to puberty as this kind of (as yet) unknown transformation: "it is not my intention to pursue the further behavior of femininity through puberty to the period of maturity. Our knowledge, moreover, would be insufficient for the purpose" (131). Puberty, despite its apparent empirical veracity, remains a mystery, and one that is moreover at the heart of femininity as a "dark continent" (134). For Freud, that is, the problem of how feminine development can happen at all is overcome, and only partially, by "the wave of repression which at puberty will do away with a large amount of the girl's masculine sexuality in order to make room for the development of her femininity" (255).

As bodily change in puberty is often represented as sexual development, sexual organs remain definitive indices of adolescence, verifying this sexual dichotomy as the foundational structure of adolescence. Puberty is held to produce a quantitative and qualitative change in sexual desire and genital form and is, in this sense, an unwilled and uncontrollable assertion of the sexual body—an anatomical destiny that paradoxically requires channeling into proper sexual practices hitherto substantially alien to the child. This idea of puberty as destiny codes sexuality as simultaneously genital and adult.[1] But the postejaculatory coding of masculine sexuality and postmenarche coding of feminine sexuality are not equivalent models of sexual desire or activity, and this narrative of puberty thus distinguishes girls from both desire and activity. Elizabeth Grosz highlights the significance of this sexual specificity for theories of the body:

> Women's bodies do not develop their adult forms with reference to their newly awakened sexual capacities. Rather her bodily development is dramatically overcoded with the resonances of motherhood. . . . Puberty is not figured as the coming of a self-chosen sexual maturity but as the signal of immanent reproductive capacities . . . the onset of menstruation is not an indication at all for the girl of her developing sexuality, only her coming womanhood. (1994:205)

The proper accomplishment of puberty in adult sexuality demands distinctly gendered performances of heterosexuality and identity. Puberty constitutes a nexus of bodily functions and privatized discipline. In late modernity puberty explains not only how reproduction becomes possible but also how gender arrives as an explanation of the subject. Understanding puberty as a psychological development still depends on sexual maturation and its social consequences, as well as their strict differentiation according to the male/female dichotomy. Representatively, Carl Jung claimed that

> Puberty is a period of illusion and only partial responsibility. . . . Into this childishness sexuality often breaks with brutal force, while, despite the

onset of puberty, it often goes on slumbering in a girl until the passion of love awakens it. . . . With man it is different. Sexuality bursts on them like a tempest, filling them with brute desires and needs. (1982b:32)

Most twentieth-century discourses on puberty endorse this interaction of physiological change and psychological development ordered according to sexual dualism, a pattern equally evident in the emotional symptoms attributed to puberty's hormonal flows and bodily reshaping. Physiological verification is important to psychological theories of adolescence, and psychological effects validate studies of adolescence as a process of physiological change. This mesh of the physical and the psychological continues to instigate contradictions and erasures in medical discourses and puberty manuals.

Everygirl presents this as a surreptitious emergence of the body that is more "exactly defined" in girls than in boys: "The physical changes which are the visible signs of puberty are due to hormones produced in the girl's body. The changes begin quietly" (30). In a 1988 audiovisual presentation titled *Growth and Development at Puberty,* no female genital category on the growth chart is analogous to the kind of data constituted by penis and testes growth. There are eleven slides of male genitals (those for penis-testes growth are repeated for pubic hair growth) but only one slide of female genitals, and that depicts the "prepubescent."[2] A second slide in the section dealing with the development of female sexual characteristics shows male rather than female genitals—as a point of comparison. This presentation is designed to support counselling of adolescents concerned about little or slow physiological development. At the conclusion of the slide series a comparison of three naked fourteen-year-old boys supports this assurance but is followed by the statement that girls cannot be reassured that variations on "normal" development are unimportant, supported by an image of a clothed reclining girl. This presentation is representative of several tendencies in dominant discourses on puberty: an understanding of male/female puberty as respectively visible/invisible; an attribution of greater difficulty, mystery, and importance to feminine puberty; and the articulation of puberty as physical development with irreducible social implications that are more pervasive for girls than for boys. The elaborate collapse of a psychosocial adjustment to maturity and the physical changes usually called puberty in late modernity brings with it an apparently contradictory imperative to distinguish between the physical and the psychological. Adolescence makes the difficulty of marking this distinction highly visible and, by interpreting it as a question of maturity, has impelled a range of social reform movements and the expansion of psychology as a therapeutic discourse.

Languages of Puberty

In *Birth of the Clinic: An Archaeology of Medical Perception* Foucault presents the emergence of perceptions of the body as anatomical as a new collaboration between language and the gaze he calls "the clinical optic." In defining bodies with an expanding vocabulary including the specular division of bodily form into anatomies, this optic produced a new form of the body's visibility. Foucault argues that this collaboration of discourse and gaze restructures the threshold of visibility so that what is seen appears to be self-evident. Anatomy proceeds through discursive articulations equivalent to diagrams that make the body appear to naturally take the form of that articulation. This is an "ideal of an exhaustive description" where the collaboration of seeing and knowing is imagined to be complete and coherent in that articulation (1973a:112–13). In this discursive form puberty is distributed in public, popular, and theoretical fields as an exhaustive gaze/articulation. I want to take this understanding of the collaboration of seeing and knowing to a consideration of the ways in which puberty is articulated for girls.

As Judith Butler argues, the gendered body is "the repeated stylization of the body, a set of repeated acts within a highly regulatory frame that congeal over time to produce the appearance of a substance, of a natural sort of being" (1990:33). This gendered body is a norm to be cited, and this repetition is recognized as taking on definitive form with puberty. Following from this premise, puberty is no more a bodily change than an educational space where an already but incompletely gendered subject learns which gender norms are available for what kinds of citation and what body styles are acceptable or possible. It is in this sense as well that a discussion of female puberty always raises the question of whether a woman is defined by specific organs or hormonal complexes. The sex/gender distinction that forms a central tenet of feminism insists that women or girls should be distinguished from their bodies as sexed by such disciplined observations as gynecology and puberty, and that female bodies should be distinguished from the more or less feminine meanings cultures assign to them. Gender is thus seen as the obvious basis of any concern with the social condition of girls, even when this is directly articulated as or directly impacts on statements about the female body. Moira Gatens argues, however, that while there is a distinction to be made between sex and gender, framing feminist concerns solely by gender pretends that the body is neutral and that women are "constructed" solely as a type of "consciousness" (30). This entanglement of the body and a social self in gender mirrors the entanglement of adolescence— and the conjunction of these in feminine adolescence might be instructive.

Although infancy is the first recourse for identifying what is innate to the late modern subject, this can only proceed by translation into adult roles— a translation that relies on the articulation of bodily facts in puberty. Puberty is initially differentiated according to sex, but it is not only gendered but also *gender* itself insofar as it reformulates and replaces rather than merely activating the genders of childhood. As a child, the girl is positioned as not fully female or feminine, and at adolescence she both loses and gains sex/gender identity. Puberty is only one component of feminine adolescence that inscribes the girl's body as sexed/gendered, but it indicates the degree to which sex and gender cannot be clearly differentiated. While gender is clearly overlaid onto sex in the unfolding of puberty, it is also evident that an already gendered body takes on its sexed identity in puberty. The particular pattern of puberty is only possible in the context of patriarchy— where the girl's sex will be mainly figured around an evaluation of reproductive capacities; and in the context of late modernity where this evaluation will be understood as a sexuality integral to her personal identity. It remains difficult, however, to think puberty in ideological terms because of its attachment to the physiological and the natural. Neither gender nor sex are cultural constructions laid upon a body, and both are entwined in the problem of sexual difference, which is neither discretely body nor socialization, even when it is understood as, to use Grosz's phrase, an "irreducible cultural universal" (1994:160). The pubescent body makes vividly visible something apparently prior to culture but also instantiates the self's place in culture. Puberty is a representation of the gendering of the body, which doesn't mean that the body before puberty is gender neutral but, rather, that before puberty the gender of a body is held to be an inadequate and perhaps unstable map of the body. There is thus no such thing as female puberty (detached from representations, ideologies, histories) but only feminine puberty—a field of discourses on gender within which the girl is especially privileged.

Puberty is usually analyzed from positions that recognize cultural meanings as a superstructure interpreting corporeal effects. Sexology formed one such position in the emergence of puberty as a popular discourse, attempting to delineate which phenomena were physical and which were socially generated. This project relied on a biological model explicated in Havelock Ellis's influential *Studies in the Psychology of Sex*, which he framed with the claim that "it has not hitherto been usual to enquire into the facts of normal sexual development" (preface), despite his evident interest in locating and analyzing perversions. Girls most often appear in Ellis's work as a neutral object for this analysis of "normal sexual development," a position he elaborates by explicitly feminizing the child and infantilizing women. By contrast perverse young women are exceptions to the norm supplied by girls, and "inverts" (a category including many lesbians) are not girls at all but an "intersex."

While puberty is often used to locate a "real" delineated by medical sciences, it is also employed to question the parameters of the biological. Such reference to puberty is common in feminist analysis and often proceeds by comparing accounts of the biological impact of puberty to more sociological approaches, such as behavioral studies of adolescents. This approach to puberty does not refute the equation between puberty and biology or question the empirical fact of the biological. Feminist studies of puberty often eliminate the claim that something is natural by an analysis of its cultural variability, a process designed to delineate the genuinely biological. Examples of this approach form some of the most influential texts in second-wave feminism, from Germaine Greer's *The Female Eunuch* (1971) to Naomi Wolf's *The Beauty Myth* (1990).

When contemporary feminist theorists approach questions of the body, they often mark out a philosophical terrain rather than producing such comparative social or cultural analysis. For example, Simone de Beauvoir's use of phenomenology and psychoanalysis in *The Second Sex* (see chapter 6 below) gestures to the interpenetration of subjectivity and materiality in the body but also posits an indecipherable real foundation for that process. Beauvoir describes female puberty as a "time of unrest" in which "the child's body is becoming the body of a woman and is being made flesh" (332). For Beauvoir, hormonal differences hold the girl at an infantile stage, as if only proper menstruation and other reproductive development allow one to "become" a woman. Puberty thus manifests for Beauvoir a simultaneous transformation of sexuality and consciousness: "She becomes an object, and she sees herself as object; she discovers this new aspect of her being with surprise: it seems to her that she has been doubled; instead of coinciding exactly with herself, she now begins to exist outside" (361). Beauvoir draws here on Freud's insistence on the psychosexual significance of childhood, which also relies on a model of puberty:

> To suppose that children have no sexual life—sexual excitations and needs and a kind of satisfaction—but suddenly acquire it between the ages of twelve and fourteen, would (quite apart from any observations) be as improbable, and indeed senseless, biologically, as to suppose that they brought no genitals with them into the world and only get them at the time of puberty. What *does* awaken in them at this time is the reproductive function, which makes use for its purposes of physical and mental material already present. (1953, 7:158–9)

For Freud, puberty is not the arrival of sexuality but the scene of its proper deployment, introducing both the normative force of sexuality in place of a more polymorphous erotic life and multiple occasions for psychological and physical disorders: "Since the new sexual aim assigns very different functions to the two sexes, their sexual development now diverges greatly. That of males is the more straightforward and the more understandable, while that of females actually enters upon a kind of involution" (1953, 8:73). Explicating the life of the self as both physiological and psychological might seem a proper resolution of an arbitrary but necessary distinction, but, rather than undermining distinctions between the physiological and psychological, psychoanalysis tends to occlude and in some cases reinforce them.

Debates over whether it is natural to align any psychology with puberty, let alone a psychosocial crisis, have often instigated attempts to locate puberty in cultures outside modernity and thus by implication outside culture. Ancient history and anthropology have thus been important resources in attempts to delineate puberty. Debates over the inevitability of crisis and trauma around puberty escalated with Margaret Mead's studies of primitive puberty, which were important contributions to the naturalization of puberty as integral to but distinct from adolescence. Mead's studies claim that the girl's initiation into womanhood is predominantly marked by pain. In one tribe a girl's "brothers build a menstrual hut for her, and in this she is attended by female relatives who rub her body with stinging nettles: They tell her to roll one of the large nettle-leaves into a tube and thrust it into her vulva; this will ensure her breasts' growing large and strong" (Mead 1939:93). The more the girl suffers, the better woman she will be. In Mead's work female puberty is the condition for a girl's ascent to social relevance; while at the same time domesticity is a social effect of this sexual maturation.[3] Her analyses proceed explicitly from late modern concerns with understanding the natural force and effects of puberty, yet they are only more explicit than Freud's analytic observations, which equally appropriate girls' specific experiences to identify the generic parameters of puberty as a physiological, psychosocial, and cultural field of knowledge and visibility. Because analyses of puberty identify a field of representations rather than a set of discovered facts, feminine puberty differs according to sites and contexts and can only be analyzed as it is articulated in specific appearances. Such analysis can not proceed by importing a model of puberty against which these articulations will be measured, and yet, paradoxically, no other analysis of puberty is possible given that puberty itself is a product of the late modern discourses that make it visible as a representation of embodied changes.

Representing the Body as Puberty
Menarche

Feminine adolescence as it is articulated in relation to these late modern conceptions of puberty is always a space, delay, and period of stasis as well as transformation. The rites of passage assigned to girl-becoming-woman appear to mark bodily changes that alter girls without any necessary reference to personal experience. Feminine adolescence represents these changes as a specific space and time of life, referring directly to the periods of suspension discerned in what appear to be puberty rituals in "premodern" societies. The changes and rites prioritized in such reference center on menarche.[4] Menarche remains important to late modern Western societies even though it does not appear to involve any public recognition of maturity in the sense discerned in analyses of supposedly primitive societies. Late modern menarche does, however, work to signify a form of psychosexual maturity in the private sphere.

The progression from girl to adolescent nominally depends on physical change, but that from adolescent to woman relies on an apparently indeterminate combination of social events. Accounts of female adolescence depend on a transition from menarche to an unpredictable point of maturity historically reliant on the idea of the hymen and variously defined as sexual intercourse, marriage, or childbirth. While menarche is mostly figured as a physical change not necessarily heralded, signalled, or followed by any change in identity, this second break is often represented as social or psychological rather than physiological.[5] But menarche is also understood as an interior change in being for which the physical visible event is merely an indication. Moreover, menarche indicates a range of invisible activities in the unseen reproductive systems of girls, activities understood to inhibit growth hormones and thus halt external developments more readily comparable to the puberty of boys. Menarche thus helps sustain the invisibility of feminine adolescence despite its arrival as a visible sign of imminent womanhood.

No comparable morphological event signifies the onset of masculine adolescence, but if menarche is an urgent rupture in whatever growing-up is prescribed for her, it does not make a girl a woman. Menstruation concretely defines the difference of the feminine, but its principle function is to represent not the assumption of womanly roles but removal from childhood. First ejaculation is sometimes used to designate a comparable watermark for masculine adolescence, but it less clearly locates a beginning point, and just as first ejaculation is understood to be triggered by psychological activity, masculine adolescence is overwhelmingly represented as a social development. Menarche, by comparison, is perceived as a universal female experience independent of social or psychic initiation and thus continues to encode feminine puberty as closer to nature, if not as definitively natural. It is arguable that menstruation, even more than maternity, is the primary ground for claims about the irreducibility of sexual difference. If the initiation of a girl's becoming woman is generally held to be menarche, a larger ontological claim is at stake in defining femininity by menstruation. Some popular discourse on menstruation, such as that exemplified in Penelope Shuttle's *The Wise Wound*, specifically claims the menstrual cycle as a more or less mystical process where an individual woman is dispersed into a movement that exceeds the individual. But many feminist writers position menstruation as marking a feminine temporality that is cyclical and fluid, with a pervasive import in women's lives. This feminine temporality draws on a long history of images of womanhood continuous with modernity. Ellis and G. Stanley Hall refer extensively to the "periodicity" of women as a pattern that structures women's lives. According to these narratives, girls are positioned in relation to a corporeal, natural world by their entry into menstruation. This is especially significant if girls can not place themselves in time/history by either monumental maternity or the Subject's reproduction.[6] But not all women menstruate: there are pre- and postmenstrual women, and many women never menstruate or cease menstruating for significant periods of time, including pregnancy. A genre of woman thus cannot be defined by menstruation, however important it may be to histories of figuring and experiencing womanhood.

The menstrual cycle has a pervasive analogical power in discussions of womanhood, but discourses on menstruation in some important sense circulate around feminine adolescence. A feminine temporality is often invoked with reference to cycle myths in which the central figure (e.g., Persephone) is the girl as bride and sign of fertility—but specifically of *potential* fertility and its delay or avoidance. At a more historically specific level discourses on menstruation, including those on menarche, regularity, and other aspects of menstrual health, or the feminine hygiene associated with menstruation in the twentieth century, are especially linked to girls rather than women. Menstruation in late modernity is a highly significant construction of the feminine body that habitually invokes the rule of the normal body over puberty.[7] Menstruation in discourses on girlhood, feminine adolescence, or female puberty articulates revelation, explication, reassurance, and disgust. Menstruation is the most explicit object for the important structure of abjection in discourses on female puberty. Julia Kristeva influentially defines "abjection" as a relation to the body as Mother; specifically as the failure to abject the Mother.[8] In representations of menstruation as well as maternity the visibly feminine body foregrounds the permeability of boundaries between self and other, nature and culture, body and self. Abjection materializes an alienation from this body not through the dominant psychoanalytic figure of castration but by constituting the female body as "leaking, uncontrollable, seeping liquid; as formless flow; as viscosity, entrapping, secreting; as lacking not so much or simply the phallus but self-containment" (Grosz 1994:203). Unlike maternity, the menstruating body is not understood as itself useful to a patriarchal society—the menstruating girl is no longer a child(daughter) but not yet a mother(wife). As an experience shared by women (as an imaginary construct) and denigrated symbolically, menstruation speaks the body as abject and also feminine.

The continuity of menstruation as a figure for the abhorrent signifies an imperative to avoid and reject the feminized body, including among women and girls. Examples of this imperative are easy to find in popular narratives for girls. Sally Mitchell asks whether the motif of illness in Victorian girls' stories invokes the "wound of adolescence—the illness and suffering that turns a girl into a woman—a code for the onset of menstruation" (1995:161). In twentieth-century fiction for girls, however, illness has become a less central motif and romance (rather than other forms of suffering) is foregrounded as the key to and form of becoming a woman, in comparison to which menarche is in fact rarely visible. This is partly because the adolescent who centers these stories is presumed to have already passed menarche, but preteen fiction that dramatizes entry into feminine adolescence also rarely displays menarche. Even advertisements for menstrual products conceal menstruation—displaying that avoidance with bright blue liquids in place of blood and by reference to activities that are pointedly not specific to menstruation. Nevertheless, this aspect of girlhood becomes increasingly, if obliquely, visible through its technologization in the twentieth century. The dimension of menstruation represented as illness is, within this technologization of menstruation, complimented by the care and practice ethic that constitutes a dominant theme of girl culture. The imperative to ward off, minimize, comprehend, and manage the effects of menstruation, rather than surrendering to the biological fallibility of womanhood, is a central theme of advertising for menstrual products, the puberty manual, and the girls' magazine.

In considering the more consistent elements of popular representations of female puberty in, for example, girls' magazines and other girl-directed products, an important and sustained critical reflexivity inherent in popular culture might become apparent. Popular culture is not only a field productive of and constituted in interplays of power and identification, as has been pointed out by several generations of cultural studies practitioners (see chapter 6); it is also a field that recognizes and articulates those processes. Representations of puberty in popular culture present themselves as interplays of power and identification: as interactions between embodied selves, cultural forms, and social structures rather than as mute objects of consumption. These representations are not only available to theories of girlhood but themselves cite and form theories of girlhood. It is highly important to the lived experience and dominant representations of girlhood that puberty, as a period of training in bodily identity and power relations, explicitly constructs knowledges about the body.

Menstruation for Girls

Twentieth-century girls' magazines prioritize monitoring of both puberty and menstruation in their interrogation of girls' maturity. As I suggested with reference to visual aids for education about puberty (which is often termed sex education), the privileging of the visual in popular and theoretical discourses about puberty reinforces an understanding of puberty as an empirically verifiable process located on an objective body. No page of a girls' magazine lacks a picture of a girl, and the text and the visualizations form interpretative frameworks for each other. Through a cult of normality and an eroticization of the adolescent woman's concern with normalizing her body, the feminine adolescent body is constructed in girls' magazines as a range of desires trespassed upon by a variety of physiological imperfections. Collapsing the public and private obligations of self-control into the public/private surface of this body, these texts present the feminine adolescent with a fantasy that control over her body is both necessary and possible.

Menstruation has been one of the central objects of clinical discourses on women's bodies, and this centrality has particularly devolved upon the ignorance of girls. A. G. Hall's 1845 guidance manual, *Womanhood: Causes of its Premature Decline,* calls itself of the "New School" (xv) in advocating the dissemination of knowledge concerning "the female constitution" for the education of mothers and their daughters. Although directed to "the Turn of Life" (what might now be called the menopausal woman), this text sources the possibility of this "decline" in a process beginning with "First Mensis" and "The Young Female."[9] Menarche is figured as a fall or crisis—an internalized and compact parallel to the storm and stress of masculine adolescence. A 1970s' puberty manual asserts that:

> Reaction to menstruation may also be beset with problems for the adolescent girl. Very often her first period will depend on the type of and amount of knowledge she has of the event and on her mother's attitude to it. The girl with no preparation may become panicky and hysterical, fearing that something is wrong with her, so that the whole process is loaded with fear and anxiety, which may cause her to reject the female role. . . . The handling of the menstrual crisis can have critical consequences for the girl's future development, since menstruation emphasises and confirms the differences between the sexes and the feminine identity. (Harper and Collins 1978b:150)

The discourse of menstruation aimed at girls creates a norm—the ideal menstruating girl—to which girls compare themselves. Girls' magazines presume an audience of adolescents, but the plethora of information explaining menarche, puberty, and supposedly less dramatic sexual experiences (such as kissing) indicates both the educational rubric of the girls' magazine and that the actual audience of the genre is presumed to be pre-pubescent. The girl of girls' magazines is in the field of puberty and yet not in control of it—she is in need of instruction, guidance, and helpful illustrative models.

Among the conventions of girls' magazines, puberty, menarche, and menstruation are both visible and invisible. Jessie Lymn's thesis on menstrual discourse for girls (1999) discusses the general concealment of blood and the fact of menstruation in fiction, advertising for menstrual products, and the information provided in girls' magazines. Magazines such as the Australian *Dolly* are dominated as much by menstrual advertising as by fashion, often containing five or more ads for tampons or sanitary napkins in each issue, and also including features on menstruation among their regular columns about bodily changes and sex advice. Lymn offers the "Dolly Period Files" in 1999 issues of the magazine as her example. This advertising campaign for Tampax menstrual products, like other similar campaigns, mimics the layout of the magazine's advice columns. Girls can write to the "Period Files," or call a toll-free help line if they are "confused." Such mechanisms for reader interaction around menstruation—quizzes, surveys, and personalized guides—participate in the genre's broader rhetorical stance as a combination of identification, invitation, and discipline.

Foucault notes that the "chief function of the disciplinary power is to train," but not by creating a "single, uniform mass." Instead disciplinary power "trains the moving, confused, useless multitudes of bodies and forces into a multiplicity of individual elements" (1980:188). The disciplinary practice of guidance manuals as mass-production of feminine adolescence does not create any "single, uniform mass" but instantiates girls as individual members of a group identity. The central premise of such puberty education is that girls lack knowledge about their own bodies or the means to attain it. Education about puberty in general and menstruation in particular regularly resorts to the diagrammatic to emphasize both the objective knowability and the everyday invisibility of the feminine adolescent body. Figure 3.1 is typical of the scientific mode of these diagrams—scientificity being inferred by linearity and highly selective detail and by direct opposition to the identificatory possibilities of photographs, which might raise other than objective and exhaustive informational relations to the illustration. These diagrams, like the instructional leaflets in tampon packaging, constitute rather than indicate a need for directions about touching this part of the body. Repeated reference to puberty reminds the girl that she is taking up a place as becoming a woman that inevitably refers to normative body images. In discussions of menstruation and other modes of puberty these educational discourses emphasize the difficulty of feminine adolescence, reinforcing the need for such dissemination of knowledge about girls' bodies.

Lymn notes that menstrual product instructions often defer mention of menstrual blood through terms such as "flow" and "fluid."[10] Information on how to use tampons thus generally reinforces concealment and discretion, reinforcing menstrual taboos while reassuring girls that they can control the menstruation process. Girls privately engage their puberty in such magazines and leaflets, but as guidance manuals these texts also belong to a more public forum, claiming to engage the girl's social roles and identities. The girls' magazine discourse on menstruation claims to be more personal and less authoritative than other guidance sources, repeatedly deferring to puberty manuals and other more serious and less dialogic or peer-oriented texts such as help lines and medical specialists. This privatizing narrative scene is repeated in such other guidance manual forms as "What's your menstrual story?" (Pallotta-Chiarolli 17)—a game I have also played in the introduction to this book. The story of menstruation will be both a physical instantiation of feminine adolescence and the signal of its end in womanhood—a history of the girl-adolescent-woman in one event.

Grosz understands puberty as separating the biological from the social body, as "a period in which the biological body undergoes major upheavals and changes as an effect of puberty. It is in this period that the subject feels the greatest discord between the body image and the lived body, between its psychical idealized self-image and its bodily changes" (1994:75). In response to such dominant discourses on the sexed body in relation to the self, Grosz aims to displace the understanding of self or identity as truly interior, an understanding that disavows the materiality of knowledges and experiences of the body. In *Volatile Bodies* Grosz's understanding of the "volatile body" that "performs I" (see 121–37) resists being pinned to a single identity by recognizing the fluidity of bodily experience and by displacing the clear distinction between body and mind with a "corporeality" that acknowledges the entwining of body and self in any subjectivity. Grosz's references to puberty in this argument highlight the sexed specificity of cultural inscriptions of embodied subjectivity and the insufficiently acknowledged importance of adolescence to theories of subjectivity, including feminist theory.

The Ideal Girl's (Social) Body

Body Imaging: Girls and Dolls

The girl of the girls' magazine is a body/subject in process, a collage of identification and discipline through a profusion of technologies of the self. The uncertain borders around girlhood and puberty enable this dominant mode in discourses on feminine adolescence. These body-self processes of feminine puberty are also evident in the girls' toys that are marketed to and consumed by predominantly prepubescent girls. Taking up the possibility that all girls are adolescent, are processes of fraught and passionate subject formation centered on a disciplined relation to bodily change and social transformation, this section considers one of the most recognized icons of Western girlhood, the Barbie doll. A genealogy of Barbie should be useful to a genealogy of feminine adolescence, intersecting discourses on puberty, girlhood, feminism, consumption, and the teenager and marking movements in the public constitution of feminine adolescence in changes to Barbie production. However, such a history of Barbie is not possible here. Instead I want to deploy Barbie as an instance of imaginary and material relations to girlhood.

Many critics have used Barbie to discussed socialization, body image, desire, pleasure, and corporate motives. But Barbie is rarely discussed as a mode of becoming a girl/woman—of feminine adolescence. Barbie is an important mass-cultural representation of femininity, but she is not a representation of Woman. Feminist approaches to Barbie often express anxiety about why and how girls play Barbie, but Barbie is a zone of paradoxes, and the feminine adolescence she models is always distinguished from the body of Woman as representative system. It is inadequate to understand Barbie as a dominant ideology or, following Slavoj, as a *sinthôme* (symbol, image, symptom) of late modernity (see Žižek 1989). Instead I want to think about Barbie as an assemblage of girl-doll relations. Barbie puts girls into relation with a gender machine. She is woman/not-woman and human/not-human, a game that can seem to denaturalize gender despite the anxieties of interested parties. Barbie displaces the question of girlhood—of feminine development of various kinds—onto something gendered only by the effect of a machine on other machines. Barbies appear to be punched out at different points on a developmental line—Kelly, Skipper, Teen Queen, Teacher, or Mommie Barbie—but there is no sequence involved. She is stamped out in a pose, and you can move her forward or backward in purchases or other

Barbie play. Barbie's occupations and activities have no function except as a space or machine for the recording and consumption of desire.[11] Barbie is also machinic in the sense of being something that works: always a forceful model of gender, sometimes a literal machine (legs that bend, neck that twists—often at an angle so that she haughtily and demurely looks up and away rather than simply turning).[12]

Barbie's multiplicity is counted not only in numbers of bodies, faces, styles, or releases but also by girls and moments of Barbie play. Barbie might be the ultimate clean and proper body for which the girl-subject of puberty manuals impossibly strives, but Barbie is never complete, which is why she accessorizes everything, including semiotic and pragmatic functions: occupations, families, names, ethnicities, and identities. Feminist appropriation of Barbie may thus be a critique or a deployment—in the Barbie Liberation Army or small circulation zines such as *Hey There Barbie Girl* as much as in feminist cultural studies. And such appropriation may still venerate Barbie, as all modes of Barbie collection (including analysis) work as appropriation. Feminist critique of Barbie, however, sometimes participates in the mainstream devaluation of girl culture. It may be useful to argue that Barbie imposes undesirable models of femininity on girls, but it is also the dominant public discourse on girls who like to play Barbie. It is not radical to imply that Barbie enthusiasts are co-opted or stupid or to see Barbie as an ideological template, because these criticisms of girl culture are proper to positioning girls as definitively malleable gullible consumers. The assumption that Barbie's multiplicity precedes her purchase and must be understood as a marketing practice is too simplistic. On the other hand, the idealization of Barbie play that assumes that her multiplicity arrives only after purchase also misses the attraction of Barbie as a group identity. Barbie maps girls in relation to each other as well as in relation to norms that may be constrictive. This map is produced in every purchase or reading of Barbie as permanent state of becoming-a-woman, always aligned with a shifting discourse on feminine adolescence that is itself a commodification.

Barbie can thus be considered a representation of puberty. Barbie cites the distracted marginality of girls who are not and never will be the Subject but will unfold in relation to a set of mobile identities fixed unpredictably to a gender machine articulated primarily as an intensely social body image. Barbie herself is less important to this proposition than the couple "girl-doll," but there is no Barbie outside that couple (even for adult Barbie collectors and other fetishists). When you wind Growing-Up Skipper's right arm her body lengthens and breasts begin to protrude from her rubber chest. Growing-Up Skipper is a machine-girl as well as being Barbie's younger sister according to Mattel's guidelines. She is not a daughter, although she is not detached from social relations, and her fascinating "growing up" can not be explicated by reference to psychological models—her puberty is a reversible gender machine that has no certainly predetermined meanings or uses. Growing-Up Skipper articulates a range of questions about Barbie's age, social position, and sexual status: If she is a girl, why is she hanging out on her own in Hawaii? If she is a woman, why doesn't she wear underpants? Through such questions Erica Rand's *Barbie's Queer Accessories* discusses Mattel's move in the 1970s to divest Barbie of all narrative fixity, including her name, parents, and a clear context for her age or "developmental" position (Rand 58–64). Despite celebration of the doll's fortieth birthday, Barbie is twenty, or fifteen, and always will be.

Doll play often takes up a mothering role, but Barbie maintains a decisive distance from maternal figures. While there are many possible ways of playing Barbie as a mother, there is only one authoritative Barbie maternity: "Mommie Barbie." As Skipper's growing-up is eminently reversible (she grows up in order to reverse it), Mommie Barbie's latex stomach rolls up to reveal a removable baby, after which Mommie Barbie's stomach snaps back into an apparently unchanged body, a game that plays on its own reversibility. Both Mommie Barbie and Growing-Up Skipper explicitly state Barbie's role as gender manipulation and more strictly regiment modes of Barbie play than most other models. Barbie's more typical development is incorporeal (a state of affairs) rather than just reversible; she is adolescent rather than developmental. But Barbie does map the construction of the body as a space marked and crossed by lines of inclusion and exclusion, such as puberty, and this raises the specter of Barbie's body image. Barbie is not responsible for the tyranny of slenderness in which she participates, which doesn't make her ungainly impossible body a good thing. Barbie does reinforce sameness by association with such bodily norms, which also pivotally include the racial marking of Barbie's body and her related association with the territoriality of America.

Barbie's relation to race has been discussed in various forums, notably Ann Ducille's analysis of ethnic Barbie friends (1994). The absorption of the specificity implied by Colored Francie or Julia into the umbrella Barbie of Hawaiian Barbie or Malaysian Barbie, which Ducille discusses, is not necessarily a greater homogenization of Barbie or Barbie play. It may not deterritorialize the ethnic primacy of white Barbie, but it may position Barbie as the doll desire, the girl/doll thing, rather than definitively the white girl.[13] Ducille correctly points to this marketing ploy as "an easy and immensely profitable way off the hook of Eurocentrism" (52), but the uncertainty of what Barbie might be supplements, rather than being absorbed into, the series that defines Barbie as the one we all know she is. Barbie is thus an interesting point for juxtaposing this image of feminine adolescence with a consideration of whether global girl culture is homogenous or Americanized. In part, Barbie's definition of girl culture as American is nostalgic for the globalizing wave of U.S. youth culture in the 1950s. Barbie as teenage doll was accompanied by the soldier doll, GI Joe, but Barbie's Americanness is not just about ethnic codes or standard models for gender identity but also about factories. The raised plastic trademark on Barbie's body traces a history of exploitation and development—from made in America to made in Japan, to Hong Kong, Korea, Taiwan, China. . . . But Barbie can only continue to articulate gender norms by being unfixed, by emphasizing the mobility of such norms: not only Princess Pink Barbie and Astronaut Barbie, but also Japanese and liberated Barbies are "Barbie." Understanding Barbie as an oppressive body type (feminine, white, American) disavows the multiplicity of Barbie, including all those games that Mattel would not put on boxes and that Barbie-friendly feminists like to cite. Girls play Barbie with both intense respect and passionate disregard for her hegemonic positions.

Before Culture: Body and Subjection

Barbie play is gender performance and might be referred to Butler's proposition that gender only consists in such performance. In *Bodies That Matter* (1993) Butler discusses the materiality of the body as a "constitutive outside"—as that which cannot be spoken and on which all else depends, and that is understood and articulated through "materialization."[14] This materialization is a process of both constitution and inscription. Butler understands it as construction, defined "not as site or surface, but as *a process of materialization that stabilizes over time to produce the effect of boundary, fixity, and surface we call matter*" (9). Insofar as the biological facts of the body are already a representation, which is how they can be thought or exchanged, this includes the body's crucial developments at puberty. Puberty is a set of discourses on the body that articulate a bodily norm by which the significance of bodies is measured. Puberty might thus be not only an example of such materialization but in fact a crucial index for what materialization means for embodiment, although Butler principally refers to Lacan's "mirror stage" and thus a nominally childhood scene of self-production. Butler's theories also enable further discussion of where culture arrives for the subject and thus where the Subject itself arrives. The question of how we know where culture begins (and the body stops) is the foundational and often unacknowledged question of any discourse on puberty.

In *The Psychic Life of Power* (1997) Butler argues that becoming a subject is an operation of power, and that "as a form of power, subjection is paradoxical" (1). In this text Butler aims to engage Foucault's insights about power with rather than against psychoanalysis. She begins the chapter "Between Freud and Foucault" with an epigraph from Foucault: "what I would like to grasp is the system of limits and exclusion which we practice without knowing it; I would like to make the cultural unconscious apparent" (quoted in Butler 1997:83).[15] Psychic Life thus also suggests ways of thinking about the processes of feminine adolescence as both operations and effects of power.

Butler's model of subjection here is paradoxical because the subject can never be separated from the forces that enable it—the same forces that continue to shape subjectivity threaten its very possibility. Butler writes:

> We are used to thinking of power as what presses on the subject from the outside, as what subordinates, sets underneath, and relegates to a lower order. This is surely a fair description of part of what power does. But if, following Foucault, we understand power as forming the subject as well, as providing the very condition of its existence and the trajectory of its desire, then power is not simply what we oppose but also, in a strong sense, what we depend on for our existence and what we harbour and preserve in the beings that we are. (1997:2)

The body is clearly a condition for puberty, but the sheer fact of the body doesn't necessitate our particular understandings of puberty, or indeed any reference to puberty at all. Puberty is a powerful regulatory discourse, a dominant because naturalized assertion of norms. Puberty relies on a scientific or detailed empirical observation of the body and its development, but also on a personalized positioning of the body where variations on a presumed generality are as important as that naturalized event and on a discourse on normality that arises from that contradiction.

Foucault describes the conjunction of bodies, power, and politicized forces that produces subject positions as "bio-power" (see Foucault 1977a). Bio-power in modernity is the possibility of mastery over life itself. This is most evident in the way that subjects are placed in relation to political mechanisms that have power over life and death, but it is also evident in the regulation of proper modes of living and understanding life. Although the authority of the state over life does not work through puberty in the same way as through a death penalty, puberty does still allow state intervention in ways of living and understanding life—through educational and health programs, for example, and other social institutions that delineate and police the activities of immature and mature bodies. Foucault observes that bio-power produces "life as a political object" (1977a:143). The conditions that make puberty possible in its modern sense are all affected/effected by relations of power and all demand that we consider how cultural forms enable girls in making themselves as well as categorizing them. As Butler suggests, "subjection consists precisely in this fundamental dependency on a discourse we never chose but that, paradoxically, initiates and sustains our agency" (1997:2).

Butler understands this subject as a relation of power in which the individual is both enabled and contained. She claims that "the form this power takes is relentlessly marked by a figure of turning, a turning back on oneself or even a turning *on* oneself" (1997:3). The reconstitution of a girl's body in puberty is in a very similar sense both beyond her control and obsessively controlled by herself and others. A girl experiences puberty by a process of reference to norms and categories that may condemn or dismiss her but are never external, particularly in relation to her pubescent body.[16] Within the realm of the mutely biological it seems impossible to think of puberty as a process of power, although it is lived as such. Far from being the merely bodily component of adolescence, puberty is a set of narratives about social positions and cultural belonging; about lived bodies, identities, and power. In fact the lack of fit between puberty and adolescence grounds much of the difficulty attributed to feminine adolescence, because dominant models of physical maturity do not in fact provide a foundation for any claim to social maturity. And yet feminine puberty is a discourse on owning a subject position and a culture, as girls' magazines, puberty manuals, and Barbie dolls all suggest.

Puberty exemplifies the "irresolvable ambiguity" that, Butler says, "arises when one attempts to distinguish between the power that (transitively) enacts the subject, and the power enacted by the subject" (1997:15). This attachment to the conditions of subjection might be thought as the processes of identification that enable access to subject positions. But the argument that one is tied to the processes of subjection might also imply that adolescence's processes of self-production can never be completed, not even in the field of puberty, as evidenced by the permanent attachment of girlhood to discourses on bodily formation and reformation. After adolescence, the residual but permanent attachment to the body in discourses on the self remains associated with adolescence, perhaps especially insofar as an ideal adolescence both rejects and is defined by the body. This is exacerbated within models of subjection that make the rejection of a feminized body the ground for identity formation. Kristeva analyzes the production of the body in the Symbolic Order (a body she aligns with femininity and "non-language" [1986b:162]) as *anterior* to that order, in which "the body must bear no trace of its debt to nature: it must be clean and proper in order to be fully symbolic" (1982:102). The onset of feminine adolescence, of the girl's sexed identity, is marked by exactly this trace of the body, if it is not the writing of it.

Kristeva's understanding of the subject's constitution across boundaries between dichotomous terms will not admit an analysis of power. Grosz suggests, partly in reply to Kristeva, that a different understanding of the body is available through phenomenology, for which "it is only through existence that facts are manifested" (Merleau-Ponty quoted in de Beauvoir 39). Drawing on Maurice Merleau-Ponty, as well as on Gilles Deleuze and Felix Guattari's critique of psychoanalysis, Grosz argues that

> Questions related to subjectivity, interiority, female sexual specificity, are thus not symptoms of a patriarchal culture, not simply products or effects of it, but are forces, intensities, requiring codifications or territorializations and in turn exerting their own deterritorializing and decodifying force, systems of compliance and resistance. (1994:180)

In thinking about the body as action and affect rather than cause and effect (Buchanan 74), Deleuze and Guattari invoke a "body without organs"—a body without hierarchically arranged organs such as penis, phallus, vagina, even mouth. I will discuss the possibilities of Deleuze's philosophy for thinking about girls in chapter 6, but it is worth noting here that Deleuze and Guattari's interrogation of the organized body might be especially significant for thinking about puberty. This body is "opposed not to the organs but to that organisation of the organs called the organism" (Deleuze and Guattari 1987:158). This organism is a conceptualization of the body as unified, and it is difficult to conceive of gender or puberty as other than such organization. Puberty clearly attaches the Subject to a delimitation of what the body can do, and trying to rethink adolescence through the "body without organs" (BwO) seems likely to divest adolescence of both puberty and, it would seem, gender.

Puberty constructs dichotomous body types as social meanings that enable particular functions tied to patriarchal, capitalist late modernity. It is thus a vital field for feminist questioning. However, feminism may also have a stake in puberty as it is currently practiced. Late modern puberty reproduces the contemporary subject of feminist politics, and feminism has a stake in guiding both what will count as the real biological imperatives given form in puberty and what will be seen as their contestable social implications. In complicating an apparently clear structural account of self and body (in puberty) I may seem to be unnecessarily complicating a useful model of what happens in puberty—one where sexual forms can be separated from both sense of self and social meanings and that is thus highly useful to feminist theory. But puberty understood in structuralist terms as a set of exchanges between separate fields of bodily organs and social roles simplifies the processes of puberty in a way that can speak to no girl's experience of it because it avoids the complex power relations that make puberty possible and articulate its current forms. It thus seems both difficult and imperative to consider a poststructuralist account of puberty and of feminine adolescence.

Part 2
Becoming a Woman

4.1 Detail of Simone Martini, *The Annunciation with Two Saints* (c. 1333); tempera on wood *(Reproduced with permission of the Italian Ministry of Cultural Assets and Activities. Held by the Galeria Uffizi. Further reproduction by any means strictly forbidden.)*

four

Daughters: Theories of Girlhood

Woman has not yet taken (a) place. . . . Woman is still the place, the whole of the place in which she cannot take possession of herself as such. . . . She is never here and now because it is she who sets up that eternal else-where from which the "subject" continues to draw his reserves, his re-sources. . . . She is already scattered into x number of places that are never gathered together into anything she knows of herself, and these remain the basis of (re)production—particularly of discourse—in all its forms.

—Luce Irigaray, *This Sex Which Is Not One*

A GENEALOGY of feminine adolescence must consider the power of theoretical discourses to constitute meanings of and for girls. This chapter surveys the major Marxist, psychoanalytic, and feminist axes of contemporary theories of feminine adolescence, explicating the girl's dominant role as daughter in these influential discourses. Such a broad approach inevitably produces some generalizations, and in some cases the best work in these fields becomes invisible when one looks for major tendencies, but this exercise is important. The daughter is the apparently inevitable point of theorizing girlhood relative to patriarchy or maternity—that is relevant to the family understood as biologically complementary heterosexual unit. The daughter is indeed a necessary foundation for biologically complementary heterosexual families, far more so, I will contend, than the son.

While not all daughters are called or identify as girls, all girls are daughters in some respect and daughterhood is always inflected by discourses on girls. Although daughter and girl are not equivalent terms they are mutually defined in a series of oppositions to other more stable terms such as father, woman, and citizen/brother. This chapter proposes that the girl's role as a figure for late modern culture entails an important role for the idea of the girl in critical theory. I will particularly focus on the figure of the daughter in relation to conceptions of property, maternity, and subjectivity.

Marxism: The Daughter's Economy
A Girl's Place: Patriarchy, Capitalism

The emergence of feminine adolescence is historically coincident with a move from industrial to commodity capitalism and with the emergence of Marxist theory. As a relation to the production of subjectivity and other social forms, feminine adolescence is necessarily shaped by and a component of capitalism as the dominant political organization of late modernity. Karl Marx's critical analysis of capitalist modernity always suggested that modernity and capitalism were historically but not necessarily tied together. I have already suggested that modernity requires the girl, but does capitalism require girls? This first section examines how Marxists might discuss girls with reference to the daughter's role in capitalist family units.

Girlhood and daughterhood are consistently articulated in relation to a future role—who or what the girl will be or do as a woman. For this differential definition there is no necessary relation between significations of girlhood and femaleness. While the girl is thus a set of meanings independent of any essential identity located in the body of a young female, this is not removed from the realm of the material. Materiality describes a place in history and the systems of social exchange that constitute history. Although girls do not fit the dominant model of progression toward the mature coherent independent Subject they are integral to the reproductive sequence daughter-mother, which constitutes a highly visible role for girls across diverse cultural and historical contexts.

Economies are systems of exchange and flow around social structures, and capitalist economies are dominated by discourses on property and propriety, which also define a particular relation to the most owned and not-owned of territories, the Mother. In relation to the Mother as a necessary component of capitalism, and necessary asset of the patriarchal capitalist family unit, girls may be seen to represent the exchange, flow and movement of property. The transitions of feminine adolescence are material exchanges of one kind of role for another, but the girl herself often seems to be the object rather than agent of these exchanges, a possibility that is frequently referred to the sexual economy of patriarchal marriage structures.[1] Frederick Engels more directly emphasizes the equivalent importance of familial and economic organization and suggests that preexisting patriarchal forms were bound into, and changed by, the development of capitalism (see Engels, and Rubin 537–8). Marxist theory, however, often seems to place Woman, or some of her attributes, in the realm of the natural, following Marx's proposition that "the direct, natural, and necessary relation of person to person is the *relation of man to woman*." The Western family within capitalism is definitively patriarchal, and although patriarchy remains historically and culturally specific rather than a static system of facts, it requires a specific range of positions and functions from daughterhood.

In noncapitalist versions of property the daughter is also often a site for negotiating the relative value of property through dowry and related marriage systems. This daughter is a kind of money—an evaluation of property and wealth and an extension of reproductive and familial labor into the world. While these systems have been widely superseded by capitalism, and popularly understood as proper to primitive societies, they retain some relevance to modern capitalism. In capitalism the daughter's role as money is more fully privatized but can still take the form of evaluating status and wealth or representing the continuity of reproductive and domestic labor. But more specifically in capitalism the girl has represented ideas of consumption or commodification. Analogies between girls and commodities are widely promulgated, and commodities are often aligned with girls (and their desirability). Girls are thus also important to images of late capitalism, including the processes of commodity capitalism, mass production, and changes to labor and employment. Siegfried Kracauer's equation of girls with the crisis of mass-production suggests, as Sabine Hake argues, that "the role of the girl was the price woman had to pay for her demystification (caused by her participation in the work process)" (Hake 158). Advertising of various kinds—Kracauer refers to dancing troupes and girls' fashion—is presented as a process of remystifying girls as the process of commodification or desire for commodities. Wolfgang Haug discusses the same modernist commodity culture as a "technocracy of sensuality" (17), replacing Marx's exchange between (men as) owners of commodities with a "commodity aesthetics" deploying the figure of a girl:

> the beautifully designed surface of the commodity becomes its package, not the simple wrapping for protection during transportation, but its real

countenance, like the fairytale princess who is transformed through her feathered costume in which she seeks her fortune in the marketplace. (50)

The significance of late modern girls to consumption is not that they consume (everybody does), or that their sexuality is in fact bound up in commodification, but that they are perceived to derive an inordinate amount of pleasure from commodification and commodity fetishism.

Marx's analysis of surplus/added value was primarily interested in the value that capitalism adds and extracts from the material, and this process can be seen as analogous to those by which value is attached to girls within a heteropatriarchal economy, sometimes seen as a system of selling women. Sociologist Gayle Rubin's "The Traffic in Women" constitutes an influential discussion of the idea that women are foundational objects of exchange for capitalism, drawing on the work of anthropologist Claude Lévi-Strauss as well as Freud. If girls are the preeminent gift exchanged in the patriarchal (incest-taboo) system explored by Lévi-Strauss, Freud, and Rubin, then they are not constituted as agents of social exchange in the same way as other members of that system. With reference to Marx and Engels's work on "reproduction" from "females as raw materials," Rubin argues that "classical Marxism" fails to "fully express or conceptualize sex oppression" (534). She nevertheless maintains that "there is no theory which accounts for the oppression of women—in its endless variety and monotonous similarity, cross-culturally and throughout history—with anything like the explanatory power of the Marxist theory of class oppression" (534). Rubin thus insists that social analysis must consider "women, marriage and sexuality," including "surplus value extracted in the form of daughters" (555).

Capitalism is not responsible for "sex oppression," but has appropriated that system to its own ends as a preexisting "historical and moral element" of the reproduction of labor" (Marx quoted in Rubin 547). This element relies on the patriarchal devaluation of daughters, and if Woman has value as a bearer of children it is primarily as the bearer of male children. However, Rubin's discussion of the relations between women and capitalism does not refer directly to any labor specific to girls—such as that involved in becoming the bride/object—but rather to "housework and the reproduction of labor" (535), often seen as the sum or core of what women produce in a patriarchal capitalist economy. Luce Irigaray, also questioning Marxist theory's exclusion of women as agents, does ask how daughters are significant in the scheme of patriarchal continuity: are they, she asks, only commodities to be exchanged for the Mother; and what relations apart from competition can they have among themselves (1985b:170–91)? The relations between feminism and Marxism have been described as an "unhappy marriage" in which women's place in capitalist economics comprises the entire relevance of the "woman question" and the relations of women to men (Hartmann 184). Although Marx himself presents even these economic relations as a foundationally natural relation, much Marxist theory has approached Woman as an ideological construct blinding women to their real position in society. For such, often feminist, Marxist theories, girls are systematically disenfranchised so that they will accept and desire a place as Woman. While boys learn class/labor roles, girls learn not only these certainties (which they must share in order not to disrupt) but also privatized and privatizing ideologies centered on the family. Class demonstrably affects both puberty and adolescence as an experience of social placement and transformation, and feminine adolescence must thus be specific to whatever constitutes class formations.[2] But given that the prolonged dependence of adolescent lives has clear economic and ideological functions, might this added ideological burden attributed to girlhood distinguish girls as a class position?

The Sheer Economy: Girls and Work

Despite emphasis on the (maternalizing) economic exchange of their potential rather than actual labor in Marxist analysis, girls are also employed as workers, and the process of defining a girl has always been one of defining a relation to labor through association of girls with certain kinds of work. The working and career girls that emerged in late modernity have continued to present girls' employment as transient and peripheral to the meaning of feminine adolescence, or a girl's life. The dominant assumption that girls do not aspire to careers in the same way as boys has relied substantially on the image and status of the kinds of work with which girls are associated. Servants, typists, shop girls, and, later, service workers in general, are not (according to the dominant mythology) desirable positions for the girls who often hold them except as places where some other transformation might happen or be offered.

A class distinction has long been evident between dominant images of girls' work. While working-class girls are constructed as holding undesirable jobs out of economic necessity, bourgeois girls are principally represented in temporary labor, taking jobs until their place in the world is settled. For working-class girls such temporary labor would instead, it seems, constitute an ideal. Although boys also work temporarily as part of the process of learning a particular social role and class position, work is figured as a continuum in their lives. Women too are represented as having more diverse relations to employment than girls do, while dominant discourses on feminine adolescence present work as either necessity or marginal pleasure rather than as a central choice. Of course, this narrative is specific to Western culture and is a dominant discourse rather than a description of girls' lives. In most cases girls do relate to work as a permanent element of their lives, but this is not broadly figured as characteristic of girls in popular culture or much Marxist theory.[3]

Girlhood has also been significant to Marxist analysis of late modern capitalism as a metaphor for alienation through mass cultural production. Nineteenth-century questions about child employment and women's suffrage helped form a new mass industrial version of the subject-citizen within an economy of workers, defined partly by opposition to the girl's position in society. The subjects of capitalism are mobile worker units whose individual agency (instantiated in suffrage) is crucial to the Marxist idea of alienation, because it means that work is something you should own and from which you can thus be alienated. The daughter/girl also maps a space between labor and work and between paid and unpaid labor. Paradigmatic unpaid domestic or reproductive labor does not make you a girl—and in fact other things must compensate for that position as Wife/Mother in order to place you as a girl. Insofar as maternity is seen as the defining feature of women's place in capitalism, girls signify the exchangeable form of that value—as potential reproduction—but they are more often associated in cultural and social criticism with the unpaid labor of consumption—a labor on the self as object, which is particularly disparaged by Marxist analysis. In summary, dominant discursive regimes in both popular culture and critical theory place girls as not valuing work, as embodying potential reproduction, and as working principally on themselves. This refuses girls' work an equal place as a marker of citizenship, a refusal that is reinforced by popular and public representations of the kind of work for which girls are chiefly employed. Although the service industries in which girls are most represented as working do not constitute easy work, they are represented as ornamental labor—including secretaries, air stewards, waitresses, or staff in retail stores. The difficulty or effort of this labor is displaced and concealed by its construction as decorative.

Despite the frequent presentation of Marxism as reducing everything to simplified economic functions, Marxist theory opposes the idea that people have no other role or interest than laboring, as well as the idea that laboring, consuming, and making profit summarize anyone's experience of the world. Marx was specifically critical of capitalism for reducing everything to economic functions, deploying a division between economic base and cultural superstructure to describe how such a reduction worked. A range of critical thinkers have debated how these structures relate and what they entail, often referencing Antonio Gramsci's theory of hegemony to describe the cultural means by which dominance is maintained.[4] The economic positions taken by girls might be used to question these structural operations, including the operation of hegemony. In the systematic reproduction of girls' dominant relations to capitalism discursive regimes clearly not only reinforce but are also constituted in interaction with real economic prospects for employment. Michel Foucault, who is often critical of presumptions deployed within accounts of hegemony, concurs with Marxist contentions that the science of economy redefined the family's role in the management of individuals and wealth, which economy helped redistribute across the field of a state. Economic relations not only structure class relations and wealth but produce foundational concepts and techniques of population management and other aspects of the modern state and systems of governance in which girls must be trained to cooperate.

In the twentieth century, according to Paul Willis's *Learning to Labour*, boys have been systematically taught to identify with the class positions of their fathers as lifestyles shaped in relation to dominant ideologies. For girls these processes must involve not only the learning of unpaid labor that is the destiny of Woman, whether or not women work, but also the equally unpaid labor of being girls. Phil Cohen argues that the difference between girls' and boys' transitions into the working adult world relies on a different relation to structural subordination and on the additional requirement that girls resolve a contradiction between adolescence and femininity (226):

> For girls the wage form offers a brief encounter with an autonomy which bears all the traces of "domestication": but for boys it signifies a licence to deny the fact of continued dependence on the family, in assuming masculine rights without adult responsibilities. (371)

The domestication of even girls' paid labor doesn't necessarily produce such brevity. Linking patriarchy with work, class, and growing up, Cohen problematizes notions such as "growing up working class," noting that since the

1960s class mobility has expanded and the determinant significance of gender in relation to employment has been reduced. Nevertheless he still assigns to the feminine and masculine definitive relations to work and society: "boys may be able to identify positively with certain aspects of their feminine positioning (instead of disavowing it) while girls may be freer to construct territories of desire quite independently of the peer group romance" (233).

Work is now presented in public and popular culture as a necessary aspect of maturity for all Western or Westernized citizens and seen as predominantly (but not exclusively) an economic necessity. Changes to the distribution of capital, production, and employment in Western cultures have meant the tripartite divisions between owners of the means of production, the bourgeoisie, and workers is less likely to describe what work means to any subject's place in the world. These changes to the relations between capital, nation-states, labor, and technology circulate and produce the late-twentieth-century concept of globalization. This has also changed the circulation of commodities, locating a range of nonlaboring relations to capitalism, which has its own apparently firmly gendered structures, as I will discuss in part 3. But these changes have also changed ideas about youth, and not only through consumption practices. Unemployment is an important aspect of late modern youth and youth cultures, which does not imply separation from employment markets or from pivotal definition in terms of work. The unemployed are occupied by looking for a job, or at least by looking like looking for a job. Girls are still less likely than boys to be understood as occupied in this more expansive sense as they are represented in relation to a (never necessarily materialized) future role independent of employment. The entry of women into the labor market is understood in classic Marxist theory as the necessary expansion of a capitalist labor market. But this assumption needs to be contextualized in relation to what is sometimes called the postindustrial economy, for which full employment is not required, and by the recognition that work takes a pivotally different role in feminine rather than masculine adolescence (a statement that does not empirically describe employment rates or attitudes to work).

Questions about the occupations and labor of girls might usefully be stressed by Marxist analysis of girls as much as analyses of paid/unpaid reproductive labor and girls' relations to ideological forms, but they tend not to be. While economic trends and employment patterns are just as relevant to girls as to young men, most Marxist analyses continue to predominantly refer to girls in discussions of unpaid labor or of commodity fetishism. Employment statistics for girls suggest that such assumptions are sociohistorically specific, but the idea that girls' relations to paternal family and husband/children determine their economic position (if not their lived situations) also crosses many cultural boundaries. This relation of girls to capital and work is partly determined by patriarchy, although the effects of this determination may be very diverse. In fact it is because girls' dominant economic positions are not determined by capitalism independently of patriarchy that they are so much more amenable to naturalization within Marxist analysis. Girls' roles in capitalist economies, let alone the significance and meaning of their employment, are not homogenous, a fact that warrants more attention in Marxist theory, where the worker-citizen and his complement/foundation in Woman/Mother remain insufficiently problematized. Attention to the specific forms of girls' relations to labor is necessary not only to distinguish between different economic structures but also to recognize divisions within capitalist societies. For example, what are usually called ethnic or racial differences dramatically differentiate girls around these material questions concerning employment, occupation and economic sustainability. While this difference is also crucial to categorizing girls within a society in terms of marriage, motherhood, education, crime, and health (among other things), these distinctions are generally understood by social analysis not as straightforwardly economic but as ideological relations to economics.

How would girls live, or would they even be possible, outside of capitalism? Given that socialist or communist cultures depend on a capitalist history we cannot look there for an answer to that question.[5] While studies of what are presumed to be precapitalist societies have often focused on daughters, the degree to which daughter or girl has the same meaning there is hard to determine. The observation of feminine adolescence is certainly proper to capitalist late modernity, and changes to girlhood as a popular and public culture have accompanied major changes to capitalist structures. Nevertheless, girls continue to be positioned in ways that strikingly resemble the functions of the daughter observed in those precapitalist societies. Girls are not usually considered in terms of the material or value they produce, or even will produce in the future, but, rather, through their value in systems of exchange and in relation to (or as) consumption. Moreover, the fact that daughters are positioned relative to mothers in patriarchal economies is often translated into a claim that girls exhibit a certain psychological specificity. The position of late modern subjects in relation to capitalism is always understood to be in part psychological, and this is especially true of Marxist theory after Freud. The Frankfurt School in particular worked to intersect psychoanalysis and Marxism, a move that has continued to trouble Marxist theory. Marxist critics such as Louis Althusser, Ernesto Laclau and Chantal Mouffe, and Slavoj Žižek have helped form an influential mode of Marxist theory shaped by Lacanian psychoanalysis.[6] But drawing as it does on psychoanalysis to supplement Marxism, this stream of Marxist theory remains implicated in complex metaphoric relations between the material and the maternal, in relation to which a material analysis of girls seems impossible.

Ideology

Many elements of a girl's life are not directly determined by her economic relations and would often be understood as cultural. Several Marxist critics, including such influential figures in cultural criticism as Terry Eagleton and Frederic Jameson, have questioned the effects of elevating the cultural in social analysis. Cultural criticism, cultural theory, and the "cultural turn" are equated with both ideology and consumption, and a focus on cultural criticism is seen to leave the structures of society unchanged. But distinctions between culture and society are difficult to make:

> Today it is not only as a seller of labour-power that the individual is subordinated to capital, but also through his or her incorporation into a multitude of other social relations: culture, free time, illness, education, sex, and even death. There is practically no domain of individual or collective life which escapes capitalist relations. (Laclau and Mouffe 346)

In the domain of critical theory the term "cultural" has expanded to encompass these terms (including labor power), a process that has been seen to relinquish attention to the economic foundation of social relations. But the Marxist study of culture privileges the concept of ideology. Ideology in this sense is false consciousness exemplarily instantiated in mass culture in studies ranging from Theodor Adorno's claim that every trip to the cinema left him "stupider and worse" (1967:45) to Žižek's account of cultural participation framed by a cynical consciousness: "they know very well what they are doing, but still, they are doing it" (Sloterdijk quoted in Žižek 1989:27). An ideology is a discourse on society in the interests of the capitalist status quo. As girls have provided images and exemplary instances of life mediated by mass production, commodity fetishism, and other modes of systemic and personal conformity, ideology has been important within accounts of girls in late modern culture. In fact girls' relations to culture have often exemplified ideology as false consciousness.

The idea of youth is itself important to Marxist analysis because capitalism requires individuals be taught to be and, Althusser would suggest, to *want to be* participants in this system. For Althusser, "ideology represents the imaginary relations of individuals to their real conditions of existence" (153). Althusser's theory of ideology not only names mechanisms of power but also analyzes subject-positions in relation to them. While ideology is sometimes used to mean a worldview, it is more properly the noneconomic means by which the status quo is maintained, usually distinguished from any forceful oppression. Althusser's analysis of state apparatuses claims that while repressive state apparatuses such as the police or army are social structures that punish noncompliance, ideological state apparatuses position subjects as wanting to behave in ways society endorses. While organizations such as school and family may clearly take both these forms with regard to the kind of girl any girl may be, literature, television, magazines, and the majority of supposedly cultural forms seem to have exclusively ideological effects. Although this mutable and shifting distinction might be more problematic than useful, the theory of interpellation Althusser deployed to discuss the ideological constitution of the self is crucial to late-twentieth-century work on youth.

Interpellation describes the way in which a social context or discursive regime calls you into "being" (Althusser 160); names you as a particular kind of person—worker, middle-class, student, delinquent, perhaps even as raced or gendered. Interpellation refers to a mutual recognition wherein society, sometimes manifest in an individual or an institution, recognizes you (e.g., as possibly delinquent) and you recognize that recognition and are called into being by that exchange. Ideological apparatuses that urge girls to want to be a particular kind of subject include structures such as the family with its shared images of good and bad families or girls. Some state apparatuses are clearly organized in order to address girls—such as age-of-consent legislation and related discourses on birth control restrictions and marriage limitations—

but ideological apparatuses also address girlhood. To be named/recognized as a girl implies a range of approved and valued behaviors differentiated from women, boys, or children.

This does not simplify the question of who is recognized as a girl and thus able to name herself that way. If Woman is an ideological construct then it depends on girls learning and wanting to be Woman/femininity. Women may be continually learning to be women, but feminine adolescence represents a space in which this learning will principally take place. This recognition does not require that girls' culture be the ideologically compromised space it often seems in social analysis. To ask whether girls' culture expresses the real interests of girls or constructs those interests ideologically is irrelevant within an Althusserian frame because even the expression of girls' interests would be part of the ideological apparatus (although no more so than other social forms). Ideology sometimes seems to relegate the effects of power to psychology and to the scene of the individual. Moreover, it often relies on a hierarchical structure of power in which girls must occupy some of the lowest levels of a power pyramid. While for Althusser it is not clear what persons or positions could have power over ideological apparatuses and not themselves be enabled and limited by those apparatuses, ideology as a structure still privileges macroeconomic structures and avoids the ways in which girls have power within specific social/cultural formations.

Foucault (a student of Althusser) proposed in place of this model an understanding of power as "discursive" (see Foucault 1980). Not all power is exercised to the exclusive benefit of the status quo, nor are the actions of power opposed to something more truthful—such as a mechanistic model of social control disseminated through apparatuses. Within this critical conception of power Foucault also critiques the individualist model of the Subject—the idea that a person is a self-contained recognizable and coherent agent. In *The Archaeology of Knowledge* he proposes a model of the subject as "not the speaking consciousness, not the author of the formulation, but a position that may be filled in certain conditions by various individuals" (115). The subject-position is a space into or through which things may move and is always subject to and the subject of power, and every statement about subjects or subjectivity is thus an exertion of power. Foucault asserts that forms of knowledge, such as observation and interpretation, are also exertions of power. Foucault's "micro-relations of power" (see 1984a:92–102) critique standard ideas about ruling classes and the maintenance of hegemony, not denying that extant systemic power relations privilege some subjects but thinking differently about how this privilege works.

Psychoanalysis: Becoming Mother
Freud

Ideology requires a system of value judgments and thus enables the discussion of girls as bad or good girls. From Adorno's jibes at flappers to John Fiske's valorizing reference to Madonna fans, girls have been pictured as the primary consumers of not only culture industries but also conservative social programs and ideologies of the family and sex. This compatibility with the interests of the status quo appears to conflict with the difficulty of feminine adolescence—the difficulty of taking up a place in society that girls are also seen to embody. One highly influential account of this contradiction is made available by psychoanalysis. Freud represented girls as both difficult and conservative, particularly because of their containment by romantic ideologies reflecting their destiny in Woman. The daughter's role positions feminine adolescence as a development toward the natural end of Womanhood, and psychoanalysis has produced some very influential accounts of this process. The importance of girls and young women to seminal case studies and pivotal psychoanalytic theories has remained relatively unacknowledged. Bourgeois daughters, hysterical (nonmaternal) women, and other female patients as well as women analysts, have been crucial to the formation of psychoanalysis.[7] It was Freud and Bruer's patient Anna O who first nominated psychoanalysis as "the talking cure," and Freud's patient Dora who was responsible for the reconception of that theory as a dialogue or system of transference between analyst and analysand. The scrutiny of these women, even when framed as therapy, was not directed toward producing more submissive or well-behaved women but toward maintaining a manageable (scrutinizable) girl/Woman identity. This self-fulfilling agenda required the instability of feminine adolescence and the girl's need for instruction whether pathologized—usually as sexualized deviant (victim)—or as normal feminine adolescent problem. In "Psychogenesis of a Case of Homosexuality in a Woman," for example, Freud traces the arrival of deviance through a familial trauma but indicates that such a narrative is largely continuous with the normal lives of girls (18:170).

This section details some of the key claims of psychoanalytic theories of girlhood. Girls (always primarily daughters) are the model on which Freud's theories of subjectification are formed, but they differ and are excluded from the standard against which subjectivity will be measured. The girl case studies and theories about girls are the crucial exception to an implied norm of boy-becoming-man. Psychoanalysis places the daughter in opposition simultaneously to the Mother/Woman and the Subject. If the Mother problematically grounds the formation of the Subject—being both his Other and what sustains and identifies him—she is a much more uncertain point of comparison for a girl. While Dora's rejection of her mother (and her "housewife's psychosis" [8:49]) is entirely comprehensible to Freud, and a necessary part of her oedipal stage, her failure to convert that moment into the proper attachment to her father and his surrogates is a failure to negotiate an Oedipus complex. Changes in Freud's own understanding of what constituted femininity and adolescence somewhat undermine his presumption of stable psychic patterns such as the oedipal stage and female shame. Freud nevertheless sets the unconscious partly outside of history, and it is in the unconscious that the sexualized components of this development are determined (or predetermined). For example, while many of Dora's experiences are specific to an historical context, as Freud recognizes, the structure to which she is compared and relative to which she could be cured operates in the unconscious and thus paradoxically requires and defies analysis. As Freud puts this many years later: "If you want to know more about femininity, enquire from your own experiences of life, or turn to the poets, or wait until science can give you deeper and more coherent information" (22:135).

The Mother constitutes a space of departure for the (oedipal) hero of psychoanalytic narratives. Teresa De Lauretis argues that anthropology and psychoanalysis are interdependently indebted to an exclusion of feminine development from the familial narrative of Oedipus, which describes women as space and yet refuses any place for women:

> The hero, the mythical subject, is constructed as human being and as male; he is the active principle of culture, the establisher of distinction, the creator of differences. Female is what is not susceptible to transformation, to life or death; she (it) is an element of plot-space, a topos, a resistance, matrix and matter. (1984:119)

This is the same relation that founds theories of capital on the maternal real—the material is a real converted to property by ownership that can be paralleled in the self-control of the body (ideally) perfected in puberty. De Lauretis retells Freud's narrative as follows:

> Leaving home, she enters the phallic phase where she comes face to face with castration, engages in uneven battle with penis envy, and remains forever scarred by a narcissistic wound, forever bleeding. But she goes on, and the worst is still to come. No longer a "little man," bereft of weapon or magical gift, the female child enters the liminal stage in which her transformation into woman will take place; but only if she successfully negotiates the crossing, haunted by the Scylla and Charybdis of object change and erotogenic zone change, into passivity. If she survives, her reward is motherhood. And here Freud stops, But let's go on. . . . (1984:132)

But moving beyond this point is impossible for psychoanalysis, which stops feminine adolescence at an unspecifiable apotheosis into mother/wife/vagina, where she will ground psychic dramas other than her own.

The Oedipus complex figures the Mother as both powerful (Lacan would say "phallic") and castrated, and this has been an influential image for twentieth-century understandings of familial development. Irigaray argues that the girl-child within this dominant model of development cannot develop as a woman but only as "not a Man." Irigaray's principal intervention in psychoanalytic discourse proceeds from a claim that this model excludes any kind of sexual difference by excluding any development specific to girls. The developmental account culminating in the Oedipus complex is what replaces and requires Freud's famous rejection of his earlier "seduction theory." Despite its influence, however, Freud is unsure whether the girl ever surmounts the Oedipus complex and is even uncertain as to when she reaches that developmental crisis. Freud writes in "Femininity" that "in the absence of fear of castration the chief motive is lacking which leads boys to surmount the Oedipus complex. Girls remain in it for an indeterminate length of time; they demolish it late and, even so, incompletely" (129). Irigaray's deconstruction of Freud's ideas about femininity sees the "phallic organization" (Freud 19:178) of the girl's oedipal stage as an absence of distinction concerning the daughter, which demands that "the little girl can thus have *no value* before puberty" (Irigaray 1985a:25). After puberty, Irigaray contends, she will still be denied a valid sexual self because puberty leaves her waiting and wishing for the man/penis/child. In this model, then, "woman never truly escapes from the Oedipus complex. She remains forever fixated on the desire for the father, remains subject to the father and his law, for fear of losing his love, which is the only thing capable of giving her any value at all" (Irigaray 1985b:87).

The girl's becoming woman must therefore be an inexplicable leap from one kind of being to another—if not more than one such leap. Although a woman is neither child nor adult, and most particularly makes no movement between the two, the difficulty of feminine adolescence as explained by psychoanalysis nevertheless presumes "that it is necessary to *become* a woman, a 'normal' one at that, whereas a man is a man from the outset" (Irigaray 1985b:134). The difficulty of the transition from girl to woman is the point of many feminist revisions of Freud's narrative, although these mostly focus on resignifying Woman or the maternal rather than specifically considering girls or feminine adolescence (see, for example, Janine Chasseguet-Smirgel and Nancy Chodorow). But the reproduction of daughters warrants further consideration, and not only through the mechanisms by which the Woman/Mother involves a certain erasure of a woman's own history. The daughter locates and performs the naturalized dramas of femininity for psychoanalysis, including penis envy and the rejection of femininity in hysteria or abjection. The daughter thus also verifies the inevitability of all rejections of femininity.

Irigaray claims that an unreconcilable tension as well as multiple intersections exists between the Mother and women—"For the sex of woman is not one" (Irigaray 1985a:239). This is partly a play on words, which notes that woman's sex is both not the sex of the subject and not coherently singular. Elizabeth Grosz's "A Thousand Tiny Sexes" takes this further, drawing on the work of Gilles Deleuze and Felix Guattari to critique the organization of the body in psychoanalysis according to any dichotomous binary structure. This multiplication of feminine sexes allow us to ask whether the girl's sex is not only different from the woman's sex but also not continuous with it—that is, whether girls are a different sex/gender than women. These critiques also depart from the significance of sexual organs to psychological development, a subject long debated by psychoanalysts with respect to girls. Freud declares that the girl moves to a vaginal leading zone during puberty, before which she is in a state of anesthesia. Ernest Jones instead emphasized the role of the clitoris in female development, accusing other analysts of a "phallic bias" (1927). This criticism is particularly appli-cable to analysts such as Helene Deutsch, who understood female sexuality as dominated by a passive sucking vagina opposed not only to phallic/cli-toral sexuality but to orgasm.[8]

The oedipal trauma is founded on incest, which is one of the reasons why Carl Jung's Electra complex was never comparable to the Oedipus complex. By coining this term Jung intended to ascribe an archetypical specificity to the girl's sexualized familial drama. Jung is generally specific about the roles he sees young women or girls playing in his psychodiorama. The girl is the virgin, *Kore*, bride, or anima—the reflection and complement of the Sub-ject. This girl constitutes a function of the transhistorical psyche and is thus less central for the processes of Jungian psychology than girls are for psy-choanalysis. Jung anxiously directed his women patients away from visions of the archetypal Kore, which is opposed to the natural commitment of women to heterosexual attachment (see Jung 1982b:159).[9] This figure of the girl as potential has remained important to popular cultural understandings of the girl, particularly for discourses on essential embodied femininity.[10] The girl of Jungian psychology also continues to appear in therapeutic nar-ratives that are less about family or other groups than individual psychic structures. But Freud's narrative of familial sexual development continues in many respects to dominate both cultural theory and popular culture.

In their well-known *Anti-Oedipus* (1977), Deleuze and Guattari oppose most psychoanalytic tenets and even reject the fundamental importance of the incest taboo, aspiring to the revolutionary potential of desire released from the "bedroom of Oedipus" (116). Deleuze and Guattari argue that Oedipal models are not just prescriptive—if you negotiate your Oedipus complex in the right way you will be normal—but constrictive. Under the hegemony of psychoanalysis, they argue, every action, desire, and power re-lation is explained by the oedipal code, and every desire falls back onto Oedipus for its explanation, justification, and correction. Given that the pre-oedipal is still defined by the oedipal, psychoanalysis can be seen to re-duce "every social manifestation of desire to the familial complex" (Seem xviii) and to presume the Mother's body and Father's name are the only sur-faces upon which desire is recorded. While sexuality within the nuclear fam-ily is patterned on a triangle of parents and child, the daughter does not in fact belong to this triangle. The daughter can become neither the father nor the mother for psychoanalysis, given the truth status of sexual difference and that the mother is not a Subject.

While the daughter is not continuous with and does not perpetuate the Mother, let alone the father, she is imperative to perpetuating the structure of patriarchy. Kristeva for example considers the girl as a relation to the mother's exclusion from the symbolic, describing the girl's love for the mother as "like black lava" lying in wait for the girl "all along the path of her desperate attempts to identify with the symbolic paternal order" (1986a:157).[11] The popular embrace of Freudianism has been crucial to the popular dissemination of feminine adolescence in part because the girl is both central to the oedipal scenario—interpreted broadly as a normative familial model of cross-gender attachment, same-gender resentment—and not there at all. The uncertain duration of the feminine Oedipus complex constructs a girl who neither experiences nor passes adolescence, a paradox central to dominant models of girlhood. This unfinished process of girlhood, which also avoids relegation to the role of founding other subjectivities proper to motherhood, moreover raises the possibility that identity might function in other ways than those described by the resolution of the Oedipus complex.

Jouissance: After Lacan

In the early 1970s the French psychoanalyst and celebrity academic Jacques Lacan made the infamous and influential statement: "Woman does not exist" (1982a:145). Lacan theorized that in a language structure predicated on a masculine subject, woman cannot have the affirmed identity of the Subject. And, more complexly, woman (like man), exists only in that relation: "There is woman only as excluded by the nature of things which is the nature of words" (1982a:144). Post-Lacanian psychoanalytic models presume that desire and language, reproduced in the nuclear family, are templates for one another: a stratification that organizes bodies and identities. Lacanian theory does not claim that women have no identity but that what constitutes woman is not "representable" and that the Woman/Other that founds dominant symbolic structures has reality only in that symbolic order that cannot represent her. Any subject's development is, for Lacan, a sequence of misrepresentation and fantasy in relation to first an Imaginary mother-child relation and then a Symbolic Order centered on the "name of the Father." But the girl's development is thus far more inexplicable than the boy's, given that the Other on which a daughter's Imaginary relations should be grounded cannot be defined by a mother definitively other than herself.

Entry into the Symbolic Order within which a mature (separate) identity is articulated depends on recognition of an ideal coherence Lacan calls the "phallus." While no one, including men, really achieves or possesses this ideal, it remains intimately tied to symbolic association with the penis. Girls are thus distanced from the phallus as an image of identity, even though they may embody the phallus as an ideal desired by the Subject (see chapter 8 below):

> Freud's presentation of the problem puts the female child in a situation that is not at all dissymetrical with that of the male. . . . As for the boy, he decides he's just not up to it. And as for the girl, she gives up any expectation of gratification in this way—the renunciation is expressed even more clearly in her case than in his. (Lacan 1977a:46)

For the daughter the Oedipus complex, which manifests this mourning, is not origin but destiny. Only the girl's finalizing womanly identification with the Mother allows her to be attractive to the man "*whose Oedipus attachment to his mother it kindles into passion*" (Freud quoted in Irigaray 1985a:109).

That the subject is predictable according to this foundational, and sometimes apparently naturalized, dualist structure is the basis for the therapeutic undercurrent of psychoanalysis. Gender is central to this structure. Kristeva, for example, privileges passionate moments of undoing or threatening the Symbolic Order and, simultaneously, gender, but also relies on their inevitable continuity to structure her analyses.[12] For Kristeva, only the maternal offers a place for the feminine in the Symbolic Order, while Irigaray's work consistently asserts the daughter's difference from the mother and from the fantasy of the Father's daughter—the phallic girl or subject of penis envy. Irigaray and Kristeva agree that the bond to the Mother is denied by the Law of the Father, and within its codes is accessible only through perversions of order. But Irigaray also insists on a self-valorizing rather than self-obliterating maternity embodied in the mother of a daughter, although the daughter herself remains secondary in Irigaray's writing on the mother-daughter relation.

The psychoanalytic Subject requires the Mother as a stable space of origin from which to individuate himself and to which corporeality may be relegated in the articulation of himself as Subject. This Subject is produced within temporal hierarchies of parent-child relations that position the daughter in a state of suspension before use. Critiques of such naturalized development might both dislodge the Subject's stable space of origin and avoid the Mother's erasure of feminine adolescence. Whether and how it will fulfill the mother's story are questions too often directed at feminine adolescence, through modes of reproduction that both rely on and exclude the daughter.

Feminism
Daughters and Sexed Identity

Feminine adolescence emerged at a nexus of various late modern discourses, but in a particularly tense engagement with feminism. Feminine adolescence as a popular and theoretical category and feminism as a public movement are contemporary in their development and their cultural visibility, and they were and still are bound together in a critical relation to patriarchal models of identity production. The significance of feminine adolescence for feminist subjectivity is partly evident in this concurrent emergence from a range of public discourses on women's development—on what a modern girl might become. The suffrage debates were often arguments about how women were formed, including debates about the essence of woman, and girls have been crucial to considering current and future forms of womanhood and femininity.

Feminists have extensively debated patriarchy's dependence on the re-production of Woman as desiring, supporting, and signifying the phallocentric Subject, but this dependence also necessitates the re-production of girls who desire to become Woman or find no alternative to that development. Feminism and psychoanalysis are also concurrent redefinitions of relations between gender and social reproduction that have repeatedly engaged one another. If it appears self-evident now that feminists might critique the presumptions of oedipal subjectivity, much feminist theory still assumes a psychoanalytic model. Grosz points out that feminists who critique Freud as well as those who endorse him

> agree that his account of sexual difference, with its references to the phallic mother, the castration complex and the Oedipus complex, provides an accurate description of the processes which produce masculine and feminine subjects within our Western, patriarchal, capitalist culture. Their

disagreements arise regarding . . . the necessity of the domination of the phallus. (1994:57)

It is also significant that both daughter and feminist have been represented by psychoanalysis as problems or disturbances of a stable psychosocial order.

Feminist references to girlhood (like feminist critiques of psychoanalysis) often focus less on how women currently live than on the question of what constitutes woman at all. Such debates over essentialism have been central to twentieth-century feminist theory, and girls provide a necessary foundation for these debates, though they (again) mostly function not as their subject but as evidence for one proposition or another about *women*. The most urgent questions addressed to essentialism in recent feminist theory center on how to understand not only differences between but also, as Rosi Braidotti puts it, "within" women:

> The female subject of feminism is constructed across a multiplicity of discourses, positions, and meanings, which are often in conflict with one another; therefore the signifier *woman* is no longer sufficient as the foundation stone of the feminist project. (105)

Age can be understood as one of these differences between and within women, but I want to suggest that the significance of girls for feminism goes beyond this.

It appears that the elaboration of puberty enables increasingly scientific specification of femaleness, leaving feminine adolescence as the social process of becoming a woman—a process in need of monitoring for all too possible deviation or failure. These processes of forming women are not, however, free of essentialist-constructionist contentions. I want to approach this through Simone de Beauvoir's pivotal feminist text, *The Second Sex*, which delineates not a woman essence that determines how womanly someone is but the social construction of womanliness (relative to men). De Beauvoir writes:

> man is defined as a being who is not fixed, who makes himself what he is. As Merleau-Ponty very justly puts it, man is not a natural species, he is an historical idea. Woman is not a completed reality, but rather a becoming, and it is in her becoming that she should be compared with man; that is to say, her *possibilities* should be defined. (66)

The fourth part of Beauvoir's text, "The Formative Years," includes sections on childhood, the young girl, sexual initiation, and the lesbian.[13] This arrangement both excludes girls from the situation of women—they are only the process of woman's formation—thus excluding girls from women's liberation from that situation and also distinguishes between childhood and the girl. This distinction is crucial to *The Second Sex*'s status as high modernist feminism and reflects the importance of the emergence of feminine adolescence to modernism.

The wave of feminism that Beauvoir strongly influenced often insisted that sex (denoting the biologically female body) differed from gender (denoting norms and expectations defining femininity).[14] The generational narrative that positions post–World War I feminism as a second wave itself arrives after the institutionalization of feminism. While this model often clumsily groups together different positions and ignores continuities between these generations, breaks between (not necessarily temporal) movements in feminism can be identified in terms of how feminists understand sex/gender.[15] For feminism sometimes labeled social-activist or egalitarian, Woman signified what patriarchal culture requires and demands of women—Woman in these terms is the enemy of feminism. Beauvoir exemplarily writes that it would be better for a girl to "identify herself as a human being who happens to be a woman. It's a certain situation which is not the same as men's situation of course, but she shouldn't identify herself as a woman" (Beauvoir in Simons 33). While Beauvoir does not see the secondary status of women as natural, she thus accepts that becoming a woman is not a path to coherent self-recognizing existence—mobility, independence, and a detached and thus healthy ego.[16]

Teresa De Lauretis contends that a distinction between sex and gender does not avoid defining women as relative to men (1987:1). Once the selective differentiation of bodies into two forms is invested with meaning, it is clearly already cultural, a "sex-gender system . . . intimately interconnected with political and economic factors" (5). In her essay "Technologies of Gender" De Lauretis aims to free the conception of a (female) subject from the impossible burden of "describing" women:

> The subject of feminism I have in mind is one *not* so defined, one whose definition or conception is in progress, in this and other feminist critical texts. . . . The subject that I see emerging from current writings and debates within feminism is one that is at the same time inside *and* outside

the ideology of gender, and conscious of being so, conscious of that twofold pull, of the division, that doubled vision. (10)[17]

The strongest version of De Lauretis's claim is that the sex of bodies is a form of knowing and enacting the self, and that sex does not denote but constructs the body. In her book *Gender Trouble* (1990) Judith Butler claimed that woman was a performance not dependent on a female body. Butler insists that sex is a construction of the body, that it is in fact a form of gender according to the usual parameters of the sex/gender distinction. This performance resembles De Lauretis's thinking gender as a technology of the self overtly interested in the disciplined knowledge of the body.[18] Education, the family, and other modes of disseminating rules and norms function to shape and discipline girls' experiences of and knowledge about gender. Both feminism and psychoanalysis are ideas about the gendered self that endorse or prohibit ways of being by continual surveillance and discipline, though their prescriptive practices work very differently.

Insistence upon the coherence and unity of the category "women" effectively refuses the multiplicity of cultural and social intersections in relation to which women are constituted (see Butler 1990:14). The most forceful question arising from these exchanges between writers who want to change the meaning of woman and those who want to problematize its possibility is how to "reconcile the post-structuralist project to displace identity with the feminist project to reclaim it" (Fuss 1993:107). Poststructuralist feminism must necessarily abandon and critique the preexisting binary structure "man/woman" and look for more disruptive terms of engagement with the effects of that structure in the world. Some feminists, such as Irigaray, utilize deconstructive reading practices to look for terms that exceed and undermine the ways sex/gender is predominantly thought to operate. The daughter might work as such a third term with which to interrogate the dominant binaries of father/mother and man/woman. If a girl is not and will never be either woman or man, father or mother, her unfixed positions relative to dominant sex/gender structures might provide a point for poststructuralist consideration of identity in relation to sexed/gendered development.

Mothers or Sisters: Gender Maturity

Lesley Johnson's *The Modern Girl* (1993) notes a pervasive characterization of feminism as a process of growing up that defines itself against a relation between young women, commodities, and self-determination: "an account which continues to hold considerable force in popular and more academic understandings of the emergence and project of second-wave feminism" (2). Feminine adolescence is separated from feminism by feminist discourses on maturity, autonomy, and individualism. Positioned in opposition to the stabilizing centrality of the transcendental Subject, girls are also positioned as always in the process of their own production. However, feminism mostly aspires to that Subjectivity defined against immaturity and femininity. Feminist practice is dominated by models of subjectivity determined by an adult or mature conception of what a woman is. Woman is presumed to be the end point of a naturalized process of developing individual identity that relegates a vast range of roles, behaviors, or practices to its immature past. The patriarchal capitalist coding of feminine adolescence as desirable commodity and undesirable identity is thus fully effective in most feminist theory— while the continuance of feminism requires the identification of girls, girls are not identified as feminists. Girlhood in feminist work appears to be defined less by age or body than by socialized characteristics that resemble those outlined by Beauvoir's chapters on girls and young women, and girls are presumed to be more subject to ideological manipulation than women.[19]

Tension between young women and feminism was clearly apparent in the nineteenth century and took many of its current forms in the 1930s, in the generation that followed the suffrage campaigns. Elaine Showalter's *These Modern Women* collates an exemplary series of feminist autobiographical essays published in the *Nation* in 1926–27. Showalter argues that being a "modern woman" was not defined by "youth or the new generation" (3), but the essayists are nevertheless bound by their concern with development, by resistance to finalizing definition by maternity (and related emblems of maturity), and by their representations of and desire for transformational identity. Even if, as the psychological commentaries published with these essays assert, autobiographies can be distortions of actual life experiences, they interact with dominant and emerging discourses on women, identity, development, and feminism. By 1926, they demonstrate, any woman's identity unavoidably referred to the formative influence of adolescence, an influence seen as at best problematic for feminists.[20] Showalter attributes the decline of feminism in the 1930s to political failures and factionalization but also to "the younger generation's disavowal of the ideals and goals of the women's movement" (9). Emphasis on the new among modern girls was seen to challenge rather than contribute to feminism, and the freedom they desired was seen as individualist rather than collective.

William O'Neill claims that feminism in the 1930s was superseded not by the achievement of suffrage but by the new sexual practices of young women:

> when the great changes in female sexual behavior became visible in the 1920s, feminists were unable to react to it in such a way as to command the respect of emancipated young women. It was their sexual views more than anything else that dated the older feminists, after World War I, and made it difficult for them to understand or speak to a generation marked by quite different ambitions. (32)[21]

While these older feminists had been significantly responsible for disseminating theories such as sexology and psychoanalysis in the first two decades of the twentieth century, in 1925 Dora Russell also insisted on generational differences over sex: "the older feminists meant the equal standard to mean more virtue for men: the young ones mean it to be more freedom for women" (98).[22] The modern girl was represented as free, but also as embodying both hedonism and distraction. In the early twentieth century the feminist espousal of agency focused, after suffrage or alongside it, on transforming heterosexual relationships—changing marriage and allowing more positions for women outside of marriage. Young women were seen as rejecting these changes for different sexual freedoms and bonds. However, both visions of sexual independence and the concurrent return to marriage were embraced by the modern girls as compatible with personal independence precisely because of that feminist history. This same pattern has been repeated in post–second-wave feminism.

As a signal force in the progress of modernity, nineteenth-century proponents of women's rights, including the suffragists, prioritized majority, citizenship, and other designations of individual maturity for women. Feminism is historically inseparable from theories of feminine adolescence, and its own developmental model necessarily defines a stage prior to and inadequate to the feminist identity that it explains and counters. This stage prior to feminist identity is undoubtedly not childhood but, rather, an immature and unconscious womanhood most often identified in the twentieth-century roles of housewife and adolescent girl. Feminist discussions of girls more rarely engage with feminine adolescence than construct girls as opposed to, and thus defining, the mature woman as feminist subject. Feminists and feminism are interested in girls, but less on their own terms than as necessary precursors to women/feminists. Girls are even positioned as embodying what must be given up in order to become a feminist. Becoming-feminist manifests simultaneously awakening and renunciation, and what feminists awaken from and renounce is girlishness as much as patriarchy. Feminists mostly approach feminine adolescence by assessing feminist content in girls' everyday lives and relations to popular culture. For Kate Peirce, for example, "teen magazines have a unique opportunity to shape the world of the teenage girl" (66) but oppose feminist aims insofar as their fiction remains stereotypical, and "nonfiction editorial copy is *not* teaching girls to become new women" (Peirce 61). Narratives of feminine adolescence narrowing in or shutting down women's potential are crucial to many feminist texts as a principal mode of explaining the operation of patriarchy and the grounds for feminism. If feminist narratives about how women are constrained by patriarchy were deprived of girls as vulnerable object of sexualized gender roles, they might be quite different narratives.

Feminism has consistently opposed the dominance of women's lives by maternity. Some commentators have seen this as a more or less pathological animosity toward the mother. Kristeva writes:

> Let *jouissance* be forbidden to the mother: this is the demand of the father's daughters (given that a man can fulfill the office of daughter). . . . The Electras—"deprived forever of their hymens"—militants in the cause of the father, frigid with exaltation—are they . . . nuns, "revolutionaries," even "feminists"? (1986a:152)

While critics such as Kristeva and Marianne Hirsch argue that feminism dictates a separation from the Mother, feminism also presumes the Mother (the "fully-developed" woman) within the subject of feminist theory. Woman defined as adult heterosexual partner and Mother is the subject of most feminist inquiry. Nevertheless, Hirsch is correct to point to the significance of daughter/sister figures to feminist narratives. Motherhood is generally consigned to special interests, such as child care, the commonality of which is taken for granted, and the feminist bond between women is instead articulated as a sisterhood (which presumes daughterhood). Such contradictions will not be productively resolved by simply allotting equal time to mothers and girls in feminist analysis, because the mother-girl distinction in fact grounds feminist relations to patriarchy. A conception of feminist subjectivity is at stake here.

If new feminist subjectivities are to escape being confined to the opposite of a positive term such as the Man/Subject, how will they develop from a girl identity understood as fully framed by patriarchy or conceived as the ground from which women depart? Feminist theory often notes the way in which Woman grounds the boy-subject of psychoanalysis/Marxism/patriarchy, but the feminist-subject is equally tied to and equally negates the girl. The girl is an obstacle in relation to which the figure of womanly maturity emerges in opposition to the dominant narrative of women's immaturity. This maturity can be seen as mirroring the Subject's maturity (Beauvoir), or as radically different.[23] For example, Carol Gilligan's argument against the maturity of detachment, which she understands to be coded masculine, does not question any established developmental model but asserts instead that the girl's attachment is more mature than the boy's detachment.[24] If the essential feminine ethics Gilligan desires is based in maternalism, as both Butler (1992) and Sabina Lovibond argue, it also resembles a dominant feminist model critiqued by Juliet Mitchell as a "sisterhood" that "doesn't allow for conflict" (Mitchell in Moi 933). Feminists thus reproduce gender/sex and norms as much as any discourse operating in relation to dichotomous sexual schematics. As De Lauretis argues:

> The construction of gender goes on as busily today as it did in earlier times, say in the Victorian era. And it goes on not only where one might expect it to—in the media, the private and public schools, the courts, the family, nuclear or extended or single-parented—in short, in what Louis Althusser has called the "ideological state apparati." The construction of gender also goes on, if less obviously, in the academy, in the intellectual community, in avant-garde artistic practices and radical theories, even, and indeed especially, in feminism. (3)

Girls are not the only possible subjects excluded by feminism's dominant model of subjectivity.[25] Feminist insistence on the coherence of its subject has accompanied other empire-building projects of the late modern world. As feminists such as bell hooks and Gayatri Spivak have discussed, feminism often remains invested in the certainty of racial or ethnic difference. The women not encompassed by the maternalized white woman of mainstream feminism—including postmenopausal women, racialized/ethnicized groups, third world women, or lesbians—are often aligned with immaturity through their inadequate identification with a generic woman. Just as significantly, accounting for girls, and the discourses on feminine adolescence that constrain and inform them, necessarily entails critiquing the individual adult Subject to which girls can only fail to conform—as Woman has always done. Feminism's comparative silence on feminine adolescence except in defensive if not actually accusatory modes almost requires young women receive it in reactionary ways. And yet feminine adolescence has much to offer feminists interested in avoiding stagnation of their practice and predetermination of their subject.

The Thing About Generation F

Feminism's detachment from girls operates by assuming that feminists are formed in the experiences of women rather than girls. Feminism's investment in its own maintenance remains antagonistic to transformations that do not promise to reproduce it, and the desire to reproduce the same within feminism remains a block on an active feminist politics. Consequent to this antagonism, feminism not only often alienates young women but also helps to confine feminine adolescence to a chronological period circumscribed by various utilitarian criteria. In this context it is crucial to also consider the particularity of girls in forms of popular feminism that are distinguished from and sometimes opposed to feminist theory defined by academic practices.

As an example of institutional organized feminist politics, Peggy Orenstein's *Schoolgirls*, supported by the National Organization for Women, focuses on where girls are placed in relation to feminist goals. More individualist popular feminist publishing, such as Naomi Wolf's best-selling *The Beauty Myth*, presents the events of girlhood as stages on the path to being "myself" (as feminist woman). These retrospective views of girlhood are not confined to the speaking position of older woman/feminist. Paradoxically, this position is available to younger feminist writers as well, including for example Barbara Findlen's collection *Listen Up* and, very differently, the postfeminist positions of writers such as Katie Roiphe. Girlhood also functions in popular feminist discourses as a field of lost possibilities: this is true of *Schoolgirls*, Mary Pipher's *Reviving Ophelia*, and Emily Hancock's *The Girl Within*. Feminine adolescence functions in these texts as the process of limiting women's lives, and strength and transformative potential are consigned to young girls or adult feminist women.

Findlen's *Listen Up: Voices from the Next Feminist Generation*, a collection of essays by young feminists that is also sponsored by a wider feminist community through *Ms.* magazine, addresses feminine adolescence as the autobiographical context for the development of feminist consciousness and predominantly maps that development as becoming unlike average girls. Several of the essays stress the importance of communicating with nonfeminist women and girls, but even these stress the young feminist's difference from other girls. While these voices outline debates within feminism, notably over race and sexuality, they are, as the introduction states, "not 'daughters' rebelling against the old-style politics of their mothers," but young feminists who "cite the writings and actions of older feminists as an integral part of their own development and beliefs" (Findlen xv). All the stories are narratives of developing independence, not only toward feminism but, mostly, away from being a girl. Once, Abra Fortune Chernik writes in *Listen Up*, she had "dismissed feminist alternatives as foreign and offensive" as she had "insisted on the title of 'girl' " rather than "the *W* word" (Chernik 76). Girls are presumed to be mainstream, and if the feminist revolution is not evident there, as another girl in *Listen Up* writes, that might be "a good sign. As soon as mainstream culture picks up on it, they'll try to co-opt it" (Lamm 86). While there are suggestions here that feminism does not have all the answers— telling a girl to "throw away her tight jeans" might be neither astute nor successful (Shah 118), for example—becoming feminist remains the project of all these girls, which is why they are included at all.

The gulf presumed to lie between girls and feminism is equally apparent in the much debated field of postfeminist publishing. Writers such as Roiphe want to derail certain versions of feminism by addressing girls before they become feminists—once they are feminists (of the wrong kind) they are lost to a more progressive position by the all-encompassing blindness of the bad versions of feminism. Avowed postfeminist Rene Denfeld's version of this schema includes two types of feminists. The first is obsessed with sex, through either a desire to censor it (i.e., antiporn/sex academics) or an attempt to focus feminism on it (i.e., lesbian separatists), while the second type focuses on what she sees as the real work of gender equality. These feminists—reformists, liberals, equity feminists—are opposed to the first group, whom she calls "the New Victorians.'[26] Denfeld supports riot grrl groups, which I will discuss further in chapter 9, as an example of "the independent, assertive, and empowering attitude of many young women who are not only entering previously male-dominated fields (and rock music was certainly one) but are completely convinced they have every right to do so" (263). She sees the riot grrl as a sign of feminist action, if not a feminist movement:

[Riot grrls], as well as young women's participation in abortion-rights marches, show we are not apathetic. We do care. As one young woman told me, "That's one argument I get into with my mom. She says my generation is apathetic. I say, 'What did you do? You gave us Reagan. Sure, thanks a bunch.' It makes you wonder." (263)

In Australia, Catharine Lumby's version of this generational model aligns girls with a vibrant cultural life that feminists simplify in order to censor. In *Bad Girls: The Media, Sex and Feminism in the 90s* (1997), Lumby positions mistaken feminists, though this comprises a less sweeping conception of feminist positions than in work such as Denfeld's, as opposed to the "bad girls" of popular culture, for whom much feminist action in public culture is seen as irrelevant.

Some of these claims about generations of feminism recognize opposition to the girl in previous feminist positions.

In 1983 Alice Walker's *In Search of Our Mother's Gardens* defined womanist as follows: "Womanist 1. From *womanish*. (Opp. of 'girlish,' i.e., frivolous, irresponsible, not serious.) A black feminist or feminist of color. From the black folk expression of mothers to female children, 'You acting womanish,' i.e., like a woman." (Siegel 62)

In the introduction of her *To Be Real*, Walker's daughter, Rebecca Walker, cites this definition but also lists "contradiction" as a generative force for her collection, setting up third wave feminism as a "hybridity" (xxxi) opposed to what she describes as a rigidly ideological second wave feminism:

Constantly measuring up to some cohesive fully down-for-the-feminist-cause identity without contradictions and messiness and lusts for power and luxury items is not a fun or easy task. . . . For many of us it seems that to be a feminist in the way that we have seen or understood feminism is to conform to an identity and way of living that doesn't allow for individuality, complexity, or less than perfect personal histories. (xxxi)

Third wave feminism needs to be distinguished from postfeminism, which usually has no more interest in poststructuralist concepts such as hybridity than does the public feminist activism it opposes. Carolyn Sorioso records the refusal of such theories by the darling of American postfeminism, Naomi Wolf:

Wolf thinks American female feminists seize on post-structural French feminist thought as if to prove that we are as complex as many male intellectuals. "Here's something of our own that's just as hard," she imagines academics reasoning. "We'll teach it to our own kids, and no one will know what *we're* talking about either." (135)

Wolf has been seen as a "recovering feminist" (Sorioso 136), but her work has been highly successful in both its feminist and postfeminist forms through books that dealt predominantly with girls (for example, *The Beauty Myth* and *Promiscuities* respectively).

Generation F has also been used to designate the complexity of feminism for girls raised after the achievements of feminism in the 1970s and 1980s: "Call us 'third wave' feminists, or, perhaps more pointedly, white middle-class feminists on the cusp of a generational divide" (Heywood and Drake 42). Kathy Bail's collection *DIY Feminism* replies to representations of girls as uninterested in feminism:

Riot grrrls, guerrilla girls, net chicks, cyber chix, geekgirls, tank girls, super-girls, action girls, deep girls—this is the era of DIY feminism. For young women, rather than one feminism there are a plethora of feminisms going under new and more exciting tags. . . . This change is allied with a do-it-yourself style and philosophy characteristic of youth culture. (3)

This is sometimes seen as a commodified feminism, which cannot be oppositional because it is part of a saleable youth culture that implies no political maturity: "Rebel only temporarily, through what you wear or the music you buy. Don't learn anything from these excursions into alternative cultural styles" (Heywood and Drake 41). But these modes of feminism claim the girl as more empowering than she might seem, even if this maneuver is only tangentially referred to interests, positions, or behaviors ordinarily associated with girls.

Debates over feminist generations have been publicly played out in polemical texts that rarely consider the historical context of relations between feminism and girls or girl culture. Does being able to identify generationalism in first, second, and third wave feminists mean it is a necessary element of feminism? Deborah Siegel discusses the importance of generationalism in feminist writing as "a chronologically informed positivist epistemology . . . an understanding of eras and consciousnesses that can be labelled 'pre' and 'post' " (56) that produces simplification in the work of post-feminists:

> in their incorporation of a masterful rhetoric of repossession, in their articulation of a "good" feminism, and in their righteous condemnation of a monolithic "bad" feminism, Wolf, Roiphe, and Denfeld make feminist history the story of a product rather than that of a process. (59)

Criticisms of feminism as a fundamentally negative practice come from a very wide range of perspectives. Kristeva claims "that a feminist practice can only be negative, at odds with what already exists so that we may say 'that's not it' and 'that's still not it' " (1986c:197). Other critical theorists who agree on the limitations of such a negative politics, concede its pragmatic necessity:

> It is, of course, indispensable for women to conduct a molar politics, with a view to winning back their own organism, their own history, their own subjectivity: "we as women . . ." makes its appearance as a subject of enunciation. But it is dangerous to confine oneself to such a subject, which does not function without drying up a spring or stopping a flow. (Deleuze and Guattari 1987:276)

Marxism, psychoanalysis, and feminism are closely tied together by historical placement, and they exchange between them critical and concerned narratives about girls. One of the effects of their interaction has been the explanatory category of feminine adolescence and a reconceptualization of the significance of girls, particularly in their roles as daughters. The construction of girlhood as a problem, and the dismissal of girls and their interests as trivial, belong to each of these critical models—in which girls will always be not yet Subjects and not yet women.

five

Sex and the Single Girl:
Studies in Girlhood

> It is true that two years ago you were very young. But you told me yourself that your mother was engaged at seventeen and then waited two years for her husband. A daughter usually takes her mother's love-story as her model. So you too wanted to wait for him, and you took it that he was only waiting till you were grown up enough to be his wife. I imagine that was a perfectly serious plan for the future in your eyes.
>
> —Freud, *Fragment of an Analysis of a Case Study of Hysteria*

FEMININE ADOLESCENCE has been overwhelmingly explicated as a sexualized mode of development, and studies of girls and girlhood have perpetuated an emphatic association between sex and girls. This association of girls and sex has underpinned public discourses on gender, sex, age, power, and agency, and the sex of single girls has been an object of concern in numerous fields. The single girl's apparent distance from functional sexual relations has motivated concern with her behaviors, opinions, actions, situation, and relations.[1] This chapter is interested in studies of girlhood and considers this focus on girls and sex through the modes of analysis this concern produces and that make it visible.

I have divided this chapter by disciplinary fields: textual studies, social sciences, and ethnography. These are not in fact easy to distinguish, but they locate important tendencies in understanding exchanges between the lived experience of girlhood and representations of girls. These modes of analysis themselves depend, moreover, on ideas of girlhood, not because all social analysis focuses on girls but because the emergence of feminine adolescence formed an integral element of constituting late modern definitions of culture, society, and its mediation of individuals.

Imagining the Virgin (Textual Studies)
The Virgin's Image

While the term "virginity" may be used to refer to persons of any sex or age, it is predominantly associated with girls. The valorization of girls' virginity long associated with patriarchy implies that process and change should not be relevant to girls, who should always enter womanhood in original condition. Virginity appears thus in conflict with adolescence. It may also, however, be used to ask a range of questions about dominant images and ideas of girl sexuality, including about how girl sexuality is constituted as a knowable and containable object and as exemplary of problems with knowing and containing objects. I want to begin this discussion of studying images or representations of girlhood with a consideration of how virginity is seen and known.

The virgin is a woman without sexual history. In one sense she is free from sexual taint (knowledge), in another she is proof against tampering with paternity: source of the strange state of technical virginity that allows sexual experience while still protecting paternity. The hymen to which virginity refers, however, does not support this image of technical wholeness. It is not the taut web visualized by images of defloration as puncture but in fact, as Giulia Sissa notes, "a lunule bordering the labia minora" (2): a protrusion of flesh that varies in shape and solidity.[2] Yet, as Sissa also notes, "neither mariology nor psychoanalysis nor forensic medicine nor erotic literature can renounce belief in this material token of female intactness, which makes it possible to conceive of a woman's first act of sexual intercourse as a definite, recognizable wound" (2). The hymen underscores the inscription of virginity on and as a feminine body, credited with social and psychological import as a border between girl and woman but also signifying a field of undecidability rather than innocence or knowledge. Signified by the invisible and able to be simulated, virginity exemplifies the constructedness of the body while also articulating a truth presumed resident in the body and its experience. Virginity seems to be a static position, a truth claim, but the virgin acts across a space between child and woman that is actively open and closed (fluids pass from her, yet she is sealed). Sissa claims this enigmatic quality explains the religious significance of virgins, but saints and oracles are only more overt forms of the virgin's ambivalence. The virgin functions less as a liminal point between innocence and knowledge than between girl and woman.[3] The girl *comes to be* virgin, the term forming an early figure for feminine adolescence, and late modern virginity presumes pubescence as well as the abstention from (or concealment of) mature sexual activity.

Freud's essay "The Taboo of Virginity," subtitled "Contributions to the Psychology of Love," discusses the patriarchal need for virginity as an object of psychosocial trade: "The demand that a girl shall not bring to her marriage any memory of sexual relations with another is, indeed, nothing other than a logical continuation of the right to exclusive possession of a woman, which forms the essence of monogamy" (11:193). The import distilled into a woman's first sexual intercourse detracts, Freud suggests, from her possible disappointment with heterosexual sex (193). What he calls the "taboo" of virginity is therefore a fetish image covering and accentuating the difficult question of a girl's sexual identity prior to (hetero)sexual intercourse. The virgin is, paradoxically, the exemplar of available women—she is not a mother and therefore not any potential lover's mother and not unavailable under the incest taboo. The definition of feminine sexuality by the goal of mature genital womanhood relies on an equation of virginity and feminine adolescence. The virgin is both emblematic of the future and has no future of her own if the only possible future for a girl is sexual activity, ostensibly unavailable to virgins. The virgin incorporates and represents feminine adolescence as a moment rather than a process: defloration, annunciation, or the prolonged passive suspension before these arrivals frozen in the image of an ideal. Virginity minimizes the significance of feminine adolescence and designates girls' maturity as something gifted by men. However, images are never really frozen and always constituted in exchange and interpretation despite fetishizing claims to coherence, and the problematic rather than reassuring virgin is no exception.

The virgin defines desirable femininity within what writers after Jacques Lacan would call the Symbolic Order. As identity, sexuality, and desire are all constituted in symbolic relations for Lacan, representations take on more substantial importance in theories and reading practices influenced by Lacan, although he draws much of this emphasis from Freud. From this perspective the monitoring of representations of the Blessed Virgin by the Roman Catholic church or the appearance of virginity by patriarchal families indicate that virgins represent the validity of these institutions.[4] I want to take the Blessed Virgin as a field of exemplary images. The Virgin Mary is an ambivalent relation between pollution and sanctity, and the passion of saints remains acceptable by reference to the seal of the virgin body.

Liturgy stresses a distinction between Virginity and the small-v virginity that women might imitate.[5] But the Blessed Virgin should not be confused with any repression of feminine sexuality, whatever that means in the fifth century B.C., the fourth century A.D., or the twentieth century. Suggesting that women are victims of an imposed cult of virginity fails to recognize the validation encoded in the performance/representation of virginity.[6] If virginity works as a statement of self-denial this is not opposed to its image of integrity but part of its attraction.

The claim that there is "an 'essential difference' between woman as representation ('*Woman*' as cultural imago) and woman as experience (real women as agents of change)" (De Lauretis cited in Braidotti 164), ignores how girls live and understand their lives in relation to such histories and images. If I want to think about girls, I am impelled to look at representations, images, or figures of girls as crucial benchmarks for what will be recognized as girlhood. The virgin marks the impossibility of fixing or determining meaning despite being a highly recognizable generically connotative image, stock character position, and theoretical concept. The Blessed Virgin is an icon and an ideal that has been utilized to contextualize and evaluate images of and ideas about girls but also to discuss textuality and the question of representation itself. The daughter-virgin-bride nexus dominates what can be identified as the girl in classical and biblical narratives, literary and nonliterary writings, and visual images (including painterly, plastic, and filmic practices). The focal point of modern appropriations of the virgin as a metaphor for art, text, and meaning is her status as ambivalent boundary.

The virgin remains a crucial component of Western philosophy, theology, iconography, and other histories, all of which claim to draw truth from the past through and in representations. This continuity is evident in the long iconographic history of the Blessed Virgin, which took new forms relevant to feminine adolescence in modernity. The Enlightenment figure of the girl is both sexualized and distanced from sex in philosophy and social theory, such as that of Kant and Rousseau, as well as in forms of popular culture—for example, the early-nineteenth-century French figure of Atala, based on an 1801 novel by Chateaubriand. Atala figured both modernity and the premodern as the savage, exotic girl of the New World disseminated in new and traditional visual images, including medals, icons, and mass-produced art. Atala also instantiates the entwining of girlhood innocence and death/corruption that is so often represented through icons of virginity. These visualizations of Atala—like those of Ophelia and the representations of Jeanne d'Arc around the time of her canonization more than one hundred years later—take up both the contemplative virgin of the annunciation and a history of representing the virgin's death proper to hagiography.[7]

Tableaux representing the Blessed Virgin constitute a nexus of social contexts. Liturgical debates and popular images of femininity, for example, necessarily position images of the annunciation. In the Renaissance these were dominated by both knowledge (the words, the book) and reticence (the virgin who looks or draws away). These are evident in Polonius staging Ophelia with a book and in Simone Martini's *L'Annunziacione* (see fig. 4.1), which explicitly narrates an iconographic history. The annunciation focuses Roman Catholic accounts of the passion of virginity, negotiating the question of action and will in virginity. When Mary speaks in order to empower the annunciation as discourse on feminine sexuality—"Behold the handmaid of the Lord, be it done to me according to thy word" (Luke 1:38)—a choice emerges in her movement towards or away. It is her marginalization within the Symbolic (the logic of the patriarchal family) that enables the virgin to work as a metaphor for liminality. The virgin as woman who cannot be a mother exceeds an order that comprehends women as a relation to the Mother. And yet a symbolic closure is assured by consigning feminine pleasure to this Virgin icon. Before sexual activity the virgin's sex/body seems to more clearly hold forth the other truth of the feminine.

Virginity names a body prior to the construction of sexuality proper and gives a place to the misfit of feminine puberty (the unrepresentability of the body before culture). This unrepresentability has also been figured as "the pleasure of the text": the blank page or "degree zero" of meaning inscribed and ordered by a signifying system.[8] Jacques Derrida's utilization of the hymen as a figure for textual slippage makes this analogy explicit:

> The hymen is the figure for undecidability and the "general law of the textual effect" . . . for at least two reasons. First, "metaphorically" it is the ritual celebration of the breaking of the vaginal membrane, and "literally" that membrane remains intact even as it opens up into two lips; second, the walls of the passage that houses the hymen are both inside and outside the body. (Spivak 1983:174)

Michele Le Doueff and Luce Irigaray have suggested that such figures of indeterminacy, which they link to the bride or muse (Sophia), are central to the content of Western philosophy.[9] Indeterminacy is similarly invoked in

Freud's deferential citation of poetry as the only place to understand what happens to women after puberty, despite all the evidence he uses to claim that women are centered on a predictable sexualized narrative. While embodying unrepresentability, virginity remains both a sign and the space for a sign. Virginity is a text space: the space in which meaning may be formed and the space between signifiers in which meaning is determined for any text. Derrida also uses the hymen as a figure for "style" that resists penetration and marking and thus demands the active production of meaning (Derrida 1978a:37–41). In this metaphor Derrida takes up the history of virginity as embodying representation (of the word of God) and resistance to such truth claims. Girls are *read* for the truth of their sex and in order to verify the integrity of various patriarchal structures.

As preeminent Western virgin, Mary of Christian Scripture symbolizes relations between man and god, self and other, which is how she can be mother, bride, queen, and daughter of Christ all at once (Kristeva 1986b:161). In her essay "Stabat Mater" Kristeva conflates the Blessed Virgin's role as "a 'bond,' a 'middle,' or an 'interval' " (162–3) with the Platonic *chora* as "feminine" space that precedes the Law of the Father.[10] Kristeva aligns this threshold with the maternal body as "threshold of culture and nature" (182), "purified as it might be by the virginal fantasy" (176). Judith Butler notes that in this understanding of the *chora* "materiality and femininity appear to merge to form a materiality prior to and formative of any notion of the empirical" (1993:17), and it is worth noting that both the Mother and the Blessed Virgin are necessary to form this space for knowledge prior to knowledge. However, the Blessed Virgin of liturgy, icons, and other histories of representation differs from this *chora* to the degree that she questions or remains ambivalent.

Representations of girl sexuality are inseparable from girl sexuality as a lived experience or as an object of analysis. Figures of virginity epitomize the way in which girl sexuality has formed in images claiming to represent the (as yet) unfinished process of feminine adolescence. Indeed it seems impossible in late modernity to represent girls without raising the question of sexual activity. The ambiguity of the girl's position as agent/object of sexual desire has become more visibly fraught with contradictory significations as the dissemination of feminine adolescence deferred resolution of that ambiguity in womanhood. The unfolding of modernity can be traced through distributed generic images of girls, whether on medals, calendars, advertisements, or film and television. These images are both inseparable from and yet not simply descriptive of modern girls. Images of adolescent girls, whether explicitly referencing virginity or not, mark feminine adolescence as embodying an object of contemplation, disciplined observation, and desiring interpretation. Their characteristic ambiguity—the openness of these images to interpretation (and their resistance to complete knowledge)—mean that these exemplary girls have materialized not only ideas about feminine adolescence but ideas about representation, interpretation, and knowledge.

History and Discourse

Girls are often deployed to invoke a play between what is outside of history (often conceived as the maternal body) and what is cultural (the crafting and control of girlhood) and are also used to question the effects and truth of representation. However crucial these are to conceptions of history, girlhood is lived rather than objectively knowable and thus a history of girlhood seems to invite a historiography of experience (or identity). But history encounters some important obstacles when taking experience as evidence. Using historians of sexuality as her example, Joan Wallach Scott argues that the

> project of making experience visible precludes critical examination of the workings of the ideological system itself, its categories of representation . . ., its premises about what these categories mean and how they operate, and of its notions of subjects, origin, and cause. (778)

In response to this lack of attention to how categories for understanding experience are formed, Scott recognizes that "we need to attend to the historical processes that, through discourse, position subjects and produce their experiences. It is not individuals who have experience, but subjects who are constituted through experience" (779). In positioning this work as a genealogy, I have accepted that girlhood as an historical object is best addressed by reference to discourses that constitute understandings of girlhood experience. This process of historicizing experience would aim to "make visible the assignment of subject-positions" (Spivak quoted in Scott 791). Feminine adolescence gains much of its explanatory force by reference to a naturalized, neutralized position beyond cultural or historical specificity, one that seems accessible only through individual experience. A history of girlhood would thus benefit greatly from what Scott imagines as a "genuinely nonfoundational history . . . which retains its explanatory power and its interest in change but does not stand on or reproduce neutralised categories" (797).

The discipline of history prioritizes both context and sequence in a developmental narrative. But the imperative of context—a text's relations to where it appears temporally and socially—is not the same thing as sequence—where a text inevitably proceeds from and displaces what came before it. Contemporary critiques of historiography have asked whether the now dominant linear model of history is useful for analyzing all events and have questioned the possibility of definitive historiography. Foucault's renovations of historiography enable consideration of context without reference to cause and effect or pursuit of precise representation of a given context. Because history is exclusively reliant on records or texts, it is entirely subject to the undecidability of texts more usually associated with analysis of literature or art. Foucault's methods allow shifts of emphasis among the categories used to understand history, including concepts such as tradition and progress. His work flattens temporal differences, focusing on discontinuity, series, and surfaces of emergence. For example, in his study of the human sciences in *The Order of Things* Foucault writes: "instead of relating the biological taxonomies to other knowledges of the living being . . . I have compared them with what might have been said at the same time about linguistic signs, the formation of general ideas, the language of action, the hierarchy of needs, and the exchange of goods" (1973b:x).[11] These practices of knowledge production are often called *discourse* in secondary material on Foucault.

Foucault turned this historiographical challenge to a range of discursive fields, including sexuality. In his three volumes of *The History of Sexuality* Foucault argues that sexuality emerges in late modern society, and thus in relation to both the nuclear family and capitalism, as a discourse that produces the secret of sexuality as central to subjectivity. While sexuality appears to be visible in earlier periods, he argues, how sex worked as an evaluation of behaviors or definition of personal identity does not conform to what the twentieth century means by sexuality. Nevertheless, the history of the virgin maintains some disquieting continuities across Foucault's distinctions between classical Greco-Roman, Christian, and late modern understandings of self, ethics, and sex. Virginity forms a dominant bridge between classical and Christian literature on the self, as well as on sex as both available to veneration and a motivated assumption of destiny. If Foucault's introduction to the *History of Sexuality* can be accused of occluding women,

The Use of Pleasure and *The Care of the Self* negotiate rather more complexly with gender.[12] The triads of men, wives, and boys upon which Foucault expands in these texts form a particular discourse on girls by constitutive opposition and even bring Foucault to intersect gynecology and masculine sexuality. Foucault's history also presents virginity as a point of entanglement between use and care and between pleasure and self with continued relevance to late modern girl sexuality.

Foucault's *History of Sexuality* maps "the multiplication of discourses concerning sex in the field of exercise of power itself" (1984a:18). This multiplication spans regimes of power including language, knowledge, observation, and even domination. But not only the practices of sex define it as a field of power—sexuality, the entwining of subjectivity with sex, is for Foucault the basis on which sex becomes the exercise of power itself. Foucault asks, "Is 'sex' really the anchorage point that supports the manifestations of sexuality, or is it not rather a complex idea that was formed inside the deployment of sexuality?" (1984a:152) Sexuality is not a fact of which one may be conscious or not—it is a product of modernity rather than a given against which modernity's presence or emergence can be charted. The act of sexual intercourse may be significant for Juliet but it marks no clear transformation of her self or even statement about her identity, and Antigone's sexual activity is not even this significant. Late modernity adds both sexuality and heterosexual identity to the virgin, recasting the place of the virgin's sex.

The virgin can not be encompassed in any form useful to the now of virginity (rather than an ideal past) by looking at representations for the historical truth of what develops when. Not only does historical continuity depend on terms imported into historical analysis, late modern discourses on sex were formed with direct reference to history in order to verify their universality; thus Juliet or the Blessed Virgin are naturally compatible with discourses on virginity formed in relation to them. We can explicate the historical emergence of contemporary versions of virginity, but the undecidability of texts remains crucial to making sense of that history. The constitution and effects of virginity are not best understood by an attempt to recapture the experience of virginity, which merely repeats the terms it is designed to unpack, or by focussing on changing models of girl sexuality that naturalize that experience. Virginity has long been a dominant code for acceptable sexual activity among girls, but its appearance and effects are not constrained by experience or identity. The Blessed Virgin Mary, for example, variously symbolizes aesthetic processes, social conditioning, objects of desire, and historical veracity. Sissa argues that attempts to understand "Greek virginity" were fundamental to debates establishing the parameters of modern historical method. He cites as exemplary the criticism of John Chrysostom as "the very model of a bad historian" (75) for downplaying the differences between Greek virginity and Marian devotion. But virginity was always a matter of textual interpretation.

As modern Roman Catholicism receives it, Marian legend and imagery evolve out of the slight accounts of Christ's conception and childhood in the gospels of Matthew and Luke, which in turn draw on the Old Testament and the Apocrypha and are practiced in liturgy exemplified by the rosary and the Nicene Creed. It is widely recognized that scriptural descriptions of Mary do not denote virginity as sexual abstinence but, rather, her status as unmarried woman or as woman who has not given birth. Disregarding the "sacrosanct" barrier between Greek and Christian virginity (Sissa 76), Marina Warner writes that the sacred virginity of goddesses

> symbolized their autonomy, and had little or no moral connotation. They spurned men because they were preeminent, independent, and alone, which is why the title virgin could be used of a goddess who entertained lovers. Her virginity signified she had retained freedom of choice: to take lovers or to reject them. (1976:47)[13]

Virginity as closure of girl sexuality—prescription of chastity and fantasy of controlled interiority—also necessitates a claim to sexual value. Virginity can thus be heresy when not anchored to the right kind of acceptance: "it must reflect a renunciation. A girl who wants to remain a virgin must first be persuaded that marriage is meritorious and blessed" (Sissa 74). Between classical virgins and the canonical Christian figure of Mary lies a field of questions concerning textual authenticity, historical specificity, and cultural difference. In the texts named for Antigone and Electra, the virginity of their sisters is never considered. It is thus not Antigone's virginity defined as unperforated body that obliges her to her brother's corpse (Ismene is not so obliged), but some other version of virginity, one that also obliges Electra to her dead father. We might use this passionate virginity to reconsider passionate relations to virginity situated by modern discourses on sexuality, an inversion of historical method that is not only tenable but also unavoidable given that texts are formed in webs of significance particular to readers.

Historiography is the writing of history, an epistemology that evades, desires, and depends upon what Michel de Certeau describes as "the unknown immensity that seduces and menaces our knowledge" (1988:3). Certeau frames this writing of history as a desiring inscription of an Other that is the unknown of culture—specifically of the culture from which that history is being produced.[14] Textual analysis preeminently searches for hidden and more or less reliable truths or meanings—indeed finding the central kernel of meaning in a text or statement is the paradigmatic search for truth. Freud's Dora, for example, comprises such a search exactly insofar as she is a case history, converted from the (always multiple) experiences of analysis into a text that can be searched for the truth of what she means. This search is irresolvable in part because she is a girl and thus both does not yet mean anything and is unconscious of her meaning—both presumptions that equate her meaning with her sex. Case studies, textual analyses, and history all participate in ongoing processes of inscription concealed by the fixity of the *archive*, a coherent field of objects, which manifests what is known and confirms what is unknowable. The archive can appear to locate a group of stable objects or finished processes, but in fact all texts are processes of enunciation and acts of interpretation. Writing on Foucault's historiographical practice, Certeau claims:

> Beneath thoughts, he discerns an "epistemological foundation" which *makes them possible*. Between the many institutions, experiences, and doctrines of an age, he detects a coherence which, though not explicit, is nonetheless the condition and organizing principle of a culture. (1988:172)[15]

Certeau in turn draws on both Lacan and Foucault to argue that "each individual is a locus in which an incoherent (and often contradictory) plurality of . . . relational determinations interact" (1984:xii). This interaction also describes the process of analyzing any object, artifact or text.

Textual analysis is sometimes thought to claim too great an autonomy for texts and to insufficiently consider the material conditions and social imperatives that not only frame texts but make them possible. If textual analysis, as its critics claim, involves pulling apart a particular object as if it speaks for a culture, and a focus on the figural rather than the material effects of that object, then historical analysis involves the same processes. The idea of discourse is thus often opposed to textual analysis by claiming that, while textual analysis looks at the properties of a cultural form, discourse analysis not only considers context but places texts as inseparable from their conditions of possibility. Textual analysis does usually focus on singular instances of a cultural field despite frequent reference to interpretative and other historical contexts. Discourse analysis more explicitly focuses on how objects and the categories for understanding them are mutually and simultaneously produced.[16] According to Michelle Barrett, textual or semiotic analysis asks "according to what rules has a particular statement been made, and consequently according to what rules could other similar statements be made?" while discourse analysis asks "how is it that one particular statement appeared rather than another?" (126). Barrett argues that discourse analysis thus enables analysis of "how what is said fits into a network that has its own history and conditions of existence" (126). While discourse is concerned with statements—the articulation of knowledge—such analysis is not confined to linguistic objects because, for Foucault, language and objects, things and words, are not separable in any causal way. Subject positions, and the experience articulated in those positions, are exemplary instances of how discourses constitute the objects they describe.

Sex Education (Social Sciences)
Sexual Sciences

The idea of culture is usually aligned with textual analysis as the social is with social sciences, but this distinction is far from clear-cut and the girl provides one space in which that distinction can be considered. How are girls' social relations—to family, school, law, and peers, for example—to be separated from the clearly cultural forms that mediate how those relations proceed through homes, classrooms, workplaces, leisure, etc. Girls are not only positioned by the demands of social structures—you must attend school—but by cultural forms and practices, such as popular cultural texts on school and schoolgirls and public culture discourses on education, work, and opportunity. A distinction between culture and society nevertheless marks important boundaries between methodological claims made by studies of girls—historically, a difference between seeing girls through representations and observing girls in their lived social relations. In this section I want to consider sex education, a discourse that deploys representations as a means of structuring social relations. Sex education is the institutional dissemination of knowledge about appropriate sexual behavior and identification, positioning girls in relation to dominant and resistant ideas about sex through the educational, legislative, and familial reproduction of normative social values centered on sexualized identities. Both popular and public sex education disseminate authorized knowledge about sex through institution-al mechanisms (including institutions centered on representation, such as media and publishing), and like most institutional forms this is more often considered by social science than textual analysis.

Foucault's analysis of the emergence of sexuality among the new human or social sciences (including education) of the nineteenth century contends that the modern discourses of "pedagogy, medicine, demography, and eco-nomics, were anchored or supported by the institutions of the state, and be-came especially focussed on the family" (De Lauretis 12). All of these are de-ployed in the institutional processes of educating girls about their sexual identity or their sexuality as "the set of effects produced in bodies, behav-iours, and social relations by a certain deployment deriving from a complex political technology" (Foucault 1984a:127). Foucault focuses his discussion of sexualized education on boys, and his silence regarding the gendered body of this history has sometimes been thought a serious obstacle to em-ploying him to talk about girls. Foucault's cautions that

> we must not look for who has the power in the order of sexuality (men, adults, parents, doctors) and who is deprived of it (women, adolescents, children, patients); nor for who has the right to know and who is forced to remain ignorant. (1984a:99)

We might nevertheless find the specificity of sex education for girls signifi-cant. Debra Tolman asserts that, in comparison to the processes of naming masculine adolescent sexual desire, girls are not educated about their own sex: "Rather than being 'educated,' girls' bodies are suppressed under sur-veillance and silenced in the schools" (325). As Foucault argues, however, "It would be less than exact to say that the pedagogical institution has imposed a ponderous silence on the sex of children and adolescents . . . it has coded contents and qualified speakers" (1984a:29).[17] Silence does not actually characterize those many sex education scenarios in which girls are repeated-ly observed and discussed, but a different mode of articulating sex education mediates and informs girl sexuality.

Puberty as unwilled quantitative and qualitative increase in sexual desire and activity foregrounds an anatomical destiny that paradoxically requires channeling into proper sexual practices and makes statements about sexual development and sex education inseparable. Foucault's analysis allows us to note the significance of this understanding of sex to the development of the social sciences and their key methodologies. Margaret Mead's influential studies of girls around puberty focus on sexuality as a pivotal means of constituting and negotiating relations between social members. Within Mead's studies, a girl must learn to place herself in a symbolic system:

> The little girls are taught from earliest childhood that they are desirable. Baby girls a few weeks old are laden with shell ornaments, ear-rings two or three inches long, and necklaces and belts of shells as big as slices of lemon. Thus conspicuously are they set off from their brothers, who go about in a naked, unadorned state. (Mead 1939:199)[18]

Symbols, legends, and taboos instantiated in everyday cultural practices are highly significant for anthropology, which generally understands the cultural as the inseparable materialization of the social. The science of social sciences, emphasizing methodological repeatability, prioritizes such structural approaches in which cultural forms reflect the presumably more consistent demands of social structures. Adolescence and the institutions that mediate it are key elements of these structural analyses of societies and the persons they (re)produce. And the sex of girls—the sex they have, want, and understand—has been a recurrent interest of social science analysis, in part due to the influence of feminists on new social sciences and the world they studied.

Sex education for girls evaluates girls in comparison to each other and in relation to social norms, a process operating in the very terms by which sex is understood. Celia Cowie and Sue Lees study, for example, the use and effects of the term "slag" among British schoolgirls in the 1980s: "It strikes us that it is the 'presence' of the category which is important, not the identification of certain girls" (18). This study considers girls' responses as effects of popular education about girl sexuality as structured by binary oppositions—love vs. sex, slags vs. drags. Like many other social science studies of girls, the study by Cowie and Lees emphasizes the importance of a romantic-sexual narrative in girls' shared popular culture that underpins sex education for girls, but no more than does the legislative inscription of girl sexuality, which sex education is also designed to communicate. Girls learn simultaneously the desirable/undesirable practices of sexuality and the legal limits on sexual identifications and acts. The definition of girls through their relations to sex can be linked to earlier historical discourses on consent and girlhood, but is inflected by contemporary discourses on public sex education and contemporary gender norms. Consent is about knowledge: knowing what consent is required from whom and that it has been obtained. However, consent is never shared—never, in fact, consensus. Law indicates matters of shared understanding (consensus), on which individuals are not called upon to speak to unless they want to interrupt that consensus. "Consenting to" is submission, and within a model of maturity where girls reach an age of consent—remembering that boys are not the focus of consent legislation except with reference to homosexual sex—they reach not majority but the age at which they can submit—not to the law, as must every citizen, but to another person.[19]

Comparatively little has changed in the makeup of the people whose consensus is recognized and enshrined in law between the 1860s and 2001. Girls rarely speak in public debates on sex education and consent; indeed they are necessarily *spoken of.* Even their consent to the wishes of others is determined as a nonconsent—this is not a question about whether or not girls actually consent, because even if they did consent, as minors they could not do so. While no form of public consensus involves girls, public consensus is paradigmatically about them—the age of consent and the majority it instantiates are founded on inequality and the incapacity to consent. Feminists have been highly instrumental in effecting changes to legislation to bring in age of consent laws for the protection of girls. However, its pragmatic purposes or desirable effects should not mean feminists cannot problematize what this consent means and how it works. Debates around age of consent legislation in different countries and at different times have repeatedly stigmatized the sexual activity of girls and repeatedly been linked to the criminalization of homosexuality as well as prostitution. There is more than semantics at stake in recognizing that age of consent legislation is addressed to girls as the objects of a law they can not be subjects of and that the emergence of these discourses on girl sexuality are pivotal to the emergence of a public sphere model on which, as Jürgen Habermas notes, our dominant Western ideals of democracy are founded.

By the 1920s public debates about modern love included a call for girls to be educated about sex, yet cautiously so.[20] Sex education participated in what was sometimes called a "New Morality" shaping visible changes to popular practices around marriage and sex. A modernizing educational program that distinguished between information and arousal validated these new public discourses on sex—for which Freud's hesitancy about naming sex in his prefatory remarks to his essay on Dora is an influential precursor. If a modern girl needed to understand something about sex, for her own mental health and for the good of society, her unimpeded innocence was thought to protect her against any corrupting knowledge. Discourses on new morality, free love, and sex education pervaded public and popular forums in the early twentieth century: magazines, novels, cinema, extended schooling, advertising, political movements. However, Foucault rejects the idea that sex had been a taboo subject for repressed Victorians liberated by new scientific understandings of sexuality: "Sexuality must not be thought of as a kind of natural given which power tries to hold in check, or as an obscure domain which knowledge tries gradually to uncover. It is the name that can be given to a historical construct . . . a great surface network" (1984a:105). The deployment of these sexual sciences involves more than the spread of particular discourses such as psychoanalysis—it involves diverse institutions (medical, educational, political, etc.) and practices (linguistic, popular, etc.) that bring girls to experience themselves as sexual beings of a certain kind.

This learned sexual self is not confined to sex acts. According to the sociologists and anthropologists whose accounts of culture and society became newly visible in the twentieth century, girls' sexual selves have the most pervasive effects on their social lives and determine much of the difficulty of feminine adolescence. Feminists such as Joan Brumberg have specifically attributed the contemporary dangers of feminine adolescence—including eating disorders and delinquency as well as teen pregnancy—to a disjunction between sexual maturity and sex education:

> I don't believe girls are getting honest guidance in the way sex education is taught today. . . . From menarche—when the focus of discussion is on personal hygiene rather than the social and emotional meaning of sexuality—onward, little attention is paid to the psychological and emotional needs of girls. Sex education programs focus on either "just say no" or how to hold off male advances or practice safe sex. These technical approaches don't help girls decide what is a fair, pleasurable, and responsible use of their bodies. (Brumberg quoted in Winter 16)

While a distinction between self and body might seem a particularly strange way to understand puberty, this othering of the self is crucial to institutional sex education. Sex education has produced modern girlhood as a mesh of qualified agency and discipline that defines their personal selves through their knowledge about sex.[21]

The Girl as Peer Group

While the impact of feminism and changed social conditions for young women at work and at home made girls seem like an urgent field of social inquiry at the end of the nineteenth century, the development of sociology often focused on masculine adolescence (as with G. Stanley Hall's *Adolescence*). This is evident in the famous late-1920s study called *Middletown*, comprised of interviews, questionnaires, and participation in the life of an American town (see Lynd and Lynd, 1929). This study surveyed rapid changes to Western society, and employed youth, women, and girls as markers of this change as much as and alongside technological change. Sociology's usual focus on the society in which its studies will be received, even when looking at exceptional social groups, increases the degree to which it analyzes the normative processes of a society.

Debates over legislation on sexual consent, marriage, and majority negotiate an alignment between girls and sex in their articulation of crucial social norms. In the nineteenth century these debates cited new anthropological studies of "primitive" peoples and colonial subjects, emphasizing the importance of social studies to improved knowledge of the world, which in turn verified the enlightened progress of society embodied in those laws and law makers. These debates over sex and sex/gender norms occurred at the same time as, and often with direct reference to, extensive educational reform that extended compulsory schooling to girls. New forms of education were linked to new sexual practices in public and popular forums, including reportage, legislative chambers and electoral platforms, and film and fiction. Educational policy continues to provide a good example of how public discourses and popular culture are continually engaged in redefining girlhood. Sociological research in the 1990s often suggested that changes to girls' lives and educations had produced a pluralization of potential life paths but not of likely outcomes (Chisholm 270).[22]

The instances in which a girl makes contact with social regulation and educational agendas extend far outside of schools, and this larger field is predominantly directed toward individual maintenance of acceptable ways of living, including sexual practices. Kerry Carrington notes this tendency in treatment of girls within juvenile justice systems:

The basis of their incarceration is quite transparent: not the commission of any legal offence through participating in any "ritual of resistance," but the repeated and escalating transgression of the mundane "infra-legal" norms governing adolescence and family life policed by a variety of social technicians concerned with the government of youth. (1993:32)

Laws that shape girls' lives are often translations of age of consent legislation, often directly aligning this threshold with authorized participation in other social rituals and spheres: voting, driving, drinking, access to restricted representations, working, access to some welfare payments, etc. Unlike the age of consent, however, these laws usually refer to a gender-neutral youth, although none of these activities are unaffected by gender. Unlike girlhood itself, girls' gender-specific relation to these laws regulating permissible social participation, and indeed social membership, is crucially determined by age.

Social studies of girls implicitly or explicitly (in the case of feminist analysis) presumes girl sexuality to be constituted for girls as an object of masculine desire. The dominance of this model in the pervasive institutions for sex education that frame girls' lives (school, family, law, etc.) naturalizes its descriptive power. Even those studies of girlhood that aim to account for the meanings and organizations proper to girls take related premises to the girls they observe, such as an overwhelmingly important distinction between sex and romance. Girls are repeatedly urged to responsibly understand this distinction through the mechanisms of sex education, although popular culture produced for and among girls questions whether that distinction is possible. Sex (within sex education) is a naturalized field of learned structures for desire, behavior, and pleasure, but in the context of girls' culture romance operates as the same kind of field, rather than as a directly imposed mechanism for social reproduction. Nevertheless, imposition, limitation, and distraction dominate accounts of girls and romance in studies of girls, positioning sex by contrast as both natural and unavoidable. While the forms of romance/sex in girls' culture have often changed, this structural understanding of the power of romance among girls has not.[23]

Girls' magazines provide one space in which girls' relations to each other and to social norms can be observed. Whether analyzed through textual analysis or through social science methods such as surveys, interviews, or observation of girls' engagement with the magazines, the projection of a peer group speaking for and as girls is pivotal. Girls' magazines invoke a simultaneous and equated development of gender identity and sexual identity and produce a normative image of the girl to whom they are addressed that, despite fluctuations in the responses of particular groups and in the pages of specific magazines, maintains some dominant conventions. This girl is ambivalently positioned between the heterosexual woman presented as her goal and a self-interest focused on desire for the ideal feminine body. The proliferation of eroticized images of young women in these texts, while more generally registered by readers in terms of body types and lifestyles, depend on intimate recognition of other girls. This ideal body remains enclosed, clean, and impermeable, despite the actions and desires of particular girls. Despite the cover blurbs on how many "dreams" or "hunks" are inside, this dominant image of girlhood (as body and sexual identity) is not represented as normatively sexually active.[24] This does not describe the lives of girls themselves but the heterosexually directed and homoerotically oriented ideal-average-girl in relation to which multiple readings of the genre are possible.[25] While young men enter girls' magazines as interested parties, girls are the presumed readers of the body for which these magazines are a production guide.[26] Their commonality of sexual desires and practices is less demanded than presumed by the genre, but the group identity of this readership is nevertheless formed around unresolved sexual ambivalence.

The extent of reader participation and interaction in this genre means that the division between text and the audience is, at least apparently, shifting and permeable. Nevertheless a sociological analysis of girls' magazines will want to directly engage with how girls read the magazines in the process of negotiating social relations. Patricia Gilbert and Sandra Taylor, for example, focus on what girls say about why and how they read these magazines, while Angela McRobbie closely considers the form of the magazines but as a point of comparison to other elements of girls' lives. Despite emphasis on particularity and individually negotiated meanings and functions, what matters in social science analyses is not any girl's particular reading, although particular girls may be quoted, but girls as a generality or as representative of a girl group. The analytic component of any study must draw conclusions, and the social component of social sciences must refer to groups rather than individuals, but the girl group sometimes appears in these studies as less particularized and individualized than other groups. Girls and their lives have repeatedly been represented as more closely framed by institutions than other groups. Indeed this is one of the defining features of public discourses on feminine adolescence, often attributed to a psychological structure particular to girls. Freud's study *Group Psychology and the Analysis of the Ego* (1922), along with other early-twentieth-century analyses of the group, specified two kinds of groups with different relations to individuality: organized, hierarchized groups (such as a church or army), and amorphous, shifting groups (the herd or crowd). This second type of group, Freud argued, fails to invest its members with the qualities of individuals and is linked to both femininity and immaturity.[27]

The occasions in which peer groups of girls might appear accelerated around the emergence of feminine adolescence in recognized and regulated gatherings in schools, workplaces, and leisure groups. These groups were often perceived as a potential problem, and concern over emotional contagion among schoolgirls appeared in many texts addressed to teachers in the early twentieth century; this concern about girl groups reinforced notions of the normal girl's difficulty. Freud's *Group Psychology* attempts to read the "mass" as not mere numbers and not necessarily primitive (1922:2–3)— culminating in a developmental model where the group "matures" through appropriation of individual qualities, and is hierarchized in accordance with that "maturity." The "group mind" exemplified by girls in Freud's study resembles many later accounts of girl groups: it cannot decide and decides badly; it is standardizing and homogenous, and yet tolerates heterogeneity. Freud sees these contradictions as surmountable by an "unknown"—the hypnotic power of the leader or "Father" (1922:94). In other peer groups influence often takes the form of mutual suggestions in lateral relations within the group—a "suggestibility" Freud describes, using the example of schoolgirls, as "contagion" (1922:64). The ways in which a group might constitute identity are constrained by such dominant psychologies within which peer groups signify a failure to constitute individuality (for Freud, ego-identity) or other symptoms of a pathologized feminine adolescence. But peer groups remain the dominant if not sole terrain of social science analysis of girls. Moreover, girl groups seem less amenable to the participant observation style of analysis, which somewhat resists such generalization because researchers appear to be so clearly distinguishable from girls.[28]

Sociological reference to girls as elements of a peer group can effectively intervene in the tendency to see girls as a psychological state or fact. But psychology is also a social science, however much it prioritizes individuals. Psychology also continues to be concerned with representations—in fact psychology can only be accessed through representation. For example, Carol Gilligan's much-cited study of gender difference in child psychology utilizes interviews, questionnaires, and observation of small groups and individuals as data for her representation of girls' conceptions of "self and morality." Gilligan argues that girls are more connective, responsive, and relational than boys. This conforms to a gender dichotomy presumed by previous psychologists and framed within a developmental hierarchy, but Gilligan simultaneously sets out to prove this feminine psychology is highly desirable and indeed more ethical than the individualism assigned to boys in such studies. Mary Pipher, claiming that psychologists and academics have not studied girls, and therapists have been "baffled" by them (21), turns to the cultural life of girls as the key to their psychology, focusing on "that place where culture and individual psychology intersect" to consider "why cultures create certain personalities and not others" (26). Pipher sees her girl subjects as split by cultural expectations into "true and false selves" (37), again structured according to a model by which individuals mature into a genuine sense of self.

These false selves are unilaterally aligned with peer groups and (popular) cultural pressures:

> With puberty, girls face enormous cultural pressures to split into false selves. The pressure comes from schools, magazines, music, television, advertisements and movies. It comes from peers. Girls can be true to themselves and risk abandonment by their peers, or they can reject their true selves and be socially acceptable. Most girls choose to be socially accepted and split into two selves, one that is authentic and one that is culturally scripted. (Pipher 38)

Pipher quotes Claudia Bepko and Jo-Ann Krestan's account of this as an "'indoctrination into the code of goodness,' which they argue is essentially unchanged since the fifties" (39)—that is, since the adolescence of the parents of Pipher's patients. The promotional blurbs on and inside Pipher's book attest to its success with such parents, mothers in particular, as a guide to the experience of feminine adolescence as a turmoil of "losing themselves." This lost "self" is substantially defined by the self-perception of those adults, an anxiety for lost value evident in Pipher's repeated assertion that "adolescence is the most formative time in the lives of women" (72). The girls of *Reviving Ophelia* are understood as culturally homogenous, despite individual variations, and the narrative of treatment offered to them is highly class-specific.[29] *Reviving Ophelia* thus evidences close links between the guidance manuals of girls' culture and popular discourses on self-help. The object of self-help discourse is intrinsically middle-class, regardless of actual participants, because it is premised on social mobility. Such self-help for women often plays on dominant discourses of feminine adolescence— like Ellen Fein and Sherrie Schneider's best-selling dating guide, *The Rules: Time Tested Secrets for Capturing the Heart of Mr. Right* (1996)—taking up the long-standing equation between girls and processes of self-production.

Self-help, psychological, and sociological narratives on feminine adolescence presume girls to be heterosexual even when they account for other kinds of girlhood. Whether lesbian identity is considered innately different, necessarily producing a different youth, or as produced in adolescence through cementing sexual orientation, these developmental narratives are compatible with dominant psychological models that understand adolescence as crucial to the production of sexuality. The dominant understanding of sexuality as a secret inner self—hard to talk about and difficult to know—also substantially conforms to psychoanalytic representations of homosexuality as a developmental problem. While sex/gender is played in more than one way in lesbian relations, the term "lesbian" relies on a sexualized dichotomy between man and woman that is perceived as constituted in adolescence.

The poststructuralist theories of sexuality articulated around the label "queer theory" problematize how one might form or claim sexual identity and thus dominant understandings of adolescence as the formation of sexuality (within the nuclear family and in its processes of development). If adolescence locates (as yet) unfixed sexual identities, it can only with difficulty be assigned a gay or lesbian identity, and if it may be labeled "queer," then it is only insofar as all adolescence would be queer. Such nonfixity is, I have argued, already proper to feminine adolescence as a sign of both incompletion and promise, a figure that presents the girl as permanently queer. Butler employs the declaration "It's a girl!" to understand the "performativity" of sex/gender:

> To the extent that the naming of the "girl" is transitive, that is, initiates the process by which a certain "girling" is compelled, the term or, rather, its symbolic power, governs the formation of a corporeally enacted femininity that never fully approximates the norm. This is a "girl," however, who is compelled to "cite" the norm in order to qualify and remain a viable subject. (1993:232)

Obscure Objects of Desire (Ethnography)
Anthropology and the Other Culture

What are the effects of the pivotal social science endeavor of seeking to define what girls desire, think, fear, and identify with? This chapter maps across diverse frames for studying girls and feminine adolescence a desire to incite girls to speak and explain the contradictions and continuities they have been thought to materialize. This final section reflects on the opportunities and problems of ethnography for talking about girls, as well as on the significance of girls to the emergence of ethnographic practices. It is simultaneously an introduction to girls' roles in ethnographic practice, the accounts of girlhood that ethnography tends to produce, and ethnography's significance among discourses on girlhood. The authoritative interpretation of experience produced by ethnography has been important to processes of defining, interpreting, and monitoring girlhood, and the ethnographic situation relies on relations of knowledge and maturity often associated with girls.

The category "feminine adolescence" emerged alongside a range of ethnographic methods; increasing the likelihood that research about girls would ask girls about their experience. A brief genealogy of ethnography might attest to an unexpected significance of girls or young women for ethnographic practices. Ethnography is the study of (or, more precisely, writing about) the behavior of people in a particular society. Among the many possible ways to go about such studies, "ethnography" specifically refers to a set of methods—usually to the direct observation of research subjects, including their everyday activities and perceptions. While ethnographic methods arose out of early sociology and travel writing as social commentary, ethnography often designated commentary drawn from experience of another culture, although it did not necessarily imply direct participation in that culture by the researcher. Ethnography involves attempts to accumulate data on how a significant sample of people within a particular culture live, usually undertaken by limited participation in or interaction with that culture.

Patricia Adler and Andrew Tolson, among others, have emphasized the roots of ethnographic fieldwork in social reform movements of the nineteenth century, which drew on statistics, observation, and interviews (Adler 8). Tolson details a mesh of writerly skills and scientific aims that produced the sociological interview at around the same time anthropological fieldwork was being cemented as social science. He notes that these methods were influenced by both parliament-sponsored research and criminology (116) but produced accounts of "social character" as much as they uncovered facts about behaviors and ways of living, manifesting a "cultural gaze [that] collectivizes and typifies the individual within a class" (122). Tolson sees in Henry Mayhew's early interview technique certain contradictions that still trouble ethnography.[30] While Mayhew is puzzled by some of his subjects, Tolson notes

> this element of surprise, the unexpected, never really amounts to a serious disturbance of the cultural consensus. It is capable of being read in a way which, although on one level shocking, on another level seems to reaffirm the validity of the norms which it disturbs. In the case of the Watercress Girl these are clearly certain middle-class norms about childhood innocence. So paradoxically a kind of normalizing judgement is confirmed even though the individual encountered in the interview does not, at first sight, conform to it. (124)

Direct participation by ethnographers emerged as a standard method in the early twentieth century in relation to a range of new discourses on society and culture, including the new psychologies eventually dominated by Freud. While Freud did not journey outside his own culture to locate subject groups, he drew connections between his patients and produced commentary about society as a whole from data collected through their words, which he guided and interpreted. Freud recorded as data not only their stories and his commentaries on them, but also his patients' nonverbal responses to analysis: their physical responses, hesitations, and silences. Freud's critics often accused him of drawing outrageous conclusions from the information his patients gave him, even of projecting his own theory or psychology onto his material, and Freud defended himself against this criticism by stressing his scientific methodology and personal scientific neutrality. These exchanges remain particularly resonant for ethnography. Margaret Mead's studies of "primitive" cultures directly credit Freud's influence, focusing on the sexual and psychic lives of her subjects and drawing on the symbolic associations and interpretative methods of psychoanalysis. Ethnography quickly became the preferred tool for discovering how a culture worked from people's accounts of themselves and for analyzing the production of modern identity and modern life (even, or perhaps especially, when it seemed to be studying what were seen as premodern peoples). Mead's work consistently relates conclusions drawn from research among distant and seemingly alien peoples to her own society, emphasizing issues such as adolescence. *Coming of Age in Samoa*, published to acclaim in 1928, argues that the tribulations associated with late modern Western adolescence were not found in Samoa and that therefore they were a product of culture, not biology. But Mead also perceived adolescence to be an integral structure of all cultures, enabling prediction of a wide range of social characteristics including adolescent perspectives on the world.[31]

Mead representatively traces observed social structures onto the desires of girls. For example she claims that Samoan girls must put aside their own interests for the greater goal of marriage, which yet remains "the inevitable to be deferred as long as possible" (1963:37). Mead utilizes a moral hierarchy drawn from debates on modern girls and, more specifically, girls and sex education. She sees the Samoan girls' knowledge of sex and reproduction as inappropriate based on their comparative ignorance of what are for her more important social structures (1963:109). From the Samoan girl's negotiation of remaining a good marriage option without marrying yet, Mead produces a commentary on America, depicting girls' and women's sexuality as a long narrative in which "the dating game" (1967:284–90) has obscured women's natural goal of pregnancy. Part of the popularity of her work relies on this address to the West and on the exotic distance between these "primitive" girls and late modern girlhood. Mead claims the plight of the twentieth-century girl rests on the "American theory of endless possibilities": "Moving picture, magazine, newspaper, all reiterate the Cinderella story in one form or another, and often the interest lies as much in the way cash girl 456 becomes head buyer as in her subsequent nuptials with the owner of the store" (1963:188). For Mead, girls' opportunities are magnified by Western popular culture, while modernization has actually resulted in the narrowing of their opportunities.

Both Freud and Mead prioritized the significance, and even the representativeness, of young women as subjects for social analysis. They looked at young women to see what continued in a culture and used them as focuses for studying problems with identity formation and cultural negotiation. In girls and young women processes of cultural belonging and cultural misfit were seen to be drawn out over a number of years, and girls' problems identifying with and settling into their social roles were seen as representative of psychosocial demands more generally. Freud's analyses and Mead's ethnography also deployed girls as data to discuss society—and therapy for the current ills of Western culture—rather than girls themselves. Girls were generally presented as subsumable into a model of subjectivity for which men were the norm and girls were, inevitably, not.

Ethnographic method has been subject to heated debate concerning how can one know or speak of another culture, given that the perspective of an analyst shapes the analysis:

> Ideally, ethnographers were to get close to members, participate in some of their activities, gain their trust and confidence and discover their subjective perspectives and interpretations. At the same time they were to keep themselves firmly anchored in the scientific conceptual framework so that they could analyze the observations and accounts they were gathering from a detached, objective vantage. (Adler 10)[32]

Anthropologists questioning how ethnography should be done tend to prioritize some relations between the analyst and the object culture over others. Elizabeth Bird, noting that anthropologists "tend to sneer at the communications researcher who carries out a dozen long interviews or lives in a community for a few weeks," contends that

> the methodological issues faced by "real" anthropologists are not necessarily so very different from those grappled with by communication researchers who are trying to reach an ethnographic, experientially-based understanding of reception processes, particularly when gender is a key factor. Anthropologists have learned that many years of living with a culture does not necessarily ensure understanding or communication. (25)

Bird calls instead for an ethnography that is responsive and collaborative. Hers is a postmodern critique of ethnography, claiming that it produces constructions rather than descriptions of the world, and that discourses mediate experience at every stage of the ethnographic encounter.[33]

If feminine adolescence is not simply a representation of girls or a discourse on girls, does it have to come back to experience? The problem of experience, which Scott addressed in historiography, is even more crucial to ethnography. As Rob Watts points out:

> Ethnographers generally do not value or seek to develop causal or explanatory theories paralleling alleged natural scientific models of research.

They lean more towards developing understandings and interpretations of meaning and symbolic systems of knowledge/belief/value. (56)

But ethnography is a search for the most complete and verifiable knowledge of an experience. Feminist social scientists tend to particularly emphasize the importance of experience but, as Scott points out, this concept is as complex and slippery as the various essentialisms it is deemed to replace (797). The experience of self sought in most ethnography of girls is shaped by a long history of such observation and other generic expectations.

Girl Talk: Feminism and Ethnography

Ethnographers have more recently turned to a model of the ethnographic encounter that stresses the role of research subjects as active participants in, rather than passive objects of, the ethnographic encounter. Feminist ethnographers have been particularly interested in this strategy, which seems compatible with a feminist ethics. Judith Stacey's article "Can There Be a Feminist Ethnography?" argues that ethnography is both inherently unequal, giving authority of interpretation to the ethnographer rather than the subject, and denies any continuity between the positions of feminist researcher and woman as respondent/subject.[34] Elizabeth Wheatley responds that "both ethnographic processes and products facilitate feminist movements" (quoted in Stacey 1994a:21). Ethnography involving girls provides another perspective on this debate because feminist researchers generally adopt separate and often explicitly authoritative positions in relation to girls.

Ethnography is often deployed by feminists to quantify how resistant to patriarchy girls are, often in order to make recommendations for their better self-definition and feminist potential. This is not, as some methodological purists would argue, caused by feminist researchers unprofessionally allowing politics to interfere with their objectivity. Every researcher's objectivity is filtered through politics. The problem instead is that while these researchers are interested in girls' experience of feminine adolescence, they also presume the primary importance of a feminist woman-subject—represented in this ethnographic encounter by the one who is investigating, discussing, or teaching the girls in question. The significance of girls to the development of ethnography might be related to the ways in which the ethnographic situation itself demands this kind of diagnostic or even correctional relation between researcher and respondent. Ethnography constructs a hierarchy where the researcher is informed and mature enough to be objective about the respondent's situations and experiences. Other methodological issues reinforce this disparity.

There is now a wide range of ethnographic and ethnomethodological research into girls, including many collections of solicited letters or other narratives of personal experience. The careful editorial framing of such collections of girls' lives generally aims to guide the reader in assessing these girls' lives according to an established model.[35] The collection of girls' feminist writing *Listen Up*, edited by Barbara Findlen, suggests some relevant questions for feminist ethnography of girls. That the girls' stories are repeatedly differentiated from a nonfeminist mainstream seems, on one hand, completely reasonable. But the selection of a particular demographic from which to solicit material—in this case readers of a feminist magazine—determines in advance a significant amount of the content that will be produced, considering the medium's established perspectives on these issues. What links *Listen Up* to more rigorously ethnographic feminist publications is its presumption that girls are by default mainstream and largely constituted by dominant cultural narratives. Understanding degrees of resistance to the mainstream is the overarching interest of feminist ethnographies of girls, and it is worth considering some influential examples in the light of this imperative to assess girls' responses in terms of resistance to patriarchal discourses.

Angela McRobbie's early interventions in cultural studies of youth involved interviewing girls who hung around subcultural scenes and a degree of limited participation in those groups. McRobbie and Garber argued, based on this research, that subcultural girls seemed to act very similarly to nonsubcultural girls and conformed to more than they varied normative models for girls' behavior.[36] Feminist social researchers since the 1980s have often discussed the erasure of pleasure from studies of mass culture, but this has not renounced oppositions between conformity and resistance or mainstream and alternative cultures. Ien Ang's *Watching Dallas* is an ethnomethodological project that discusses pleasure in popular cultural narratives as often proceeding by an "ironic identification" with the ideologies in which those narratives are invested. This way of speaking about relations to mass culture seems, however, to be less readily applied to girls. Studies of popular culture addressed to girls focus on their incorporation of a defining frame for reception or pleasure and thus represent girls as more passive in audience-text relations.

More strictly ethnographic studies of girls continue these emphases. Both Sara Thornton (1995) and Maria Pini (1997) investigate girls' participation in club and rave culture through interviews and participation, locating in Thornton's case conformity to gender norms where the girls concerned think there is resistance; and in Pini's case a perception of resistance that she thinks is meaningful despite apparent conformity to gender norms. Helen Thomas (1993) interviews girls in more traditional dance institutions, focusing on whether there are gender consistencies in their understanding of what it means to dance and be a dancer. Her discussion of what that identification requires emphasizes adoption of norms for body image, even in girls who recognize that adoption in others and distance themselves from it. These studies continue to focus on girls' conformity interpreted in terms of a preexisting model of conformity that belongs to the study rather than the girls concerned. It is unclear in these studies what the girls could have said to be seen as truly resistant, or why true resistance persists as a criterion in studies of girls when it has been abandoned in studies of other groups. McRobbie argues that discussing identities as textual or discursive identities limits ethnography and calls for studies that bring together text and lived experience: an approach that she calls "identity ethnography: an analysis of personal meanings of particular practices" (McRobbie 1992:730). However, the dominance of an opposition between conformity and resistance is not answered by ethnography, which despite its emphasis on particularity still often reproduces that opposition.

Ethnography can be therapeutic within the academic social sciences as much as within popular guidance texts; in fact with reference to girls it tends to be so. Sue Lees's *Losing Out* is addressed directly to girls, attempting to inform them about the structural inequity of current ideas of sexuality and to provide girls with tools to confront problems Lees identifies. Much feminist research into girls assesses their behaviors and opinions and prescribes improvement, even when positioning girls as in need of this guidance requires simplification of the material at hand. For example, Carrington's study of girls' graffiti concurs with a dominant definition of girls as dependent on groups (1989:98ff). But while she includes friendship groups in her discussion, they remain subsidiary to the girl as manifestation of heterosexuality. While Carrington insists that a vision of girls' lives as contained by the alternatives of "heterosexual but virginal girl always hopelessly 'in love' " and "slut" is a "bleak interpretation" and "not the whole story" (1989:98), she does not discuss evidence to the contrary and furthermore assigns to girls a failure of reflective capacities. This is also the case in Cowie and Lees's study where girls are portrayed as "articulating" contradictions they are unable to "grasp" (27), despite the authors' reflection at this point on their own ethnographic method:

> We have not systematically gathered and ordered facts about girls which we present as the object of analysis. Instead our paper is an organized collection of quotes, and so we must raise the question of what status these quotes have as data. Their use as evidence in support of arguments would not be justified if those arguments were not wholly an argument to make sense of what the girls have said. However, we at no point wish to imply that what the girls say can be taken as a simple reflection of reality or even of their experience of reality. But rather that what they say has a shared though hidden organization that structures, indeed produces those cultural meanings through which they relate to the world. Our analysis is therefore concerned with penetrating that hidden organization by placing question marks over the contradictions, the gaps and the often taken-for-granted terms which the girls commonly use. (18)[37]

Ethnography can provide fascinating material and even new perspectives on girls' relations to late modernity, but investment in this kind of ethnography produces a strange imbalance. If a girl says she buys a genre of music, goes to a club, or desires a particular kind of boyfriend, it remains unclear how this is more authentic than another person's critical analysis of those practices, unless girlhood itself locates an authoritative perspective on girls. This assumption depends both on a conception of experience and on an investment in the truth value of what are presumed to be naive or unreflective cultural positions. This presumption of naïveté and reincorporation of data within a preexisting set of values is not a failing of ethnography per se but of relations between researchers and girls as objects of research—a relation that ethnography, in explicitly relaying girls' experiences, makes more obvious. Erica Rand's analysis of Barbie in *Barbie's Queer Accessories* blends a semiotic/psychoanalytic inquiry with an ethnographic project, in all of which the feminist researcher speaks from a woman's place. While she has interviewed girls about their responses to Barbie and about their Barbie play, and uses those interviews in her discussion of how Barbie can be "queered"—played against the grain of a hegemonic image of femininity she might be seen to represent—Rand repeatedly finds women's recollection of their girlhood Barbie experiences more useful than her conversations with contemporary girls because the women are more focused on the subversion of Barbie and evidence the significance of Barbie within dominant narratives of femininity (93–148). Rand finds the data she gathers from girls too indecisive on these questions, preferring the women's answers, which address them directly. This retrospective girlhood is presented as more responsible to girlhood than anything girls themselves might say. Rand's ethnography produces a complex picture of Barbie use, but perhaps only avoids positioning Barbie play as conformist by referring to women rather than girls.

More consideration should be given to what about girls impels ethnographic research and why evaluations of agency and conformity continue to be at issue when they have been abandoned as counterproductive in studies of women. Girls have been pivotal to developing ethnographic strategies and to theorizations of conformity because it is not at all difficult for girls to be asked to reflect on themselves in a form appropriate to ethnography. In fact feminine adolescence is a set of discourses on self-monitoring—on analyzing yourself in relation to other girls to identify and verify the kind of a girl you are and your relations to dominant models for women and femininity. Girls are used to being interrogated in mild or aggressive ways as to what kind of girl they are. It is also arguable that dominant discourses on feminine adolescence are themselves ethnographic in this sense. Furthermore, like prisoners and inmates of asylums, girls have been ideal ethnographic subjects because they are often available in accessible groups for such research. Girls are not only practiced in self-reflection but also conveniently located in organizations such as schools, families, and leisure groups, sorted into ready-made demographic clusters with enough free time to talk about being girls. This captive subject group is, moreover, a site in relation to which conformity is interrogated because girls have constituted ways of defining conformity (a point I will discuss further in chapter 7). Ethnographies of girls tend to reproduce a distinction between researcher and the naïve analysand whose words are mined for a revelation they can not themselves make and that may be utilized in prescriptive analysis of their situation from positions that are not theirs. Collections of girls' voices are not what is required here, given that even when assembled and framed by other girls they do not avoid presenting the normative difficulty of feminine adolescence as a relation to the mainstream and as a cultural crisis.

6.1 Mariana Hardwick Bridal Designs (1997) *(Mariana Hardwick Designs)*

six

Becoming Bride:
Girls and Cultural Studies

One is not born, but rather becomes, a woman.

—Simone de Beauvoir, *The Second Sex*

CULTURAL STUDIES has changed the way in which girl-hood is likely to be studied and is currently the discipline most likely to take girl culture, rather than girls as individual instances of psychosocial development, as an object. This chapter will define some of the key terms now proper to cultural studies, consider how theories of youth and sex/gender have been crucial points of formation for the discipline, and provide an overview of how girls are considered within it. I will focus these maps of how cultural studies understands girls on the figure of the bride and the example of bridal culture—which is made up of a whole range of places and ways to circulate and negotiate the meanings of brides. The bride not only comprises one of the most consistently visible roles for girls in late modern culture but also exemplifies the supposedly natural field of heterosexual destiny and the psychological/philosophical terrain of love and desire.

This chapter demonstrates some of the most influential ways that the methods and theories discussed in the two previous chapters appear in contemporary academic work and the public sphere; it also problematizes the distinctiveness of cultural studies and its pre-eminence as a set of tools for studying girls. In particular I want to consider how cultural studies might

6.2 Still from *Muriel's Wedding* (1995)
(P. J. Hogan (dir.), Muriel's Wedding, © *House & Moorhouse Films Pty Ltd.)*

avoid objectivization of girls and instead deploy less hierarchical or dualist theories of identity, action, and desire. More than any of the preceding chapters this constitutes a methodological survey, evaluating tools and concepts that might be used in the analyses of girl culture in part 3.

Bridal Cultures

Culture

The contested terminology of cultural studies maps a more recent field, perhaps the one where girls seem most obviously significant. Cultural studies is thus an appropriate point to conclude a discussion of how studies of girls constitute girlhood. It is also the field in which studies of girls particularly address their relations to popular culture and cultural theory. This chapter will survey definitions of "mass culture," "popular culture," and "public culture," "distinction," "everyday life," and "identity politics" in terms of how they have approached girls, but any such overview must begin with the term "culture." "Culture" at the beginning of the twentieth century was usually defined as what was "good for" people and distinguished by what critics such as Matthew Arnold and later F. R. Leavis called "great minds" (circularly, defined as someone equipped to judge what should be called culture). But late modernity, saturated by the mass production and dissemination of proliferating cultural forms, also required a definition of culture that was not limited to what was deemed improving, in order to engage with the increasingly complex relations between art, politics, and mass and popular culture. Culture now names all social exchanges of meaning—from newspapers to politics to shopping to art galleries. Culture is sometimes understood as derived from society, so that a culture reflects more foundational social relations (perhaps primarily economic relations, as in much Marxist theory). However, societies produce multiple cultures that cannot therefore be reduced to reflections of a given society.

Defining cultural studies takes on all the difficulty of defining its apparent object: culture. Many cultural studies practitioners draw their understanding of culture from British critic Raymond Williams, as do John Clarke et al. in their influential *Resistance Through Rituals* (1975):

> By culture we understand the shared principles of life characteristic of particular classes, groups or social milieux. Cultures are produced as groups make sense of their social existence in the course of everyday experience. . . . Since, however, this everyday world is itself problematic, culture must perforce take complex and heterogenous forms, not at all free from contradictions. (18)

Subsequently cultural studies has emphasized these contradictions, and in the 1990s John Frow and Meaghan Morris could define culture as "a contested and conflictual set of practices of representation bound up with the processes of formation and reformation of social groups" (xx). These definitions are about negotiation, emphasizing the ways culture is made and changed. Cultural studies thus names an approach to research rather than the study of everything cultural, and what constitutes the proper research practices of cultural studies is not at all clearly established. It is often defined as interdisciplinary rather than distinguished from other humanities and social science disciplines from which it draws methods and interests.

While cultural studies can not be identified with any particular object and uses many different methods, sometimes without much apparent respect for the complex histories of their emergence, some specific interests are evident. Cultural studies is consistently framed by discourses on modernization, including new technologies and processes of urbanization and industrialization, and cultural studies practices are tied to changing modes of producing cultural subjects. Cultural studies also often analyzes culture as a field of power relations, focusing on what Morris describes as "historical and social constraints" and "pressures . . . that can, and sometimes should, be changed" (1997a:50). From this perspective many practitioners insist that semiotic analysis—the analysis of signs—is not cultural studies unless it engages with a broad cultural context for the object of study and perhaps especially with the political effects of its production. From this perspective cultural studies analysis of a bridal magazine or a wedding, therefore, should not isolate the wedding from the structures that give it meaning for participants, nor can it be detached from dominant patterns that center ideas about weddings on young women.[1]

The public images, meanings, and identities associated with youth in late modern Western culture have provided an influential focus for cultural studies analysis of how society/culture works. Studies of youth culture, rather than youth psychology at a more individual level, were crucial to the early Birmingham School version of cultural studies in the 1970s, which focused on Marxist analysis of the reproduction of class and other social structures. However, this youth was generically masculine. In this context I want to emphasize a significant cultural field not usually associated with youth studies and more generally specific to girls. Romance, fashion, and beauty culture have been widely utilized to represent girls' late modern relations to social institutions and dominant cultures, and these fields intersect in the idea of the bride. As an intersection of girls and theories of girlhood in popular and public culture, bridal culture is also interesting because it does not conform to the usual parameters of youth culture within cultural studies. While it invokes normative discourses on age, development, and gender, bridal culture does not invest its participants with the modes of authenticity often ascribed to youth culture.[2]

Bridal cultures can be discerned in all patriarchal societies, but they always take highly specific cultural forms, and the permeation of bridal rituals by mass culture appears to distinguish bridal culture in the West. However, the cultural specificity of bridal culture in late modernity exceeds such a distinction between patriarchal ritual and mass commodification. The commodity-fetishism of some dowry practices in India, for example, is not straightforwardly translatable into the commodification of bridal identity apparent in Western bridal culture. Nevertheless bridal culture does provide a possible point of intersection between different cultural practices that participate in signifying girlhood as a never fully determined patriarchal territory. Bridal culture further provides a site for acknowledging the appropriations of cultural difference to various interested ends, including not only commodification but also conservative cultural fetishization.

The expansion of new mass and popular cultural industries in the twentieth century was accompanied by increasing public and intellectual commentary. Among modernist writers, in particular, this usually took the form of highly critical analyses of mass culture industries (see part 3). Cultural studies in the 1980s began to more frequently consider popular culture as enabling and sustaining rather than limiting and deluding. Such studies do not necessarily prioritize resistance among consumers of popular culture, but they often insist that popular culture is a field for the production rather than imposition of meaning. Cultural studies often distinguishes between popular culture—all cultural forms not valorized as high culture or culture very widely circulated within a given social field—and mass culture—denoting the products of large-scale cultural industries. Not all mass culture is popular (which is why television series can fail) and not all popular culture is mass culture (for example, many leisure activities). A further distinction can be made between popular/mass culture and public culture—which describes the circulation of public statements about culture/society in fields, such as the media and parliament, which are not necessarily commodified. However, culture tends not to be readily divided according to such categories. Bridal culture clearly intersects popular culture—enthusiastically embraced by large numbers of people as a significant component of their lives and pleasure; mass culture—as a nexus of diverse industries and mass-produced forms; and public culture—the circulation of discourses on family, law, majority, and consent.

Bridal culture is thus not confined to products that are sold to brides, although this is still the most visible, and most derided, form of bridal culture. Since bridal culture took on its current forms in the early twentieth century it has been used to exemplify the superficiality of modern women's values and activities. Bridal culture is criticized for commercializing and devaluing a crucial social institution (marriage) and a fundamental human experience (love), as well as for limiting the desires and opportunities of girls. One of the most visible forms of bridal culture is the bridal magazine, which provides a cross section of many elements of contemporary Western bridal culture. Special bridal features in women's magazines coalesced out of the twin patriarchal narratives of family portraiture and the social pages.[3] The bridal magazine sells not to brides but brides-to-be, a presumed audience of heterosexual single women who are predominantly young and engaged. Not all brides are young, but the glamour of youth is invoked in the bridal look, and the bride always functions as a mode of development, requiring that bridal magazines be both fashion magazine and guidance manual. The bride of this genre is a public ideal regularly transformed by changes to the mass media and social norms as much as by fashion.

Each bridal magazine enumerates traditions and their possible variations in the wedding planner and its attendant infomercials. Bridal culture is always regional because sales are made locally even when employing a global cachet. But even at this level of sales and industries bridal culture is never simply about mass distribution of commodities. What bridal magazines sell is not wedding dresses, dinner sets, or any other commodity so much as popular discourses on the public roles of girls. The Australian film *Muriel's Wedding* (see fig. 6.1) provides an excellent opportunity to think about how selling and consuming the bride forms narratives about cultural and personal identity. The film focuses on Muriel's desperate desire to be a bride but also explores this narrative through representations of Australianness.[4] While *Muriel's Wedding* was internationally successful, it is unclear how this evident regionalism works in overseas consumption. The film does not fetishize Australianness—there are no kangaroos, koalas, or shots of Sydney Harbor—but its comedic elements often rely on the local color of exaggerated costume design, set decoration, and other elements of mis-en-scène.

Muriel's Wedding's images of Australianness resemble a themed wedding, and they make sense in various cultural contexts because the film is about weddings and, more specifically, wanting to be a bride. Muriel wants to be a bride because her life is dismal, and she knows it—she wants to escape. But Tanya, Cheryl, and Muriel's other peers in Porpoise Spit want to be brides because their life is dismal and they do not know it. A similar public figure of the bride organized according to her class can be found in the United States, where Muriel and her friends might look like white trash and their wedding dreams would equally never bring about the wedding of the bridal magazine. From inside these working-class weddings the bride looks like an escape, from outside they look like stagnating repetitions. *Muriel's Wedding* ultimately claims the wedding is no way out of Muriel's life, and while the film feels for Muriel's bridal passion it finally presents a criticism of the bride and bridal culture.

The bride constitutes the desirable end point of becoming a woman across a range of popular and theoretical discourses on feminine adolescence. Becoming a bride—or its equivalent image in debutantes, dates, and graduations—is constructed as the moment of the girl's public appearance. While various rites of passage that used to be exclusive to boys now also apply to girls, there are still few moments when becoming a woman is celebrated. If the bride is an ideal member of an ideal desiring public for popular culture industries, she nevertheless also constitutes a validation of feminine adolescence not elsewhere available to girls. In bridal culture addressed to girls—in popular film, soap operas, or bridal or girls magazines—the bride summarizes and erases but also idealizes and validates feminine adolescence. The bride can be read as a psychological proposition—a scene or object of desire or identity production—but the bride is better discussed as a cultural complex. Becoming a bride celebrates the girl's desire and potential through an everyday figure of transformation that always remains on the unfinished side of becoming a woman. As framed in social and psychological theory, the bride is both the completion of feminine psychology and proof of the masculine Subject's development (by recognizing his maturity and independence). The bride is also understood as an object of exchange moving between families as a sign of socioeconomic correspondence—a commodity. The bride is thus an ideal that undermines the significance of other ways of being a girl or becoming a woman, but it is important to recognize that the bride also refers to the desires and pleasures of girls. Girls are taught to be, and to want to be, the bride, but they also take substantial pleasures from that performance. The bride may have ideological forms and effects, but she does actually produce desire and transformation for girls.[5]

Everyday Life: Before and After the Bride

The ordinary culture studied by cultural studies covers a wide range of discourses and practices not confined to popular culture. Under the heading of everyday life, cultural studies focuses on the routine negotiation of identities and cultural locations, including familial, work, and lifestyle patterns, the occupation of social spaces, and language use. The analysis of everyday life is not confined to the analysis of consumption practices, although it can consider these. Michel de Certeau specifies the everyday as the "cultural activity of the non-producers of culture, an activity that is unsigned, unreadable and unsymbolized" (1984:xviii). The humanities and social science disciplines on which Certeau draws assume that all analysis proceeds from a position that, though rarely phrased as neutral, is at least practically more objective than everyday life. This claim to objectivity has not been relegated to the anthropological antecedents of cultural studies that continue to speak of culture through the examination of an "Other" culture.[6] Studying the everyday life of your own or a familiar culture is not that classic anthropological situation where you seek to understand the basic tenets of a culture, but analyses of everyday life observe fields to which the observer belongs only tangentially if at all, and the analysis of everyday life is not itself everyday.

Cultural studies' insistence that culture can be practiced with a degree of knowledge about ideological context does not overturn a fundamental distinction between what is organized as cultural production and what is not. Certeau's *The Practice of Everyday Life* seeks to make "everyday practices, 'ways of operating' or doing things, no longer appear as merely the obscure background of social activity" (1984:xi).[7] Going to a movie, reading a novel, or playing music are popularly recognized as cultural, while the everyday is the practice of culture, such as the wedding, which does not reflect on its relations to production. Some cultural practices are both popular culture and part of the everyday. Television, for example, can be discussed as popular culture, but it fits within people's lives as a pervasive and interactive presence in everyday life. Public culture is also engaged by people in the process of making meaning of the world under the rubric of the everyday. The everyday cuts across popular, mass, high and public culture, and forms of cultural practice unorganized by established divisions of cultural activity according to economic production—and in all these senses brides are everyday. Everyday life for Certeau is the set of tactics and technologies by which the self is constituted as a subject of culture, and bridal culture clearly comprises such a field—and if it is not one Certeau would study, it also conveys the psychological impact he focused on in studies of dying or walking.

The bride is the act of marrying; she is not a bride before or after marriage. She is a moment: the day, the movement down the aisle, the vow, the dress. But she also moves between social placements, a major relocation in a lifelong training for heterosexual desire that especially emphasizes adolescence. In this sense, feminine adolescence is a crescendo of value climaxing at the bridal moment, or else a banal expanse punctuated by bridal moments (first date, first kiss, engagement, wedding). The bride is thus central to dominant discourses on feminine desire, predicated on a woman's impossible but ideal passivity, which disavow the bride's mobility by constructing her as waiting for love. Even though weddings seem to necessarily finish the process of becoming a bride, the bridal moment is never simply in the past or the future, as both remarriages and the crucial role of wedding photography evidences. Morris has argued that

> Muriel is really on an adventure, but she sees herself in a "fairy-tale romance"—complete with wedding, confetti, and sporting-hero husband. However, her romantic object is not the man she marries. Muriel desperately desires a white dress, flashing cameras, and the admiring looks of friends; she wants to become a wedding photo in a glossy magazine. (1996:399)

The bride is both everyday and extraordinary—a symbolic pinnacle that disrupts an everyday life, including narratives of romantic love, which it in turn helps determine as everyday.

The bride is not a linear development, but she is popularly understood that way as a normative marker in a girl's expected life cycle. *Muriel's Wedding* provides a case study for the place of the wedding in everyday life. Development is a principle narrative of *Muriel's Wedding*—development of the town, the region, and of the Hesslops. Indeed, Bill Hesslop's growing up shadows Muriel's throughout the film and they jointly place the narrative as an allegory for Australia. P. J. Hogan reportedly tells the following story about the development of *Muriel's Wedding*:

> Day after day I sat there [in a café] feeling like I would always be unemployed, and nobody would ever make any of my films. I just happened to keep noticing this bridal-wear shop across the street, and girls would go in there and I could see them trying on bridal wear and they would be transformed into brides. "It was amazing. I was struck by how much just putting on those dresses and veils gave them a sense of realising their fantasies, and there I was sitting around wanting to be transformed into something myself, a working film maker. I got this idea that being invited to become

a bride was also being invited to go to the bridal-wear shop as if it was an exclusive club—not just a place anyone would walk into. You had to be chosen, you had to have a fiance." (Stack 39)

The bridal salon (see fig. 6.1) is a stage for the total makeover into a glamour doll or princess. It is a space of recognition, although it frames the bride-to-be as a star rather than a child. But Hogan's bridal story of the film is not meant to address what brides become. It encompasses a becoming of Australian culture through opposition to a popular mainstream represented by bridal culture:

> Hogan said that Australian films are undergoing a new wave, and he's pleased that "Muriel's Wedding" has been talked about as being on the cutting edge. "We've finally put behind us our obsession with our colonial past and now, with 'Strictly Ballroom' and 'Muriel's Wedding,' we are taking a good look at what we are today. It's rather daring for Australians to look at themselves in the mirror—it's a sign that we've grown up." (Stack 39)

Distinction: Choosing a Wedding

The second part of *Muriel's Wedding*, captioned "Sydney: City of Brides," moves Muriel to the sophisticated urban opposite to the rest of Australia—Sydney, site of escape, fall, and maturity. Sydney provides Muriel with a makeover, a job, a date, a new name. She reappears on the other side of her transformation playing tapes of Princess Diana's wedding as she will later play tapes of her own. After her first salon experience, on the shards of glass and showered beanbag beads (like crystal and confetti) marking the transformations of her first date and Rhonda's illness, Mariel begins her collection of bridal selves in a photograph album. Bridal culture positions the bride as always such a performance, and developmental models in which the bride circumscribes all horizons for feminine adolescence might yet involve what Luce Irigaray calls "mimicry" or Judith Butler refers to as citing the law "differently":

> What is "forced" by the symbolic, then, is a citation of its law that re-iterates and consolidates the ruse of its own force. What would it mean to "cite" the law to produce it differently, to "cite" the law in order to

reiterate and co-opt its power, to expose the heterosexual matrix and to displace the effect of its necessity? (1993:15)

Applying this theory of citation to bridal culture would not rely on subversion but on the relations between brides and bridal norms. Brides do not copy the bride (that's impossible), or simply perform their own co-option into patriarchal systems of oppression. Rather, the bride cites the laws of marriage and the wedding, including the possibility of performing them incorrectly or not at all.[8] The bridal ideal is not any internalized ideal self but a performance moving across the surface of its own recording. The wedding is a carnival, but any transgression involved is, like the bride's empowerment, strictly limited. The bridal performance does not simply replay patriarchal structures, but this is not clearly transgressive so much as a negotiation and celebration of such boundaries.

As *Muriel's Wedding*'s use of Australia suggests, Western weddings blend local culture (including family cultures) and global bridal culture, a process represented in films, television, magazines, and shopping cultures. Because they make statements about cultural continuity and cultural change, weddings, brides, and bridal culture are ways of talking about the place of any particular wedding in history. Through deployments of taste they also position girls, families, and couples in a range of social structures, including class, ethnicity, wealth, and education. Bridal culture shares knowledge about brides or weddings, mediated by a responsibility to articulate the position of that wedding in a broader social context. Bridal culture suggests what French sociologist Pierre Bourdieu describes as the construction of "taste" in his famous study, *Distinction*. "Distinction" is the means by which the everyday and the cultural are organized. Bourdieu analyzes how cultural consumption determines and sustains cultural placement and flows from the arrangement of economic production, focusing on the different tastes of people from different social groups and how they understand their own preferences:

> The field of production, which clearly could not function if it could not count on already existing tastes, more or less strong propensities to consume more or less clearly defined goods, enables taste to be realized by offering it, at each moment, the universe of cultural goods as a system of stylistic possibles from which it can select the system of stylistic features constituting a life-style. (1986:203)

Bourdieu, however, also argues that

> every change in tastes resulting from a transformation of the conditions of existence and of the corresponding dispositions will tend to induce, directly or indirectly, a transformation of the field of production, by favouring the success, within the struggle constituting the field, of the producers best able to produce the needs corresponding to the new dispositions. (1986:231)

Bourdieu distinguishes between economic capital—wealth and the "ownership of the means of production"—and "cultural capital," which means both "status" in the classic sociological sense and practices of consumption, "lifestyle," and other modes of self-expression.[9]

The style of a wedding or bride—size, expense, time, venue, ceremony, clothes, decorations, and other contents—makes statements about the wedding's position in relation to such forms of capital inflected by various cultural identifications. While the contents of the weddings in magazines such as *Italian Bride* and *Modern Bride* might differ only slightly, those differences are not necessarily less important than the substantial differences between such magazine ideals and the backyard wedding that opens *Muriel's Wedding*. Features in a bridal magazine always produce claims about the sociocultural positions of its presumed audience, not by reflecting the weddings they do or will have but by reflecting the weddings they are presumed to desire. Variations to accommodate cultural placement are evident in these ideal weddings as well as in everyday wedding practices. Statements about cultural allegiance often appear in the wedding reception, which combines the all too locally inflected ingredients of family and food. But statements about cultural position are also made in more structured variations of religious or secular form and bridal tradition.

Bourdieu's surveys of how people understand their own taste posit diverse cultural texts and evaluations as mediating self-perceptions and materializing social relations. This is not, however, a flexible system in which an individual stylistic preference will alter social contexts or even meanings. Bourdieu stresses that economic capital substantially determines cultural capital.[10] Wealth can be used to provide, for example, more advanced or exclusive education that bears its own cultural capital and educates subjects in structures of distinction that further privilege their access to appropriate regimes of taste, such as those missing from the Porpoise Spit worldview.

Bourdieu nevertheless emphasizes that taste is a process of negotiation. Taste in cultural products (whether a girl prefers a dress with veil and train, for example) is realizable because of shared discourses on what that preference means. This pattern of reproducing social structures through taste mediated by structured interventions such as education is compromised by the fact that a girl's status and taste is not devolved primarily from those structures. Not only will the wedding intersect the tastes of different parties, it is also an artificial construction of social positions, in which the bride can elect to perform tastes she does not share.

The wedding as expression of taste negotiates a social field that is both contingent—changing over time and between contexts—and personalized—manifest in its location in individuals. But a more or less shared ground enables the meanings produced by individuals and groups. This context remains external to individuals—a ground for cultural participation that Bourdieu calls "habitus": habitus is a condition—"a sense of one's place" and, simultaneously, "a sense of the other's place" (Bourdieu and Wacquant 131). Habitus is relative, a social location and "socialized subjectivity" apprehended by the self and influenced by all an individual's experiences (1990:91).[11] Habitus involves the entire complex of a subject's location and, while privileging some fields (e.g., class or race) over others, may also come into conflict with those fields. Muriel's shift in knowing/being in the world is a change in habitus. Muriel's becoming Mariel results from conflicts that impact on her relation to the bridal ideal and to her place in the social fields through which she moves. While various regimes of capital place Muriel in ways that are coded into her own habitus, habitus can nevertheless be changed or challenged.

There is no substitute for and no getting back to the wedding day—except, of course, that it is eminently repeatable, and if it produces something not quite ideal this has nothing to do with second weddings. No wedding equals the wedding of the bridal magazine, which is *the* wedding of *the* bride. Bridal culture employs the tradition in which it participates—the history of images of brides, weddings, romantic love, and marriage—as a territory where the bride appears and through which she moves. Knowing that the traditional bride is entirely fictional does not make her any less influential as an image. Stylized transgressions such as getting married on a beach or basketball court are part of being a modern bride. The multiplicity of bridal culture is not about such variations in taste or style but devolves on the fact that the bride is not an individual but a movement. Brides routinely attempt to transform the meaning of their social context and the tastes it requires and recognizes. Nevertheless, weddings remain social rituals marking continuity across generations and between families, as well as occasions for marking what matters within a culture. Mariel's wedding ceremony is both traditional and trashy, signified by the move from "Ave Maria" into "I do I do," a variation on the ceremony that the amazed congregation suggests exceeds the acceptable variations of bridal culture. This scene insists that an expensive wedding can transform any girl, but its ironic inflections also point to the gap between ideal and individual weddings.

Cultural studies analyses of bridal culture might produce textual readings, as I am doing with *Muriel's Wedding*. It also might survey the responses of brides-to-be, past brides, and/or producers of bridal culture through ethnographic or ethnomethodological studies. It is even likely to combine some of these approaches in a given study, usually framed by a critical analytic imperative. Cultural studies has absorbed this conjunction of elements and is also likely to frame such analysis with a critique of the event's foundational structures. Cultural studies very often uses poststructuralist theory and philosophy to engage with the various significances of ordinary cultural practices. My reading of *Muriel's Wedding* here, for example, is less meticulous formal analysis and much less statistical analysis than a deployment of this film as a focus for a range of critical perspectives on girls' experiences of bridal culture. The most likely criticism of such a focus is that it does not account for how girls experience bridal culture and thus cannot act on or elucidate any person or group's experience.

Identity Politics: Feminist Cultural Studies

The bride is not only a role in popular and public culture, then, but also a recognized identity, a certain kind of person (despite so many variations). The conditions for bridehood appear to be that she is a girl/woman, heterosexual, and single (unmarried).[12] Actual figures for marriage are not as important here as the fact that the bride is transforming her social status. She is not a child—as indicated by the age of consent—but not necessarily a woman, as the age for consent to marriage is not necessarily equivalent to the age of majority. There is an implied equivalence between becoming a woman and marriage but not one between maturity and becoming a bride. The rituals by which the bride is exchanged between families symbolically reinforce this distinction between capacity to consent to marriage and legal majority. The bride is a girl because, regardless of age, she articulates transformative processes of adolescence, including negotiation of sex/gender and maturity. The bride is a specific value credited to a girl who marries, although it is possible to marry without being named as a bride. Who becomes a bride and why are questions feminists seem compelled to ask. But while it seems feminists would be particularly interested in bridal culture, they more or less explicitly position participation in bridal culture as a form of co-option or delusion. While the power deployed in the bride's consent is certainly limited, it does not follow that the wedding separates girls from some power they would have had otherwise. Representing the bride as terminating a girl's possibilities accepts that marriage delimits girls. Even when romance could be reclaimed as a pragmatically important field of pleasure for women, feminists have remained dubious about bridal culture—when they addressed it all. This may be partly because, while romance can be figured as personal pleasure, the bride is a public role, but understanding the bride as deluded is exacerbated by the presumed distance between feminists and girls.

Feminist analysis has always focused on institutions that affect women, but it has also focused on the impact of cultural forms, locations, and industries. Feminist interest in the impact of late modern life on women meant that feminists were always interested in popular culture and everyday life. Analysis of popular culture particularly interested second wave feminism, including such pivotal texts as Betty Friedan's *The Feminine Mystique* (1963).[13] Many texts that helped form second wave feminism, influenced by the renovation of social analysis after psychoanalysis, focused on the not necessarily conscious repetition of social norms. Such feminist texts on self-realization and cultural analysis produced important frameworks for feminist cultural studies, realizing new ways for talking about sex/gender in public and popular culture. These analyses focused on gender distinctions mapped onto a distinction between private and public domains. In these studies, gender was an interpretation of cultural consensus concerning women and popular culture seemed to function as verification of that consensus. Popular culture has also been seen to reinforce the naturalization of a social structure in which men have access to both private and public domains and have authority in public discourses that were held to be important and historical. By comparison women were seen to have access mainly to the private domain, given authority in the realm of the human rather than the historical, the personal rather than the social. Popular culture traverses this distinction between public and private and has been a privileged focus for analysis interested in transforming patriarchal society. Feminist cultural studies has been especially interested in reclaiming popular culture directed at women from the scrap heap of mass culture, focusing on genres that provide pervasive discourses on femininity for women—such as soap operas, romance novels, and "women's films."

Since the institutionalization of cultural studies as an academic discipline, feminist cultural analysts have often claimed that earlier criticism of patriarchal ideologies in cultural fields did not account for the forms of pleasure women might take from them.[14] However, earlier feminists such as Friedan actually found women to be ambivalent about such ideological forms and did not just ignore women's pleasure in them even if they saw that pleasure as false consciousness. Nevertheless, feminist cultural studies did introduce new ways of speaking about women, culture, and pleasure. There has been a longstanding association between women and low or popular culture, and women and a kind of fanship or spectator position inclined to be, according to these analyses, conservative, passive, and malleable, as well as histrionic, excessive, and distracted. Feminists have criticized the association of women with such attributes by criticizing these supposedly lower cultural forms or, increasingly, by arguing that they were not necessarily conservative, passive, malleable, histrionic, or distracted, or at least did not preclude other possibilities.

The expansion of feminist cultural studies added gender to established patterns of analyzing class, consumption, and cultural production. Emphasis on class and the economics of cultural production has been displaced in feminist cultural studies, according to some commentators, by "a focus on reproduction, on consumption, and on the problematic of femininity" (Shiach 335). Analyses of women as productive participants in consumption as audiences and consumer groups became the dominant mode of feminist analysis of popular culture in the 1990s. Following the work of critics such as Janice Radway (1984), Tania Modleski (1982) and Angela McRobbie, feminist cultural studies focused on the production of women in and as culture through a focus on representations of and for women. This increased investment in analyzing what women want and what makes them want it has also been applied to girls, although framed by some disinterest in girls and girl culture themselves. Neither patriarchal narratives nor popular culture are indiscriminate as to age, but feminist cultural studies has presumed a subject position occupied by women of an unspecified but implicitly adult age. And yet the actual objects of feminist cultural analysis often focus on gender formation and other transitions associated with girls and adolescence, and even on fields that equally if not preeminently address girls (such as romance narratives and pop music respectively).

The model of desire, pleasure, and identification that feminist cultural studies takes from psychoanalysis positions girls as the exemplary object of patriarchal desire and exemplary instance of those forms of identification that epitomize the passivity and malleability more generally attributed to women. The bride can be understood in both these ways. However, the desire to be the bride that looks at the bride is not a desiring gaze defined by this standard heteropatriarchal narrative, and perhaps contains no narrative of sexualized possession at all. The bride is not possessed by anyone, unless by herself. For the bride, the distinction between self-validating object-love and the value that accrues to the love object is inapplicable (see Freud 1953, 14:67–104). The bride is her own ideal and love object, and any groom (the one who loves me) is a means to this idealization. While heterosexual courtship constructs her as a masculine suitor's ego ideal, the wedding consummates a love relation between the girl and the bride. While the psychoanalytic version of psychology offers many useful concepts to feminist analysis of relations between subjects and cultural fields, it also limits how those relations are perceived and articulated.

The bride is not only an individual (psychology), if she is that at all. The bride is a position that can be occupied by individuals—the object of a public gaze, a spectacle of momentary independence, desiring herself and her own elaboration in the bridal ideal. The bride is a romantic mannequin and a fashionable fairy-tale princess, but these forms of pleasure are shared and public even when they appear most personal, as in the case of Muriel and her wedding dresses. The wedding dress (see fig. 6.1) is a continual pose—a tool or machine—as well as such a subject position. Like any fashion item, wedding dresses suggest an ideal body specific as to gender, age range, and norms of facial beauty and body type. But they shape an ideal also in being staged. The dresses are not practical, and the less practical or reusable they are the more they signify both investment in the wedding and the exclusivity of the moment. All of this recurs in an array of narrative scenes and advertisements centered on the wedding dress—and it is relevant here that the fashion catwalk resembles nothing more than an aisle and the bridal procession. Wedding dress ads are clearly unrealistic, not least because the bride will not move exclusively against solid color backgrounds and in lighting designed to highlight her dress—but she will try to. The dress ideally poses the bride as center of attention as its most valued effect, centering the ceremony, the reception, and the memory-fantasy of wedding photographs. This kind of commentary on how a bride works is only a simplification of how girls get married to the same degree that bridal culture performs that simplification. The frame of the bridal photograph elides class narratives, regional narratives, and even familial narratives, as no actual wedding can. The traditional scenarios for wedding photographs repeated in bridal magazines construct this decontextualization as part of what it means to be a bride—the bride is a position taken up by a girl as the process of her own production.

While "identity" might apply to a very extensive range of characteristics—anything that particularizes a person—it tends to be applied to terms that can be made to claim an essential presence and thus function as a political foundation. Terms that are linked to identity include sex/gender, race, sexuality, ethnicity, or class positions, rather than regional location, employment, marital status, or age groups, all of which are perceived as more changeable. Slavoj Žižek and Judith Butler, among others, have suggested that such identity categories might be especially amenable to globalized commodity forms of capitalism and politics.[15] Given that it is not a term behind which people rally, can "girl" be understood in anything like the same way? Identity politics for youth are particularly difficult to maintain given youth's role as identity in flux. The bride is fixed by required attributes, such as gender and sexuality, but her transience means she is not a site for identity politics. Less symbolic girl roles, such as daughter or student, also do not provide the necessary foundations for identity politics. Feminist identity politics requires a degree of certainty attached to Woman, even if only in a pragmatic sense, and brides are not centered on the defining characteristics of womanhood. The apparent sense of this distinction is undermined by the realization that "girl" is not available as an identity precisely because of the primary essentializing power of Woman. Critiques of feminist identity politics are not concerned with feminist agendas (as is postfeminism) or feminist definitions of woman per se (as is the postcolonial critique), but with the idea that politics and identities are linked together in such a way that having a given identity demands a certain politics. This critique understands identity politics to include assertions of rights along lines of specificity or difference that support a unitary model of being. The problem with identity politics is not whether or how it resists, but its reliance on the primacy of a particular normative subject and thus its exclusion of other possible points or intersections of political engagement.

The bride is not a static object but a deployment or apparatus that can produce very different effects when engaged or cited in different contexts, which is why these alternative bridal moments can work as part of Muriel's engagement with bridal culture. Foucault used the term *"dispositif"* (translated as apparatus or deployment) to describe the combination of a discourse and a set of practices and institutions. The deployment/apparatus of bridal culture involves relations between discourses and specific institutions (law, family) or practices and their effects. Even when directly considering scenes or instances of oppression Foucault insists on the significance of asking how, not why, some thing or force appears. To take a contentious example from the diverse cultures of bridal practices, resistance to "female genital mutilation" cannot avoid essentialism when analyzing why such practices exist, or claiming such things should simply not be done to girls (a rejection of the presumed "why").[16] Paradoxically, giving up the identity-based rights discourse that says girls must be protected from such treatment allows resistance to clitoridectomy and related practices to be dissociated from the reasons why Western feminists should not intervene in the practices of other cultures. Instead the ethical question of how such practices are pursued and sustained means it does not matter why they are done. Any appeal to why will always teleologically summon insistence of culturally specific reasons and cultural rights, will only ever refer back to the cultural system that supports that practice. Asking how the practice takes effect instead addresses the ways girls come to participate in that cultural nexus. Analyzing the conditions that make clitoridectomy possible, including dominant ideas about feminine sexual development that rely on specific understandings of puberty, sex, and marriage, allows possible points of intervention in those practices.

A survey or other analysis of bridal experience or a textual analysis of representation of or within bridal culture could equally well ask how bridal culture works, so long as neither is detached from social/cultural histories and the discourses and institutions that make participation in bridal culture possible. Clitoridectomy is a marriage practice that indicates that while bridal culture does not have to be about power and pleasure for girls, it always addresses the need for and provides mechanisms for girls' validation within their specific cultural contexts. Other bridal cultural traditions such as sati (bride burning, a form of dowry death) and dowry systems also seem to more blatantly exploit girls from a Western feminist point of view than our own bridal practices.[17] These practices all locate a nexus of sexuality and gender in bridal culture as a site for articulating the normative process of defining desirable womanhood, a process that can maintain symbolic force even when contradicted by other cultural changes.[18] Bridal culture can also cross more fixed cultural boundaries, such as nation-states, in for example the international marketing of bridal culture or the irony or theatricality with which bridal narratives can be consumed as or against cultural traditions.

Analyzing bridal culture as a discourse—as a way of speaking about and knowing the world—would include observing the interactions between brides and bridal culture, including the social structures that make it possible and the cultural products by which it circulates. Bridal culture is part of a discursive complex centering on the family, love, sex, and girlhood. Paying attention to what makes weddings possible and the contexts in which they have meaning, we could note that while there are only two weddings in *Muriel's Wedding* there are other bridal moments without the social recognition required of a wedding. *Muriel's Wedding* manages to avoid simply condemning bridal culture by acknowledging these bridal moments. For example, Rhonda was always the key to Muriel's transformation, which begins with their meeting at a honeymoon resort. Muriel's move to Sydney might also be seen as a honeymoon (complete with name change). But Muriel's wedding (the only one Muriel has) would thus be the Waterloo dance routine with Rhonda, where they are both brides in white satin (complete with battling bridesmaids). The film could have had a traditional romantic closure to complete its white-wedding trajectory. This possibility is emphasized by the honeymoon-night elements of the last scene between Muriel and David: the beach resort scene outside the hotel window, the soundtrack of wedding music, the first (apparently Muriel's first) sexual intercourse. But this moment and possibility disappears. While neither David nor Muriel's perspectives are taken in this "love scene," the following scene places the viewer with Muriel as she leaves (using her maiden name) to keep her vows to Rhonda rather than David. And yet the couple riding off to the horizon—the bridal momentum—continues to be the proper ending for a girl.[19]

Muriel's Wedding is a critical account of girls' relations to bridal culture, but it is so by recognizing the force of Muriel's attraction to the bridal ideal. While critics often see the girls in *Muriel's Wedding* as extravagantly conformist and uncritical, the film's representation of bridal culture as central to ideas of becoming a woman means their relations to it are completely comprehensible. *Muriel's Wedding* demonstrates that girls buy becomings every day, including through bridal culture, and that girls (like brides) are images of transformation. The too easy dismissal of brides as conformist, ideological, or unreflective denies the public and personal significance of bridal moments within a culturally specific feminine adolescence and ignores the bride's representation of girls' significance within those cultures.

Becoming: The Girl Question from de Beauvoir to Deleuze
Desiring Machines: Deleuze and Girls

Cultural studies is not necessarily the only productive way to discuss the complexity of bridal culture and the bridal trajectory. Its reliance on structures inherited from earlier disciplines can limit its analyses of practices and forms. The primacy of the unconscious in cultural studies analysis of cultural practices and the related psychologization of its objects; a tendency to position the objects of its analysis as outside and even Other than itself; and other dichotomies based in a fundamental epistemological opposition between subject and object keep cultural studies firmly within a modern narrative about what can be known and how it can be known. Cultural studies tends to read girls through such major binary distinctions as popular/mass or high culture and mature or immature identities, employing tools such as ideology and identification that reinforce them. While some excellent cultural studies work is done on objects not often considered in other fields, insufficient attention continues to be paid to the practical multiplicity and activity of culture. Thus recourse to theory and philosophy in cultural studies work is not just an attempt to justify objects often not considered serious but can also be used to problematize the presumed simplicity of those objects and strategies appropriate to their analysis.

Gilles Deleuze's poststructuralist philosophy, according to Foucault, makes thinking possible after the epistemological shift which killed the Subject (Foucault 1984b:165). In this section I want to refer my discussion of bridal culture to Deleuze and Felix Guattari's particular association of "becoming," as antihierarchical desiring production, with girls. Various feminist critics, notably Alice Jardine, Elizabeth Grosz, and Rosi Braidotti, have argued that Deleuze's deployment of "becoming-woman" as a positive departure from established hierarchies remains problematic for feminism because of both the absence and the presence of gender in Deleuze's work.[20] Feminists have objected that Deleuze and Guattari's concept of becoming-woman is a feminization that takes the specificity of woman away from women. They at times use the terms "woman" and "man" to refer to anatomical bodies and at times to indicate an opposition between transcendental Subjectivity and an embodiment identified with women. Moreover, this becoming-woman is only a stage in a chain of becomings that seems to suggest a fixed linear path the course of which makes woman redundant. The critique of subjectification in which becoming-woman is employed also problematizes concepts such as woman's identity, and if the deterritorialization of women removes them from patriarchal ownership, it also avoids other, for example feminist, claims to territory. Other feminists seek to engage with these difficulties for feminists using Deleuze. Both Braidotti and Grosz desire a "selective reading and use" of Deleuze and Guattari's works, which might "manage to capture and put to work valuable methodologies, questions, insights that may lead in directions Deleuze and Guattari may not go or even may not accept" (Grosz 1994:180). But they rarely address the significance, in Deleuze's work, of the girl as an assemblage that escapes the foundational territory of the oedipalized family that feminist theory has inherited from psychoanalysis.[21]

When Deleuze interrogates psychoanalysis, he also questions feminist presumptions concerning the formation and certainty of gender, of the relation between bodies and identity, and the naturalization of desire as emanating from an individual toward an object. Deleuze criticizes these assumptions with new terminologies for desire and body that disrupt our commonsense connection of them to inner selves. Deleuze and Guattari describe the oedipalized unconscious—one in which repression has been instituted as necessary for existence—as an entirely interested invention: "the plane of the Unconscious remains a plane of transcendence guaranteeing, justifying, the existence of psychoanalysis and the necessity of its interpretations" (1987:284). Deleuze rejects this dichotomous subjectivity—the Subject and its structural antithesis, the Other; I and it—for a model of subjectivity that is mobile and connective rather than oppositional. Deleuze also rejects the centered subject of language and history as "the form under which the majority is based [. . .] white, male, adult, 'rational,' etc., in short the average European, the subject of enunciation" (Deleuze and Guattari 1987:292). Deleuze's "little girl" is an impossible figure of escape from this oedipal framework and this major language, a pivotally difficult figure for processes of constituting the subject. This girl is a radical singularity constituted in relations of power between statements and visibilities (Deleuze 1988:79).

Feminist discussion of becoming-woman tends to focus on woman but, like the "becoming a wolf" that Deleuze and Guattari turn against Freud, becoming-woman "is not a question of representation" (1987:32). They distinguish between "molar" and "molecular" versions of "woman" to articulate becoming-woman as a relation to majority that must be engaged in order to interrogate/escape that majority:

> What we term a molar entity is, for example, the woman as defined by her form, endowed with organs and functions and assigned as a subject. Becoming-woman is not imitating . . . or assuming the female form, but emitting particles that enter the relation of movement and rest, or the zone of proximity, of a microfemininity, in other words, that produce in us a molecular woman. (1987:275)

A molecular woman, on the other hand, is an agency of multiplicity—she is, as Grosz puts it, "a thousand tiny sexes" (see Grosz 1993) flowing over an unorganized body (the body without organs). The girl manifests and enacts this process. In *A Thousand Plateaus* Deleuze and Guattari contend that

> body is stolen first from the girl: Stop behaving like that, you're not a little girl anymore, you're not a tomboy, etc. The girl's becoming is stolen first, in order to impose a history or prehistory upon her. The boy's turn comes next, but it is by using the girl as an example, by pointing to the girl as the object of his desire, that an opposed organism, a dominant history is fabricated for him too. The girl is the first victim, but she must also serve as an example and a trap. That is why, conversely, the reconstruction of the Body without Organs, the anorganism of the body, is inseparable from a becoming-woman, or the production of a molecular woman. Doubtless, the girl becomes a woman in the molar or organic sense. But conversely, becoming-woman or the molecular woman is the girl herself. (1987:276)

But if the little girl is deployed in becoming-woman there is no causal connection between girl and woman:

> The girl . . . is an abstract line, or a line of flight. Thus girls do not belong to an age, group, sex, order or kingdom: they slip in everywhere, between orders, acts, ages, sexes: they produce *n* molecular sexes in the line of flight in relation to the dualism machines they cross right through. . . . The girl is like the block of becoming that remains contemporaneous to each opposable term, man, woman, child, adult. It is

not the girl who becomes woman; it is becoming-woman that produces the universal girl. (276–7)

Grosz recognizes that this narrative incorporates psychoanalytic accounts of the boy's oedipalization (1994:175), where a girl can not become Subject or Mother, and it retains the girl's role as opposing and defining the boy's development. Yet Deleuze and Guattari's *Anti-Oedipus* also describes this process as "the real production of a girl born without a mother, of a non-oedipal woman (who would not be oedipal either for herself or for others)" (1987:471–2).

This model suggests that Western philosophy's account of subjectivity, "in its effort to preserve the identity of the One, hardened the ontological difference between Being and becoming" (Boundas 5), and poses an alternative imagined in the girl's impossible relation to the Subject's origin. Becoming-woman produces an identity that is not an outcome of a process but is that process itself. The bride constitutes such an unfinished movement— a passage and a procession—that is not founded on any origin, being, or molar identity. I might argue that the bride is a transgressive figure, a figure of becoming-woman, a passage that is never accomplished, and that it is this unfinished moment of valorization that bridal culture successfully deploys. Women might thus gain an open-ended validation from the bride without being relegated to its proclaimed social consequences as Wife-Mother. But bridal culture doesn't certainly work that way and seems to necessarily contain the finalization of that movement and that possibility. It seems that the bride is a full stop on becoming. On the other side of the wedding she is gone. Still, the bridal moment is never simply in the past or the future and instead remains mobile between the disappointment, promise, and pleasure the bride offers. The concept of becoming might think about elements of bridal culture not usually raised in feminist reference to brides. Bridal culture is a mode of becoming a woman, but it also offers opportunities for becoming-woman, and an analysis of bridal culture through such becoming avoids the hierarchical dualisms that tend to be reproduced in studies of girls: subject-object, resistant-conformist, mature-immature.

Becoming-woman is a becoming-minoritarian, and as such is not opposed to masses and detached from judgments of maturity.[22] Girls form minoritarian cultures, however popular or populated: "All becoming is minoritarian. Women, regardless of their numbers, are a minority, definable as a state or subset; but they create only by making possible a becoming over which they do not have ownership, into which they themselves must enter" (Deleuze and Guattari 1987:106). In this distinction between "minorities as subsystems" and "the minoritarian as a potential, creative and created, becoming" (105–6), brides might be minoritarian despite the utility of weddings primarily because they cite rather than reproduce the bride. "People are always thinking of a majority future (when I'm grown up, when I'm in power . . .) when really the problem is one of a becoming-minority: not to act like or imitate the infant, fool, woman, animal, stutterer, or foreigner, but to become all that, in order to invent new forces or new weapons" (Deleuze quoted in Jardine 215). The bride can only attach to (cite) the majoritarian aspects of the bride, and then she must move on without ever *being* the bride. This movement is what Deleuze and Guattari elsewhere call nomadism. The nomad owns no territory, only a process of deterritorialization that *Muriel's Wedding* exemplifies—Muriel's bridal movement continues long after Mariel's wedding in productive detachments from such social machines as name, family, or wedding dress. The feminine adolescent is a nomad and her movement is a becoming, a continual process of deterritorialization and minoritization in relation to Woman.[23]

Becoming-woman draws on Deleuze's prior conception of "the little girl" in *The Logic of Sense*, where he appropriates Alice as the nonlinear series of the girl and becoming-woman. Deleuze glosses the "little girl" as "incorporeal"—a becoming detached from corporeal causes; "a way of being" (147). As Grosz points out, Deleuze utilizes "the girl as the site of a culture's most intensified disinvestments and re-castings of the body" (1994:174–5). Becoming-woman is a deterritorialization of the organized body precisely because it uses gender against that organizing signification. Gender is positioned in this theory as a territorialization shaping desire into a signifying and signifiable field. Deleuze's usefulness for feminist cultural studies might be more evident in a discussion of Barbie. Barbie is definitively organized by a variety of hierarchizing interests, including gender, but she is no organism—no interior body, no genitals, her breasts are mounds (which have no nipples), her mouth fixed (mostly closed), and her eyes fixed (mostly open)—she is a surface. Such a body without organs (BwO) retains a connection with gender, and might be referred to the material (in Marxist among other senses) and to the Lacanian "Real" understood as the impossible "lack of a lack."[24] But it is not confined to these molar theories. For Deleuze there is no lack founding subjectivity, society, or desire and his rejection of gender can paradoxically serve the interests of feminists questioning the history of representing women's sex/gender as lack.

Desire for Barbie might seem to operate on a presumption of lack—girls who lack Barbie, or a particular Barbie accessory—but Barbie herself is the embodiment of not lacking. Anything that looks like lack on Barbie is really the potential for further attachment, and what is produced on the surface of Barbie and in connections between Barbie and girls is not explicable by reference to lack.[25] Barbie is an exemplary BwO as a surface for desiring production, and in the Barbie assemblage girls do not imitate Barbie. Instead Barbie functions as a recording surface for desires and identities. Barbie might be for many an undesirable model for feminist theory, and she does not locate all women's desires; but there are interactions that produce Barbie-becoming-feminist, including the Barbie Liberation Army, although any girls playing Barbie might produce important unexpected things. Desire operates in relation to the BwO through the connective/disjunctive processes of desiring machines, which are not goal or object-directed and suggest a desire that does not emanate from an individual but is produced on the body among fluxes of "associative flows and partial objects" (Deleuze and Guattari 1977:287). The possibility that Barbie is a goal is what concerns most feminists about girls desiring Barbie. But subjectivities are produced along the many always discontinued lines constituting the surface/name Barbie: "This subject itself is not at the center, which is occupied by the machine, but on the periphery, with no fixed identity, forever decentered, defined by the states through which it passes" (Deleuze and Guattari 1977:20). Barbie does not represent girls or women but assembles feminine adolescence or the girl/woman question. Barbie makes money through images of gender conformity, but is not fully organized by the gendered surface of her body.

Becoming Woman

Cultural studies shares with feminism a difficulty reconciling the specificity of its position—situated within certain cultural locations such as the Western academy—with a focus on knowing and changing the world. In importing Deleuze to a discussion of girls and feminist analysis I risk using an authoritative theoretical voice to quash the problematization of that authority by feminists. In this last section I want to engage what I find useful about Deleuze with perhaps the most eminent feminist theorist of the twentieth century, Simone de Beauvoir. Beauvoir marks an important translation of canonical modernist philosophical, psychological, and cultural theories into feminist theory, and she has remained influential on contemporary analyses of gender, including those of girls and how they live.

As I have outlined above, Deleuze configures the little girl and becoming-woman as processes of moving away from dominant hierarchical understandings of subjectivity. Jardine argues that "for [Deleuze], only the paradox can move us into pure 'becoming' beyond the fixed sexual identities of intersubjectivity, of subject and object . . . [and] he exemplifies this process through the image of 'the little girl' " (113). The little girl, and women's relations to processes of becoming, are also crucial to Beauvoir's *The Second Sex*—much of which is concerned with how possibilities for women's becoming are constrained by the process of becoming a Woman. This seems to establish common ground between Deleuze and Beauvoir, but Beauvoir, influenced by existentialism and psychoanalysis, understands becoming a woman through hierarchical oppositions rejected by Deleuze, including subject and object, self and other. However, Jardine and others have correctly suggested that whatever Deleuze's becoming-woman might mean for those whose becoming woman is not necessarily a line of escape—that is, for women—does not inhere in the proposition "Woman." In *The Second Sex* Beauvoir also prioritizes becoming over the destination woman and sees "Woman" as an undesirably fixed identity and destination.

For Deleuze, Alice is a figure for understanding how we make and use meaning. Alice struggles with the identities offered to her—perhaps, she thinks, she's been changed for someone else (Carroll 39).[26] Deleuze thinks this destabilization of certain categories for understanding the self and its effects is highly important. Its special relevance to girlhood is evident in Alice's transitions in body, power and identity:

> All of these reversals . . . have one consequence: the contesting of Alice's personal identity and the loss of her proper name. The loss of the proper name is the adventure which is repeated throughout all Alice's adventures. . . . Paradox is initially that which destroys good sense as the only direction, but it is also that which destroys common sense as the assignation of fixed identities. (1990:3)

Alice's changes remain reversible, as becoming-queen does not foreclose on or guarantee Alice's becoming woman. Deleuze's reading of Alice insists that becoming is a paradox defined as "the affirmation of both senses or directions at the same time" (1990:1). Becoming always suggests a movement across time, but Deleuze wants to oppose becoming to standard models of development: the commonsense meaning of becoming woman is in no sense reversible, but he argues that the changes of the little girl and the processes of becoming-woman are. As antilinear, antimemory and antioedipal, Alice reiterates that a girl never becomes a woman in any univocal unidirectional sense. Feminine adolescence is not a transition from one state to another but a contingent and in some senses reversible movement.

Beauvoir's girl is shaped by an experience of herself, inflected through puberty, as shameful, fearful, and disgusting. While *The Second Sex* is decidedly more negative about the embodiment of the girl than is Deleuze, the main difference is that Deleuze does not see the girl's body as leading toward the maternal body. Beauvoir famously rejects the confinement of women to femininity and the maternal body, but positions the maternal body as foundation of the girl's existence. This contradiction is resolved in her work by a distinction between girl and woman, where the maternal body is the weighty destiny of the girl and the site of her anxious struggles but is not, because of that separation, the destiny of the woman-subject. Nevertheless Beauvoir sees the girl as locating not only women's learned submission and objectification but also the only space in which the situation of women can be changed. *The Second Sex*'s conclusion asserts that changing laws and other institutions bearing on the life of the girl, such as education and employment, are not sufficient. Reshaping the girl herself is the necessary and least visible path for women's liberation.

In this conclusion Beauvoir reiterates that man and woman are historical ideas. Deleuze is often less cautious with historical positions, and Beauvoir might suggest that the significant version of Alice for readers of *The Second Sex* is not the promising paradoxes of Carroll but the stilted if charming homilies of Walt Disney's 1951 animated film, *Alice in Wonderland*. This Alice is a foundational text in the girls' culture of the late twentieth century, crossing many of the cultural fields and founding philosophies Beauvoir records in "The Formative Years." Beauvoir points, in a way Deleuze does not, to the significance of historical differences between the little girl of the 1860s and of the postwar Western world. Her references to fashion, diaries, and peer groups, to the popular and the personal as resonant discourses both for and about girls, are highly important to a consideration of what

Alice can mean now. Beauvoir's phenomenology, rather than her existentialism, demands this attention to the parameters of a girl's lived experience:

> The young girl feels that her body is getting away from her, it is no longer the straightforward expression of her individuality; it becomes foreign to her; and at the same time she becomes for others a thing: on the street men follow her with their eyes and comment on her anatomy. She would like to be invisible; it frightens her to become flesh and show her flesh. (Beauvoir 345–50)

Beauvoir also suggests that these parameters include psychoanalysis and philosophy, among other histories and myths of capitalist patriarchy.

Beauvoir rather than Deleuze would articulate the significance of how, while Muriel becomes several kinds of daughter, sister, and girlfriend, shopgirl, cover-girl, lover, and consumer, she most particularly desires to be, and becomes, a bride. Muriel's relation to the bridal ideal is a measure of her autonomy and self-worth in precisely the way Beauvoir has mapped. She becomes Mariel (a bride) and then a new Muriel, with both autonomy and self-worth to the extent that she has rejected the bridal ideal. But this becoming is not a linear directed path toward Woman or any other finalization. Muriel's becoming, as Morris notes, is a "line of flight"—a concept that "is often treated as an escapist slogan, a signature theme of the ratty romanticism that 'Deleuze and Guattari' are taken to represent. In the ruined backyard of her family home, Muriel knows better" (1996:401). The risk involved in the lines of flight available to Muriel is not in fact co-optation or objectification, but destruction (the flight of Muriel's mother). The bride is neither subject nor object but a becoming, although not perhaps a figure of becoming that Deleuze would have cited despite his interest in girls, and perhaps for similar reasons to those that distance feminists from the bride. But however mainstream the bride looks, becoming-woman and related figures from Deleuze's antihierarchical philosophy are relevant to her. What passes for identity in Deleuze is an assemblage, a cluster producing momentary subjectivities at its edge that, "in its multiplicity, necessarily acts on semiotic flows, material flows, and social flows simultaneously" (Deleuze and Guattari 1987:22–3).

The bride encompasses a set of movements at a tangent to the oedipalized family and the model of gendered subjectivity/desire that relies upon it. For Beauvoir, the problem of gendered inequality was solved by existentialism, by the transcendence of consciousness over the gendered body. Deleuze's understanding of subjectivity does not organize the self into more or less innate binary oppositions and is thus useful for a feminist theory that would consider conjunctions of body and identity without relying on transcendence or other distinctions from the embodied self. Our assignation as sexed/gendered does not wholly constitute us, and assemblage may be a way of appropriating its collaborative formation with other positions. The questions this enables include: how productive a machine is sex/gender, and in connection to what other machines does it produce other than hierarchically? Contemporary critical theory often understands gender as oppositional and forecloses on gender's productive fluctuations and multiplicity, including the ways in which girls are not becoming women. Cultural studies, while blending different perspectives and methods, at least demands an intersection of lived subjectivity with fields of power and cultural forms and practices. In this sense cultural studies has inherited a range of phenomenological concerns. Like phenomenology, cultural studies can contribute to a study of feminine adolescence an emphasis on how girls live that does not prioritize psychologized interior experience or systematically elide the embodied processes of feminine adolescence. This feminine adolescence would never be finalized in Beauvoir's dichotomous options of Woman or Subject, and not bypassed in Deleuze's ideally reversible universal becoming, but coheres a series of events continually transforming the embodied self in which they inhere.

Part 3
Girls and
Cultural Production

Figure 7.1
Still from *Clueless* (1995)
(Amy Heckerling (dir.), Clueless,
Paramount Pictures)

Figure 7.2
Still from *Trainspotting* (1996)
(Danny Boyle (dir.), Trainspotting,
Polygram Pictures)

Part 5
Self and
Cultural Production

seven

Distraction:
Girls and Mass Culture

The Girls were artificially manufactured in the USA and exported to Europe by the dozens. Not only were they American products; at the same time they demonstrated the greatness of American production. . . . When they formed an undulating snake, they radiantly illustrated the virtues of the conveyor belt; when they tapped their feet in fast tempo, it sounded like *business, business.*

—Siegfried Kracauer, "Girls and Crisis"

THE TWENTIETH-CENTURY expansion of mass-cultural forms changed definitions of culture, and those changes and the identities wrought in relation to them have often been referred to girls and the new category of feminine adolescence. This chapter historicizes the much discussed relations between girls and mass culture through the example of youth-directed film genres and the immaturity of the film audience. It considers distinctions between youth film and teen film as different aesthetic and market registers and looks also at youth-directed horror film as perhaps offering performances of youth, teen, and girl that are less easily reduced to the oppositional structures that dominate the youth and teen labels.

This chapter also considers the fascination of cultural studies with youth culture and with ideas of rebellion, resistance, and the space of the subculture, focusing on the roles assigned to and produced by girls in relation to youth culture. Film is a highly useful example for these discussions as an influential mode of representing and producing youth culture as a site of tension between ideas of resistance and conformity. This chapter is thus also concerned with how a distinction between youth culture and girl culture might be made.

7.3 Still from *Buffy the Vampire Slayer* (2000)
(Joss Whedon (prod.), Buffy the Vampire Slayer, *Fox Television & Mutant Enemy)*

Youth Film: The Subcultural
Youth Subcultures

The idea of youth has been used to question how people come to be particular kinds of individuals and identifiable selves, how cultures surround and
define us individually and as groups, and how cultures are reproduced and
challenged by individuals and groups. Youth has been a fascinating object for
modernity—identified with an attitude to contemporaneity and change—
because of its association with the new, the future, and diverse social changes,
and provides an important focus for thinking about how societies work. Because youth has been understood as a crucial point of cultural reproduction
and cultural change it has been consistently important to cultural analysis (a

concept that is itself proper to the twentieth century). Youth is associated with specific social roles and cultural forms across the course of modernity, but before the late nineteenth century what might be termed "youth culture" was understood to dramatically vary between cultures. Part of the rise of youth culture has thus been an expansion of what we now call the globalization of culture, dramatically exemplified in the rise of the film industry. Youth studies have, however, predominantly focused on subcultures and on music cultures, and a focus on the mainstream and on film cultures might raise additional questions about relations among gender, youth, mass culture, and globalization.

Youth culture is a field of cultural production that represents, produces, and consumes the idea of adolescence as a transitional state for social relations and personal psychic development. Youth is associated with the production and consumption of particular cultural forms, and a range of relations to cultural production have come to be characterized as youthful in popular and public culture and critical theory. In particular, youth has been associated with the possibility of more or less overtly resisting the needs and imperatives of the society into which youth enters as a group of new social subjects. This chapter considers the effects of seeing youth as a time when rebellion is expected, but expected to be in most respects temporary, focusing on the construction of conformity and resistance in late modernity and the definition of youth culture by subcultural activity.

The circulation of ideas about and representations of youth occurs across a range of cultural fields, but popular culture has been particularly important to establishing dominant discourses on what constitutes youth and youth culture. I want to begin this discussion with the example of Stanley Kubrick's 1971 film, *A Clockwork Orange*, which has continued to be somewhat controversial in the field of films about youth. The moral structure of the narrative has been of less interest to commentators than its stylized portrait of youth delinquency—a strongly gendered and more loosely classed narrative about youth violence in relation to the state and family, and its representation of a period of rapid social change. The censorship and stringent classification of *A Clockwork Orange* devolved on the impact it was thought to have on young impressionable minds—ironic considering that the film's narrative is about exactly such discourses on youth, morality, manipulation, and nonconformity. This impact was heightened by a presumption that a young audience would identify with the young protagonist of the film.[1] Although *A Clockwork Orange*'s notorious display of "ultraviolence" is enacted against women as much as against the state or society (see Elsaesser), it helped shape a film genre in which youth was constitutionally opposed to society:

> in Britain, about 1960 . . . respectable people began to murmur about the growth of juvenile delinquency and suggest [that the young criminals] were a somehow inhuman breed and required inhuman treatment. . . . There were irresponsible people who spoke of aversion therapy. . . . Society, as ever, was put first. The delinquents were, of course, not quite human beings: they were minors, and they had no vote; they were very much them as opposed to us, who represented society. (Burgess quoted in Lund)

In 1950s' films, such as *The Wild One*, the rebel's marginalization in society was an individual situation, but *A Clockwork Orange* marks (though not alone) alienation and rebellion as intrinsic to youth as a group. For Alex and his friends alienation is not a matter of individual circumstances but of a structural social position for youth.

As a film and a novel *A Clockwork Orange* was always about youth but not for youth. In this sense they are proper to the expansion of youth studies in the 1960s and 1970s. *A Clockwork Orange* is often cited as a point of comparison when the question of ratings for or in the interests of youth is raised.[2] Youth films can in part be understood as films where it is a matter of concern whether a film is given a restrictive rating. Youth films push the border of what young people are supposed to be, do, and see. The spectacle of ratings works in part as a marketing strategy, enabling direction to the classification borderland that names a target audience. Restrictive classifications will cut down on the possible youth audience, but the youth film also identifies a market niche drawn to popular forms that break a certain range of social rules. At the turn of the twenty-first century the issues that need to be assessed in considering whether a film is suitable for youth are usually sex, violence, drug use, profanity, and nudity (with those measures differing between cultural locations). That these are the exact terms upon which censorship in general is now based—rather than, for example, political allegiance or moral norms concerning marriage and religion—is no less significant than the fact that film classifications are themselves explicitly ranked around chronological ages that periodize adolescence. Youth is a liminal position, and "the only boundaries which define the teenage years are boundaries of exclusion which define what young people are not, cannot do or cannot be," a process of definition evident in many "legal classifications, for example the age at which young people can drink alcohol, earn money, join the armed forces or consent to sexual intercourse" (Valentine et al. 5). As Gill Valentine, Tracey Skelton, and Deborah Chambers recognize, these are classifications that in practice "demonstrate how variable, context-specific and gendered these definitions of where childhood ends and adulthood begins are" (Valentine et al. 5). But as the example of *A Clockwork Orange* indicates, these liminal narratives are often focused on young men, and although these classifications affect girls as much as boys they are not often named as the subjects of such regulation.

Dick Hebdige's influential work, *Subculture: The Meaning of Style* recognizes this articulation of boundaries by publicly exceptional groups as "a diverting spectacle within the dominant mythology from which it in part emanates" (1979:94). Subcultures form just such a confirming spectacle for public and popular culture. Subcultures are smaller groups within larger cultural collectives, which form group identities and have distinguishable systems of knowledge and signification but are not identified as a separable culture. Subcultures are defined by socially binding elements focused around certain activities and values and uses of material artifacts, territorial spaces, etc., which significantly differentiate them from the wider culture. But, since they are subsets, there must also be significant things that bind and articulate these groups as part of the "parent" culture (Clarke et al. 100).

Despite a longstanding association, "subculture" does not connote anything about rebelliousness or youth. Any group self-identified through shared knowledge and signification is a subculture: primary-school girls as much as gangstas. *A Clockwork Orange* provides a clear example of a subculture at work, presenting a group identity constructed through ritual, dress, and argot; while ritual and dress are more important in the book than in the film, music and language are crucial in both. But *A Clockwork Orange* is not just a film about subcultures, it is also a subcultural film. Burgess's invented dialect (*nadsat*), for example, circulates within a field of specific cultural identifications comprising the film's fans. Its notoriety, repetition at specialist cinemas, and a fan base that repeatedly views, debates, and annotates the film comprise it as a cult film.

Introducing *The Subcultures Reader*, Sarah Thornton writes that there is no agreed answer to what a subculture is, or what distinguishes it from "the masses, the public, society, culture" (1997:1). Like all these other terms, a subculture is a group constituted by something in common: the "sub" infers that something in common constitutes the group as "subordinate, subaltern or subterranean (ibid.)." The subculture's commonality deviates from the mainstream, which it helps define. Most often this deviation is understood as deviance, so while racial or ethnic groups might be subcultural it is more usual to reserve the term for groups deviating from or resisting social norms and cultural placements that are understood to be optional, as race and ethnicity are not often held to be. Youth itself is not subcultural, but the drama of late modern adolescence does locate many points of social/cultural tension thought appropriate to subcultural formation. In *Resistance Through Rituals*, John Clarke, Stuart Hall, Tony Jefferson, and Brian Roberts argue that

> some subcultures are merely loosely-defined strands or "milieux" within the parent culture: they possess no distinctive "world" of their own. Others develop a clear, coherent identity and structure. . . . When these tightly-defined groups are also distinguished by age and generation, we call them youth subcultures. (100)[3]

Youth culture as a scene for the maintenance or change of social structures was crucial to the Birmingham School's determination to take on the questions of hegemony, ideology, and cultural coherence. Clarke, Jefferson, Hall, and Roberts argue that the highly visible and widely accessible commercially provided "Youth Culture" is only a substitute for real peer groups, a substitute that claims to represent "one vast, symbolic 'peer group': 'Our Generation' " (107). Whatever would be authentic in a youth subculture then—group recognitions and productive self-representation among youths—they find only artificially present in something like the globalized youth market into which popular films enter. As in the film (rather than the book) *A Clockwork Orange*, this perspective sees most subcultures as distractions from the real conditions of life, the economic conditions that determine what roles you can take, what you will choose to do and want, and even who you think you are. But how is youth culture distinguished from this commercial "Youth Culture"?

In the 1950s the range of commercial segments and commodity forms interested in naming youth as a normal if difficult phase of life through cultural production specific to it did claim to be new, dismissing earlier youth culture as less specialized (see Grossberg 186). This new range of self-identifying youth culture distinguished between a commodity-oriented mode (youth culture that could be bought), and a more publicly spectacular rebellious form, both of which were conceived as lifestyles and clearly associated with girls and boys respectively. The commercial side of this youth culture was represented in public commentary and guidance manuals as an ambiguous formation—both leading teenagers outside the home or compromising selected value systems and actually distracting teenagers from rebellion. Certainly this commodity culture produced a bridge that allowed popular culture to take up some of the gloss of youth rebellion. This differentiation between commodification and rebellion is reflected in that between teen films and youth films even though the term "teenager" has not been uniformly restricted to the commodity-oriented form of youth culture.

Expressing tensions between the dominant and the marginal, youth culture is simultaneously concerned with belonging and with what Hebdige has described as "that distinctive quest for a measure of autonomy which characterizes all youth sub (and counter) cultures" (1979:88). Youth rebellion in this context also connotes authenticity and authentic relations to society/culture. This includes, and not as a secondary superstructure attached to something more serious but as a key mode of resistance, rebelling against the intended use of cultural products. According to Hebdige, meanings are contested within the realm of style whereby opposing definitions are stylistically created to conflict with the dominant culture (see Valentine et al. 15). The commodities and other objects employed within subcultures are not what makes a style: "What makes a style is the activity of stylisation—the active organisation of objects with activities and outlooks, which produce an organised group-identity in the form and shape of a coherent and distinctive way of being in the world" (Clarke et al. 108). This process of using commodities affirms the correct use for that product while also verifying the authentic cultural activity of subcultural consumption.

The girls in *Muriel's Wedding* have their own ways of speaking and their own value systems, and in this way they might be subcultural. However they are too ignorant, unsophisticated, and inarticulate in their assertive discriminations. Only some subcultures are perceived as being subcultural. Athletic youth cultures, for example, are not seen as subcultural despite their strong group identifications.[4] Groups of girls also challenge dominant identifications through their diverse affiliations, and if brought to the attention of an analyst they, like the jocks, might evidently form subcultures. But girls' cultural groups are rarely seen as subcultures and within such groups they are generally marginal to its perceived rebellions. Donna Gaines sees girls within her subject group acting/identifying "as they always have . . . deriving their status by involvement in school (as cheerleaders, in clubs, in the classroom).

And just as important, by the boys they hung around with. They were defined by who they were, by what they wore, by where they were seen, and with whom" (93). "Girls" seems both not specific enough for subcultural identity and so homogenous it overwhelms other possibilities for one.

The public image of youth rebellion is often aligned with youth-directed (and teenage) popular culture after World War II but, as Andrew Tolson argues, earlier understandings of subculture might "radically recast the assumption, in several classic cultural studies accounts, that the emergence of spectacular urban subcultures is a distinctively postwar cultural phenomenon" (113). Concern about youth and the effects of youth culture are not postwar phenomena, and youth as a social problem—the familiar sigh of youth today—is repeatedly discovered in a range of "moral panics."[5] The 1960s were indeed significant for the field and object of youth culture, but not as foundational as much analysis of youth culture centered on the signal transformations of sixties rebellion suggests. Lawrence Grossberg argues that the imperative links between youth and rock and roll have been made redundant as rock and roll became a mainstream form. It is unclear why, for this kind of analysis, hip hop or new punk do not work as equally effective distinctions between forms and ideas of youth. It was not only the baby boomers Grossberg discusses "who have tried to define youth as an attitude" (185), but the post-1960s period may be the first in which youth culture and youth resistance as a marketable commodity have become a *nostalgic* point of reference. The 1960s are now an image coalescing a certain kind of youth culture as at once hedonism and protest, and a number of critics in the 1990s wondered about the void left by assigning such an iconic youth to a past historical period. Gaines even suggests that this allocation may practically set aside resistance as something to be grown out of.[6]

When the Birmingham School talked about youth and youth cultures, they substantially meant boys or young men. In 1975 Angela McRobbie and Jenny Garber cogently critiqued the exclusion of women from subcultural theories, addressing the "failure by subcultural theorists to dislodge the male connotations of "youth" (16), citing in particular Paul Willis's *Learning to Labour* and Hebdige's *Subculture*. McRobbie and Garber argued that the Birmingham studies generally support the contention that boys are more likely to resist social expectations, and that only public not private resistance matters. They also contend that girls and women are kept on the margins of subcultural studies (if not subcultures themselves), when they are present at all. McRobbie and Garber add gender to existing methods of study rather than interrogating ways of studying youth, but they also suggest that the invisibility of girls in subcultures might ask whether "Girls' subcultures may have become invisible because the very term 'subculture' has acquired such strong masculine overtones" (114). From a dominant perspective in which girls are exemplary consumers of culture industries, adolescent women form an aspect of dominant culture—and if they are resistant it must be with reference to something other than girls as a group. This is significant given that subcultures "have seemed to possess the capacity to change the direction of young people's lives, or at least to shape their focus by confirming some felt, but as yet unexpressed desire" (McRobbie 1991:ix).

The central tenet of Mike Brake's chapter on girls in his *The Sociology of Youth Culture and Youth Subcultures* is that girls are excluded from subcultures because femininity must be subordinated within such a structure (153). Brake characterizes girls' lives as constrained by school or other privatized processes of adolescence, and this explains for him the triviality of girls' subcultural lives: "Girls are present in male subcultures, but are contained within them, rather than using them to explore actively forms of female identity. The subculture may be a special focus, something to dress up for, and an escape from the restraints of home, school and work" (141). Like most analysts of subcultures, Brake discusses subcultures as mediating class inequalities (160), linking youth rebellion and economic depression, unemployment, and urbanization. Both Gaines and Brake suggest that subcultures are spaces for adolescents to perform "alternative scripts" (Brake 166) in an endeavor to find their real selves in the face of alienation. In this aspect of their analysis such alternatives are less evident among girls because girls remain tied to domesticity and separate from employment as a sum of their social positions. Recent studies have responded to these accounts of girls in subcultures by recording and responding to the voices of girl groups as themselves subcultural: for example Lauraine Leblanc's *Pretty in Punk* (1999), or the 1999 special issue of *Signs* on girl culture, which emphasizes alternative culture and lives among girls (with a particular focus on music). However, the specific focus of these studies continues to be an equation between public social resistance and authentic youth culture.

Trainspotting: The Avant Garde and Mass Culture

Trainspotting—the novel by Irvine Welsh (1993) and the film directed by Danny Boyle (1996)—might be used to focus some of the above points. *Trainspotting* was popular and well received in both these forms but enters youth culture as a subcultural film—a form amenable to youth culture in ways literature and theater are not. The film centers on a display of subcultural life spectacularly opposed to the normative standards of the society in which the book and film are set and in which they were a significant success. In its opening sequence the film quotes the "Choose Life" antidrug campaigns popular in America and England in the late 1980s:

> Choose life. Choose a job. Choose a career. Choose a family. Choose a fucking big television. Choose washing machines, cars, compact disc players and electrical tin-openers. Choose good health, low cholesterol and dental insurance. Choose fixed-interest mortgage repayments. Choose a starter home. Choose your friends. Choose leisure-wear and matching luggage. Choose a three-piece suite on hire-purchase in a range of fucking fabrics. Choose DIY and wondering who the fuck you are on a Saturday night. Choose sitting on that couch watching mind-numbing, spirit-crushing game shows, stuffing fucking junk food into your mouth. Choose rottin' away at the end of it all, pissing your last in a miserable home nothing more than an embarrassment to the selfish fucked-up brats that you've spawned to replace yourselves. Choose your future. Choose life.

The hip criticism of consumption and working-class ideologies in Renton's monologues is a similar discourse on subcultures and class to those the Birmingham School employed in their studies of subcultural groups such as punk, reggae, gangs, mods, hippies, bikers, etc. The Birmingham School often saw subcultures as disguising class positions through temporary alternative allegiances, but sometimes saw them as conscious of exploitation but taking pleasure somewhere else. Like Renton they are interested in how commodities allow people to produce sustainable pleasures within capitalist systems.

The roles taken by women in *Trainspotting* conform fairly well to McRobbie and Garber's arguments concerning girls and subcultures. They are on the edge of subcultures even when apparently participating in them. The young mother in the opening shooting-up scene does not belong to this boy's own adventure in heroin, despite her own habit. The other women in *Trainspotting* are mothers or girlfriends who do not understand, with their own small cliques and secrets covered over (however ironically) by shopping and duty. The only really characterized woman/girl in the film is Diane (see fig. 7.2), a mix of schoolgirl and club girl carefully poised on the edge of the nuclear family home. While her enthusiasm to be included in Renton's life belies her apparent sophistication, she produces through her nightclubbing and sexual life the kinds of resistance it is standard to find among girls on the edge of a subcultural life. These resistances are articulated against her home, school, and family, rather than directly against the state or society in general. The boys' greater detachment from their homes and families is only emphasized by the exceptional circumstances in which they come under the rule of the family, such as Renton's withdrawal confinement in a room dominated by motifs of childhood rather than youth. The boys' actual ages are unclear—while Diane's is of course at issue—but they are old enough to be parents and workers. Begbie in particular is aligned in the film with a parent culture, which is why Renton's parents can't see his failings, but their lives are wrapped up in signs of youth culture: games, popular music, nightclubs, illicit drugs, petty crime, and new and changing sexual, romantic, work, and economic relationships.

The *Trainspotting* posters put Diane as the girl much more in the foreground than does the book. The billboards gave her equal billing with the four young men (or displaced Tommy with her), foregrounding a possible girl audience for this boy-centered narrative. The posters evidence that despite its subcultural credibility, *Trainspotting* is surrounded by a degree of merchandizing that didn't circulate around *Muriel's Wedding*. Despite cards and posters, *Trainspotting*'s cult aura was sold most successfully through the hit soundtrack, which confirms it as a film directed to the youth market. It also suggests the retrospectivity characteristic of many representations of youth culture. The book and the film are set in the 1980s but the soundtrack does not clearly set that scene. It features Iggy Pop and Lou Reed, but also late 1990s' British "Top 20" bands such as Pulp, Blur, and Elastica. Diane draws attention to this historical contradiction when she insists that music and drugs have changed, away from rock and heroin to something new: "You're not getting any younger Mark. The world's changing, music's changing, even drugs are changing."

Attention to the direction of *Trainspotting* confirms its position as a serious as well as an entertainment film. Its filmic techniques are mostly overt manipulations of framing with some surreal insertions, but this does distinguish it from most of the established generic conventions of youth film, which push a range of social boundaries but do not necessarily involve formal experimentation. This direction draws on the formal innovation of the book, indebted to avant-garde literature, including Thomas Pynchon's *Gravity's Rainbow* (source of the toilet scene) and *A Clockwork Orange*. Kubrick's film is often cited as *Trainspotting*'s formal precursor, and the milk-bar scene from *A Clockwork Orange* is directly cited in the mis-en-scène of the Edinburgh nightclub. A stylistically avant-garde film is less likely to be defined as youth culture despite its possible popularity among youth. The 1994 film *Kids*, directed by Larry Clark and written by Harmony Korine, was both extravagantly praised by and marketed toward an art-house demographic by reference to recollections of past youth. Reviews of *Kids* often described it as hard-hitting, realistic, uncompromising, and raw, and inferred it employed an ethnographic approach to filmmaking. But despite such claims to realism *Kids*, like *Trainspotting*, reinforced the characterization of girls' lives through leisure spaces focused on domesticity rather than the subcultural.

Youth culture is not necessarily counter to any hegemony. *Trainspotting* focuses on fantasies of conformity and rebellion, from the consumer lifestyle it enumerates to dreams of belonging: families, relationships, sporting associations, friendships, clubbers, junkies. Youth culture also mostly means culture directed to, about, and for youth rather than cultural production by youth. The exceptional field in this regard is popular music, incorporation of which has become one of the key indications that a text is part of youth culture. The circulation of youth films evidences "the role played by youth sub-cultures in production and marketing for consumption":

> the intersection of sub-cultures, the hidden economy and institutions such as fashion, image and such form a complex process whereby youth styles are commercially appropriated and become part of transnational popular cultural youth forms. However, young people then reinterpret those forms, invent new forms from their own productive creativity and conspire to render the commercial forms obsolete, and so the process begins again. (Valentine et al. 24)

This participates in a long-standing anxiety that indicates some of the ways in which cultural studies of youth remained fundamentally grounded in modernist anxieties over both immaturity and mass culture. Andreas Huyssen cogently argues that "modernism constituted itself through a conscious strategy of exclusion, an anxiety of contamination by its other: an increasingly consuming and engulfing mass culture" consistently figured as feminine (vii). Modernism was, in part, a reaction against modern women and the feminization of aesthetics that was associated with new cultural forms including adolescence.

As Janice Radway argues, the production of culture and cultural consumers around this time, "standardized and feminized consumer-subjects" who were thought to respond to "culture" as a commodity which could be purchased and thus "would no longer function as the uniquely unmarked mark of human distinction" (1994:887). This world defrauded by mass culture defines modern subjectivity as

a change in personality type based on conformity to external standards rather than, as in the liberal age, on the internalization of authority. Internalization of authority, however, is held to be a necessary prerequisite for the later (mature) rejection of authority by a strong ego. The culture industry is seen as one of the major factors preventing such "healthy" internalization and replacing it by those external standards of behaviour which inevitably lead to conformism. (Huyssen 22)

These modernist perspectives were crucial to the crystallization of feminine adolescence as a public discourse: "The threat of losing oneself to mass culture, it should be recalled, was central to Heidegger's claim that the loss of self is inseparable from the specter of losing oneself to Others" (Petro 142). For example, F. R. Leavis and Denys Thompson's modernist programs for training in taste and distinction, for defending culture against the modern environment, were specifically directed at young men. This educational agenda also addresses youth's perceived antitraditionalism, an "ideal" of the new which, Leavis and Thompson claim "has had the effect of arresting the development of whole generations at adolescence" (123).[7]

The discourses that must be considered in a genealogy of feminine adolescence in relation to youth culture include the segmentation of popular film into genres such as teen film or youth film that work as classifying categories with regard to their audience. Generic distinctions between forms of youth-directed film are evident in the early escalation of the genre. The youth/teen film genres coalesced in the 1950s and 1960s, responding in part to the need for new marketing strategies attracting young people to film theaters after the emergence of television but always reflecting on earlier forms of youth culture. Classics such as *Blackboard Jungle* and *Rebel without a Cause* (both 1955) varied preexisting dramatic genres and emerged in juxtaposition with romance and party films that provided apparently less confronting images of teenage life (and are also less remembered or remarked upon, as precursors of the teen film). The significance of adolescence to dramatic narratives at this time was not confined to films marketed to youth, as developmental narratives of films such as *On the Waterfront* (1954) attest, but there was a new emphasis on this drama of youth as itself socially disruptive. After World War II, the popular impact of ego psychology, in the American media in particular, disseminated new theories about the storm and stress of adolescence, including reference to separate youth cultures. Representations of youth (and youth culture) were subsequently often sold as youth culture although also marketed to older groups through various forms of concern, interest, regret, or nostalgia. These films did not necessarily have a new audience, but they were marketed as if they did, and going to a youth film became a way to recapture youth or identify with or negotiate its difficulty.

Teen Film: Conformity and Resistance

Clueless: Teen Films

What has been called the teen flick or the teen film has been a staple of cinematic production since the 1940s, becoming widely recognized in the 1960s and then reemerging as a hypersuccessful genre in the 1980s. In the broader history of cinema, films that now seem to conform to this genre were often held to have a wide appeal, given general concern with the rapid changes of modern life and the perceived attraction and difficulty of youth. Teen films are distinguishable in a range of ways from other youth-directed films. In teen film it is unusual to talk about the success or even the style of directing, and avant-gardism is consequently almost never an issue. Commercial success has been read as a statement that the directing and the script are unremarkable or at least pose no intervention in anyone's enjoyment of the film. There are, for example, few critical or academic readings of *Clueless*, written and directed by Amy Heckerling—few critics comment on the film's social narratives and fewer are intrigued by the style of the film. Lesley Stern is an exception, and her reading of the film also recognizes the historical narrative on girlhood articulated between *Clueless* and Jane Austen's *Emma* (1816), on which the script is loosely based:

> The teen movie might be very modern (coming into prominence in the eighties) but it has a pre-history, both in the movies and in other forms such as the novel. *Clueless* not only remakes and comments on *Emma* but remakes the teen movies that precede it and also the twentieth century

apparatus of modernity that provides the preconditions of the genre; the film is alert to and permeated by the myriad influences which shape the very experience and notion of contemporaneity.

Regardless of their audience and even in spite of some of their content, teen films are received as girl films because of the transience of their form and content—their romantic narratives of transformation mediated by overt commodification.

It is difficult to discuss teen film without using examples most readers will not know—although there are definitive or watershed films in the genre, even these are subject to the presumed triviality and planned obsolescence of the genre. In a historical account of teen film at least one example would need to be drawn from the films of John Carpenter, whose 1980s films provide an excellent summary of its conventions. *The Breakfast Club* (1985), for example, dramatizes interactions between a range of stock teen film characters, including the alienated youth, easily refunctioned as romantic hero-type in teen film. The mediating influence of such boys allows films such as *The Breakfast Club* or *Heathers* (1988) to maintain a measure of serious social commentary not usually presumed for teen film. The teen genre often contains the disruptive drama of youth within specific social institutions designed for that purpose, such as family and school, and inflects it with youthful romance or sex. These conventions separate the teen film from the flaming-youth-style film of the 1920s, a celebration of youth that was less focused on life within the emerging institutions for defining and disciplining youth, although sharing the teen film's upbeat narrative closure.[8] Teen and youth film genres have interacted with each other and helped cast into public culture a distinction between rebellious youth and difficult teen life. In the 1960s films such as *To Sir With Love* (1967), *A Hard Day's Night* (1964), and the Beach Party movies (the original *Beach Party* was made in 1963) played on that distinction and were marketed as containing characteristics of each. This distinction claims that youth subcultures are eternally rebellious, whereas the teenage world based around school and home is, unless exceptional and subcultural, mainstream and conformist, with the expectation of conventionally happy endings for which particularity is only important in order to sustain interest.[9]

Mass culture industries have helped define adolescence as a functional spending frenzy in prereproductive years. This redefinition is gender specific:

the rebellious self-interest connoted by teen angst is not constituted by, though it may involve, modes of consumption, and is predominantly referred to masculine adolescence, while that coded as feminine adolescence is perceived as being channeled into and constituted in consumption. The idea of girls has consistently occupied the conformist end of even resistant models of consumption. As mass-produced youth culture is defined by consumption, by audiences and marketplaces, such films can often use much older actors than those supposedly being represented. More serious or dramatic films about young people are likely to use actors around the age of the characters, but popular cultural representations of teenagers or people in their early twenties do not rely on actors or producers of that age. The 1990s television hit *Beverley Hills 90210* or the Beach Party films of the 1960s demonstrate that the ages of teen stars are often irrelevant, while the age of the audience is far more significant than it is for a youth film. Film critic Adrian Martin argues that "the teen in teen movie is itself a very elastic, bill-of-fare word; it refers not to biological age, but a type, a mode of behaviour, a way of being. . . . The teen in teen movie means something more like youth" (66–7). Martin admires in this sense Robert Benayoun's list of "normal qualities of youth: naïveté, idealism, humour, hatred of tradition, erotomania, and a sense of injustice" (Benayoun quoted in Martin 67). There are other understandings of teen culture that do link its forms to age and to some shared experiences of adolescence or even puberty. Stuart Hall and Paddy Whannel see "teenage culture" as a response to social transition, "an area of common symbols and meanings" and thus an identifiable cultural group founded on the "natural tensions of adolescence" (70).

Hall and Whannel describe youth as a subculture attached to forms of resistance and reappropriation. This definition excludes many practices not seen as manifesting this resistant appropriation, such as those behaviors that are "compliant"—"the pops" for example (74), or teen film—exemplary forms of commodifying culture and identity especially associated with girls. The opening sequence of *Clueless* introduces generic teen plots, and cues such as pop music, to situate itself in relation to the teen film audience:

> The movie begins with a spinning overhead shot of a group of girls having fun in a car—in a white jeep which careers all over, as does the handheld camera, as do the colors to initiate a montage of Cher and her friends having fun—shopping, driving, kidding about by the pool. The colors are garishly bright, every frame is crowded, energetic, and music

pumps out. Before too long one of the girls in the opening emerges as "heroine" both on the image track and in a narrating voice over: "So OK, you're probably thinking, 'Is this, like a Noxema commercial, or what?!' But seriously, I actually have a way normal life for a teenage girl. I mean I get up, I brush my teeth, and I pick out my school clothes." (Stern)

Cher's social placement claims to be accessible to a broad range of girls, at least as an ideal. While she is privileged (rich and white), coded as happy and attractive, her life is bounded by familiar institutions and her difficulties, including a broken family and a few already obvious insecurities, prevent her being inaccessible. While Cher (see fig. 7.1) knows people are often jealous of her and that her life is not one most girls have, this degree of implied normal identification—reinforced by the placement of the camera in the car with Cher and her friend—is typical of the teen film genre.[10] The "I'm just a girl" soundtrack behind this scene merely underscores the claim that *Clueless* is about girls and is a teen film. Like most teen films this is also a film about the girls' growing-up or transformation. The genre foregrounds girl culture forms including fashion, makeup, and girl-directed pop music, and its key narratives (such as the makeover) take up similar commodified transformations. The teen film's ideal girl is a look and a lifestyle, and like other looks/lifestyles it is a commodity. However, as *Resistance Through Rituals* states:

Commodities are, also, cultural *signs*. They have already been invested, by the dominant culture, with meanings, associations, social connotations. Many of these meanings seem fixed and "natural." But it is only because the dominant culture has so fully appropriated them to its use, that the meanings which it attributes to the commodities have come to appear as the only meaning which they can express. In fact, in cultural systems, there is no "natural" meaning as such. Objects and commodities do not mean any one thing. They "mean" only because they have already been arranged, according to social use, into cultural codes of meaning. (Clarke et al. 109)

The conventions of teen film also include the youthfulness of not only central characters but most supporting characters; content usually centered on girls or young heterosexual couples; a romance plot; and subplots including the makeover, education, and parent-child resolution (although adults are often very marginal within the teen film). The ideal girls of teen film usually abide within an accepted range of behaviors and expectations, although late 1990s' renovations to the genre focused on horror or thriller plot lines accentuated the extremes that could be included within that range. While romance remains the key indicator of the teen film, as Heckerling's loose adaptation of Austen's novel confirms this is often focused on the girl's educational romance. As *Clueless* exemplifies, teen films usually take a conventional narrative point of view, mostly located outside the characters except when a main character's perspective is represented. The direction emphasizes the enclosure of many scenes and employs many close shots, except when full-body shots are used to make statements about power (including beauty). Stylistically, with the exception of glamorous male stars, the youth film uses fewer close-ups or fixed to slow-moving long shots. Renton doesn't need to walk down a staircase like Cher, although a full-body shot attributes power and coherence to his drug high. Teen films are also distinguished from youth films by a tendency to present tension between boy groups as either marginal or relative to girls. While violence between groups of boys is almost required content for youth films, teen films focus dramatic tension less on direct violence than on interiorized disciplines and exclusions. Crossover points between teen and youth films thus often appear as comedies centered on makeover or school narratives centered on boys within institutions such as schools and families.[11]

Whether or not commentary on teen film begins with a focus on gender, it will be likely to end with a position on conformity rather than rebellion or the subcultural. Promotion of *Clueless*, like *Trainspotting*, presumed its audience might not completely understand the dialect of the central characters but would not be so confused as to risk alienation, and both films approached the rituals of their lives as a bizarre but riveting spectacle. But the valley girl subculture is not subcultural. *Clueless* foregrounds the tighter knit of friendships and leisure spaces that characterize girls' subcultures for McRobbie and Garber—a space referred to a future domesticity that will absorb its transient difference and small rebellions. Cher believes she can have sex and take drugs if she wants, but chooses not to; but can she "Choose Life" or choose sex, drugs, and rock and roll (in Renton's nostalgic formation)? If relinquishing her popular girl position would not necessarily be liberating for Cher, is that merely because the narrative establishes the rightness of her conformity? And if modes of disciplining youth are operating in Cher's choices, are they also operating on Renton and his choices? When agency is evaluated according to resistance, it becomes inevitable that rebellious or subcultural youth will be perceived as more independent and individual than a girl like Cher. A Foucauldian analysis of *Trainspotting* and *Clueless* might point out, however, that agency is itself a construction of dominant ideologies, and "choosing" to belong to rebellious subcultures is part of a privileged discourse on individualism.

The eclectic consumption of Cher and her friends is not a valorized, resisting form of agency. The homogeneity across white, black, and Jewish girls has been achieved at some price. This is not just because *Clueless* is a smartly ironic film, playing with what kind of "homies" might be rolling with Tai, Cher, and Dionne. Teen film as a genre always dramatizes incorporation and exclusion among peer groups and focuses on the struggle to learn how to conform in the right ways, negotiating discipline and knowledge. There is resistance to social conventions and hierarchies among teen film heroines. *Clueless* or *Cruel Intentions* (1999) indicate that not only love, sex, and pop music but class, family, and marriage institutions are at stake in a teen film. Interpreting politics as romance seems to be a crucial part of the teen film genre, consistently framed by family and school. School was not often featured on film before World War II: fewer girls in particular stayed at school, and high schools were not represented as a shared public experience in the same way. School and college or university as scenes for playing out youth culture were increasingly prevalent after the 1950s, an emphasis that had sound financial motives as well as reflecting changing social agendas. The school film genre emerged most forcefully with *The Blackboard Jungle*, which is also credited with the first rock and roll theme song— "Rock Around the Clock." *The Blackboard Jungle* imports the wildness of rebel youth to the safer spaces of the classroom, and the school film recognizes the potential for rebellion in prescribed as well as prohibited assemblies of youth.

Distraction

The conformity of teen films is supposedly more significant than its overt generic conventions. The genre reputedly reinforces or even helps instill conformity in its audience. Cher, it would be said, reinforces a rule that independent girls must become nurturing, responsive, heterosexual partners in their processes of growing-up. In his defense of teen films, Martin insists they should be taken on their own terms, judged according to the criteria by which they become popular. Martin's "Teen Movies: The Forgetting of Wisdom" notes that teen films are packed with the "fabulously consuming trivia of everyday teen life" (65) and praises their invocation of "liminal experience: that intense, suspended moment between yesterday and tomorrow, between childhood and adulthood, between being a nobody and a somebody, when everything is in question, and anything is possible" (68).

Youth films and teen films articulate youth, with different and internally varying emphases, as both opportunity and threat or risk. These ambivalences are frequently synthesized in a gendered opposition of marginal and mainstream that defines girls by their conformity. A more outlandish or overt plotline than *Clueless*, such as that of *Tank Girl* (1995), for example, will not overturn the conformity ascribed to girl films. While the comics series on which the film is based is a cult punk form (see fig. 9.5) and perhaps only proper to girl culture insofar as it relies on an opposition to presumed elements of girl life, the film jettisons all but the stylistics of punk girl action and generic border crossing that characterize the series.[12] There is no such thing as avant-garde "teen culture." Some of the contemporary commentary Barbara Ehrenreich, Elizabeth Hess, and Gloria Jacobs reproduce in their analysis of Beatlemania attests to the same tendency, but they also counter this premise by recognizing that "conformity meant more" for girls "than surrendering, comatose, to the banal drift of junior high or high school life," and was actually a tightrope of social expectations and desires (528). This figure of the teenager is, however, preserved in the institutions in relation to which she was formed: the economic metaphor for teen girl sexuality—save yourself or be cheap—is still operating in *Clueless* twenty-five years after Beatlemania; the culture of educating girls in being girls continues; the girl is still a valorized look that requires specific knowledge and practices; and high school is still the principal form of public life for single teenage girls.

The Birmingham studies emerged at a time when the role of culture in securing domination had been elaborately investigated and there was a need for analysis of resistant struggles over meaning. But it is not certain that cultural studies now has a fully elaborated understanding of the ways in which dominant discourses and institutions are secured on the terrain of popular culture. Cultural studies is in general less interested in what constitutes conformity or more ambivalent forms of cultural participation, an emphasis it shares with youth culture. Both *Clueless* and *Trainspotting* are popular texts on youth rebellion, and youth resistance is a readily available facet of popular culture. The entertainment industries continue to be both a privileged outlet for new practices of consumption and a discourse on and mode of disciplining and producing those practices. These are questions I will consider at length in chapter 9, but an example will be useful here.

An instance of the melange of youth and teen films is Baz Luhrmann's film of *Romeo and Juliet*, which revived a range of romantic action films for youth. It is both a teen film, taking up ideas about young love set to pop music, and a youth film, packed with angst, anger, action and violence articulating a public rather than familial generation gap. *Romeo + Juliet* as both romantic comedy and youth-rebel tragedy draws on Shakespeare's play. This juxtaposition works by never overlapping the Juliet scenes with the gang scenes, but in fact separating them by every element of the film's style. A mix of slow-moving or close-up and fast-paced filmic styles allows Romeo (Leonardo di Caprio) to cross this border and connect the teen and youth elements of the film. Romeo and Juliet only appear together in this film in enclosed otherworldly spaces: the fish tank, the pool, the church, the bed (enclosed by sheets), the church again. Given the cultural capital of Shakespeare, setting *Romeo + Juliet* in the present is necessary in order to make it any kind of youth film. If teen films and youth films are terms connoting a hierarchy that mirrors a gender distinction, this is not a description of the audience, in which girls would watch teen films and boys youth films, but rather a feminization and masculinization of the forms. *Romeo + Juliet* was marketed as both teen and youth film, and the most obvious element of its crossover between these markets is its highly successful soundtrack. The soundtrack is a mix of romantic ballads and dance tracks to cover the teen/pop market, with name rather than generic artists and alternative artists to carry the authenticity of youth cachet. *Romeo + Juliet* thus also claims knowledges that incorporate it into a self-identifying youth culture. In a *Cineaste* symposium on Shakespeare films Luhrmann states that he expects his film to date, while Franco Zeferelli (who directed an seventies film adapting the play) claims an eternal essential relevance is inherent in the play, expressed "more nobly, more fully, than young people do today" (Brook et al. 53). This now and then division distinguishing the teen market from aesthetic integrity remains a standard maneuver in cultural production and commentary on it.

Understandings of mass culture as eroding the singular taste of the cultured individual have consistently exemplified mass culture by reference to girls. Such feminization is well known in accounts of the rise of mass culture (such as Huyssen's), but debate over cultural consumption continues, with a remarkable consistency, to deploy girls as figures of late modern conformity, a deployment often evident in feminism and feminist cultural studies. In high modernist version of cultural criticism, writers such as Theodor Adorno argue that capitalism's new forms of cultural production—for example the mass-produced forms of popular cinema and music—no longer produced art with social effect or relevance. These new forms, they thought, no longer presented the highest forms of culture or possibilities for human improvement but instead comprised a distraction from the real lives of individuals, while at the same time encouraging them to live compliantly within their social contexts. At times this has been called the culture industry. The popular cinema of this high modernist period was a privileged example of these culture industries and their new practices of consumption. Seigfried Kracauer's much cited essay, "The Cult of Distraction," presents an analysis of relations between dominant ideologies and mass culture that is rather more hopeful than anything produced under the heading of the culture industry, although Kracauer's work nevertheless positions girls as the most ambivalent point of contact between the self and ideology through mass culture.

The audience of mainstream cinema in the 1920s and 1930s was predominantly represented, in public discourse and critical theory, as populated by girls. Moreover, cinematic pleasures were represented as processes proper to girls. The audience of early mainstream cinema was figured as feminine and adolescent and as vulnerable to or indeed characterized by forms of identification particular to girls. Producer Irving Thalberg claimed in 1929 that motion pictures were particularly able to represent "the attitude of modern life": "the attitude of children towards parents, the family life or the lack of it, is so quickly and so normally and so clearly brought out in pictures" (Thalberg 46).[13] These characteristics combine to associate girls with "distraction," an influential term in discourses on politics and mass culture in the 1920s and 1930s, particularly in the work of Martin Heidegger and the Frankfurt School writers such as Adorno, Max Horkheimer, and, more tangentially, Kracauer.[14] Rather than being simply passive, or an embodiment of impressionability, however, the concept of distraction actually suggests a mobility of interest.

The relations between women and the cinema at this time have been widely discussed. R. W. McCormick notes that in Weimar Germany "the new art of the century, the cinema, depended both on the visibility of women as actors on the screen and on their presence in front of the screen . . . they made up a majority of the audience" (644). But the immaturity of this audience—its girlishness—has been less often noted. Girls in the audience were figured by writers such as Adorno as ideal copy-machines, and generally as desirously impressionable.[15] Kracauer describes the "little shopgirls" through which he narrated contemporary popular cinematic experiences for his newspaper columns in these terms. He emphasizes, moreover, that this audience is constructed in the films themselves: "According to the cinematic testimony, a human being is a girl who can dance the Charleston well and a boy who knows just as little" (301). Kracauer is referring to the same Weimar audience as McCormick, but the significance of girls for cinema audiences of the United States and Great Britain is also widely attested. This figuration does not rely on assessments of who bought tickets but theorizes how a film audience works, within and outside film industries, describing processes of participation, capture, and identification evident in theories of feminine adolescence at the same time.

Rachel Bowlby finds in the marketing discourses of the 1920s and 1930s "two standard models of the consumer"—the "classical" discerning consumer and the romantic dupe or hedonist (98–9). Radway's discussion of the new book clubs of the 1920s details a similar opposition between the "abstract, universal, deliberating-and-freely-choosing reader" and the standardized consumer-subject (Radway 1994:887). A conception of the audience as vulnerable has been widely shared by theorists of modernity and by public debates in popular mediums with higher cultural capital than those directed to youth: by journals and intellectual magazines; by artists; and by feminist criticism. And by educational programs:

> This ignorance, this immaturity, of large sections of the population, are due chiefly, I think, to lack of emotional education when young. . . . There are thousands who will day-dream and night-dream in a cinema while idly allowing meaningless clap-trap to float pictorially before them. (Leavis and Thompson 107)

New discourses on the girl audience helped constitute modern girls as a failure of distinction and as a particularly internalized and sometimes difficult to perceive disciplinary problem. But Kracauer is alternately charmed and horrified by those shopgirls in the audience, and the divide between distinction and distraction is rarely unambiguous. Even Adorno and Horkheimer, as Miriam Hansen recognizes, "ascribe the effectivity of mass-cultural scripts of identity not simply to the viewers" manipulation as passive consumers, but rather to their very solicitation as experts, as active readers" (1992:51). Advertising addressed to feminine adolescents cites such expertise as part of its appeal and as the framework for its comprehension. Such critics repeatedly refer to girls as exemplary dupes of culture industries, but this did not lead to an equal emphasis on girls in later studies of the resistance possible in relation to popular culture. If popular discourses on consumption continue to detail an opposition between active consumption and passive malleable consumers with poor taste, there is nevertheless a pervasive ambivalence involved in the mobile interests of the feminine and immature, and their economic and cultural force.

Horror Film: The Girl's Role
Girls on Film

This image of the malleable, gullible audience never applied to all audiences; instead, it largely feminized the conception of the audience as a group consumption of culture, as a process of identification. This final section links such identification with market imperatives through popular generic conventions that articulate specific relations between the girl in the audience and on the screen. Much anxiety over the moral dangers of mass entertainment, and the social decay inferred from its popularity, articulates a fear of women looking (de Lauretis 135) and of the passivity of the audience for visual culture. Significantly, these dangers rely on imitation and identification rather than just looking, on the extreme identificatory practices supposedly produced by the impact of cinema on impressionable audiences. This permeability has seemed terrifying to critics extolling social independence and cultural maturity.

Cinema's "illusory plenitude" supposedly particularly entices the female spectator, "who proves the most susceptible to the cinematic illusion, who is unable to achieve a critical distance from it" (Petro 119).[16] Laura Mulvey's influential essay, "Visual Pleasure and Narrative Cinema," claims, moreover, that the dominant narrative conventions of popular film are inherently patriarchal and heterosexual, positioning the viewer by a voyeuristic gaze on women as passive and always incomplete objects of screen desire:

> The beauty of the woman as object and the screen space coalesce; she is
> no longer the bearer of guilt but a perfect product, whose body, stylized

and fragmented by close-ups, is the content of the film and the direct re-
cipient of the spectator's look. (22)

Woman is presumed by such film theory to be the object of the camera's vision and of dominant narrative conventions. Subsequent film theorists have
supplemented or critiqued Mulvey's argument by recognizing more diverse
possible relations between an audience and a film. Mulvey's reply to her
critics explicitly addressed the question of women in the audience, and how
women might be part of this cinematic gaze as well as the on-screen look.
But while *looking* and *looking at* are crucial to film, the on-screen image
is not a coherent object and takes its meaning from multiple processes of
signification.

Following the work of Christian Metz and influential debates in film
journals such as *Screen*, an intersection of psychoanalysis and semiotics became in the 1980s and 1990s the dominant mode of analyzing film form.
While these theories often represented cinema as an "apparatus"—"a technological, institutional and psychical 'machine'" (Petro 120), they remained
focused on the reception of film by individuals, mediated by such institutions. Gilles Deleuze further emphasized the machinic character of cinema
at the expense of the psychological theories of film production and reception produced by critics such as Metz, Mulvey, or Slavoj Žižek. For Deleuze
the screen image is assembled or organized by the camera as a machinic conjunction with the audience.[17] These are social processes of constructing
both cinematic genres and modes of film spectatorship. The film spectator,
as Stephen Heath argues, "is produced by the film as subject in process, in
the process of demonstration of the film, with the repetition an intensification of that process" (169). This account of film as a social field of repetitions aligns cinema itself with the production of normative models for self-
production, such as gender. Teresa de Lauretis cites cinema among the
apparatus or technologies of gender: "gender . . . both as representation and
as self-representation, is the product of various social technologies, such as
cinema, and of institutionalized discourses, epistemologies, and critical
practices, as well as practices of daily life" (2). Film has not only participated in coding some attributes as masculine or feminine but has changed or
produced new formations of gender including new formations of girlhood
as both to be looked at and as a mode of being in the audience.

While the next two chapters focus on marketing to girls and the girl as
market, demographic, and audience, the girl also deploys a range of symbolic functions articulated in the conventions of popular film. That some

genres presume girls to form an important mode or possibility within its audience does not necessarily refer to whether or not girls watch that kind of film. Girlhood is invested with a range of meanings by film genres and dominant understandings of the film audience. Some of these meanings are framed by repetitions of dominant social structures and ideologies attendant on them, but generic conventions provide not only frames for reception but also modes of reception. Genres always intersect culture industries and other modes of cultural production with audiences as recognizable public groups. Martin notes that "genres are not categories or boxes—they are a set of cues to the audience as to which loose assortments of situations, moods, characters and topics to expect" (65) and locates teen movies as necessarily hybrid forms: "the syntax of the plot is always borrowed from elsewhere, from war movies, musicals, romantic comedies, relationship dramas, horror movies" (66). While horror film is not associated with girl demographics in the same way as romantic comedy, it is more than one among these possible hybrid teen genres. Teen horror is articulated in a range of conventions that are significant for historicizing ideas about girls and what we might think of as girl culture.

Never Answer the Phone

Jonathan Bernstein claims teen films emerged in the 1970s and 1980s, in direct relation to teen horror films such as John Carpenter's *Halloween*.[18] Horror film has been understood to generically presume a male audience, and teenage horror films are predominantly discussed as directed to an audience of young men.[19] The comparatively limited range of available criticism on horror film indicates the degree to which this is a teen film genre rather than any apparently more complex form of mass popular culture (such as action or even youth films). Slasher films apparently resemble youth films in their display of violence, but in other respects they conform to the teen film world without adults (except as monsters) and dominated by the peer group and the familiar (often even in the selection of weapons—knives and other domestic tools rather than guns). Critical attention to horror film mostly appears from a feminist perspective. Carol Clover's *Men, Women and Chainsaws* (1992) and Barbara Creed's *The Monstrous-Feminine* (1993) are exemplary instances: Clover analyses the politics of horror film's generic conventions and Creed the significance of the abject feminine to the genre. Discussing the wave of 1980s teen horror films Clover observes the solidification of a singularly relevant convention, which she calls "the final girl."

Successful horror films of the time constructed youth or teen horror as a slasher genre, where mode of death is more important than the question of death. Clover notes that these films, often spawning long series of sequels (*Halloween* [1978]; *Friday the Thirteenth* [1980]; *Nightmare on Elm Street* [1984]), manifest a convention by which a certain type of girl would be the only survivor of the slashing field. Creed also focuses her reading of the horror genre on gendered conventions for representing the embodied subject and object of horror film. She notes a pervasive "monstrous feminine" in which the girl's "literal castration is depicted in films in which she is usually a victim, such as the slasher film, where her body is repeatedly knifed until it resembles a bleeding wound" (122). As Creed suggests, teen horror can be understood as a narrative turning on abjection, and Julia Kristeva's model of abjection can be effectively used to consider some of the effects of such display: "The body's inside . . . shows up in order to compensate for the collapse of the border between inside and outside. It is as if the skin, a fragile container, no longer guaranteed the integrity of one's 'own and clean self' " (1982:53). The abject is about structural permeability, the continual (unclosed) recurrence of threats to the Subject as framed by a Symbolic Order. Creed draws on Clover's genre study for this argument, but without Clover's recognition that the lead female character in horror film is usually coded as a girl rather than a woman.

Both Creed and Clover deploy psychoanalysis to understand the feminine role in horror: "Figuratively seen, the Final Girl is a male surrogate in things oedipal, a homoerotic stand-in, the audience incorporate; to the extent that she 'means' girl at all, it is only for the purposes of signifying lack" (Clover 119). But Clover's identification of the girl's role cites quite a different position within the field of psychoanalytic theory (see chapter 4 above). Having referenced her analysis to psychoanalytic theories of girlhood, Clover is left with a contradiction between these theories and the activity of the teen-horror girl. To resolve this contradiction she overstates the gender ambiguity of this girl. Creed responds that "the slasher film does not, as Clover suggests, simply 'eliminate the woman.' " It represents "woman in the *twin* roles of castrated and castrator, and it is the latter image which dominates the ending in most all of these films" (127). In contrast to both these positions I would contend that the "regendering" of the "final girl" (Clover 59) does not position the girl as a boy but as a girl, outside identification with dominant models of Womanhood (including psychoanalysis). Within the context of late-twentieth-century girl culture this assertion of the girl as girl is fully compatible with teen and youth film genres, in which agency, action, and even violence are not unthinkable for girls (especially given extreme circumstances). It is unnecessary to see Ripley (of the *Alien* series) or Nancy (in *Halloween*) as "boyish" (Clover 40) or masculine-identified in order to comprehend their agency in a dominant cinematic field. Girls in teen films have exactly this kind of compromised, enclosed agency. This is one of the conventions shared by teen and youth/horror film genres, along with fraught peer relations and a focus on "sex and parents" (Clover 49). Youth/teen horror films certainly play on the centrality for images of adolescence of gendered modes of social and psychic violence. *Nightmare on Elm Street*, for example, takes up the domestic alienation typical of teen film and makes a nightmare out of it; the incomprehension and self-interest of parents (often placed offscreen and thus excluded from possible identification) is responsible for the monster that stalks their teenage children.

The teen/youth horror film genre also represents sex as destruction, a narrative proper to teen rather than youth culture forms. Clover claims that in the slasher film "violence and sex are not concomitant but alternatives, the one as much a substitute for and a prelude to the other as the teenage horror film is a substitute for and a prelude to the 'adult' film" (29). This seems misleading in terms of what girls do in horror films. In teen horror the innocence or naïveté of the central girl is always eventually undermined—she is "the only one . . . whose perspective approaches our own privileged understanding of the situation" (Clover 44), and her final triumph is a transformation aligned with adolescence and, more viscerally, with puberty.[20] Like the gothic, the horror film is a discourse on knowledge that tends, in its teen formations, to the ironic. Clover understands this "self-ironizing" or, as she puts it, "camp" element in slasher films as an ironic relation "to taboo signifiers." While she remains uncertain about the effects or significance of this convention, beyond its constitution of "a remarkably competent audience" (41), her own analysis recognizes that these films turn on an opposition between what the girl "*does* and what she *seems*" as "opposed to what she *is*" (58). While the teen horror film has not been particularly indexed to girls in the audience, it inherits many of its central conventions from genres that are identified with girls—not only teen film but also the gothic.

Many gothic narratives center on a girl who is both the first and the final girl, and threat to the girl is articulated as enclosure and breach of personalized and often clearly domestic security and integrity. Horror films including *Frankenstein* and various incarnations of Dracula have taken up the gothic heroine as a girl who is both innocent and knowing. The gothic is about horror rather than terror because the girl always *knows*, even if uncertainly or ambivalently. The inflection of horror films with the spectacle of adolescent turmoil was made far more overt in a series of possession films, such as *The Exorcist* (1973) and *Rosemary's Baby* (1968), in which it is literally the girl's body rather than her consciousness that knows. While Clover wants to see these films as in fact films about men (65), they clearly turn on abjection—on horrifying transgression of bodily and self-other boundaries that I have already suggested are especially relevant to feminine puberty. The demon-girl in these films is a problem daughter and often opposed to the maternal that a Kristevan analysis of this abjection, such as Creed's, would prioritize. These can also be revenge films, including the classic *Carrie* (1976), which explicitly frames the demon-girl as pubescent drama of peer groups, sexual tension, and familial alienation.

While what is sometimes called feminine gothic is dominated by scary interiors, domestic scenes full of threat, things that appear genial and are in fact terrorizing, and familial and marital patriarchal oppression, most gothic narratives conventionally focus on a central girl. Teen horror takes up this location of the girl in a house identified with a more or less uncertain threat to her. Although the threat of the slasher film ubiquitously penetrates from the outside, "the same walls that promise to keep the killer out quickly become, once the killer penetrates them, the walls that hold the victim in" (Clover 31). In the 1990s the gothic elements of youth horror film further emphasized an ironic gothic form. The precursor to this gothic irony might be found in Jane Austen's parody of feminine gothic, *Northanger Abbey* (1818), directed to a presumed audience that significantly included young women. Feminine gothic texts are narratives of development that make gothic a genre of some significance to the formation of feminine adolescence. In *Northanger Abbey* Catherine Morland insists on thinking that the world resembles gothic fiction after the model of Anne Radcliffe's *Mysteries of Udolpho* (1794), all mansions with hidden passages, ancient murders, and horrifying secrets. These horrors do surround Catherine, but in the form of rather pedestrian social machinations around marriage and property.

The *Scream* cycle (beginning in 1996) marks a resurgence of the teen horror genre, parodying the slasher series such as *Friday the Thirteenth*. *Scream*'s "Final Girl" Sidney Prescott openly criticizes slasher films: "It's stupid. They're all the same. Killers stalking some big-breasted girl who's always running up the stairs when she should be running out the door. It's insulting" (Craven 1996). The *Scream* films both parody and follow the teen horror conventions: "the heroine sees the extent of the murders; the heroine sees the killer; the heroine does battle with the killer; the heroine kills or subdues the killer; the heroine survives; but the heroine is not free" (Dika quoted in Clover 25 n. 11). Clover recognizes that "the films following *Halloween* present Final Girls who not only fight back but do so with ferocity, and even kill the killer on their own, without help from the outside" (37). In *Scream* Sidney does have help, although not predominantly from men, but her own vigilance, resilience, and agency are what saves her. The final girl should be "presented from the outset as the main character" (Clover 39), a convention *Scream* also plays on by opening with a sequence casting well-known actress Drew Barrymore in a classic teen slasher scenario that seems to play her as central girl and then kills her.[21] While slasher films shift the filmic point of view and audience identification from the killer to the girl in the final stages of the film (Clover 45), the initial identification with the killer is not a requirement of teen horror.

The slasher film's final girl intersects with the teen film in the subgenres of pop horror and teen gothic. Teen gothic includes a diverse range of filmic texts from the cynical *Heathers* (Martin calls it "dark anti-teen" [65]) to the romantic *Edward Scissor-Hands* (1990) and the moral fables of *The Craft* (1994) and *Beetlejuice* (1988). In all these cases teen gothic is distinguished from horror by comedic elements and by its veiling or avoidance of the display of death and bodily permeability. On television these comedic elements help distinguish the teen romance of *Buffy the Vampire Slayer* (see fig. 7.3) and *Charmed*. Buffy's displays of the horrific are not very horrible. Death and hell are reversible, temporary, and amusing rather than alarming. This teen gothic is also tinged with irony, not confined to reflexive forms of situation comedy. More important, it also undercuts the developmental narrative of some earlier forms of feminine gothic. *Northanger Abbey* is a novel of false developments in which Catherine learns that her truths are false while the narrative knows they are true. The teen gothic film or television series is an instant of development with its own reversals built in, which is why Buffy could convert so successfully into television, where all growing-up narratives have to be abortive and repeatable so they can appear again next week.[22] In series four, Buffy goes to college but (as with other teen series, such as *Beverly Hills 90210*) the plots barely change.

While Buffy is privileged and exceptional in many ways (and, sure, a supernatural killer), like Cher, her life is bounded by familiar institutions and her difficulties—including teachers who don't understand, a broken family, a mother who wants to mother her, and a few obvious insecurities—prevent her being entirely inaccessible. Nevertheless Buffy (Sarah Michelle Gellar) is the star, and the audience is positioned by the camera alongside Buffy, looking at her. An analysis of the fight scenes indicates that while we see the monsters through her eyes some of the time, and occasionally her through the monsters' eyes, we mostly watch Buffy from slightly to one side of the action. It would also suggest that we are looking at Buffy's visual style as much as her fighting style. *Buffy* is as much about feminine adolescence as it is about monsters. Buffy's family or peer-group dramas and her unhappy or impossible love affairs pull these narratives together. While Buffy is framed as completely desirable, she never gets the guy except to discover that loving him will destroy him, her, or the world. One way in which *Buffy* exceeds the teen TV genre, though, is in its use of this central narrative of frustrated romance. It's not endless deferral of Buffy's romantic happiness that's a problem—after all this is something the show takes from soap operas, where all the thrill is in the achievement or winning of a lover, or in the love's impossibility or dissolution, never in a period of happiness. But Buffy remains an exception to the generic convention of romance as growing up because she cannot proceed to any absorbing future domesticity. The destiny articulated for Buffy is magical and deathly rather than heteronormative bliss.

Sunnydale, where the series is set, is built on a hellmouth, and like all mouths and most images of adolescence it is a place of border crossings—of incorporation, transformation, blending, destruction, and expulsion. Vampires get a special place in this as an instance of crossing the border between human and demonic. Vampires within this tradition are not only a crossing of the human/demon border but themselves cross a range of borders that, as much commentary on vampires attests, are crucial to defining the human—borders between self and food but also self and other, the inside and the outside of the body. But rather than abjecting these transgressions, Buffy lives them. For a story about essential good and essential evil, the ethical parameters of Buffy's narratives are surprisingly complex. *Buffy* is a story about consequences rather than fixed principles, and the evil or good of a being is mutable by their choices, and the evil or good of an action is mutable by its consequences. While *Buffy* seems to have an established metaphysics, a story about what is outside the material world, populated by essential characteristics, immortal souls, and divine principals, this map of living in the world repeatedly changes and supposedly immutable principles are adjusted according to the choices people make. This community of girls (in which the central men, boys, and vampires must be included) negotiates, as girl culture always does, discourses on individuality and group identity, regimes of power and powerlessness. *Buffy* as girl culture fending of the horrors of loss, self-doubt, and adulthood is an index for specific technologies of the self—locating the contact or exchanges between disciplinary powers (such as school, state, and parents) and self disciplines (processes of producing a self).

Without the teen inflection, gothic horror continues to center on the innocence/knowledge boundary articulated by a girl. Dana Scully from the successful series *The X-Files* resembles a late twentieth-century Catherine Morland. Every scientific ideal Scully has learned from television, educational institutions, and assorted other mentors and parents implodes as she is confronted with the instability of those truths and institutions.[23] In classic gothic mode *The X-Files* plays out its conspiracy theory in the imagination of the hero Fox Mulder, and on the body of Scully. The aliens that present dubious elements of the show's "real" narrative manifest as narratives about Mulder and Scully's families—especially Fox's sister—and in a storyline about Scully's sexuality. Not only has she been abducted (a gothic staple), but her body and especially her reproductive capacities have been invaded. Scully also intersects with the teenage girl narratives of television gothic through her insistent reference to institutional narratives of faith and doubt. In comparison to *The X Files* the teen gothic of *Buffy* or *Charmed* takes up exceptionally ordinary scenes for extraordinary experiences of self-revelation. While the framing distinctions between heaven and hell, good and evil, are not at all ambivalent, each of these narratives plays on the internal possibility of good and evil becoming their inverse. Sharing the everyday settings of the teen horror genre these girls encounter a mode of gothic horror threading through most banal workplace romances and high-school or college anxieties. These intersecting genres materialize girls as both threat and banality. They have little or no rebellious cachet, although various *Buffy* media/cultures indicate they can certainly work as subcultures, but they insistently return gothic conventions to the difficulty and promise of the girl's role in contemporary culture.

eight

In Visible Bodies

Only what happened on the streets mattered.

—Angela McRobbie and Jenny Garber, "Girls and Subcultures"

IF "GIRL" indicates uncertain narratives about identity, development and social position, if girls are marginal to narratives about culture and yet central to them, does girl culture have to reflect those uncertainties and displacements? In this chapter I want to return to the dominant privatized, psychologised discourses on feminine adolescence through the spectrum of youth culture's place in late modern culture. This chapter provides a context for thinking about how youth culture's narratives of public placement appear within the privatized discourses of what we might call girl culture and its primary definition by and understanding of feminine adolescence as narrative of embodiment.

This chapter focuses on contemporary intersections of public/popular culture and critical theory in representations of girls and embodiment. Popular culture and public discourses are not only shared across specific cultural locations but extend into girls' lives, including their experience of self. In the expanding body cultures of the twentieth century, feminine adolescence paradigmatically materializes theories about bodily presence, identification, and pleasure. This chapter specifically considers roles for girls within body cultures such as sport, beauty regimens, fashion industries, and eating disorders; theories about the importance of body image to girlhood; and the

8.1 Tracey Moffatt, *Nativity* (1974)
(© Tracey Moffatt. From the Backyard Series (1988). Roslyn Oxley 9 Gallery)

placement of girls' bodies in disciplinary orders including self-defense, dietary advice, and bedroom culture. Across this range popular culture for and representing or imagining girls itself provides theories about culture.

Feminine Adolescence and the Mirror Stage

In the Mirror: Girls and Identification

Sigmund Freud's most influential contributions toward a theory of feminine adolescence appear in theories that occur outside his strict theses on feminine development, in texts on narcissism and group identity. In *Group Psychology* Freud produced a highly influential model of identification, divided into three forms with developmentally arranged implications. The first form of identification is prior to proper individuality and exemplarily constituted in the identification of the boy child with his father. The second form of identification is proper to developing subjects and even adults, a modelling of one's self on an ideal figure (ego ideal). The third mode, which he sees as proper to girls in particular, is a group identification:

> Supposing, for example, that one of the girls in a boarding school has had a letter from someone with whom she is secretly in love which rouses her jealousy, and that she reacts to it with a fit of hysterics; then some of her friends who know about it will contract the fit, as we say, by means of mental infection. The mechanism is that of identification based upon the possibility of putting oneself in the same situation. (64–5)

Freud sees this form of identification as an immature positioning of the self. While identification has been important to late-twentieth-century critical theory—in film theory, feminist theory, and postcolonial theory—the first two types of identification rather than the third have usually been prioritized. In the first part of this chapter I want to focus on the work of some postpsychoanalytic feminist theories that enable us to think about identification in relation to body image as a useful concept in analyses of feminine adolescence.

Elizabeth Grosz proposes a feminist theory that does not distance itself from the body; a corporeal feminist theory that might displace the dominance of (Cartesian) mind-body dualism in Western philosophy (among other cultural theories). Grosz understands this dualism to found the preeminent distinctions between visible and invisible, and subject and object, which are the conditions of possibility for late modern ideas about body image. A discussion of girls and body image clearly raises many of the same questions as a discussion of puberty, and puberty can certainly be conceived as a systematic institution of the self in relation to normative body images. The understanding of adolescence as significant for "the development of the body image" relies on its close alignment with "major upheavals and changes as an effect of puberty" (Grosz 1994:75). This model of puberty is indebted to psychoanalysis, which has strongly influenced contemporary theories of identification and body image. Luce Irigaray also aims, within her critique of psychoanalysis as a continuance of Western philosophy, to deconstruct this dominant dualist separation of the body as visible object from the mind as invisible subjectivity. For Irigaray the feminine body insists on the entwinement in the flesh of the visible and the invisible, the object and the subject (Irigaray 1985a:168).

Drawing on the work of Maurice Merleau-Ponty she claims that the body is both visible and materially invisible because, if the subject is one who looks and sees himself, his body as visible object must be distanced from himself. Further, while the subject relegates this body (both me and not-me) to the Other (the feminine), which is thus the object and not the subject of vision, he only sees himself in this way within a field of vision conditioned by that possibility of his being seen.[1]

According to psychoanalytic theory, the subject is put together as an organism by the identificatory fantasy of the mirror stage: the successful production of body image as a kind of prescriptive map-making. Grosz's *Volatile Bodies* turns away from this visible materiality of the body in psychoanalysis, neurophysiology, and phenomenology toward the invisible materiality of the body mapped by Nietzsche, Foucault, and Deleuze. In this text Grosz argues against certain key psychoanalytic theories and prefers in some respects the Deleuzean model of a body without any organs to be cathected in its development. As Moira Gatens suggests, the mind-body division is always unstable: "mind is constituted by the affirmation of the actual existence of the body, and reason is active and embodied precisely because it is the affirmation of a *particular* bodily existence" (57). But this division remains central to psychoanalysis, which continues to delineate the concerns of much feminist theory. Psychoanalysis develops " 'the mysterious leap' from the body to the mind" (Grosz 1994:51) into a hierarchization whereby the mind is interpretable by its effects in the body, understanding the body as a reflection of the mind—hence the bodily speaking of hysteria and the potent reliability of the symptom. Grosz even describes the psychoanalytic ego as "both a map of the body's surface and a reflection of the image of the other's body" (1994:38)—as a body image.

Body image locates a unified representation of the self, but it is not necessarily stable and never independent of sociocultural definitions of body, image, and self. Theoretical and popular understandings of body image privilege the visual because the divisions self-other and subject-object are not only visually reinforced but also visual by necessity. We can never see the body image of another, only our interpretation of their relation to norms and dominant tendencies among images of the body—that is, in relation to our own body image.[2] Body image thus supports a fantasy of sociality: that others see you as you see yourself. These visual metaphors are especially significant to girls because in both popular culture and critical theory feminine adolescence has been strongly associated with visualized self-image. Girls' body images are predominantly understood in psychoanalysis as structured by visual metaphors, including the phallus and castration, and Lacanian psychoanalysis implies that girls are balanced, in relation to these terms, between acceptance of lack and a fragmentation characterized by fluidity of ego boundaries indicating a failure of subjectivity and body-image at once. Jacques Lacan's work on feminine sexuality (see Juliet Mitchell and Jacqueline Rose), following Freud, identifies a "narcissistic alienation" that contributes to hysteria (Lacan 1982b:68). But if women do not possess a certainty recognized as the ego they paradoxically embody the mirror or body image, and it is significant that while the ego represents salvation from psychosis, the mirror image and mirror stage constitute a failure to fit.

The girl in these theories is of course an abstraction—not any particular girl or girls. She is aware of the invisible mirror as the plane of her self-construction and of its ambiguous equivalence to her body image. She also knows that the body image is a nexus of power/knowledge with the body, a proposition that Lacan concretely genders when he writes that, in the mirror stage, "the subject anticipates in a mirage the maturation of his power," his "self-mastery" (Lacan 1977b:94–5). If women never resolve an ego in this way, what kind of mirror stage do they have? If something approximating the mirror stage is necessary to the formation of body image, feminine adolescence might locate processes comparable to the mirror stage. Uncertainty of body image is especially associated with adolescence, which as new body image already questions what is produced in the infantile mirror stage. As feminine adolescence is understood to especially emphasize the renegotiation of body image, the girl can not be assumed to have already either unified her body image or necessarily accepted her body as lack in ways that ensure an identity separate from and superior to her body. The continual processes of reforming body image characteristic of girl culture suggest a prolonged and vacillating mirror stage—an endless production of different unities that are never certainly separate from the body. The feminine adolescent desires her-self as she might become—a potential visualized in connection to other girls and constructed through observation of her own and other girls' bodies.

Narcissism

The specific forms by which the gaze addresses girls in modernity all leave room for the question: who looks at girls? Girls are often seen as exemplary objects of "being *watched*" (Freud 14:95), becoming-beautiful, and, of course, narcissism. Being watched—as Freud, Foucault, and John Berger differently assert—equally suggests processes of self-observation:

> A woman must continually watch herself. She is almost continually accompanied by her own image of herself. . . . From earliest childhood she has been taught and persuaded to survey herself continually.
>
> And so she comes to consider the surveyor and the surveyed within her as the two constituent yet always distinct elements of her identity as a woman. (Berger 46)

While psychoanalysis characterizes women by retarded superego development, it also accounts for girls as obsessively self-observing, and this self-regulation is particularly devolved onto her body image. Girls are, apparently, narcissistic. What Freud called normal or primary narcissism is a difficult but necessary transitional phase in ego development (14:77), but the secondary narcissism considered common among girls does not conform to this progression. For men, narcissism is an exception to the norm—avoiding his Mother as model for the sexual object (Freud 14:88)—but narcissism characterizes "the feminine form of erotic life" (88–9).

Bela Grunberger argues that narcissistic girls are attempting to compensate for the absence of valorizing recognitions of women. This "maternal deficiency" (73) as a sexual object demands that feminine adolescence be "the narcissistic stage *par excellence*" (71). Grunberger argues that "her body self will become increasingly important, extending from her body to her clothes and accessories to her 'home': her house and the material promises of her love life" (70). The currency of this model extends beyond psychoanalytic terminology or practice but draws on the ambiguous exchanges between castration, shame, and narcissism in Freud's account of femininity. Freud describes a woman weaving to cover her shame and to adorn herself—a self-love defined by self-hatred—as a significant analogy for femininity or female sexuality (which seem to be undifferentiated in this account). The girl, realizing her own devaluation, overcompensates for that loss in her self-image: "they are bound to value their charms more highly as a late compensation for their original sexual inferiority" (Freud 22:132). But refusal to pass through narcissism toward the Subject is perverse, and if girls cannot become the Subject they can nevertheless avoid perversion by moving toward him (Freud 14:73). Narcissism, in opposition to this development, is an avoidance of proper object-attachment, which is the anaclitic or Subject-object attachment girls are incapable of within this model. This desire to-be-looked-at still derives pleasure from the self in relation to others, and the girl's narcissistic identifications and gratifications are maintained in relation to an intensely social body image. The self-contentment Freud sees as characteristic of some young women is their certainty of being-loved.[3] While the girl's resemblance to the external object of her desire conforms to Freud's account of love rather than narcissism as it usually understood, he explains this satisfaction as regressive self-love rather than indicating a substantially satisfied ego ideal (which is possible for loved men). The classification of women as loved rather than loving suggests not only their passivity but also that girls manifest an inferior type of love. This inferiority informs rather than opposes what is widely discussed as girls' obsession with love.

These premises inform much contemporary feminist theory—as well as public discourses on and popular representations of girls. For Judith Butler's understanding of the body's materiality as "constitutive outside" (1983:8), body image might be an inscription of sexual difference: a gender performativity. Grosz imagines the body as a Möbius strip entwining inside and outside in order to examine

> the complex intertwining relations of mutual production and feedback of materially different bodies, substances, forms of matter, and materially different inscriptions, tracings, transformations, the interchanging between writing and bodies, bodies as the blank or already encoded surfaces of inscription. (1994:189–90)

The fashion model or the star might materialize such an inscriptive body image, entwining the imagined body and desire. The beautiful woman is utilized by Freud as exemplifying both narcissism and women's value as object of desire:

> The importance of this type of woman for the erotic life of mankind is to be rated very high. Such women have the greatest fascination for men, not only for aesthetic reasons . . . another person's narcissism has a great attraction for those who have renounced part of their own narcissism and are in search of object-love. (14:89)

This model is a display of self-love, but it is unclear what position is taken by women who find the model attractive—how is their unrelinquished narcissism attracted to this narcissistic display (given that the female homosexual is presumed by Freud to love in a *masculine* way). The narcissistic woman nevertheless forms herself at the expense of heterosexuality:

> The narcissistic woman strives to make her body into the phallus. She devotes loving time and energy to the image she has for others, her representation in the world. She paints/shaves/plucks/dyes/diets/exercises her body, and clearly derives pleasure from compliments about her looks. Her whole body becomes the phallus to compensate for a genital "deficiency," which she is able to disavow through her narcissism. The art of illusion and semblance become her greatest assets. She can utilize these techniques to mask, or cover over this "secret" insufficiency. (Grosz 1990:133)

Clearly these techniques are only the most open of secrets (see Sedgwick 1990), a "masquerade." Irigaray defines "masquerade" as "in particular, what Freud calls 'femininity.' The belief, for example, that it is necessary to become a woman, a 'normal' one at that, whereas a man is a man from the outset" (Irigaray 1985b:134). Girls who identify with the model do not achieve identity as the model (or on the model as screen for fantasies) but in connection to her, perhaps becoming but never achieving her.

The status of sexual difference as ontological fact remains vital to Grosz's analysis (1994:189), but her representation of the body as "quite literally rewritten, traced over, by desire" (56) resembles Butler's understanding of materialization. Body image is the self-location of the mirror image, the visible meshed with the invisible perception of one's own body. Like the ego, the body image is not a point to point representation of the body, but an own body map inseparable from dominant cultural models of order and identity. Grosz notes Lacan's claim that "the phallus has an a priori privilege in the constitution of the body image" (1994:59). When she asks whether there is "somewhere in woman's psyche, a representation of the phallus she has lost?" (1994:73), Grosz not only accepts the explanatory power of castration as a psychosocial constraint but also this privilege of the phallus in ordering the visual imagination of sexualized subjectivity.[4] The question remains, from Freud to Grosz, whether the girl produces a body image other than as self-observing identification with a phallocentric image of women's bodies.

Body Culture and Body Image
Fashion, Makeup, Self-Production

Irigaray points to a continuum or a consistency between the girl's mirror fascination and patriarchal images of motherhood: "And so she is one [une], at least for the gaze, covering up her lacerations with dazzling makeup, or her mothering persona" (1985b:54). A similar continuum is visible in Naomi Wolf's *The Beauty Myth*, which erases specific differences between maternal and feminine adolescent body images in order to see beauty myths as an attack on maternity. Wolf's text emphasizes the significance of body image and body cultures among late-twentieth-century women and, in particular, girls, referencing a wide range of popular discourses on feminine adolescence as body image. Mary Pipher's case studies also reflect this general absorption in body image, and Pipher explicitly aims to cure her patients of unhealthy attention to body image at the expense of other interests diagnosed as more significant. Protecting against this unhealthy interest in body image—and thus unhealthy bodies and selves—is a longstanding feature of girls' guidance manuals. While this is also true of texts for women, these are often positioned as a mature adult perspective on girls or immature women's lives—a pattern evident in the guidance culture of women-directed television talk shows.

Continuities between psychological and sociological theories of body image and popular discourses on girls' relations to diet, fashion, makeup, or body image, suggest that clear distinctions between the evaluations produced as popular culture and as theory might be problematic. Fashion and makeup as techniques of self-production provide excellent examples of this entwinement. Before modernity, dress was mostly discussed as a cover for whatever constituted the person. Disapproval of this concealment was increasingly addressed to young women, and modern discourses on girls have focused on dress as exemplary of mass-cultural identity. The moral foundation of this concern is evident in Eliza Linton's "Girl of the Period," who

> cannot be made to see that modesty of appearance and virtue in deed ought to be inseparable . . . we are willing to believe that she has still some modesty of soul left hidden under all that affrontery [sic] of fashion . . . if she could be made to see herself as she appears to the eyes of men, she would mend her ways before too late. (110–11)

Linton's opprobrium indicates the extent to which attitudes to dress mark girls as particular types, an understanding shared by feminist dress reform movements, the regulators of school uniform, and fashion designers.

In 1929 developmental psychologist Elizabeth Hurlock, a student of G. Stanley Hall, discussed modern fashion as a sex function or, following Havelock Ellis, a secondary sexual characteristic. Fashion pages, and the emergence of fashion magazines out of a blend of dressmaking and society magazines, record changes to fashion as paralleling changes to women's lives at this time. Linking fashion to the new psychologies of her time, Hurlock also notes that girls of a certain age ("The 'Show-off' Age") are "apt to look more like a caricature than like a copy of an original fashion plate" (184). Late modern girls are mass consumers and producers of fashion who record and thus materialize fashionable identities. The interpolation of identity in fashion is equally apparent in articulations of subjectivity produced in relation to the face. Cosmetics gave way to modern makeup at around this time—making up (openly suggesting dissimulation and masquerade) was the routine production of the kind of girl women wanted to be. The craft of glamour as an expanding discourse in the 1930s and 1940s (attached to more and varied beauty products) was even more publicly explicit, as a guidance column in a Hollywood star magazine attests:

> Contrary to general opinion, Hollywood beauty is not skin deep. It is not alone the rose-textured skin of sixteen or the gold of youthful curls. Hollywood beauty is, however, largely the result of self study, of effort and determination to correct a fault and a development of personal allure. (Van Wyck 182–3)

The Hollywood mode of glamour was an industrialized response to new roles for femininity in response to changed work, marriage, and education patterns. It was also a discourse on effort and self-production; a new version of the technologies of the self apparent in Victorian girls' guidance. Becoming-star (and later becoming-model) shares in the makeover theme of films and other popular cultural productions addressed to girls: girl transformed into an ideal girl through her effort and because of her innate value. While this revelation is always more spiritual than physical, it is pivotally manifest in the girl being seen.

Such technologies produce and display the coherent self that adolescence is supposed to achieve. A 1940 grooming handbook advocates to this end,

> clothes that have one thought in mind . . . if that thought is YOU . . . express a definite idea: "Susan is romantic" . . . "Susan is Victorian" . . . "Susan likes sports" . . . "Susan is a good scout" . . . "Susan is in love" . . . Susan is Smooth. And this one-ness is the beginning of a definite sense of style. (Giles 19)

Fashion provides a range of already sanctioned codes for coherence and recognition to be cited by the girl in pursuit of identity. In synthesizing this unified character, the beauty routine and the fashionable look are synecdochic of the process of adolescence. Fashion is not an individual aesthetic but a process of simultaneously producing, recording, and consuming the self. As with all advertising technologies, the seller exaggerates (makes up) the value from which the commodity is detached. As desirable commodity and exemplar of unfinished processes of self-production it is the girl that modern makeup signifies and modern fashion outlines. While there are diverse genres of desirable looks in contemporary beauty and fashion advice/coverage, the ideal girl maintains a highly desirable position as both practiced and yet not artificial.

Beauty cultures are not necessarily external effects of interiorized psychological practices. They are not concretely individual performances, although they are singular in their individual relations to the sociality of beauty culture, and they are not determined by the dictates of mass culture, although such dominant discourses are part of a girl's social field. Fashion is now generally represented as mass produced, but if it is not necessarily an expression of individuality it is always a production of identity. Girls clearly inflect the most required and most homogenous fashions (such as school uniforms and midriff T-shirts) with their own lives or social positions. This is unavoidable because fashion is subject to regulation (school rules and public laws, for example) and limitation (available finances, for example), but it is also always an articulation of girls' cultural identities. Within girl culture there are many positions on the dominant late modern demand for girls to (want to) be fashionable, encompassing many different modes of discipline and identification. While even the most standardized objects do not produce standardized people (despite the anxiety of much cultural commentary), all fashion presents standardization as one possible response to the social imperatives of feminine adolescence. Fashion is both change and continuity, an ambiguity particularly associated with youth, and in this instance with girls. In the most conformist fashion modes girls are often considered subject to a planned obsolescence operating within the fashion industry. However, girls repeatedly reject or abandon fashions that those industries would have them take up, and the plethora of new lines all the time is only one element of girls' diversity. Girls are also involved in antifashion fashion—styles that do not appear fashionable but that, in order to be recognizable as not fashionable, nevertheless require a degree of standardization. Unrecognized clothes could signify bad taste, fashion failure, or poverty, while antifashion is carefully coded. Punk or riot grrl fashion, for example, is recognizable as not mainstream by producing a particular identifiable style.[5] Articulating a position beyond or opposed to fashion is thus also a way of marketing clothes to girls.

Critiques of beauty culture often presume it does not provide girls with access to valuable modes of self-production, but instead distracts them from real achievement: "Women have become The Face, yet their achievement of face paralyses other social practices" (Craik 95). Visual girl cultures clearly constitute girls as not only what is seen but as an audience and a viewing subject.[6] But dominant theories of the gaze and visual culture claim that how girls/women are brought to look at themselves is not self-recognizing in the same way as the valorized gaze by which the Subject knows himself. As with Wolf's beauty myth, these theories are not always explicitly psychoanalytic but have been shaped by a series of popularly received psychoanalytic premises about subjectivity. For psychoanalysis this gaze is presumed to be necessarily heterosexual in the sense that it affirms the Subject against a feminized object. For example, girl readers looking at the girl in a girls' magazine are expected to be framed by expectations of appropriation and thus to reinforce a subject-object gendering, utilizing the homoerotic for what Eve Sedgwick calls "the preservation of an essential *heterosexuality* within desire itself" (1990:87).

Rather than looking at themselves being looked at, however, girl readers of girls' magazines are looking at each other as desirable. The heterosexual frame provided by the magazines does not erase what Diana Fuss identifies as "the articulation of lesbian desire within the identificatory move itself" (1992:730). Fuss's psychoanalytic account of "Fashion and the Homospectatorial Look" argues that eroticized images of women in women's magazines compel that audience "to verify herself endlessly, to identify all her bodily parts, and to fashion continually from this corporeal and psychical jigsaw puzzle a total picture, an imago of her own body" (1992:718). In girls' magazines, moreover, this picture or totality is a collage surface like the surface presented by any given page in the genre, laying out images, words, and advertisements in barely differentiated proximity to each other. The profusion of homoerotic images in girls' magazines is shaped by a claimed immediacy of identification, while apparently similar images from women's magazines differentiate between woman and product. Fuss discusses the "spectatorial" object of women's magazines "not as an object of desire but rather a point of identification" (1992:714). She thus differentiates between desiring to be and to have the woman (716), but identification functions in girls' magazines to produce desiring the girl as being the girl. This contradiction produces girls among girls in an *identification as becoming* that does not erase desire.

Visual images of girls in girls' magazines are of two main types: partial and situational. The partial image fragments the girl's body and focuses on the possible perfection of that formal component of her body, while the situational explains how this perfectible body should be used. As Wolf's discussion of "beauty pornography" (1991:132 ff.) suggests, these image-types are strikingly similar to "light" pornography in men's magazines. In both genres these types may be discussed as the fetishization of body parts and the externalization of fantasy.[7] The genre's processes of identification thus also produce anxiety based on difference between girls (and girls' bodies) manifest in body and beauty problem pages and coverage of body image problems and bodily health problems (which are kept distinct within the genre). Commodified as both consumer and marketplace, the girl is produced as not only the space in which Woman will be delineated but also, because of this incompleteness, as full of diverse possibilities for self-production. This feminine adolescent identity is the ultimate commodity on sale to girls. This is not about a future lack for which current commodities/pleasures compensate. Girl as ideal heterosexual object conflicts with feminine adolescence as pause before heterosexuality, and here the girl desires other girls as images of herself and herself as a mirror of other girls, all guarded by a limited homosociality allowed to girls. In relation to this genre, and visual girl culture more generally, girls are not confined to imitation. Identification is always more productive than imitation, and it is the connective process rather than the product that is necessary to identification as becoming.

Eating Disorders

As Lawrence Grossberg notes in his essay, "The Deconstruction of Youth," forms of youth culture are among the most visible processes of the modern disciplinization of youth. While Grossberg focuses on a public youth culture dominated by young men, the understanding of discipline he draws from Foucault for this purpose can also be deployed to think about girl culture. Foucault argues that the displacement of spectacular punishment by discipline produces observation as a preeminent mode of exercising power, one that does not straightforwardly distinguish between the subject and object of that power. Foucault's example is an ideal prison he calls "the panopticon"— a circular prison designed to see everything a prisoner does and impose upon them regimes of being seen.[8] Foucault's "The Eye of Power" claims, "There is no need for arms, physical violence, material constraints, just a gaze. An inspecting gaze, a gaze which each individual under its weight will end by interiorizing to the point that he is his own overseer, each individual thus exercising this surveillance over, and against himself" (1980:155). A model of power within which observation exercises power without reference to external imposition is clearly relevant to girl culture, which so often works through normative self-observation. Feminists such as Susan Bordo have aligned this modern disciplinary mind-set with the self-monitoring that produces conformity to fashion codes and body images. For Bordo, as for Wolf, beauty practices "train the female body in docility and obedience to cultural demands while at the same time being *experienced* in terms of power and control" (Bordo 1993:27).

Eating disorders have provided a key example for such discussion of girls. Accounts of the anorexic or other eating disorders as self alienated from body generally fail to account for the significance of the processes of feminine adolescence to such a position. As guides for teenage girls and their families state or imply: "as the adolescent girl's body approaches an aesthetic perfection found at no other time in the life span, she becomes more dissatisfied with her physical appearance than ever" (Harper and Collins 1978b:46). Many critics have subsequently understood eating disorders as a struggle and recognized power as a central issue in these disorders, constituted through the presumed perfectibility of a girl's body. Most feminist responses to eating disorders focus on anorexia, which constitutes an excellent allegory for the disappearance of self often assigned to feminine adolescence. These analyses tend to consider it an effect of castration, focusing both on the tragedy of anorexia's appeal to the most promising (intelligent, successful, beautiful) young women, and on anorexia as a rejection of femininity. Bordo claims "the relentless pursuit of thinness is an attempt to embody certain values, to create a body that will speak for the self in a meaningful and powerful way" (1993:47). Grosz indicates that

> neither a "disorder" of the ego nor, as popular opinion has it, a "dieting disease" gone out of control, anorexia can, like the phantom limb, be a kind of mourning for a pre-Oedipal (i.e., precastrated) body and a corporeal connection to the mother that women in patriarchy are required to abandon. Anorexia is a form of protest at the social meaning of the female body. Rather than see it as an out-of-control compliance with the current patriarchal ideals of slenderness, it is precisely a renunciation of these "ideals." (1994:40)

Joan Brumberg, on the other hand, rejects such claims as "venerating" and "romanticizing" anorectics as "heroic freedom fighters" (in Bordo 1993:65).

This body is defined as immanent womanhood, and these studies tend to ignore the ways in which girl culture not only eroticizes the normalization of the body but also normalizes a scene in which girls are never as perfect as the girl they are practicing to be. These accounts are also shaped by psychoanalysis, which has closely linked girlhood to negotiations of sex/gender in relation to food. They figure anorexia as a mechanism for coping with a particular body through obsessive control or rejection:

> Anorexics seem to take to extremes the egalitarian disdain for female corporeality in their attempts to think the subject as a pure transcendence, a pure will unbounded by bodily needs and limitations. They exhibit a kind of wishful megalomania, the fantasy of the self-made and completely self-controlled subject, the subject who needs nothing and no one. (Bordo 1993:212n)

Anorexia rejects the body's controlling mechanisms: the instinct to eat but also in turn the sexed functioning of the body, including menstruation. This can only be a rejection of the feminine body if that body is essentially characterized by these attributes. This rejection thus specifically addresses a body coded exclusively as maternal-heterosexual.[9] Grosz responds to this model of anorexia as a crisis of self-control by insisting that

> the very status of the body as product—the question is whose product?— remains at stake here. While psychological investigations are clearly useful and necessary in accounting for women's—and, less frequently, men's—entwinement with dietary and exercise procedures, such approaches risk duplicating the mind/body dualism and taking the body as a kind of natural bedrock. (1994:143–4)[10]

The anorexic body, like the hysteric, has also been seen as a positive self-assertion—the anorexic, "demands the positive presence of the absence of food: she demands 'no thing,' 'no food' " (Grosz 1990:64). Both the anorexic and the hysteric practice a femininity otherwise coded as positively desirable. Foreshadowing contemporary accounts of anorexics, Freud writes that "the majority of hysterical women are among the attractive and even beautiful representations of their sex" (14:99). Feminist diagnoses of anorexia repeatedly refer to an interpenetration of fashionable femininity and body image.[11] Produced by the inscriptive power of an observation in which she takes the principle part, this idea of the anorexic is an agent only in complicity with the model's power. While the model proclaims apparent coherence and self-control, the anorexic appears to make desire for and anxiety over the mind-body distinction visible. Anorexia is not defined by a goal— it is a becoming (not thin but thinner) that could never reach a thin state. The anorexic is a captivating image, not as the model or other beautiful body she might refer to but as extreme control and disappearing. Analyses of anorexia that insist only the strongest and most promising young women become anorexic deserve more interrogation than they have been subject to, principally because the selection of subject-groups and subjects' identification with the label are at issue in that research. But the anorexic certainly is an intimacy with power, practicing with excellence a mode of the observation that characterizes feminine adolescence.

The anorexic body is also a powerful assertion of boundaries not apparent in public constructions of the bulimic body, which has a different relation to those *objets à* that define the abject: to food, vomit, feces, and menstrual fluid. According to Julia Kristeva's theory of abjection, even drawing the gaze toward corporeal boundaries can risk the symbolic order that defines how and as what girls should live. The simultaneous rejection and sacrilization of the body that Kristeva aligns with the abject inform the imaginary relations of girls, a drama that the anorexic powerfully evokes. But Kristevan abjection relegates the body to the place of the Mother or Woman, while eating disorders struggle with that process of relegation. A girl's abjection turns upon a corporeal self dramatically separated from her desirable body image. A clean and proper identity (one capable of speaking) becomes the reflection and not the girl.[12] While Grosz questions the maternalizing account of anorexia as fear of pregnancy (1994:139), she still considers anorexia a relation to the mother through abjection. Anorexia is recurrently diagnosed as resistance to the periodization of the feminine body. Even Hilde Bruch, who emphasizes a link between anorexia and fashion, describes "the anorectic's 'battle' against the adult development of her body" (quoted in Bordo 1993:45).

The model is the preeminent modern type of desirable woman, and one always produced in relation to feminine adolescence. The model and the anorexic are effects of and effect negative inscriptions of feminine adolescence, but while feminist theories of feminine adolescence must recognize the importance of body image to this inscriptive crisis, they must also recognize the significance of such self-production. The model foregrounds relations between the self and the body/object, but has no self insofar as she embodies the veiling function of the phallus. The model can be understood as Jean Baudrillard's "simulacra," which

> marks the triumph of the image, the represented object, of the visible in so far as it becomes visual—that is, an object of scopic consumption. Hyper-realistically over-represented, this object remains profoundly absent (like "the body," "the woman," "the feminine," and so on).
>
> The bodily surface, and the complex montage of organs that composes it, is thus reduced to pure surface, exteriority without depth, a movable theater of the self. (Braidotti 1994:49–50)

The model is not about any solid identity—she is made-up, masked. This mask is inscribed on a surface someone, but impermanently; the mask is about change rather than definition. The anorexic is also a model body, herself a style. No girl becomes anorexic without reference to discourses on anorexia (usually popular as well as medical discourses). The anorexic thus makes explicit the processes of transforming and producing the self and foregrounds the technologies of the self by which girls are formed in relation to the sociality of a body image—not as individual psychopathology but as a lifestyle.

Life Styles
Health Cultures

Philosopher Alfonso Lingis characterizes modernity by the "civilized" reduction of the erotogenic sites of the body (see Grosz 1994:138–44). Beauty cultures do not conform to this narrative and retain an association with the primitive as well as with technological or artificial sophistication. This modernization of body image is often represented as a process of commodification: "The civilized body is constituted as a use value and its dimensions and capacities become purchasable commodities, capable of selective augmentation, replacement, or transformation" (Grosz 1994:141). The anorexic, the model, and other craftings of body image materialize labor at becoming beautiful, but the labor of the self rather than for another. Because the anorexic is presumed to be an effect of commodification, and the model the embodiment of that process, they are not understood as viable forms of self-production. But similar processes of manipulating body image are positively coded forms of feminine adolescence, and the most validated of these are sport cultures for girls.

The nineteenth-century institution of schooling for girls included and often emphasized exercise as a bodily regimen with crucial psychosocial effects. Observation of girls' development and bodily maintenance (often the precise measurement of these within discourses such as anthropometry) combined with dietary advice and formalized exercise programs to help constitute feminine adolescence as a technologized scene for self and body discipline. Sport for girls was not unambiguously embraced by these institutions, but health cultures were, and forms of individual and team sport often participated in that drive to methodically produce better-quality girls. The ideologies deployed in these exercise cultures directly addressed the significance of girls both as future mothers—that is, as useful bodies—and as images of social morality. Sherrie Inness claims the scientific of physical education in the United States in the 1890s "aimed at making women better mothers rather than at giving them 'an exhilarating awareness of physicality and the potential significance of body control' " (221).

These girl culture forms often aligned individuality with maturity after the fashion of dominant discourses at the time, but this was to some degree conflicted by the new arrangement of girls into peer groups. While caution was inspired by the danger that excessive or inappropriate exercise for girls might reduce their naturally attractive girlishness, sport for girls was also framed by concern that team sports would provide excessively strong allegiances between girls (Inness 223). In the early twentieth century this concern was displaced by the institutionalization of new ideas about the healthy body-type, which emphasized an obligation to produce that healthfulness in visible body cultures. Dancing troupes, sporting stars, and other active displays of bodily health became part of a young woman's expected range of enjoyments and concerns. Jill Julius Matthews accounts for how ideas about modernity were mapped onto women's bodies in the 1920s and 1930s through emerging discourses on beauty (see Matthews 1987) and exercise and dance (see Matthews 1995). A young woman's pleasures, and even her concern with beauty, were thus valid components of normalizing institutions: "The modern female body was . . . different in the same way for everyone. It was young, slender, tanned, fit not muscular, attractive but not sensual" (Matthews 1987:31).

Health models are highly visible in late modern everyday life, from educational systems through changing medical standards to media dissemination of diet and weight-loss narratives and advertisements. Although an alignment between health and weightlessness remains specific to certain cultural contexts, this is also influenced through global promotion of the Western body.[13] Within this discursive regime, sport and other health cultures for girls form a continuum with the dominant body-type often thought responsible for trapping girls in subordination to normative fashion and body images. Healthy bodies may be preferable to unhealthy ones, but the condemnation of beauty culture draws much of its force from positively coded discourses on managing one's body. The healthy body can equally provide a tyrannical body image in relation to which some girls (with different bodies) are coded as inferior, or as manifesting insufficient attention and effort concerning their body. Discourses on the virtuous healthy body are especially directed at girls, and health and beauty cultures consistently overlap with girls' guidance culture. In the late twentieth century in particular, beauty culture was dramatically invested with the positive social program of health by new discourses on fitness. "Fitness" not only produced new commodities and new lifestyles that utilized them but also recast existing lifestyles. A new proliferation of dietary models appropriated the alternative rejection of processed food, as well as the new acceptability of muscle bulk for women engaged with previously marginal images of the beautiful feminine body.

In relation to these shifts in public and popular body images and the lifestyles that produce them, athleticism has become more relevant to Western girls' everyday lives. The cultural circulation of sporting bodies through such forums as the modern Olympic Games as much as popular cultural texts, film, magazines, and television programs promotes a fitness-modified feminine body that is coded as youthful and often as girlish. While Pierre Bourdieu correctly notes that the Olympic spectacle is mediated by media coverage tailored to various audience interests—"The sports given prominence and the individual games or meets shown must be carefully selected to showcase the national teams most likely to win events and thereby gratify national pride" (1998:80)—this spectacle is equally tailored to meet expectations concerning the gendered performance of the spectacular sporting body. The body produced in certain sports merits more attention than others, regardless of national success, and girls' and women's bodies are specified and differentiated by sport according to dominant aesthetics that are also not dependent on success within a particular sport.

Certain sports (such as athletics) are seen to produce exceptional girls while others are associated with ideal bodies for ordinary girls. Some sports, moreover, focus on the display of feminine bodies in similar modes to fashion modeling.[14] Health cultures are generally both beauty cultures and lifestyle industries, and they appear as such in public forums where the sports star works as image of health and beauty (as well as locus of national or regional identification). This is specifically the case in girl culture forms, such as television series and girls' magazines, where sports stars make guest appearances. Sports stars also function as model fashionable bodies in calendars and magazines. Although not reliant on age or maturity this "fitness" actually cites and mirrors adolescence. Youth is the presumed index of fitness—the pinnacle of complete physical development unmarked by the degeneration of age—but fitness is also a discourse on subjectivity as process and a preoccupation with personal training highly familiar to modern girls.

At the end of the twentieth century popular culture spotlights sports stars and, in a different way, sport and fitness as a field against which the sports star is articulated in her singularity. However, some sports do not produce stars because they lack either the necessary cultural capital or a dramatically sculpted body on which coverage could focus. While spectacular (televizable) girls'/women's sports are amenable to the representation of individual star beauty, they are at the same time covered by mass media as masculinizing or a deferral of womanliness. They nevertheless remain overwhelmingly less visible than the prowess and heroism narratives in media coverage of men's sports. Everyday girls' sports—weekend or school sports—are not spectacles of prowess or star beauty, nor will they be so in their grown-up forms. Sport as part of girls' lives continues to be propagated in educational institutions as a compulsory element of Western schooling for adolescent bodies. As the same compulsory shaping of the body through sport is not applied to any other group, where sport and health are a matter of individual choice/agency, this continues the monitoring of adolescent bodies through health policy.

Within contemporary Western health policies girls mostly appear with reference to the dissemination of dietary and body-image advice, and sexual or reproductive health.[15] This is especially the case for girls' puberty manuals and health or personal development classes, where a discourse on chastity phrased as sex education provides information about contraception, sexual practices, and sexually transmitted diseases. These health cultures involve a complex interpenetration of self, body, and culture and present the performance of healthy body image as directly reflecting a healthy self. Like eating disorders they train the self as a body and constrain the body's movements and pleasures in the interests of performing the proper girl's body-self image. The practices of a girl's body image are thus morally inflected, and girls are, moreover, trained to see their bodies as continually under threat—not only from the meanings attached to their own femininity, as suggested by eating disorders, but also from the outside world. This is especially apparent in dominant discourses on self-defense for women.

Self-defense training, as distinct from martial arts training, focuses on consciousness of threat and crafting a sense of body via a sense of space. The dominant rhetoric of self-defense for women is directed primarily at an image of the single girl as mobile and unprotected and presumes its participants attend as victims or potential victims rather than for physical training. The pivotal rhetorical move of this field of courses, pamphlets, books, and posters positions the girl's body as intrinsically vulnerable. It defines the girl by a sexualized embodiment founded on threat, rhetoric all the more troubling for employing a language of empowerment. Girls are surrounded by ideas about their own fragility, and self-defense for women is premised on this sexualized vulnerability, encoding the feminine body as an eminently violable vessel. Self-defense scenarios are very often rape scenarios, and within them rape is often construed as the preeminent threat to girls and as almost equal to death. The preeminence of learning to defend yourself with "things you carry in your bag everyday" is both an arming of girls against possible danger and a presumption that enough personal consideration of risks and defense will enable protection. The other staple element of this self-defense is the modification of an attitude presumed to be proper to girls—a timidity, passivity, and incapacity for violence—which reinforces the normative image it transgresses in a good cause.

In this context girls' bodies are rehearsed as subject to assault within a developmental language proper to the presumed dependence and vulnerability of girl sexuality. Because the body is inseparable from its cultural inscriptions, which may invest women's bodies as elements of personhood differently than men's, the gendering of violence is pragmatically necessary. But legal recognition of difference, for example, between a woman's and a man's breast remains different from claiming girls are personally determined by the inviolate form of their bodies. Rape and sexual assault are predominantly committed against girls/women with the overt effect of diminishing their ways of living. But girls are not bounded quantities of sexual availability and these discourses on defense, as well as the violence they protect against, define girls by a conception of their bodies as sexualized territory—by a reterritorialization of their possible movements. Deleuze and Guattari's conception of how different cultures of violence interact with one another articulates such binary oppositions between territory and movement as the interaction of "war machines" (see Deleuze and Guattari 1987). While their theoretical excursions with war machines are concerned with violence and the state, the idea of a self to defend as a mode of being in the world is determined by relations to the state. The body of the self-defending girl is as much an artificial body as the padded dummy attacker—it is a body image detached from herself; an ideal and an abject body image folded into the girl's ideal and abject relations to the world. This body image is a fragile sexualized territory over which women have a duty of care that also claims to reflect their healthfulness as a person. "Scream; Run; Be aware of your surroundings" are mechanisms that fix, bound, and contain the territory to be defined as much as they put up barriers against attack. This self-defense predicated on a girl's physical inadequacy presumes that these sexualized threats are both external to her home and inscribed upon her body.

Bedroom Culture

Bordo adopts Foucault's model of power and discipline to assert that in "the organisation and regulation of the time, space, and movements of our daily lives, our bodies are trained, shaped, and impressed with the stamps of prevailing historical forms of selfhood" (1997:91). Girlhood is represented across various forms of girl culture as a process of containment. The most significant of these appears to be her containment in relation to her own body. This section considers the representation of girls as especially determined by a domestic subspace. Girls often seem to be not only produced in relation to the nuclear family but to live their adolescence closely contained within its territory. Even when participating in cultural practices specific to them as a genre, girls are seen to remain within enclosed domestic spaces:

> Boys are thought to occupy the public world for their leisure and subcultural activities, while girls are thought to resort to the private sanctuary of the bedroom where they read teeny bopper magazines and indulge in fantasies with their girlfriends about rock stars and *Jackie* pin-ups. (McRobbie 1991:72)

This is also a relation between bodies and public visibility that influences possible modes of being-in-the-world.

In the ethnographic component of *Teenage Wasteland,* Donna Gaines quickly differentiates between girls' and boys' interaction with public space:

> it was usually the guys that I hung round with. It was easier to hook up with them. If I saw them anywhere, any time, with rare exception, I could be included. Mostly we did nothing. The girls, though, always had a mission pending; some shopping, an errand, a planned chance meeting with

"him" which meant they had to travel light. . . . Unless they are involved in some heavy drug scene, girls will normally be gone from the street by the time they reach legal age. (117–18)

Gaines describes these girls as "insular; they mostly hang out in pairs, rarely more than trios. . . . You have to be a best friend to get really close. Their conversations tend to be more local, personal, private. The girls are a subculture within a subculture" (118). Girls are excluded from youth culture defined as public spectacle of resistance, disenfranchisement, and threat by narratives about girls' developmental psychology and by discourses on girl as public victim, but also by popular models of girl culture. While girls occupy a wide range of social spaces and lifestyles, they are publicly understood as marginal participants in youth as spectacle, and as proper to more enclosed spaces—houses, bedrooms, and shopping centers. As central participants in activities that are not spectacular, or even invisible, girls thus do not conform to many of the defining characteristics of youth culture.

Mike Brake figures girl culture as a period/space wherein a girl learns skills necessary for her mostly private functions within a heterosexist patriarchal schema. As these skills seem trivial in terms of public life he contends that girls need subcultures to retreat or escape. Yet Brake details only one example of girl subculture, which therefore becomes, in his analysis as in so many others, the archetypal girl subculture:

The TeenyBopper subculture is a retreat and a preparation for young girls. They can relate to their best friend (girls often emphasize the importance of their best friend, whose friendship they see as continuing after marriage) and together practise in the secrecy of girl culture for the rituals of courtship, away from the eye of male ridicule. (143)

Celia Cowie and Sue Lees object to this confinement of girls "within subculture theory" by the identification of separate gender-spaces—which means, for girls, "namely a bedroom culture and a lavatory culture" (28).

Defining youth culture by reference to visible subcultures and in opposition to the domesticity or other enclosed ways of living considered proper to girlhood also works to naturalize that division. Phil Cohen notes that feminists have centrally criticized the overwhelming gender blindness of youth research. Several decades of work by male social scientists had done little or nothing to challenge the popular view that youth was boys being boys, usually in the street, while girls went on practising being little wives and mothers somewhere else, usually indoors, where from this vantage point they were both out of sight and out of mind. (Cohen 202)[16]

Appearance in public spaces enables identification of youth culture practices as active lifestyles, while youth culture operating in a domestic space appears constrained by a parent culture. Girls do, of course, appear in public. Cowie and Lees contest McRobbie's claim that the figure of the "street walker" limits girls' appearance on "the streets," arguing instead that it "pronounces the terms on which they can be seen on the street i.e., as girlfriend or slag" (Cowie and Lees 30). There are other options for occupying the street as a girl—as worker, for shopping, in groups of friends—but girls are predominantly understood as less likely to occupy public space. Kerry Carrington notes, moreover, that "most public spaces are not 'public' at all" but in fact available to a specific range of groups in different ways: "the female toilet would not need to exist to fulfil girls' unfulfilled leisure needs if girls had equal and self-determining access to alternative leisure facilities and social resources" (1989:92–3). It is relevant here that although girls are aligned with the private, home, or domestic field, girls were not named in the same way as women by the pervasive organization and mechanization of domesticity during the interwar years and are thus not assigned a public role by their domesticity.

The private and public spheres, and their intersection in fields such as the marketplace and the family, have been reconstituted in late modernity through various disciplinary regimes. Following the spectacles of youth resistance in the 1960s many forms of public youth culture have been positioned in public commentary as, by comparison, futile exhibitions of social displacement rather than resistance. But such a comparison ignores changes to the public and private mechanisms by which young people's lives and actions are defined and interpreted. Foucault's analyses of governmentality interrogate the state apparatuses that tactically produce and arrange populations, economies, and knowledges. He notes that the "finality of government resides in the things it manages and in the pursuit of the perfection and intensification of the processes which it directs"

(1991:95). Gordon Tait, claiming that the Birmingham School homogenized diverse experiences under the categories of youth and subculture (2), suggests that Foucault's work "necessitates a re-evaluation of the dominant assumptions underlying subculture theory and offers in its place a model which re-locates street kids, and youth itself, as artefacts of a network of governmental strategies" (1). As Carrington asserts, these strategic agencies are not "the necessary effect of the essential structure of society (capitalist, patriarchal) and the replication of its logic of control through the institutions of social government, as generally suggested in the cultural studies literature on youth subcultures" (1990:30). Consideration of governmentality allows analysis of girl culture to recognize how public strategies make contact with the everyday lives of girls and are differentiated along gender lines by culturally specific expectations, including those of subculture theory.

Private spaces and domestic cultures, rather than public space and subcultural styles understood as self-expression, seem to structure girls' lives. While in feminist studies the possibility that the private might be a field of resistance has been recognized, in youth cultural studies this has not been equally apparent. Most researchers contend, however, that girls make different use of private space than do boys. McRobbie suggests "that the development of tightly knit girls' friendship groups may serve to give girls private space—centring on imaginary encounters with the help of images and commodities from popular culture" (1991:14). Feminine adolescence and modern girlhood have been formed at an intersection of the domestic field and developmental theories, and it is thus unsurprising that research on girls should find their development dominated by domesticity. Emerging discourses on feminine adolescence have in fact helped constitute such distinct social fields. While the popularization of the teenager as extended familial dependence further refined apprehension of the girl as a way of being in the world, the home that boys and their subcultures are thus seen to exceed is also the ground of their formation (see Grossberg 1994:188). Girl culture articulates cultural activities and situations found specific to girls and, moreover, framing a culturally specific model of consumption situated by reference to a domestic girl space. While boys as much as girls might participate in bedroom culture, girls' association with this space belongs to preexisting discourses on girls' lives.

The phenomenon of bedroom culture could be approached through phenomenological theories of being-in-the-world, the feminist idea of the situated body, or through Pierre Bourdieu's concept of "habitus." Bedroom culture is referenced not only to the popular distribution of the teenager but also to legislation on majority and property, and disciplines related to families, employment, and sex. Education locates girls as more closely defined by curricula and school disciplines in comparison to boys; girls' occupations are frequently domesticated by being framed as ornamental or service oriented; girl sexuality is popularly constructed as passive and oriented toward domesticity; and it is generally accepted that "parents control girls' spare time much more closely" than boys' (Brake 142). Bedroom culture is chiefly defined in relation to the idea of the daughter and presumed to reflect not only a position in the world but also a specific range of psychologies. The gendered space of bedroom culture is both normal and pathological, both personal and public. It is also a subfield materialized in opposition to the public field of youth culture. Both bedroom culture and youth culture are commodified styles of being in the world, but produced and sold with different presumed relations between individuals and collectives and different relations to law and public space. Youth rebellion often connotes the public dissatisfaction and disenfranchisement of youth who may have attained majority in any effective sense but still remain dependent on external authoritative definition of their place in the world. But if bedroom culture is highly determined by its location—indexed to the personal, the ornamental, the popular, attenuated to the nuclear family—this does not have to be harmonious. Bedroom culture can be a form of isolation from or resistance to family authority.

The concept of habitus when applied to feminine adolescence must intersect with a range of visualizations of the self and the self's location—it can neither be confined to nor avoid the importance of visual cultures to late modern girlhood. Fig. 8.1, the Australian artist Tracey Moffatt's recapturing of a backyard girlhood in "Nativity" provides a suitably multilayered example of this. This image is both an image of imagining an everyday girl relation to images of girlhood (partly contextualized by the discussion of the Blessed Virgin as icon and image in chapter 5) and a representation of habitus—enmeshing self, location, space, and self-perception with the social standards for those important discourses on the personal self. This girl game, this home, this region, this nation-state, this socioeconomic specificity, these friends, these knowledges, this image, this act of representation are all part of what makes habitus a rich version of self-perception as well as a structural analysis of social location.

Cowie and Lees argue that "there can be no 'different space' that is not always and already the product of gender relations" (21). All culture takes place not only in a particular context but with reference to a certain highly specific foundation for making sense of it. Bourdieu terms this personalized ground for meaning "habitus." This might be referred to the semiotic "notion of 'ground' (a sort of context of the sign which makes pertinent certain attributes or aspects of the object and thus is already a component of meaning)" (de Lauretis 39–40), but Bourdieu means something even more negotiated and relational. Habitus resembles the phenomenological position as well as the semiotic ground. In phenomenology, as I have inferred above, "for the subject to take up a position as a subject, it must be able to be situated in the space occupied by its body. This anchoring of subjectivity in its body is the condition of coherent identity, and, moreover, the condition under which the subject *has a perspective* on the world" (Grosz 1994:47). In *The Second Sex* Simone de Beauvoir does not distinguish between physicality or history and consciousness; indeed, she suggests these are inseparable and she demonstrates this inseparability with reference to phenomenology by utilizing girls' lives as exemplary.

The being-in-the-world with which phenomenology is concerned needs also to be linked to the networks of discipline that normalize some modes of being in the world and attempt to exclude or punish others. These forms of discipline, which Foucault terms "governmentality" at the level of public culture, do not act on practices of living but in fact make them possible. In *The Practice of Everyday Life*, Certeau famously concludes that "if it is true that the grid of discipline is everywhere becoming clearer and more extensive, it is all the more urgent to discover how an entire society resists being reduced to it" (xiv). These theoretical concepts are all useful for thinking about how girls live in the world. Girls intersect particular if not singular combinations of social fields and engage a habitus that does not preexist them but is constituted and continually renegotiated in relations between habitual body and social positions. It is this sense of a highly specific and yet socially structured habitus that determines even what is desirable or thinkable that ethnography cannot capture in the life of any girl or other social agent. Habitus articulates how interactions between individuals and their social placement, including public discourses such as feminine adolescence and the modes of cultural identification produced as definitive of girl culture, are crucial for mapping girlhood. Body images and lifestyles are themselves theories about being-in-the-world, and feminine adolescence as public and popular negotiation of body image produces particular analyses of gender/sex and power. Popular culture and critical theory have different places in economies of production and different cultural forms, but both provide ways of engaging with culturally located subjects.

9.1
The Spice Girls
(Artist: Jon C. Allen, one sheet design.
Sony Pictures [Columbia], 1997)

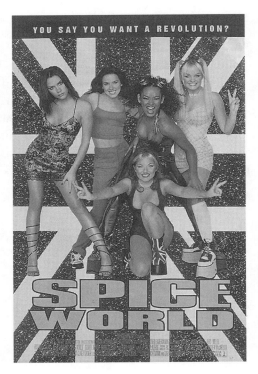

9.2 Bikini Kill
(Kill Rock Stars)

nine

The Girl Market and Girl Culture

As one reads the captions beneath the style photos, the columns of beauty advice and the articles on the co-ordination of wardrobes and furnishings, one senses that those who bought these things were not varied as to age, marital status, ethnicity or any other characteristics. Out there, working as a clerk in a store and living in an apartment with a friend, was *one girl*—single, nineteen years old, Anglo-Saxon, somewhat favouring Janet Gaynor. The thousands of Hollywood-associated designers, publicity men, sales heads, beauty consultants and merchandisers had internalised her so long ago that her psychic life had become their psychic life. They empathised with her shyness, her social awkwardness, her fear of offending. They understood her slight weight problem and her chagrin at being a trifle too tall. They could tell you what sort of man she hoped to marry and how she spent her leisure time.

—Charles Eckert, "The Carole Lombard in Macy's Window"

THIS FINAL CHAPTER discusses the deployment of girls in mass-produced popular culture as one site for debating relations between girls and conformity and then negotiates a definition of girl culture through both popular and alternative movements in contemporary girl culture. It surveys continuing reference in cultural analysis to the girl market as a site for understanding mass consumption and global popularization and considers how the girl market as global category might raise useful questions about how not only girls but also globalization are understood. Finally it thus also considers the role of cultural specificity—defined in relation to nationality, class, race, and ethnicity—in understanding girl culture's relation to the globalization of popular culture (and cultural analysis).

9.3 Naoko Takeuchi, Sailor Moon (1995) *(Naoko Takeuchi/Kodansha Ltd./Toei Animation Co., Ltd.)*

Girl Culture

Rebel girl, rebel girl, rebel girl you are the queen of my world . . .

> —Bikini Kill, "Rebel Girl"

I wanna be the girl with the most cake . . .

> —Hole, "doll parts"

I'll tell you what I want, what I really really want

> —Spice Girls, "Wannabe'

Circulating the Girl

What girl culture might name, or how it might be used, is difficult to strictly delimit because what seems most obvious about it—girls—is what makes it hardest to define. How do the ambivalences of girlhood affect the definition of girl culture? Would girl culture be a mode of youth culture, comprised in generic variations, or would it be more strongly inflected by physiological and/or psychological discourses on girlhood? In this final chapter I want to focus on the circulation of a range of cultural products that must be included in girl culture because they explicitly constitute girlhood in modes circulated among girls. These examples include much-discussed instances of girl-directed popular culture, such as pop music and girls' magazines, in both globally and more locally successful forms, and some less frequently discussed elements of girls' lives, including their occupation of electronic and other public spaces. But I will begin with the idea of the girl market.

Emerging forms of cultural production are inseparable from emerging forms of cultural analysis, and the idea of mass marketing emerged alongside the expansion of mass culture, within which girl culture took on highly public new forms. In the first half of the twentieth century the association of girls with mass culture already drew on new marketplaces of women, adolescents, and girls. Repeated references to girls as exemplarily deluded consumers of culture industries and as figures for the distraction produced by engagement with mass culture are entirely contemporary with the new science of market analysis. The development of a girl market has been pivotal to defining the characteristics of marketing and, in particular, the global market. The girl market is the kind of market segmentation often described as a demographic, a group defined by shared socioeconomic characteristics. But girls were and are a proliferation that does not entirely conform to its reputation as consuming prototype. However carefully girls were defined in these discourses and strategies, they were not fantasies of the advertising industry or of discourses on developmental psychology and social welfare that also helped define them. Nevertheless, unmarried women without children were more being often named as disposing of individual incomes, and extensive supervision dedicated to girls' development at this time worked to emphasize, expand, and guide this disposal.

Girls who like particular products do not form a demographic—that, is, they are not defined as individuals by their similarities as girls. It is not that individual girls differ; rather, my strong claim here is that demographics do not exist except as marketing concepts. The idea of a girl market locating a specific demographic of girls is confounded by the difficulty of defining girls, who dramatically exceed, even for marketing discourses, any singular age range or other criteria. Demographics belong among what Michel Foucault identifies as sciences constructing life in the service of economics. According to Foucault, "population" emerged as a cause for the modern state and effectively segmented subjects into population groupings with economic effects. Demographics are proper to the state identification and governance of population, elaborating on existing governance of households and families (Foucault 1991:94) to help produce the population as a field of visibility organized by economic categories (as well as majority).

An idea of the girl market is employed to sell participation in girlhood. The commodities marketed to the new (global) girl consumers discussed above included the idea and the means of feminine adolescence. But rather than being equivalent to the girl market, girl culture names the circulation of ways to articulate identities as girls. Girl culture does not denote advertising, sales, or commercial discourse on who buys what popular cultural products, because these do not delimit circulating representations of girls or necessarily identify any social group as girls. There continue to be two dominant tendencies for discussing the girl market, and while these are reductive as summaries of any particular analysis they are recognizable as tendencies. The first might be characterized as the culture industry position, in which girls are exemplary of mass consumption and its pervasive construction of identities amenable to that consumption. The second is an ethnographic position wherein girls are an identifiable cultural group to be accessed for accounts of its typical consumption practices. Both of these tendencies inadequately consider the problems with using demographics: with assuming that you can locate and describe a girl market. They both insufficiently interrogate whether girls, or even a given market that could be proven to consist mainly of girls, constitute a coherent demographic, and both interpret the behavior of that group as a multiplication of individualist psychologies characterized as adolescent. Consumption articulates identities and communities, but according to influential models for talking about it the girl market describes a demographic wrapped up in negotiating their own power and powerlessness through consumption. This idea underlies specific analyses of how girls consume, which also tend to focus on assessing the conformity or nonconformity of girls as consumers or girls as products. This is how the girl market has characteristically worked, but any marketing strategy works by trying to manipulate conformity, including conformity to the image of nonconformity.

The girl market has always utilized nonconformity and, in particular, relations between conformity and nonconformity. But the opposition between pleasure in consumption figured as conformity and pleasure against the grain of such conformity does not provide a useful model for considering girl culture, where resistance is often just another form of conformity and conformity may be compatible with other resistances. Girl culture is often presented as exemplary of cultural conformity, an attribution explicitly dependent on the dominant modern gendering and codification of maturity. In comparison to the spectacular claims to be exceptional produced in the realms of the subcultural, or the resistance to everyday hegemonies, conformity and the mainstream are more rarely considered in cultural studies. Such studies of resistance presuppose a model of agency that is problematized by naming the subject as a girl. A dominant presumption that valid subjectivity requires an agency understood as independent choice continues to prioritize cultural forms viewed as maintaining individualist authenticity. Given that girls are seen to be influenced if not defined by identification with dominant cultures or ideologies, an agency defined against these attributes would produce at best highly ambivalent ideas about girls and girl culture. The girl market thus contributes to the valorization of terms for cultural production, consumption, and analysis that exclude girls.

For example, the conventions of girl pop are more often presumed than enumerated. Although dominant models of pop music change, variations in relation to a current dominant model seem comparatively slight. While girl pop cannot be defined without reference to its musical and, now, audiovisual conventions, the differences between particular pop acts are even less remarkable when viewed as cultural processes that extend beyond the musical form.[1] Pop music as a generic description, while it has been attached to certain musical structures, mostly describes patterns of production and consumption and thus its attribution to segments of the music industry confuses different ways of using the term "pop." Marketing, identification, gender roles, and the question of conformity, are more important to analyses of pop music than attention to formal conventions. In his famous essay, "On Popular Music," Theodor Adorno claims that the "standardization of song hits keeps the customers in line by doing their listening for them. . . . Pseudo-individualisation . . . keeps them in line by making them forget that what they listen to is already listened to for them, or 'pre-digested' " (1994:208). What Adorno calls predigestion works by repetition within the song itself and within the music genres that historically and socially frame it:

> the harmonic cornerstones of each hit—the beginning and end of each part—must beat out the standard scheme. . . . Complications have no consequences. This inexorable device guarantees that regardless of what aberrations occur, the hit will lead back to the same familiar experience, and nothing fundamentally novel will be introduced. (208)

While this essay resembles formal criticisms of girl pop music, it is in fact about jazz. While its conceptual framework can perhaps be used without its condemnatory tone, it is Adorno's dismissal that continues to most resemble ongoing commentary on girl pop.

Spice Girls, Riot Grrls, Cyber-gurls

Established readings of girl fans of pop music invoke identification along the psychoanalytic lines discussed above. Stuart Hall and Paddy Whannel claim that the pop stars girls admire "are not remote stars, but tangible idealisations of the life of the average teenager" (35). This argument, framed as it is by denigration of pop stars, implies that girls' (over-)investment in objects reflects a fear of separation and difference. These pop stars are often assumed to be boys rather than men. The counterpart to this argument has usually been that there are very few girl performers for girls to look up to, and that boys with a degree of effeminacy will do instead as nonthreatening role models and objects in relation to which a moderately more independent self might be produced. This structural narrative has persisted in the face of increasing success for girls in the girl pop market.[2] According to these accounts, girls' consumption of pop music is bound into a transitory freedom between childhood and impending adult domesticity. Lawrence Grossberg counters as follows:

> [Simon] Frith and McRobbie have argued that the antidomesticity of rock and roll is an expression of its basic male orientation and its antifemale ideology. I disagree: the antidomesticity of the rock and roll apparatus is an attack on the place in which its own youth is constructed. (1994:188)

As Grossberg suggests, domesticity is the required terrain of youth culture, but an engagement with the special intimacy between girls' popular culture and the familial space of youth's construction is still necessary.

The pop group Spice Girls (see fig. 9.1) was founded in 1996, comprising four young women from different parts of Britain. A number of similar all-girl singing groups appeared in the wake of the Spice Girls' success—and that success is also attached to a global boy bands pop phenomenon, which relies on similar performance strategies and musical styles—but the Spice Girls remained singularly recognizable in the late 1990s. As hard as their critics derided them as conformist the Spice Girls sold themselves as radical. The Spice Girls also suggest that contestation over the meanings of girl culture and "girl power" surrounding and pervading popular culture for girls might have produced new relationships between popular culture, girls, and feminism. Whether or not the Spice Girls are good, for girls or as music, is not a question that interests me here, except to consider why it is an issue—why so many people cared about whether the Spice Girls were good, as musicians or for girls.

While generic expectations, and the releases of Virgin Records, place Spice Girl consumers as girls, this only comprises a set of expectations.[3] The forms in which the Spice Girls were marketed indicate that, whoever actually bought the Spice Girls, they were marketed as for girls.[4] Most responses to the relation between the Spice Girls and their audience assert that their everygirlness appeals to a phase of pop conformity, and that girls who like the Spice Girls will grow out of it (and the accompanying products). Girls who like the group know that they are not the same as the Spice Girls, and will not be, and yet they are also responding to statements that the Spice Girls are just like them. Moreover, the Spice Girls are figured as doing something in the place of all the girls who can't—like kick over tables in a men's social club in the "Wannabe" video clip. I'd like to prize this identification as and as not a Spice Girl out from the assumption that young women are particularly bound up in identifications. With implicit reference to girls' intimacy with identification, indiscriminate consumption is supposed to be the main problem with Spice Girls' fandom. But the modes of identification deployed in Spice Girls' fandom might be comprised of the very real imaginary relations people sustain with commodities in their lives, and the conditions of girls' production as a relation to power rather than a psychological phase.

The Spice Girls did not rely on an opposition between agency and conformity or subsume their feminist messages into an account of personal experience. If their everydayness conformed to generic expectations for girl music, or even for girls, this might also be a vivid recognition of and accessible commentary on the way power and identification work. The Spice Girls claimed to be what girls want, and they were very successful at it. The usual grounds for dismissing this claim is that they were just a glossy prepackaged commodity. Popularity doesn't establish value or the absence of it, yet manufacture, fad, and popularity were accusations repeatedly leveled against the Spice Girls. Given that these terms are applicable in different ways to much globally marketed music, they inadequately account for the broad dismissal of the Spice Girls, which also takes up debates over what constitutes feminist politics or comment and over the ways girls might identify with other girls or, more unusually, with politicized slogans. Can feminism be a mass-produced, globally distributed product, and can merchandised relations to girls be authentic? The Spice Girls' claims to authenticity invoke the experience of girls restrained by being good girls and related claims to show how things really are for girls now—or how they could be. The "Girl Power" slogan was the most prominent aspect of Spice Girl authenticity, although the visual representation of their songs as filmic narrative was important to the identifications that comprise being a Spice Girls fan. In fact, the idea (marketing concept) of girl power is also part of this visualizing system, and it too must be seen. The back of the "Spice Girls' Hour of Power" video exclaims: "We don't only talk about girl power, we live it! Just watch!"[5]

Despite these strategies and slogans, the Spice Girls were widely discussed—in the mass media, including specialist publications, and in a variety of public forums—as having no kind of authenticity at all. This is an attribution that gains a great deal of weight from being perceived as a girl thing. The more considered of these accounts claim that the real desires of girls have little outlet and are thus understandably if regrettably projected onto a commodity invented by marketers. This equally dismissive interpretation claims that the machinery that produces the Spice Girls is hostile to and destructive of a real girl culture, perhaps offering some expression of their desires, but encouraging passive conformity in the long term. The model of pop music consumption situated in a domestic girl space informed by privatized discourses on heterosexual reproduction is held to be distinct from the stylistically and/or technically informed, participatory relation to music belonging to more independent forms of youth culture. Alternative forms of girl culture often question what constitutes girl-space, and in comparison the Spice Girls seem more amenable to the sometimes limited range of spaces allowed to girls. The Spice Girls generally address the same demographic as that surveyed as participating in Beatlemania and other scenes of teenybopper culture, and indeed the attribution of stupidity to Spice Girls fandom resembles that attributed to Beatlemaniacs (see Ehrenreich et al. 528). Given that such excessive and trivial fandom is now anticipated as a part of feminine adolescence, the Spice Girls constitute an acceptable interest and means of grouping for many girls. But they also suggest the powerful self-interest noted by Sheryl Garratt's semi-autobiographical analysis of pop fans, in which she comments that "our real obsession was with ourselves; in the end, the actual men behind the posters had very little to do with it" (402)?

Agency is a very problematic criterion for understanding how culture is produced for the simple reason that no one person produces a culture, and yet circulating shared meanings—the definition of cultural activity—often seems to compromise a desired cultural authenticity. Raymond Williams notes that

> the existence of the possibility of opposition, and of its articulation, its degree of openness, and so on, again depends on very precise social and political forces. The facts of alternative and oppositional forms of social life and culture . . . have then to be recognized as subject to historical

variation, and as having sources which are very significant as a fact about the dominant culture itself. (1987:210)

So do alternative girl cultures deploy different cultural modes? The Spice Girls are often compared to the riot grrl bands, usually in order to condemn one of them. While riot grrl zines and sites decry such pop phenomena as the Spice Girls, some of the Spice Girl fan material describes the riot grrls as dull and dour, whining, self-pitying, and sexless—interestingly some of the same accusations riot grrls have leveled at second wave feminism.

Riot grrls are easier to define than such loose girl culture scenes as teeny-boppers, despite heated debate over their interests, allegiances, and even how to spell them.[6] There are one-, two-, and three-r versions of the girl that riots, mostly defined in relation to girl music scenes influenced by punk. Sometimes the two-r grrls accuse the three-r grrls of claiming a superior badness: "maybe that third 'r' is like a proud scarlet letter, a matter of haute transgression and baaadddddness stumbled over, a door slammed, a curse hurled." This is from the "Pop Tart" home page, where the owner claims: "It's actually [sic] pretty cool that grrrl/grrl/grl has entered the language as such. Nobody 'owns' it, ya know" (Kile). But owning is the explicit focus of this antagonism. The *Riot Grrrl* e-zine apparently changed its name from three to two rrs in order to patent "*RiotGrrl*," prompting outrage that seems telling concerning the parameters of riot grrlness (and its distinction from cyber-gurls).[7] But Riot grrls are easier to define because of these re-peated attempts delineate themselves, particularly in small circulation zines and electronic or e-zines. In 1999 *RiotGrrl* had on its home page the slogan "RiotGrrl changes lives!" It featured stories, competitions, quizzes, games—such as "Feed the Supermodel: Feed her Now!"—letters, and lists for ex-changes with other grrls, a format derived directly from girls' magazines. It included a section on feminism, as well as international sections that frame it as part of a global movement.

Bikini Kill is often identified as the premier riot grrl band, and I will use them as exemplary although a more extensive list of groups helped form the label.[8] The various riot grrls war over representing themselves (fig. 9.2 is an unusually pop star pose among images of "the Kill"), but they are all sup-posedly different from the Spice Girls because they interrogate the repre-sentation of girls. The Spice Girls are, by contrast, extensively visualized across multiple media. The emergence of MTV is important to this dis-tinction between the accessibility and coverage of the Spice Girls and groups such as Bikini Kill. But much of the dominant girl-band aesthetic at the end of the twentieth century, and which the Spice Girls and MTV referenced repeatedly in their own changing visual styles, draws on riot grrl and other punk-influenced groups. As one fanzine notes, riot grrl bands not only produced feminist texts but also "inspired a new type of dress, short, little girl dresses as well as Hello Kitty pocketbooks and backpacks" (Angie) as part of their resistance to a perceived desexualization of girls among feminists. Punk and alternative bands can be televised or filmed, despite Bikini Kill stressing their rejection of this mediation. In the 1994 liner notes to the CD version of Bikini Kill's first two records Tobi Vail writes: "We have been written about a lot by big magazines who have never talked to us or seen our shows. They write about us authoritatively, as if they understand us better than we understand our own ideas, tactics, and significance." This is a presumption no one challenges with reference to the Spice Girls. Bikini Kill fear they are being misunderstood as popular: "We want to be an underground band. . . . We don't want to be featured in Newsweek magazine." Andrew Goodwin summarizes this subcultural musical credibility as a "perceived authenticity [which] derives in no small measure from . . . [an] antipathy to popular culture," supposedly based on "both its sounds and its sentiments" being opposed to "commercialism" (109).

Marketing and commercialism are necessary to even alternative popular music. Riot grrls cohere loosely by opposition to specific aspects of their own conditions of production, including the idea of the girl audience—the riot grrl group Bratmobile has a song with the double-edged title "Fuck Your Fans." The Spice Girls and riot grrls both question whether girls have a special need for expression specific to them, but the girls they reach seem clearly distinguishable. The Spice Girls direct their slogans and appeals to include home-oriented teenagers or preteens (what would have been called the teenybopper audience), while Bikini Kill has primarily a college/university or adult audience. It is possible to be a fan of both the Spice Girls and Bikini Kill as popular profeminist girl groups, but given the definition of girlhood in relation to domesticity and dependence, clearly far fewer girls have a space (habitus) that allows listening to Bikini Kill. In the context of middle-class grunge looks and riot grrl fashions, though, the mainstream is not self-evident, and while less punk-inflected riot grrl groups such as Hole are more widely accessible, they may not be consumed as riot grrls.[9] As Pierre Bourdieu notes, "facility with the games of cultural criticism—their 'I know that you know that I know'—is not universal. Nor is the ability to spin out elaborate 'readings' of the 'ironic and metatextual' messages" (1998:8–9) that might be located even in Spice Girl lyrics.

Preferring Bikini Kill to the Spice Girls is not a matter of free choice in which distinctions between products equal distinctions between consumers. Degrees of resistance are not adequately understood by dividing popular music up into hierarchies of popularity or taste. Taste is relative and not in the least independent of culture industries or the globalization of entertainment. The generic conventions of pop and rock music, rather than political content, distinguish the Spice Girls from Bikini Kill, along with the language in which they speak (both statements about their presumed audience). Similarities between them seem as interesting as oppositions, including the modes of identification between girls to which the politics of both Bikini Kill and the Spice Girls are attached. This does not require homogenizing all forms of music addressed to young women. As Holly Kruse points out "as much as the word 'identification' seems to imply a sense of belonging, perhaps even more it describes a process of differentiation. . . . Senses of shared identity are alliances formed out of oppositional stances" (34). Beatlemaniacs, the Spice Girls, and Bikini Kill all also appear in that stratum where girls have often been allowed some resistant or even subcultural activity—in the field of what McRobbie and Garber call "sexual deviance" (29) and Ehrenreich, Hess, and Jacobs align with "subversive versions of heterosexuality" (534). Questioning whether either this identification or this subversive heterosexuality characterizes girl culture, I want to juxtapose these examples with one outside popular music.

The "cyber-gurls" or "cybergirls" are a broad but allied range of Web sites, mailing lists, and cyberpractices interested in girls, technology, and the image of the future. Although I am interested here in cybergirls rather than cyberfeminism in general, cybergirls, like riot grrls and the Spice Girls, manifest in explicitly feminist practices. Cybergirls intersect with riot grrls as a mode of do-it-yourself girl expression, and cybergirl pages, books, and review sites—such as *Surfer Grrls*, a riot grrl guide to the Internet—often cite Bikini Kill as a soundtrack. Cybergirl revolution explicitly privileges appropriation and insurrection from within—a kind of computer guerrilla warfare or mission to negotiate the Internet as manifestation of patriarchy. Cybergirls are thus required to make a space within the discourse they oppose, which is one of the reasons why feminists have found them an attractive metaphor for new feminisms. Under the search terms "feminism," "women," and/or "space," you will find Planet Cybergrrl® and the Cybergrrl village. The trademark matters insofar as cybergirls like riot grrls belong to a system of commodities but disavow the importance of their delimitation by commercial interests.[10] The music industry by which Bikini Kill circulates, and the Internet by which both riot grrls and cybergirls circulate, are not fundamentally opposed to the circulation of the Spice Girls on Virgin records. Localized production by girls, which differentiates these alternative forms from the Spice Girls, is an important mode of contemporary girl culture, but it is an inequitable basis for devaluing Spice Girls fandom. The personal, communal, educational, financial, and technical resources necessary for such practices are not equally available to all girls.

Cyberfeminism utilizes the girl as an emblem of women in the future—the newly born technological woman. Cybergirls broadly emphasize and oppose the patriarchal control of technology—variously phrased as "phallocentric," "cyberhegemony," or VNS Matrix's "Big Daddy Mainframe." The VNS Matrix computer game *Bad Code* "moves the player through a labyrinthine hive of subcultural tribes, assisting the viral intelligence 'Gen' on her mission to sabotage the databases of Big Daddy Mainframe, thus activating the germ of the new world disorder" (VNS Matrix 75).[11] Under the aegis of VNS Matrix you can locate various cybergirl identities, artifacts, and realms, such as Gender Filth World: "Tired of bleaching the grime of social conditioning? Then join our tribe of anarchogendaterrorists in Gender Filth World. Explode the binary with deviant software bombs! Feel your gender markings dissolve! (Children admitted free.)"[12] Cyber-**gurl** does not rely on any type of body: its significations of gender are mutable and disposable while its -url (Uniform Resource Locator) continues to articulate a concretely located speaking position. But its highly specialized location and address are not relevant to, and do not often refer to, any generic girl experience. This avoids unfortunate generalizations but also separates cybergirls from girls, who thus continue to manifest an undifferentiated and conformist mainstream. While riot grrls interrogate dominant discourses on femininity—as they put it "smash the mask"—and cybergirls challenge the reliance of girlness on having the body of a girl, both groups are troubled by their reliance on the systems they confront.

Girls and Complicity

The critical perspective or anger of these girl culture forms (including the Spice Girls) is directed against a range of global economies, and emphasizes the circulation of cultural forms for and about girls. Patriarchy—understood as the frame in which girls are constituted in utilitarian ways as daughters, and future heterosexual partners and mothers, and as the process of properly conditioning women to repeat this constitution—is not global. It is precisely local in all the ways that problematize feminist accounts of other cultures from within their own. But patriarchy has global forms, and the globalization of entertainment is one of these fields in which feminist politics might also be enacted. Although broadly technophilic, the antagonism of much "alternative" girl culture toward global capitalist interests is often expressed as an ecological stance, a protection of the planet (often by, perhaps paradoxically, technological means). The *Tank Girl* comics (see fig. 9.5) provide representative motifs—set in a postwar desert, the recurring image of girls battling for justice in a wasteland brought about by industrial stupidity belong to an often unspecific opposition to how patriarchy has organized the world. The wasteland is also that place outside the fixed civilizing space of social order—including humanism, heterosexuality, and the nuclear family—and much alternative girl culture operates on the borders of these terms because of the centrality of girls to marking that territory.

When feminist analysis of girl culture recognizes that girls are not merely dupes of patriarchal capitalist systems, it often focuses on nonconformist consumption among rebellious (understood as subcultural) girl groups or redefines consumption as itself resistant at the expense of ignoring what conformity might entail or produce. A hierarchizing of girl culture according to an authenticity understood as individual production also infers that neither distribution nor consumption is productive. Riot grrls are presumed to belong by choice—activism—rather than by the consumption of any products: their products in fact constrain their articulation of riot grrlness. It does matter that the Spice Girls are more widely distributed than riot grrl music/writing or cybergirl feminism, and this ease does testify to their complicity with the system that distributes them, but that does not exclude the possibility that girl power is a more complex set of practices. Some girls, many girls, buy things. Girl culture consists in circulating the things girls can do, be, have, and make, and in that process defining what processes are particular to girls. This circulation of things—this economy of girl culture—includes the unresolvable tensions located by tensions between agency and conformity. To actually embrace the community alternative girl culture imagines requires a degree of complicity with systems with which they claim to be incompatible, and they produce legitimated models of agency within the systems they say exclude them.

Girl culture provides a means for considering the coherence of popular culture, or the processes by which something qualifies as resistance, given the regularity with which studies of girl culture, and girl culture itself, define a tension between conformity and resistance. This section reconsiders the complicity of girl culture and the figure of the girl participant in girl culture as a conformist mode of resistance, particularly among feminist studies of girls. The chief feminist objection to girls' magazines, for example, is that they propagate a model in which women's work, interests, and ambitions are both inferior to and encompassed by their familial and sexual responsibilities, while at the same time compensating for this with an array of personal and commodity-oriented pleasures. Criticism that such magazines restrict girls' interests (and their knowledge and images of themselves) to subsidiary, private, and domestic roles presumes that they accurately describe their readers' lives and aspirations, but also that girls read them in such a way as to be unduly influenced by their content or else to take pleasure in complicity with their own oppression. On the levels of both information and pleasure girls' magazines are seen as letting girls down and selling girls out; as not interrogating the lives girls are usually asked to live and the pleasures they are most encouraged to take.

Studies of girls' magazines have generally seen them as complicit with patriarchal ideologies about girlhood and as trivializing girls' lives with beauty regimes, fashion models, and discourses on romantic love. But there are compelling arguments for the seriousness of these things in the everyday lives of girls. The expansion of girls' magazines does belong to the expansion of mass consumption, particularly in the domestic and leisure spheres. But to assign to these economic factors the genre's sole productive force vastly undervalues their importance to women's cultural positions and identities and ignores the importance of the audience text—the way in which girls as presumed readers are included within the magazines—to the success of the genre. Magazines for adolescent women developed alongside the greater allocation of spending power to girls and the proliferation of new forms of advertisement and discourses on marketing. Luxury goods such as cosmetics or fashionable clothes dominate advertising in girls' magazines, but they are not necessarily experienced as luxuries by girls for whom a decisive lifetime direction is presumed in becoming beautiful. As consumers whose perceptions and desires concerning feminine adolescence must be divined and shaped in the direction of purchasing the magazine and the products it advertises, what girls actually do and like is central to these publications. Any causal model of the relationship between magazines and readers will thus be teleological and misleading. Neither the discursive regulation of progress among her peers, nor the sale of products necessary for successful adolescence, undermines the genre's facilitation of girls' identities and voices.

Girls' magazines, and girl culture more generally, demand, incite, or offer a wide range of uses and practices. Many kinds of girls' magazines conform incompletely to the broader genre's conventions, including magazines in genres mostly read by girls, such as pop-music magazines. There are also girls' magazines, some of which are only locally distributed, which offer overt critiques of the girls' magazine genre, but these depend on the recognizability and accessibility of the formal as well as discursive conventions of mainstream girls' magazines. No girls or women's magazines exist in a prefeminist state. These genres are all affected by the now inevitable question of whether and how a woman is employed, feminist critiques of beauty culture, and other feminist propositions or practices (which does not mean they take a predictable position on these issues). Feminism itself belongs to the popular cultural field, a point feminist discussion of popular culture often seems to ignore even in fields where the influence of feminism is most palpable.

Returning to my earlier discussion of feminine adolescence as a field of power relations, I want to consider the possibility of detaching Judith Butler's analysis of how subjection is tied to the means of its own production from individualized psychology and use it to think explicitly about cultural relations. As Butler argues, those thought to "pursue or sustain their own subordination are easily represented as responsible for it" (1997:15). It's in this context that Butler's *The Psychic Life of Power* might be used to think about girl power, complicity, and the conformity of girls. Complicity and vulnerability are crucial to feminism as a discourse on empowerment; they are the grounds for feminist politics. This recognition might relegate feminism to a reactionary politics, but in fact such dependence on the conditions in relation to which agency appears is unavoidable. Complicity and empowerment are not separable, though neither are they opposed by one being the rectification of the other. Butler asks in her introduction "how to take an oppositional relation to power that is, admittedly, implicated in the very power one opposes" (1997:17) or, more appropriately still, whether there "is . . . a way to affirm complicity as the basis of political agency, yet insist that political agency may do more than reiterate the conditions of subordination?" (29–30).[13] These recognitions are important for an account of girl culture, and if the terms seem defeatist then perhaps they can be rephrased as the vulnerability and promise of identification. "Complicity" might mean an unavoidable and productive identification with the discourses that enact and enable any subject; that is, it might be the risk and condition of any politics. Butler claims that "agency exceeds the power by which it is enabled" (15) but remains bound to its own subjection: "exceeding is not escaping, and the subject exceeds precisely that to which it is bound" (17). Butler understands this within a psychoanalytic frame—as an individual psychic structure—but this might be evident in the recoil of girl power's processes of identification and in the ambivalence of a subject-position such as that of the normatively unruly and obedient girl. I want to note that the Spice Girls are subject to those models of agency, originality, and authenticity in opposition to which they are constituted, and that their momentary eclipse of that opposition is significant for feminists thinking about girl culture.

The Spice Girls sell feminism as compatible with many traditional roles for girls. Many feminists see better options for girl culture, and many see the Spice Girls as reducing feminism to a collection of empty slogans and the bad girl end of conventional images of girl sexuality. In response to such dismissal Susan J. Douglas claimed:

> When adolescent girls flock to a group, they are telling us plenty about how they experience the transition to womanhood in a society in which boys are still very much on top. . . . So while it's easy as pie to hold a group like the Spice Girls in contempt, we should be wary when music embraced by preteen girls is ridiculed. . . . The Spice Girls tell them that feminism is necessary and fun. Hey, when I was 10 we had "I Wanna Be Bobby's Girl." Crass commercial calculation and all, the Spice Girls are a decided improvement. (Douglas 29)

The Spice Girls talk about feminism and about the relations between politics and popular music in a massively popular field. Riot grrls and the cybergirls make similar moves, often in more sophisticated or confrontational modes, but the Spice Girls are less likely to be credited with this agenda or its effects. Their articulation of feminist politics occurs on the terrain of international multiple-platinum-selling pop music articulated as by and for girls. This marks a shift in the dominant paradigms of girl culture the effects and limitations of which are worth considering.

Assemblage: Theorizing the Girl Market
Globalizing Consumption

The girl consumer and the girl demographic are entwined with the expansion of transnational mass production, the dissemination of new marketing technologies, and the category of feminine adolescence. The globalization of certain modes of production/consumption demands stable cross-cultural categories that could be used to explain how people could be brought to consume products not differentiated along specific cultural lines. By constructing certain consumer groups as innately, naturally, interested in specific products it is possible to sell an idea of belonging to groups, such as girls, which can cross cultural boundaries although they do not always do so. Are the Spice Girls or Bikini Kill consumed as British or American, or as global? "Global" does not mean "universal" but a specific mode of distribution that organizes flows of products and money between groups, nations, and so on. It is associated with Anglo-American popular culture rather than, for example, Japanese popular culture, insofar as the consumption of Asian popular culture is differentiated from the global in the largest markets for global products. The global popular music market, for example, is located by demographic and musical generic segments distributed across an English-language base. Even when it appears global, girl culture is manifest in the local and the everyday, as evidenced by the strategies for promoting the Spice Girls, where a reference to Margaret Thatcher as a "Spice Girl" claimed to rescue Britain from losing its identity to globalism and Americanization.[14] And while cybergirls appear to be definitively global—always enabled by the World Wide Web—the North American specificity of not only most cybergirl narratives but much of the Internet remains clear. Although this Anglophone dominance may be changing, participation in the Internet, as in all domestically located cultural forms, is constrained by the local space and time of the user.

In the 1920s the process of creating a transnationalized consumer was often referred to as Americanization. Globalization as Americanization is also the context in which youth culture emerged in association with the distribution of film, music, and other leisure products, rapidly accelerating after each of the world wars with the new global technologies they produced.[15] Hall and Whannel argue that when they

> come to deal with "teenage" entertainments and culture, the distinction between media and audience is difficult to maintain. For one thing, the

postwar spurt in the growth of the media and the change in adolescent attitudes have gone hand in hand—apparently two aspects of the same social trend. (69)

Before the twentieth century what might have constituted youth culture varied more dramatically between cultures because cultural products were not distributed widely between different cultural locations. New consumer groups accompanied the expansion of transnational mass production, but this is not a process of simply utilizing group identities within a globalized market place. Rather, the globalized market place helps produce new identities and collectivities. As theorists of globalization have suggested, late modern culture is characterized not only by mass production but also by global distribution of that production, which demands that we are all familiar with an idea of a global marketplace. Globalization refers to the historical acceleration of the organization of production and consumption across national boundaries. As Simon During points out, "It is tempting to call this larger process globalization, but, except in quite specific instances, it constitutes something less—transnationalization" (808). Nevertheless, as During argues, "the global popular is a category that challenges (though it does not overturn) current cultural studies' welcome to difference, hybridity, and subversion" (808–9). It seems, that is, to be a process of homogenization rather than an expansion of ways in which difference is recognized. The global popular music industry markets itself to, and thus names, not finely differentiated individuals but categories that seem increasingly universal as the products designed around them become more popular.[16]

Cultural studies of popular culture very often proceed as audience analysis, but this tendency does not avoid or subordinate a focus on individuals; rather, it multiplies just that focus in audience analyses. Evoking the audience as a collection of individuals demands a theory of identification that presupposes a psychological model. Having already questioned the deployment of demographics in audience studies, perhaps audience is even the wrong way to think about global or transnational fields such as the popular music market. The girl market and girl culture are identifiable effects within popular culture industries. The girl as figure for consumption, which underlies specific analyses of how girls consume, is a universalizing point of reference for assessing girls as consumers or as products. The girl market is an index for specific technologies of the self—locating the contact or exchanges between disciplinary powers (such as global capitalism, the state, and parents) and self disciplines (processes of producing a self). Girls' magazines, films, fashion and dance cultures, and pop music all produce modes of self-production in relation to groups. In fact identification might be the only way of understanding what a girl market is if it is not defined by the circular idea of a demographic. According to this argument, girls buy the Spice Girls as selves who might identify as "girls" (named as the Spice Girls' audience). Not all girls will so identify, but what that identification means thus becomes the question for analysis, rather than an assumption about girl consumers (as knowable and predictable; the effect of demographics). With reference to the previous chapter, by "identification" I do not mean the familiar story about girls' exemplary investment in objects as a fear of separation and a transitory freedom. Reference to this model of identification is used to verify the girl demographic—an individual personal history generalized to the level of a cultural unconscious.

Thinking about the girl market as identification rather than demographic positions girl consumers as an assemblage of cultural positions and normative lines. The girl market mediates identity and power through popular cultural codes and generic conventions for becoming a woman and belonging to different cultures: to both nationalized and globalized culture, for example—and there is nothing more natural about the idea of the nation than the idea of the global. It remains important to analyze the movement of capital across national borders and examine the companies that define the kind of culture global consumers will want (which is not the same as being able to predetermine tastes or purchases). The global market is a distribution of power across individualized practices, like buying CDs or going to clubs, predominantly linked as practices producing identities and communities, including the construction of the global consumer. Questions about whether diversity is encouraged or stifled by this globalized consumption are less problematic than more materially specific questions. Does popular culture subsume all girls into a singular field referenced to the girl—the global girl consumer defined as the white Western girl that global markets still privilege? And, when consumers identify themselves in relation to a global girl idea, does that posit some form of universal girl subject?

Assemblage

Global markets are neither an impersonal economic system nor a huge conglomeration of individual psychologies. The girl market might be thought without relying on an individual (or a group) subject of choice, through what Gilles Deleuze has called a "practical assemblage, a 'mechanism' of statements and visibilities" (1986:51). The global music market assembles discursive statements into a field of high visibility that might be used to analyze how late modern cultures are constituted in relation to an idea of the global. As Deleuze's chapter on power in *Foucault* suggests, an assemblage, affected by certain regimes of force, such as a media event or global marketing campaign, may appear as the kind of stratification that is called a demographic, but it is not reducible to such consistency. An assemblage is not only a contingent or occasional conjunction but also a surface, which can be striated by power and thus form strata—coherent positivities that are inseparable from the contexts that name them—such as girl pop fans.

If girl culture exceeds relations between resistance and conformity, perhaps not only individualized agency but even identification is unnecessary to understand the girl market. The globalized girl market may be thought as an assemblage of singular connections between group identities. The global girl market, like the concept of girlhood, can be understood as a performance and a knowledge rather than as any universalizing point of reference. Deleuze's concept of assemblage seems productive for studies of audiences and markets that want to avoid the certainties of demography. Deleuze and Guattari argue that "assemblages are necessary for states of force and regimes of signs to intertwine their relations" (1987:71). That is, an assemblage is a way of being and a mode of signification simultaneously and can thus recognize the discursive power of terms such as "subject" and "girl." While this theoretical proposition draws on philosophy, I would suggest that this is also how the girl market, and feminine adolescence more generally, works in popular understandings of girlhood. Through the concept of assemblage even resistance can be understood without prioritizing individual agency. A girl does not buy a CD because she is convinced of any true or false need for the Spice Girls, but in so doing she practices socioculturally specific knowledge about what girl culture is, even about what the girl market is.

The girl market is an assembled knowledge of girl culture. It envelops a territory that appears on a plane of consistency, which may thought as global but that is not definitively confined there. The series (sales, desires) that the girl market populates, and the surfaces and names assembled in it, constitute an emergence that takes on the appearance of a singular object within certain discourses. This may also be understood as the strata Deleuze invokes in reading

Foucault—the terrain mapped by an archaeology: "The stratified element is not the indirect object of a knowledge which would subsequently emerge but instead something that directly constitutes a knowledge: the lesson of things and the lesson of grammar" (Deleuze 1988:50). The girl market does not precede knowledge of the girl market, which is not the same as accusing it of being manufactured. The kind of "stratified element" that the girl pop consumer constitutes is not a stable prior object of any knowledge, including market analysis. Instead, market analysis constructs that object, making up a girl or a global consumer in the process of its own constitution: global marketing is defined by defining a global consumer. If there is no clear distinction in girl culture modes between desiring and being the girl, or between production and consumption of the girl, this is an entwining of knowing and practicing girl culture. Identification with producing the girl (a production of desiring *as* being) is thus also an attachment to the conditions of producing girl culture. This approach intersects Butler and Deleuze, despite other incompatibilities, through their different attempts to come to terms with Foucault's analyses of power.

The girl market is not organized by an ideal girl or by one set of parameters for ideal girlness, but has different shifting boundaries for the embodied assemblage of different girls and girl markets. In a process of assemblage what attaches to a meaning, or cultural production, can and will also detach from it. The girl market is a visible distribution of consumption and production, but it is also a field of statements about cultural identity as a practice and a knowledge. The simultaneous semiotic, material, and social flows of the assemblage I have referred to the girl-doll relations around Barbie can also be used to see the Spice Girls performing in Turkey as something less totalizing than the permeation of a global market by yet another anglophone girl product. Thinking this scenario through the concept of assemblage does not require that the audience be girls or even an audience for a girl object. They are instead a momentary assemblage of products, media forms, and diverse and de-individualized desires, a mobile consistency that is not homogenizing. It is not necessary to ask if or why Turkish girls like the Spice Girls but, rather, how Turkey, girls, and the Spice Girls are assembled in that broadcast as the girl market: a knowledge that is not owned by media conglomerates even if it is authoritatively expressed by them. Assemblage is connected in Deleuze and Guattari's *A Thousand Plateaus* to nomadic culture, an antihierarchical model of culture directed against the state organization of property and materiality. If girl culture is institutionally directed from some territories toward others—territories that include home, school, market, public space, childhood—these exiles are also escapes and movements in relation to a territory, a group identity cohering around feminine adolescence.[17]

The global pop music audience does not consist of demographics who buy globally marketed pop music, supposedly because of their gullibility with regard to worldwide corporate advertising. It is instead an assemblage of diverse, partial, and mobile images and identities. Analyses of pop music markets that focus on global economics and corporate marketing recognize that such partial identities negotiated through mass consumption often serve the interests of transnational record companies marketing to a globalized idea of the popular music consumer. And the global music consumer is also a group of predictable demographic attributes. Global success depends on a mode of cross-cultural translation, mostly phrased in terms of national cultural divisions. Girl culture presumes global popular culture and depends on conceiving of marketplaces in terms of categories transferable between cultures. The shared girl experience that is often invoked in marketing to young girls becomes more problematic when referred to youth culture, where the specificity of cultural context is seen to have been established. Feminine adolescence and girlhood are thus produced through a range of consumptions upon the collage surface of girls as a group identity. In consumption of girl culture, girls are recorded as producing and desiring themselves at the edge of such group identities: not simply a peer marketplace but a multiplicitous production of interest in themselves.

Cultural Difference?: Japanese Girl Culture
Comparative Culture

What do terms such as "Western," "global," or "Japanese" mean with reference to girlhood, especially insofar as it is attributed transcultural and even transhistorical significance? Are dominant modes of girlhood as an object of thinking and talking about girls in the twentieth century specific to Western cultures? And how does that translate into our conception of cultural production as operating on a global scale? This final section looks for a point of comparison for girl culture as it is understood in the West: an agglomeration loosely defined as Western Europe, North America, and Australasia. This is clearly a fantastic coherence necessitated only by orientalizing opposition to

9.4 Chikatoshi Enomoto, *A Walk Around the Pond* (1932)
(Art Deco and the Orient (1920–30), *Tokyo Metropolitan Teien Art Museum*)

the East, but is also a material certainty within the global field of girl culture. This section discusses Japanese girls' culture, considering both possible specificity and necessary divergences from that Western girl culture. Because my position in relation to this culture is external, I will particularly emphasize texts translated into English and other modes of consumption of Japanese girl culture in Anglophone contexts where my cultural knowledge is more complex. I will focus on examples from girl pop music and publishing for girls. Japanese girls and girl culture are both external to an idea of Western hegemony and provide a crucial test case for Western and materially global popular industries. Moreover, Japanese girl culture presents some specific and important relations to cultures outside of Japan through public discourses on Japanese assimilation of the foreign or the West. This process of assimilation, like Japanese girlhood itself, is often represented in popular and public culture as a positive term "but also in a relatively negative, self-defensive or self-ironical manner" (Iwabuchi 1998b:73).

The formation of girlhood I discussed with reference to Victorian girls in many ways resembles the formation of late modern Japanese girlhood, though they did not occur at the same time or in the same way. The institutionalization of girls' schools, around discourses on appropriate education for womanhood, escalated in the Taishō period (1912–1926) as part of a process of modernization reaching into conceptions of girlhood.[18] This educational reform somewhat resembled the reform movements of late-nineteenth-century England, and they were contextualized by new globalized discourses: training organized around age groups, dissemination of group psychologies, and woman suffrage. The emergence of feminine adolescence and the establishment of a distinct girl culture thus seems to have occurred in Japan around forty to fifty years later than in Britain, America, and Australia, for example, and in a period in which new global communications made those comparisons possible. Indeed such comparisons between cultures were at times articulated directly around Japanese girls, heightening tensions around the idea of the new or modern girl (which also accompanied this process elsewhere). However, these changes to discourses on girls did not occur at the same time or in the same order in all Western nations. Moreover, the globalization of much popular and public consumption means that this Japanese history doesn't have to map onto the West in order to produce a recognizable contemporary girl culture.

Japan is an example that allows consideration of discourses on modernity in relation to girls that are not centered on Europe. Following the Meiji restoration, a series of modernizing projects in Japan disseminated a massive escalation of technology, urbanization, and modern disciplinary and governmental structures (Taishō democracy) as well as a rapid modernization of everyday life in Japan, including public conceptions of girlhood. This modernization was always relative to public discourses on Japaneseness. Koichi Iwabuchi notes that

> in the face of apparent Western domination, the concept of an "uncont-
> aminated" Japanese essence has become part of the construction of Japan-
> ese national/cultural identity. Westernisation had to be balanced by
> Japanisation. The slogan, *wakon yousai* (Japanese spirit, Western tech-
> nologies) after the Meiji restoration in the mid-nineteenth-century was a
> manifestation of this need. (1998b:73)

The relations between avant-garde and popular arts in European and Japanese cultural production during the 1920s exemplifies the ways in which Japan
seems to have been "conscious of the Western gaze when claiming its cultural
uniqueness" (Iwabuchi 1998a:179–80). The modernist fetishization of the
orient evident in art deco and other modernist cultural forms in Japan appeared alongside equally modernist discourses on girls' special relation to
modernization. This is, for example, evident in Chikotoshi Enomoto's *Walk
Around the Pond* (fig. 9.4), where technology meets traditional Japanese girlhood and articulates a specific Japanese modernity in that conjunction.

    This modernization did not overturn prior conceptions of womanhood,
but it did rearrange them in relation to modern discourses, including feminine adolescence. Jennifer Robertson notes, without foregrounding, an apparent synchronicity between feminine adolescence and the term "*shōjo*":
"In Japan, the key indicators for females of social adulthood are marriage
and motherhood. [*Shōjo*] is the term coined in the Meiji period for unmarried girls and women and means, literally, a 'not-quite-female' female"
(64–5). *Shōjo* is often identified with a unique culture for Japanese schoolgirls, which is also used to convey something more like girl-life (*shōjuki*—
time of *shōjo*). John Treat argues that "the modern concept of the [*shōjo*] coalesced in the late nineteenth and early twentieth centuries, when rapid
economic changes produced a social utility for 'adolescence', i.e., a period
between childhood and adulthood during which labor is trained for its role
in industrial culture" (280). *Shōjo* thus covers much of the same terrain as
feminine adolescence and also maps the emergence of girl culture—a "special [*shōjo*] world" (Treat 280).

    An example of this mesh of public and popular renovations of girlhood
and womanhood is the Takarazuka revue, an extant all-female theater
troupe established in the Taishō period and the subject of Jennifer Robert-

son's history, *Takarazuka*. Designed as a more popularly inflected complement to Kabuki theater it was also, according to Robertson, designed to socialize "new women" into sanctioned modes of femininity. The revue was even established with a connecting school. Two further relevant aspects of Robertson's analysis are evident in the following quotation. Robertson claims the company

> tempered the revolutionary potential of the [Takarazuka] actor by denying them maturity. Whether Academy students or Revue actors, all [were] . . . referred to as students (*seito*), partly to create an aura of innocence and amateurism to minimise the distance between stage and spectator, and partly to keep their wages low relative to those of professional actors. More important, [this] relegates the players of women's roles to the status of daughter, with its attendant connotations of filial piety, youthfulness, pedigree, virginity, and being unmarried. (16)

The girls were assigned to male or female roles at the end of the first semester but, in effect, "gender assignments notwithstanding, all the actors . . . were daughters" (16). While the revue displayed girls as dramatizing cultural marking it also presented a specifically malleable and even fluid gender identity, and these elements have retained currency in Japanese girl culture in ways that are not so straightforwardly apparent in anglophone girl culture.

The emergence of discourses that can be understood as feminine adolescence are also apparent in *shōjo* magazines (*zasshi*) of the period, where the overlap between European and Japanese images of girls as emblems of modernity through mass consumption was reproduced in popular images by artists such as Le Pape and Takabakate. If a stylized address to girls and an idealization of a particular discourse on the body in fact define girls' magazines, the appearance of these same themes in Japanese girls magazines would suggest a significant continuity not only in that genre but in the meanings of feminine adolescence. Contemporary Japanese girls' magazines do train, in a way that resembles the Western genre, an audience and a marketplace for the products they advertise. Japanese girls' magazines also participate in similar discourses on consumption, fashion, and identity as Western girls' magazines; and indeed some anglophone girls' magazines are sold in Japan. These generic characteristics focus on an image of the girl as becoming a woman (in the future) but also on a girl specifically differentiated from womanhood. This differentiation is often apparent in the younger field of anglophone girls' magazines, but is more dramatically evident in Japanese girls' magazines. In an extreme case, catalogue magazines such as *Happy Girls* profile in minutiae the life of the happy or good girl-subject without any reference to possible alteration. But Japanese girls' magazines should not be dissociated from a field of girl-directed publications with no clear parallel in Western girl culture: girl-directed *manga* (graphic magazines), including the more specific *shōjo manga* form. *Shōjo manga* are not as product-oriented as girls' magazines; rather, they are highly metaphoric fiction for girls about girls. Matt Thorn claims that the genre, especially in comparison with boys' (*shōnen*) *manga*, is stylistically sophisticated, less realistically representational, and closer to the everyday lives of its readers.[19]

Japanese girls are highly visible, central to the iconography of Japanese life and culture, and yet often represented in public discourse as marginal to Japanese citizenship. From a Western perspective the gender of Japanese girls may seem unambiguous and tending to uniformity. Thorn writes on his Web site:

> They can be seen giggling in groups of three or four; school uniforms of black, navy or gray neatly ironed; handbags decorated with cute characters dangling from one arm; hair plainly styled to meet school appearance codes. They present an image of untainted innocence and childlike naivete. . . . Peeking over the shoulder of one of these girls, you, the outsider (whether foreign or native), are not likely to revise your initial impression on the basis of what you see [in their *manga*]: fashionably dressed characters gazing into each other's sparkling, saucer-like eyes as flowers float inexplicably in the background. But if you don't have anything to read yourself and keep glancing over long enough, you might come to a curious realization: you can't always tell which characters are male and which are female. ("Unlikely Explorers")

These narratives are focused on everyday girls' lives framed by familial, school, and love relationships. While heterosexual romance dominates the genre, the phenomenon of "boy-love (*shōnen-ai*) *manga*"—*manga* directed at girls/women that narrates love relationships between boys—has attracted the most commentary in the West, and with academics, as a form singularly alien to Western girls' magazines. The possibility that the sexing and gendering of Japanese girls does not, in fact, precede in the same way as in Western culture is suggested by the significance of sex/gender shifts in *shōjo-*

manga. However the intimacy between the content of this genre and its girl readers, and the collage-style layout of the pages, indicates why it needs, from a Western point of view, to be included in the genre of girls' magazines, rather than comic books.

Some Japanese girl culture manifestations would be very hard to export and are not apparent in Western girl culture. These are often identities and looks: such as the blackface makeup (with short skirts, high heels, and dyed hair) popular at the end of the twentieth century and often called "cool girl" (with the inflection of "colored girl" as well); or the weekend kimono-girls who parade contemporary inflections on traditional dress in public traditional spaces such as Asakusa and Meiji-jinju. Other Japanese inflections of girl/youth culture belong to a distribution of space (rather than body/identity), the best known being the youth-dominated shopping and display spaces of Harajuku and Shibuya. What would be recognized as the girl in Western-dominated cultures, and thus circulates as the girl of global culture, registers in Japan through marketing of icons such as Barbie or Mariah Carey, as well as in the manifestation of girl culture products with slightly longer histories in the West. These forms include various fashion and pop-music cultures, as well as girls' magazines and the schoolgirl. Each of these forms has what look like specifically Japanese inflections and vary within Japan according to class and region. The inflection of Western culture with "Japaneseness" is often conceived as a form of hybridism, and these girl culture forms might be read that way. A range of critics identify dominant discourses on cultural hybridism within Japanese public and popular culture.[20]

Iwabuchi counters this theory of hybridization with a discourse on cultural influence, focusing on the export of what he calls "culturally odourless" products—that is, "products which, in contrast to American export icons such as Coca Cola or McDonalds, do not immediately conjure images of the country of origin" (1998a:165). He juxtaposes the undisputable "self-Orientalising discourse in Japan" (1998a:167) with an erasure of Japaneseness in cultural exports, particularly *manga/anime* characters that do not look Japanese. These he describes as *mu-kokuseki*, which "literally means something or someone lacking any nationality, but also implies the erasure of racial or ethnic characteristics and any context that would embed the characters in a particular culture or country" (Iwabuchi 1998a:167). However, seeing animation as culturally odorless also depends on its different relation to a referent than live action film. Claiming that animation as non-mimetic representation of Japaneseness is culturally odorless presumes that only a mimetic index could signify Japanese identity or embodiment. It also neutralizes these cultural forms, occluding the patterns of gender, nation, and age formed by audiences in relation to them.[21] Disguise, mimicry, masquerade, and performance styles can just as effectively convey cultural location, as the Takarazuka and the cool girl indicate.

Girl Orientalism

The exaggeration of facial features in Japanese animation is often described as Caucasian, even as a fetishization of the Western body, but they have no such clear referent. These are not Caucasian features and evoke nothing so much as a Japanese *style* of animation. They are recognizably Japanese more than they are echoes of the infant faces of Disney cartoons.[22] Japanese girl culture is not culturally odorless even when it appears to be *mu-kokuseki*, as toys such as Hello Kitty exemplify. The *manga* and *anime* series "Sailor Moon" were marketed more broadly than to young Japanese girls, but from a Western perspective they are identified with the younger girl audience comparable to Barbie's main market. "Sailor Moon" names a number of series created by Naoko Takeuchi, beginning in 1992 with *Bishōjo Senshi Sailor Moon* (Pretty Soldier Sailor Moon) and finishing in 1996.[23] Sailor Moon is "an ordinary girl" named Tsukino Usagi who lives with her parents and annoying brother and has an alter-ego life as the warrior princess Sailor Moon.[24] This standard comic-book premise is indebted to American superhero comics but also proper now to a long history of Japanese *manga* and its globalized derivatives such as "The Mighty Morphin Power Rangers."

Usagi, the homeworld girl (the series is set in Tokyo) who is still from another planet (the Moon Kingdom), finds boys to be both the enemy and her romantic destiny on the other side of a transformation conceived as both spiritual and physical. Such themes might indicate questions concerning becoming a woman and femininity that are encountered by all girls everywhere, even if the specific questions differ, and even suggest a somehow universal girl subject with the same basic interests, desires, and fears. Considerable effort was directed toward promoting Sailor Moon for U.S. audiences. This was articulated in fan material, industry publications, and author appearances, in terms of links between Japanese and American girl culture. But the U.S. adaptation emphasized the alien element of the narratives, making the series as a whole more familiar in an American science fiction context, and Takeuchi herself stresses the magical aspect of the series and of Japanese girl culture.

The Sailors are each warrior-girls identified with a planet, but all also have intricate private identities, points of girl-audience identification that are standard across twentieth-century Western cultural products for girls. Usagi's favorite foods are cake and ice cream, her favorite subject is home economics (the worst are English and math), she's fickle, a show-off, curious and deceptive, prone to crying, and afraid of dentists. Her blood type is O. In an overt recognition of the mainstream identity this poses for Usagi, the warrior princess dreams of being a bride. But through all of this everyday girlness, violence is not only part of Sailor Moon's life but defines her. She attacks not only in self-defense but when she judges her culture or world to be threatened; or even to improve it. This violence is bizarrely mediated by femininity and markers of girlhood—her weapons include a range of moon rods to engulf enemies in ribbons and hearts, and her tiara can be used as a discus to stun or even kill. Sailor Moon (see fig. 9.3) looks amenable in many ways to Western girlhood. She could be used to relate girlhood in Japan to girlhood in other places and might even infer a shared girl experience that underpins any culturally specific consumption—for example, the ways in which Western girl culture consumes Asian culture. Such consumption mostly occurs iconically, as with Atom/Astro Boy T-shirts and Hello Kitty backpacks, participating in an appropriative and interpretative system that could be called global girl culture. Anglophone girl culture tends in particular to utilize Japanese girl culture as an iconography of a childhood that is both familiar and alien but remains proper to a discourse on feminine adolescence.

While it often subsumes the drama of the adolescent experience into more otherworldly narratives, Japanese girl culture also produces a range of teen/youth-centered dramas. But *manga/anime* media do something different with relations between the ambivalently engaged terms of feminine adolescence. They are, for example, more explicit about enfolding knowledge, innocence, sex, vulnerability, and power into the girl figure. Sex is explicitly raised by Sailor Moon's passion for Tuxedo Mask, and Takeuchi has stressed that two of the Sailors, Uranus and Neptune, are intended to be lovers. They are thus not only sexually inflected schoolgirls but also suggest that Robertson's analysis of gender diversity in the Takarazuka can be extended more widely to Japanese girl culture. Robertson identifies a Japanese narrative of girlhood in which "heterosexual inexperience and homosexual experience" (65) are recognized, but not necessarily sexual behavior (resembling the homoerotic images in Western girls' magazines). The gender and sexual ambiguities of these girl culture figures are not distinct from the prominence of schoolgirl figures in mainstream men's pornography, which are particularly public in Japan. However, other desires manifest in Sailor Moon are just as explicit in the West. As reflected in Sailor Moon, the *shōjo* is generally presented as a consumer, a dominant emphasis in the field of girl culture.[25]

When cultural criticism in Anglophone contexts discusses Japanese popular culture, it mostly does not center on girls, but when they appear it is usually as fantastically object-directed and centered on an aesthetic known in Japan as *kawaii* or "cute." As a common descriptor *kawaii* is not confined to girls—men and women news readers may readily concur that an image of a small child with a rabbit is *kawaii desu-ne*. But as a statement of taste, *kawaii* is popularly associated with girls, especially when inflected with a rising exclamation as a total description of an object. This visibility as object-directed infers a special childishness in Japanese girls based on the developmental model by which objects are relinquished for external normative sexual objects—a model with apparent relevance to discourses on girlhood in Japan. A *kawaii* girl, indisputably girl as object, is often construed as "attractive . . . but lack[ing] libidinal agency of her own" (Treat 281). As Treat phrases this link, "the [*shōjo*'s] own sexual energy, directed as it is towards stuffed animals, pink notebooks, strawberry crepes and Hello Kitty novelties, is an energy not yet deployable in the heterosexual economy of adult life" (281). In this context Treat also considers Robertson's rather cautiously deployed argument that "in Japan, one might well argue that [*shōjo*] constitute their own gender" (Treat 282). Caution with such a claim is required in Western commentary in order to protect the developmental priorities of the girl-woman unit, a model that, as I have already detailed, serves a range of different and even conflicting interests.

The Western formation "girl culture" most likely refers to Japanese girl culture by looking for its presumed specificity—its different and yet familiar segmentation of girl culture. But how might the idea of girl culture be deployed in Japan? In 1999 Audrey (Shisaka) Kimura welcomed visitors to the Web site of Benten Label, which produces only young women artists, with a comparison of girl culture production in the West and Japan:

> Girls in Japan don't use words like feminist or Riot Grrl, etc. There are not even any Japanese words that equal these ideas. The girls in 1990 non-feudal Japan are freed from all sexually discriminating issues. When they decide what they want to do, they do it, and nobody stands in their way.

Young people in other countries may strongly support a band that has an intese [sic] political message, while Japanese girls (and boys too) have the same enthusiasm and great sympathy for a silly, crazy band who are shameless, courageous, and who love to entertain people. (Kimura 1999)

Japanese pop music (J-Pop) provides an excellent opportunity to think about markers and ideas of Japanese girlhood. Within Japanese popular music, "idol" singers, because they are explicitly marketed to teenage or pre-teen girls, are the most obvious points of focus for this discussion. Idol singers are framed by a system of repeatedly producing teen stars and promoting them extensively across various mass media. Discussions of idol singers in English very often conform to similar descriptions of manufactured pop in Western countries, and it presumes a comparable if not even greater degree of investment and intimacy in its marketing. Although there are many boy acts to choose from, Namie Amuro (formerly of Supermonkeys) might exemplify spectacularly popular girl-pop and is credited with equally spectacular success in the late 1990s as a saleable look resembling a more everyday cool girl: the "Amura" required "penciled-in eyebrows, mini-skirt, dyed hair" (*Billboard*, 2 August 1997:59).[26] J-Pop production takes place on a massive cross-media scale and also at a highly localized level, such as the sale of idol cards at convenience stores and street stalls.

Iwabuchi limits his argument about cultural odor to products that succeed overseas. He notes that "If 'culturally odourless' products consciously or unconsciously lack Japanese bodily images, the imagery of TV programmes and popular music is inescapably represented through living Japanese bodies" (1998a:169). The J-Pop music industry is often discussed as heavily specialized and not easily translated into global music genres based around Western music: "It's not just a question of language—it's a question of musical culture" (*Billboard*, 24 February 1996:58). Despite both internationalization and Westernisms, Japanese music is overwhelmingly the most popular form of music in Japan.[27] Some forms of Japanese popular music resemble Western genres, including in the late 1990s cult boy and girl singing groups, and some distinctly J-Pop forms cite a mesh of putatively Western styles—such as the "*visual-kei*" boy bands, which mesh glam and goth styles with the boy band phenomenon. Conversely, successful J-pop is rarely popular in foreign markets, where the more successful acts are usually quite different to idol J-Pop and may be perceived as alternative—examples include Pizzicato Five, Towa Tei, and Shonen Knife.

Shonen Knife are not particularly young nor are their music or lyrics clearly marketed to girls, but they are produced in their images and fan communities as girls. Many of the materials circulating Shonen Knife resemble those for Sailor Moon or the Spice Girls. Despite what seem like obvious pop conventions, Shonen Knife are not mainstream in Japan, but when they are taken up in America as pop with a twist their Japaneseness is coded as mainstream. Most Shonen Knife albums sell better overseas than in Japan, and they are often described in terms of overseas success to their Japanese audiences too. Along with other Japanese girl culture products they are regularly appropriated as an other girl world by alternative American girl culture. This appropriation—as pop; as figures of conformity being redeployed as something more than pop—only works by ignoring Shonen Knife's more alternative status within the Japanese pop music scene. It is also crucial that, because of the historical integration of Americanness in Japanese popular culture, J-Pop is accessible to U.S. cultural forms while still looking like the orient. And yet, commercial success in Japanese popular culture rarely translates into success in anglophone contexts, as Sailor Moon and Shonen Knife both indicate in different ways.

The appropriation of Asian girl culture by anglophone girl culture (and by academic reference) is often an imagination of girls everywhere, but also an orientalizing opposition to the complexities of modern Western girls after feminism. Because this mode of consuming girl culture must serve as that coherence, it is not likely to embrace the contradictions of Sailor Moon or recognize the complexity of Shonen Knife's generic placement. Japanese production of girl culture often plays out contradictory images of femininity. This is evident in Kimura's welcome to Benten Label: "The key concept of Benten Label is silliness and seriousness; we enjoy the siillyness [sic] of our music seriously." Some popular music genres in Japan exist outside of a pop mainstream, but despite the recognizable Western labels used to describe them (such as punk or thrash metal), they do not easily fit the genres as they appear in Western/global popular music. It has been claimed that Japanese alternative music genres are purged of any political/ideological content they would have in the West. Japanese alternative genre fans do not necessarily concur with this assessment, but it seems to be a staple of commentary on Japanese pop music.[28]

While pop, mainstream, and alternative do not segment the music market in the same way in Japan as in America or Australia, these are the categories by which anglophone commentary understands Japanese girl culture. Cross-cultural studies of reception are in fact often confined by the repetition of categories circulating as marketing strategies. The mobile categories for Japanese popular music produced in fan Web sites and zines, CDs, music and pop magazines, and record company releases evaporate in cultural commentary on J-Pop or girl culture. Instead the guiding categories used to discuss these fields clearly distinguish between conformity and social critique (or other associations with authenticity) used to segment a girl culture conceived as universal. The difference of Japanese girl culture within globalized contemporary cultural studies is used to underscore the naturalization of demographics and categorical hierarchies of conformity and resistance. This perspective presumes these categories are firmly in place within Asian cultures in forms easily comprehensible outside them and reinforces the certainty that critique of these forms will originate externally. Their Asianness is represented as constitutive and not as a site of negotiation. Both anglophone girl culture and studies of girl culture construct oriental objects as an alien yet familiar pop that explicates the natural elements of dominant Western girlhood.

This imaginary coherence attached to productions of Asianness in Japanese culture differs from what Edward Said calls "orientalism" (1995), a term reserved for those discourses and representations that employ Asianness as an imaginary coherence that conceals hierarchies and ambivalences. However, Rey Chow's understanding of orientalism as "structural ambivalence" (1993:1–54) might enable a discussion of how Asian cultural production employs orientalism. Chow cites Arjun Appadurai's account in *The Social Life of Things* of a process by which the specificity of culture is divested in cultural analysis. Appadurai discusses a "commoditization by diversion" and "the aesthetics of decontextualization" in which "value [. . .] is accelerated or enhanced by placing objects and things in unlikely contexts" (as quoted in Chow 134). Chow further suggests that this commoditizing diversion is also applicable to human subjects, and especially to "ethnic specimens" (134). Michel de Certeau insists that

> we . . . cannot discuss culture or its global aspects without, first of all, recognizing the fact that we are . . . dealing with it from only one site, our own. It will be impossible either to eradicate or to overcome the alterity that experiences and observations, rooted in *other* places, hold before us and outside of us. (1988:123)

It may be impossible to avoid translation and homogenization when comparing different cultures, but it is nevertheless worth asking whether Western feminist cultural studies is a productive perspective from which to approach Japanese girl culture. This cross-cultural comparison (which is of course between more than two cultures) might at least offer important questions to an analysis of anglophone girl culture—a form of orientalism that is unavoidable and not necessarily hierarchical. The widely asserted difficulty of applying feminism to girl culture and girls in Japan might question the ease with which feminism is applied to girl culture and girls sanctioned by a belief that we are looking at the same or even our own culture.

The girl life and girl spaces of Tokyo provide a set of scenes across which cultural specificity appears as a striation of cultural fields. The Harajuku-dori running up to the Harajuku rail station was for a period of time regularly closed on Sundays and turned into an outdoor stage for bands, dance groups, and other performers. The small streets near the JR station are filled with boutique stores stocking youth fashions in clothing, toys, accessories, and pop-culture products, and the station itself borders on Tokyo's major Shinto shrine (Meiji-jinju). Harajuku maintains this reputation although it no longer closes. The shrine, shopping precinct, or station platform provide forums for the public enactment of a range of girl lives: from the *kawaii*, cool girls, and other merchandised lifestyles in the shopping district, through the validated cultural romance of the shrine visit (often with kimono-style display), to the alternative pop culture scenes of the platform and plaza above the station. Girls dominate the alternative displays of clothes, music, and peer associations in these spaces in the late 1990s. Though boys/men still more often play instrumental music in public spaces, the gathering of costumed youth is comprised mainly of girls in fairy-tale, fantasy, gothic, or otherwise extraordinary costumes, or in the regalia of various subcultures. Girls assemble here to do the things girls are often thought to do within bedroom culture (though with different accessories).

The Japaneseness, the Asianness, of these scenes and styles are under negotiation in ways sometimes evident to me and often not. But interviewing Japanese girls in these spaces or even walking among them invites a recognition of girlness, of the malleability and publicly recognized transience of a girlhood not so much suspended before womanhood as figuring a separate space of and commentary on sex/gender/culture. These girl culture forms have a globalized frame that does not disavow their specificity, because the global form produced the collective identities of Japanese or Asian anyway. Orientalist girl culture foregrounds the idea of the girl circulating as the central product of girl culture within globalization. If distinct cultures have specific conceptions of feminine adolescence, late modern girls are nevertheless a global formation. If girl culture assembles imaginary groups and not demographics, questions about control of distribution and about the particular meanings of consumption remain possible within an understanding of girl culture as specific assemblages of practices and knowledges.

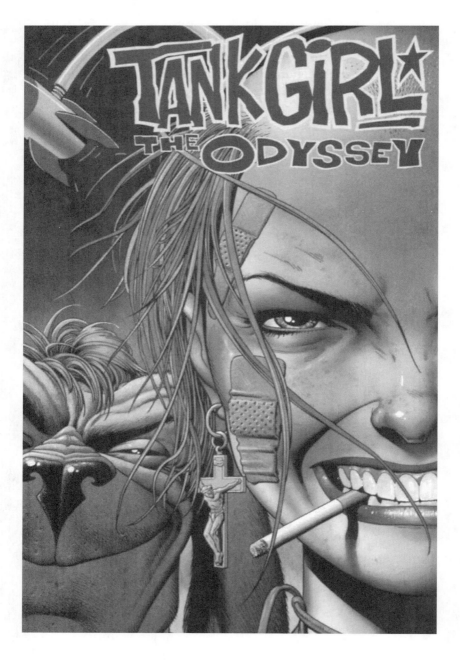

C.1 Jamie Hewlett, Tank Girl (1991)   *(Tank Girl © Hewlett/Martin/Deadline. Illustration by Jamie Hewlett)*

Conclusion:
The Girl of the Century

> The critique of what we are is at one and the same time the
> historical analysis of the limits that are imposed on us and an experiment with the
> possibility of going beyond them.
>
> —Michel Foucault, "What is Enlightenment?"

IF GIRLS are not a demographic and there is no direct link
between girls and girl products, is there such a thing as girl culture? What
field would girl culture describe—all of a girl's life and all fields she enters;
or specific fields of cultural production directed to, produced by, or perceived as particular to girls? Neither the naturalized force of girlhood nor girl
culture's highly visible exchanges between homogeneity and deviance grant
girl culture a coherence that allows it to be descriptive in this sense. Girls and
culture are, discretely, too problematic and in fact fill the function of the
problematic for late modernity, and in conjunction—to paraphrase Stuart
Hall on popular culture—girl culture is almost impossible (1990:456). Girls
have been employed to represent conformity and the mainstream, reflecting
by opposition the authentic Subject of culture, though central to the field of
culture more generally. Girls also provide a figure for a failure of development and thus a place to engage with the traps laid for the individual by the
modern world. Girls figure both the pleasures and threats of technologized
cultural progress and the promise and failure of the modern. Girl culture
might be asked to encompass the production of terms and categories such
as "girl" and "feminine adolescence" with reference to the dissemination

amongst girls of artifacts, behaviors, values, roles, and meanings, including those to which girl is put in discourses such as cultural studies. Girl culture is a territory that allows new ways of looking at the range of cultural fields in which girls are articulated and provides a new and yet familiar map of modernity, and perhaps of the twentieth century in particular.

Girlhood in late modernity is constituted in processes rather than stable terms such as "demographics" or "identity categories." The association of girlhood with immaturity has interpreted these processes as uncertain and as opposed to majority, agency, citizenship, and other markers of maturity. But such a minority status can produce unexpected as well as predetermined possibilities. Feminist cultural studies can recognize such possibilities only by questioning the position from which girls are understood to be merely observed or subject to power, while at the same time acknowledging that it is the categorical disciplines of subject formation that enable girlhood. Feminism was one of the most influential discourses of the twentieth century, and it shares this history with the emergence of feminine adolescence. A history of girlhood enables reflection on feminist relations to dominant discourses, and this is more significant than feminists often acknowledge. As soon as feminist theory—analytic or activist—begins to look only for its own repetition, as soon as it is certain of where it comes from and what its effects are, then it begins to expect merely its own repetition. It also thus ceases to be a vital force in political life, let alone in the lives of individual women and girls. A feminist focus on girls is thus desirable for pragmatic reasons, but it also draws attention to the model of subjection presumed by feminist theory and the ways the Woman-feminist subject is formed, deployed, or avoided within the experience of individuals.

A productive feminist analysis of girls and feminine adolescence must recognize the specificity of girls and girl cultures as singular assemblages in relation to historically and socially specific dominant cultural fields. In order to pursue the ideological imperatives that continue to make feminist analysis vital and significant, it must analyze what makes singular formations of girls and girlhood possible in given contexts. Such analysis of girl culture is not a matter of just finding out more about girls, or talking about girls, however fascinating and pleasurable those things are, but of considering their interaction with discourses that name and constitute them. Girls have been deployed by twentieth-century popular and public culture, and various kinds of cultural analysis. For example, girl culture provides an opportunity to consider whether the oppositions between conformity and the mainstream on one hand and nonconformity, resistance, and authenticity on the other, which have been so important to positioning the ordinary and the exceptional girl in late modernity, are in fact viable concepts for thinking about Western/global popular culture. The marginalization of girls in relation to Subjectivity, and ethical and political agency, constitutes a productive position from which to consider the contemporary repetition and reformulation of those models for the modern self in the modern world.

The ambivalences around girlhood invite a history of its formation that acknowledges the limitations of all historiography, as well as the possibilities that this recognition opens up. Given its new visibility as a discipline for enquiring into such subjects, this history would also interrogate the way that cultural studies and cultural theory conceive of subjectivity, of materiality and change, of the body, of affect and thought, of discourses on agency, authenticity, and authority. Not only sex/gender normativity but the conceptions of the person/citizen have constituted the girl of late modernity—have made feminine adolescence possible—and girls have been crucial elements of the processes of producing these categories. The twentieth century was the period in which girls in this sense emerged as a dominant visible force in public life and in the representations and objects that form and explicate it. A genealogy of the girl has seemed the most useful way to approach this problem because it provides simultaneously an account of new disciplinary and ideological mechanisms specific to the context in which girls are produced and an account of the pleasures, actions, interests, and limitations through which girls are articulated.

The twentieth century was dominated, in cultural theory and popular culture, by a discourse on the Subject in crisis. Adolescence and femininity have been crucial instances of this popular and theoretical focus. The conjunction of these discourses on self and social formation in the figure of the girl has enabled the girl to figure as an image of change, crisis, and personal and cultural tensions. At the turn of the century, is there any reason to think the next century will not prioritize this conjunction of adolescence and femininity in conversations about power, complicity, ideology, change, culture, authenticity, and selfhood? The late twentieth century witnessed an increase in the forms by which interrogations of masculinity entered public discourse. At present, however, these interrogations of gender remain dependent on a constitutive binary division—as girls were present to flesh out the experience of subcultural boys for the Birmingham School, so girls remain a relatively unspoken but foundational opposition for new writers on masculinity or on the new conception of a boy problem. This perception of a boy problem draws partly on the extended possibilities for women and girls, and partly on a decline in discourses centering on masculinized individuality in general, which were nevertheless constitutive of persons rather than men—for example, unemployment and globalization in relation to statehood. Masculinity in crisis continues to be articulated relative to the girl of the twentieth century.

The twentieth century marks a field in which feminine adolescence emerged as an important category for understanding the production and evaluation of sexed/gendered subjectivities in relation to transforming cultural production and theoretical and popular relations to culture. The mass-cultural production that crucially defined the twentieth century, and the new cultural forms attendant on it, are inseparable from new forms of cultural analysis that also arose there. Girls might finally provide a significant focus for considering relations between popular culture and critical theory insofar as they have not only been pivotal to a series of renovations of the modern as an object of analysis but have also been constituted by the formation of late modern critical theory as much as popular culture. It is thus not only possible but imperative to recognize the significance of girls around us, and the folding of major public discourses into the highly visible formation of late modern girls.

Notes

Introduction: Toward a Genealogy of Girlhood

1. The relations between the terms "sex" and "gender" are highly important to the functions and presumed difficulty of feminine adolescence. From the outset I want to acknowledge that sex is not simply the biological form of the body to which social or cultural gender norms are applied. Sex is a way of knowing the body and a construction of the body—although one that may be distinguished from gender.

2. The distinction between society and culture is primarily a matter of emphasis. My reference to culture and to cultural theory is designed to indicate that large-scale political and economic systems are not my first concern. I am not suggesting that such systems do not have effect on the lives of girls; rather, I would question whether they have effect as large-scale systems rather than as more localized effects and relations—this could be discussed either through various discourses on ideology or through what Foucault called "micro-relations of power." See chapter 4.

1. The Girl of the Period

1. Ben-Amos continues: "this implied that the period of adolescence and youth was tremendously long rather than short, for if life expectancy was 35 or 40, most people spent nearly half their lives in a position of 'youth,' during which time they were barred from assumption of the primary role of adults; namely household headship" (6). For writers in agreement with the prolonged adolescence theory, adolescence and youth equate to the early modern terms youth and young adulthood (Ben-Amos 9).

2. Ben-Amos uses "work" as the principal point of distinction between girls and boys and subsequently as the only point for extensive discussion of girls,

generally positioning women's youth as a compromise between adolescence/youth and gender norms.

3. The age of consent effectively based on British common law is generally held to have been twelve, lowered to ten in 1576, then raised from ten to twelve in 1861, to thirteen in 1875, and finally to sixteen across a serious of changes from 1879 to 1893. In practice, ages of consent varied according to location, enabled by prosecutions using lesser charges, the deployment of religious law, and variations in colonies.

4. The canons of 1604 "forbade the marriage of persons under twenty-one without the consent of parents of guardians" although there were clearly ways of avoiding this prohibition, which conflicted with other laws "as a product of the distinction between church and civil courts" (Stone 31). Cook appends that "if quite youthful affianced partners had sexual intercourse (prima facie evidence of maturation), that act carried with it the presumption of consent to their union, and there was even a proviso that lawful marriages could occur at ages younger than twelve if puberty had been attained. Elizabethans and Jacobeans thereby recognised that adulthood could not be defined by a set number of years, as could wardship or legal minority" (20).

5. Stone attributes increased ages of first marriage in Renaissance and post-Renaissance England to greater choice concerning marriage partners, changing medical opinion, extended education and training periods, and delays in inheritance and majority (42–4).

6. The ambivalence of girls' gender performance in Shakespeare's plays is also important. A range of girls including Rosalind and Viola perform being boys (and boys performing girls performing boys). Moreover, characters including King Lear, Othello, and Hamlet comment directly on the difficulty of discerning the truth from a girl's appearance.

7. I will discuss both of these propositions—that psychoanalysis permeates public and popular understandings of adolescence, and that these understandings are no more popular than they are theoretical—in part 2. My own experience of teaching *Romeo and Juliet* to undergraduate students suggests that a broad range of students from different social backgrounds and positions are very familiar with the pattern of adolescent psychology and the socialization of youth Dalsimer and others describe, in fact seeing it not as a theory about youth but as the natural pattern of human development.

8. Ernest Jones's extended reading of *Hamlet* through psychoanalysis enables much of this discussion, posing psychoanalysis as a means of "solving" the problem of *Hamlet*. Rose sums up psychoanalytic accounts of the play as fol-

lows: "The relationship of psychoanalysis to *Hamlet* has in fact always been a strange and repetitive one in which Hamlet the character is constantly given the status of a truth, and becomes a pivot for psychoanalysis and its project" (133).

9. For Lacan this positions Ophelia as "the phallus, exteriorized and rejected by the subject as a symbol signifying life" (1977a:23); "she has become for him the very symbol of the rejection of his desire" (Lacan 1977a:36).

10. Pipher does mean this reference, moreover, to infer a project of reclaiming cultural certainties lost in a late modern adolescence in which "with puberty girls crash into junk culture" (13). I will return to *Reviving Ophelia* as a successful narrative on feminine adolescence in later chapters.

11. Thus "when Hamlet immediately interprets her presence in exactly the way he is intended to, he is to be imagined as responding to an established iconographical language" (Lyons 60). This is particularly indexed to annunciation images of the virgin reading (see fig. 4.1). The tableau of the virgin in spiritual contemplation is also utilized by Juliet to escape her parents' house and is apparent in the popular iconography of Atala in eighteenth-century France (see chapter 5).

12. Appelbaum's essay on Romeo's manhood, which deploys a more complicated version of psychoanalytic theory than Dalsimer's book, notes that Romeo does not have the authority to simply cite the law as a protection and that this failure of authority brings about Mercutio's death and thus the tragedy of the play.

13. For example, through texts such as James Frazer's *The Golden Bough* and Jessie Weston's *From Ritual to Romance*, as well as modernist poetry, drama, music, dance, and novels.

14. The classical girl can also be discussed through the apparently more delimited position of the virgin, but attempting to apply "virgin" to classical girls is an exceedingly difficult maneuver. While I will discuss the ambiguity of virginity in chapter 5, I want to note here the difficulty of overlaying our conceptions of girlhood, or even virginity, onto the classical period. While the latter concept is influenced by classical texts, the alignment between the two in the classical world is often exaggerated.

15. Notable among works on this topic is Judith Butler's recent contribution, *Antigone's Claim* (2000).

16. Within Hegel's reading of *Antigone*, Irigaray argues, "both sexes, male and female, have already yielded to a destiny that is different for each [. . .] as Hegel admits when he affirms that the brother is for the sister the possibility of recognition of which she is deprived as mother and wife, but does not state

that the situation is reciprocal. This means that the brother has already been invested with a value for the sister that she cannot offer in return, except by devoting herself to his culture after death" (1993:217).

17. Chanter asks what Hegel conceals "when he reduces Antigone's 'knowledge' to intuition, when he claims that her ethical sensibility is not true ethical knowledge, because it does not know itself as such, because it is immediate rather than reflected, because it consists of divine feeling (madness?) rather than well considered (speculative, determined, mediated) thought?" (76)

18. Various writers outside of feminist theory have recast Hegel's Antigone in the light of Freud's oedipal theories, including Derrida and Phillip Lacoue-Labarthe. For Soren Kierkegaard, Antigone is "a (modern) daughter of Oedipus who is neither the fully responsible, Kantian (male) person of modernity, nor simply a token of the family to be punished by (pre-modern) Fate" (Battersby 172).

19. This book is a sequel to Stuart's 1926 *The Boy Through the Ages* and focuses on the relations of girls to clothes, food, law, social mores, and, particularly, education. She states: "I feared that a certain amount of overlapping and duplication would be inevitable . . . [but] I encountered such multitudes of picturesque and engaging little girls that I decided that *The Girl Through the Ages* would be quite as good a subject as *The Boy*—perhaps even better" (7).

20. Margaret McFadden locates in a series of letters between Boston girls an interesting example of the way in which girls participated in this debate, rather than merely being objects of it. Nelson and Vallone argue the letters reveal "that both the terms and the spirit of key feminist arguments of the nineteenth century were part of girls' culture . . . [and this] demonstrates that girls' culture was not monolithic but multivocal" (2).

21. Sally Mitchell notes that the status of young persons was renegotiated in the factory acts: "Those laws defined children, whose work was increasingly regulated, as under fourteen, and men and women as those nineteen and over; the 'young person' aged fourteen to eighteen, was in an intermediate and partially protected category" (1994:244).

22. On Victorian guidance for girls see also Rowbotham (1989) and Vallone (1995).

23. Described by Sally Mitchell as "the first broadly successful magazine for girls" (1994:246), this seems to have been widely preserved because of both the length of its success and its sponsored dissemination. *The Girl's Own Paper* was published by the Religious Tract Society for one penny a week to provide, as Mitchell puts it, "the increasingly literate young people who benefited from

the 1870 Education Act" with healthier reading material (1995:246–7). Mitchell describes its assumed audience as "middle-class" but notes that letters indicate servants also read it (246).

24. For Foucault power is diffuse, operating across and through all social forms, and it is also open to resistance across and through those spaces. This model of power is neither a top-down model nor a model of concerted forces that have any single point of origin.

25. This process is evidenced by extracts from a story, "Attraction," in the *Girls' Own Paper*: "She was nearly nineteen in years; in some things she was twenty-nine, and at times she did not exceed nine" (23 November, 1889, 123); and, in the story's denouement—"what a silly 'little muslin schoolgirl' I was to think I could resist you, when our marriage was made long ages ago by angels in heaven!" (141). Here the concrete ending of the engagement and the retrospective construction of a sexual identity for our heroine overcomes the girl's adolescent transitions.

26. In the end Alice's checkmate of the Red King is ignored, emphasizing her challenge to the queens and sidelining the conflict between her and the passionate father who may be dreaming her—or may be something she dreams has the power to dream her: "he was part of my dream, of course—but then I was part of his dream too! *Was* it the Red King . . . ?" (Carroll 344).

27. Richards identifies discourses on feminine adolescent sexuality in nineteenth-century advertisements, girls and women's magazines, and novels, focusing especially on the advertising icon of "the seaside girl," which continues with different significations in contemporary popular culture.

28. Gorham argues that "our perception of this period in the life cycle causes us to perceive distinct differences in needs and in personality developing over a single year, or even a few months, during adolescence. But in the 1880s both the purity reformers and their opponents used arguments that were drawn from an older conception of youth, in which youth was defined not in terms of chronological age, or psycho-sexual development, but had to do with the status of the individual in relation to other groups in society." (369) The Law Relating to the Protection of Young Girls (1881) is covered in Hansard Parliamentary Debates, 3d ser. vol. 289 (1884).

29. In the context of such debates a notion of the "public good" drawn from Rousseau instantiates a public sphere that will later be espoused as the goal of modernity by critics such as Habermas. Lynda Lange points out that "the common good is held by Rousseau to be an objective reality, whether or not the majority knows it or appreciates it. This good is most likely to be apprehended by

citizens of a certain character and capacity. This in turn requires proper education, and above all equality, in the sense of freedom from dependence on others" (97).

30. In England the age of consent was again negotiated in "An Act to Make Further Provision for the Protection of Women and Young Girls and the Suppression of Brothels and Other Purposes" (1893). Gorham notes that these " 'Other Purposes' included (under part I, section 11) stringent penalties against male homosexuality" (354n). This inclusion foregrounds the degree to which girl sexuality is an improper, and according to these legislative principles, nonproductive sexuality.

31. Freud also indicates that maids could be re-named and dismissed, had little right to expression, and were disbelieved on principle. The sexual vulnerability of servants, as with feminine adolescents more generally, is interpreted as sexual irresponsibility, if not evil. Emma Eckstein, a patient and colleague of Freud, wrote in 1889 that "our laws, which protect all our property, do not recognize the honour of somebody who serves, and these poor young girls are without rights and without protection even in the eyes of the law" (quoted in Masson 249).

32. Previous related legislative changes had occurred across almost twenty years, and we can retrospectively understand a range of debates and legislative amendments to have foreshadowed this conception of consent. See Simpson (1987) and Walkowitz (1993).

2. Feminine Adolescence

1. The disjunction between maturity and majority in public discourse—ideas dependent on puberty and law respectively—enables the pervasive representation of young men caught between these terms as a threat. They are figured by this gap as capable of action, but not of responsible action. While I will not pursue it here, debates on the disenfranchisement of young men need to critique this impossible relation between maturity and majority.

2. The adolescence of this history means masculine adolescence, but despite compartmentalization of the life cycle around various physical and social criteria, classical adolescence is not so specific. Whereas the Latin *adulescentia* was "the age of *adulescens,* the time between the age of the *puer* and *juvenis,* i.e., from the 15th to the 30th year, the time of youth," *adolescens* referred to a process of growth and included older men (*Cassell's Latin Dictionary*).

3. Leavis singles out an educated minority who have custody of culture, categorizing everyone else as immature: "The critically adult public is very small indeed: they are a very small minority" (16).

4. Dyhouse is specifically interested in Hall's account of adolescent women. Dyhouse goes on to deride Hall for a "glutinous, leery prose" style (122), and by this she insinuates a lecherous response to the adolescent subjects he is discussing. In noting Hall's alignment of women with adolescents, Dyhouse mostly does not quote *Adolescence* itself, in which adolescence is valorized for its energy and creativity, although she does include his advocation that "this calf or filly stage should be prolonged by every artifice" (123, quoting Hall 1904 2:1).

5. Spacks contingently defines adolescence as "the time of life when the individual has developed full sexual capacity but has not yet assumed a full adult role in society" (7). While this definition is obviously teleological, presuming the "full adult role" as the natural end of adolescence, it recognizes the gendering of adolescence in relation to gender distinctions between full adult roles.

6. Participants in a 1999 survey of Australian high-school girls emphasized the following milestones as the end of girlhood (in order of decreasing importance): getting married, becoming an adult, becoming a woman, finishing puberty, attaining legal majority, having sex, and (interestingly) "never, you're always a girl." Options rarely selected included having a child, leaving home, or getting a job (Driscoll 1999).

7. Christine's narrative is not transcribed like Dora's because "Christine Beauchamp" is definitively unlocatable. Prince's text is divided into two parts: "The Development of the Personalities" and "The Hunt for the Real Miss Beauchamp."

8. Proponents of Prince's form of psychology opposed the associative methods of psychoanalysis, preferring hypnosis as a method of revealing the alternative state of consciousness that both movements believed to be revelatory of the deep self and the means for constructing a functionally integrated personality. Prince is best known for developing, in relation to Christine's case study, a theory of "co-consciousness" and "dissociation." See Leys's discussion of hypnosis and mimesis between Freud and Prince.

9. For discussion of this convention see D. Gaines (1990), Grossberg (1994), Davis (1999), and Douglas Coupland's *Gen X Reader*.

10. Mitchell's claim that girl culture in any effective sense ceased to exist in the early twentieth century involves two separate assumptions that require more

support than she offers and seem to me to be inherently flawed: that girls' culture shares an overarching aim in relation to which it may be effective or not (including the possible aim of authentically representing girls' lives); and that girls' culture was not initially a commercial category and that the commercialization that brought about its expansion disrupted an authenticity it had previously maintained.

11. Patrice Petro's discussion of modernity and mass culture in Weimar Germany quotes a 1929 "magazine for intellectuals": "Berlin is a girl in a pullover, not much powder on her face, Hölderlin in her pocket, thighs like those of Atalanta, an undigested education, a heart which is almost too ready to sympathize, and a breadth of view which charms one's repressions" (115). A further example of the periodization of modern women as girls might also include: Wyndham Lewis in the avant-garde journal *Blast* in 1915—"I see every day in a certain A. B. C. Shop at least three girls who belong to a new and unknown race. They would furnish an artist looking for an origin with a model of a new mankind" (quoted in Symons 7).

12. De Tocqueville wrote in 1835 that "long before an American girl arrives at the age of marriage, her emancipation from maternal control begins: she has scarcely ceased to be a child, when she already thinks for herself, speaks with freedom, and acts on her own impulse" (quoted in Helsinger et al. 175).

13. Gaines argues that as this family was often not present in the lived experience of boys, the state, which relies on its disciplinary presence, took an ideologically compensatory role: "State reform schools were not viewed as prisons, and the guys were not being punished they were being 'trained.' . . . *Parens patriae* and the idea of adolescence worked well together to keep wild boys and angry boys behind bars" (121).

14. Mason's study *The Girl Sleuth* is structured to trace an alignment between increasing sophistication in girl's detective fiction and girls' personal development. Mason constructs the girl as reading "to assuage a confused longing" (47) linked to sexual knowledge (63).

15. Although Grossberg concedes in a footnote that adolescence has a longer history than postwar youth cultures, he otherwise focuses exclusively on post-1950s youth culture, identifying a radical shift in knowledge about youth around post-1960s music industries (183). The rock'n'roll" youth of the 1950s and 1960s coalesce certain ways of knowing about youth, but they did not intervene in a previously homogenous or unimportant history.

16. This has been attributed to a backlash against feminism: "during the decades from 1870 to 1910, middle-class women were beginning to organize on behalf

of higher education, entrance to the professions, and political rights. Simultaneously, the female nervous disorders of anorexia nervosa, hysteria, and neurasthenia became epidemic; and the Darwinian 'nerve specialist' arose to dictate proper feminine behavior outside the asylum as well as in . . . and to oppose women's efforts to change the conditions of their lives" (Showalter 18).

17.   Dyhouse quotes the promise on the back of a membership card: "We, the Members of the Snowdrop Band, sign our names to show that we have agreed that wherever we are, and in whatever company, we will, with God's help, earnestly try, both by our example and influence, to discourage all wrong conversation, light and immodest conduct and the reading of bad and foolish books" (109). The word "try," here, as Dyhouse points out, allows for error and imperfection, but it also articulates the impossibility of ultimate attainment. This is an ideal progression with no material endpoint, like the Christian perfection of the soul in relation to which Foucault maps the development of technologies of the self out of demands for religious self-examination.

18.   This selection also represents texts from the United States, United Kingdom, and Australia, respectively.

19.   Brumberg writes at the conclusion of her *Body Project* that "more than any other group in the population, girls and their bodies have borne the brunt of twentieth century social change, and we ignore that fact at our peril." She extols Pipher's work as an important response to this crisis: "The popularity of this much-talked about book is a sign that Americans are finally waking up to the jeopardy their daughters are in" (quoted in Winter 14). I will return to *Reviving Ophelia* in the context of feminist writing on girls.

20.   There is perhaps a resurgence of the young girls' magazine in the appearance of texts such as *Barbie* magazine, which is clearly directed at an audience preceding the pre- and early pubescent demographic that constitutes the main market for girls' magazines. However *Barbie* draws its generic conventions less from popular culture for small girls than from adolescent girls' magazines.

21.   In McRobbie's more recent work on feminist readings of girls' magazines, she analyzes the variations on normative models for girls that have more recently entered that field. See McRobbie 1997.

3. Puberty

1.   Schilder exemplifies this position: "the development from pre-genitality to genitality is also of fundamental importance for our attitude towards our own body. We experience our body as united, as a whole, only when the genital level

is harmoniously reached. Fully developed genital sexuality is indispensable for the full appreciation of our own body-image" (quoted in Grosz 1994:82).

2. In the copy I obtained this slide had been removed.

3. Mead blames cultures of silence and misinformation around puberty for tying girls to an unhappy postadolescent life, torn by their mystified biology from the childish preadolescent happiness of "primitive life": "At menstruation the girl's pact with her sex is sealed for ever" (Mead 1975:121). Mead identifies this with a process of "shaming" (122), and while she does reflect on puberty as a time of learning it figures chiefly as a period of more or less mute incubation from which a woman will emerge.

4. The recognition of masculine rites of passage "in terms of the need for some visible sign of changed physical maturity on the part of the male" (Harper and Collins 1978b:175), can be seen as an attempt to compensate for the lack of a visible statement comparable to menarche.

5. "Rites of passage or ceremonies in which the child or adolescent is initiated into adulthood take place in many different cultures but, for males, physiological and social puberty are essentially different and rarely converge. The event of menstruation in girls provides a pressure for a recognition of a change of status so that where specific rituals occur they tend to be more closely tied to physical development" (Rutter 5).

6. Theories of women's time often define recurrence as a temporality specific to women's bodies and women's continuity with Nature. This is "*monumental time*" as proposed by Nietzsche and taken up by Kristeva: the larger view of history determined by "symbolic determination" of relations of *reproduction* "and its representation" (Kristeva 1986c:189–90). Kristeva argues that "modern sciences of subjectivity" all support the equation of the Mother with space evident in "matriarchal religions" and classical philosophy (191). This is widely held to be one of the founding dichotomies of Western Subjectivity: material space, the matter of birth and the body, is equated with the Mother while the Father represents social process and experience—the time of the mind: "As for time, female subjectivity seems to provide a specific measure that essentially retains *separation* and *eternity* from among the multiple modalities of time known through the history of civilization. On the one hand, these are cycles, gestation, the eternal recurrence of a biological rhythm which conforms to that of nature and imposes a temporality whose stereotyping may shock, but whose regularity and unison with what is experienced as extra-subjective time, cosmic time, occasion vertiginous visions and unnameable *jouissance*" (Kristeva 1986c:191).

7. Extensive research has been dedicated to explaining the mesh of nature and culture in menstruation—discussing the effect of diet on menstruation, for example, is about both body and culture. Such research has also considered the lowering age of menarche (see Brumberg 1997), an event with extensive implications for girls given menarche's role as physical and psychic break with childhood.

8. This is the only place women can take in this psychoanalytic schema of abjection. The meaning that collapses in abjection (see Kristeva 1982) is the Symbolic organization of dualist sexual difference under the weight of any suggestion that Woman is not fixed as Other-than-the-Subject.

9. The definition of postmenstrual women as having "passed the term of their sexual life" (Ellis 1974:255), reinforces the equation of feminine sexuality with childbearing that helps construct feminine adolescence as prior to both femininity and sexuality.

10. As a resistance to these educational and medicalized discourses, Lymn argues that girls have other opportunities, in girl or women-girl groups and in more local forms of cultural production, such as Web sites, to seek and create their own knowledges about their menstruation, supporting Foucault's contention that there is room for resistance in the power/knowledge process (53).

11. According to the vice president of design and development of girl's toys at Mattel: "Barbie has no fixed identity, no "self." Barbie *is* change. . . . There was Barbie the model (1959), Barbie the career girl (1963), Barbie the surgeon (1973), and Barbie the aerobics instructor (1984)" (quoted in Carter 54).

12. These machines are not incidental but pivotal to Barbie play. Sports Barbie came complete with a complicated mechanism that did little except enable her to be attached to a machine that would mediate between the hand that twisted and the twisting of her body into tennis strokes or golf shots (she also came with a riding outfit, but the horse was extra). Some of Barbie's arms bend and some had mechanized hands for grasping televisions and drinks trays—in her jointed-hand incarnations she rarely came with the more dreary domestic appliances that are crucial at times when her attachment to these commodities is less direct. Even the stiffly poised Growing-Hair Barbie openly conceals machines—a ponytail that snapped back into a sophisticated "adult" style, to which braids and other wigs could be attached if you didn't want her default hair.

13. Ducille's discussion of Mattel's attempts to design and produce a specifically African-American girls' body provides an important instance here of how Barbie interacts with changing relations between bodily form and social identity.

14. "There is an 'outside' to what is constructed by discourse, but this is not an absolute 'outside,' an ontological thereness that exceeds or counters the boundaries of discourse; as a constitutive 'outside,' it is that which can only be thought—when it can—in relation to that discourse, at and as its most tenuous borders" (Butler 1993:8).

15. Foucault's cultural unconscious, or his versions of discourse, are not equivalent to "ideology" in its negative sense as that which cultural studies is often mobilized to critique—as the failure or inadequacy of popular reflection on culture. Butler's text does tend to make that reduction. Despite the way in which she foreshadows her project, Foucault drops out of the argument when it turns to Althusser. From the beginning of the chapter "Althusser's Subjection," there are no substantial references to Foucault, indeed the index to the book doesn't refer to one.

16. This might be glossed in the more recognizable psychoanalytic language of *Bodies That Matter* as identification. It is not that the forming subject turns back on itself, but that power does (Butler 1997:4), and this is the actual process of forming the subject or subject-position: "the subject is the effect of power in recoil" (Butler 1997:6).

4. Daughters: Theories of Girlhood

1. This is one of the implications of Hegel's idea that even Antigone's direct action is unconscious and outside of history (because referenced to the Divine). What Marxism chiefly takes from Hegel is the idea of the dialectic as an opposition between apparently dichotomous terms, which can be synthesized in the progress of history. This history, I contend in this chapter, is that of the worker-brother-citizen.

2. Late modern analysts have often focused on how "puberty is considerably influenced by alimentation and hygiene—that is to say, by the social class to which the child belongs" (Ellis 1974:36). Class also effects this construction of adolescence as "conflict"—"psychosocial adolescence" being "a luxury afforded by the affluent" (Rutter 6).

3. Exceptions are usually found in specific studies of girls in relation to work and employment (for example in McRobbie and Nava's *Gender and Generation*) rather than in more general accounts of work, capitalism, or labor relations.

4. Raymond Williams identifies a structure in which every society includes "a central system of practices, meanings and values, which we can properly call dominant and effective" (1987:209), but this is not, he argues, "in any sense a static system. On the contrary we can only understand an effective and dominant

culture if we understand the real social processes on which it depends . . . the process of incorporation" (209). Williams identifies these processes particularly with education, but the incorporative processes of a dominant culture are far more extensive, multiple, and intertwined with what Williams calls "alternative" or "oppositional" cultures than with an education system. Families and popular and public cultural fields are all crucial sites for such incorporation.

5. Available material on girls in the U.S.S.R., however, suggests that when monitored equalization of the educational and career expectations of girls took place they had significant effects. Urie Bronfenbrenner (1974) compared U.S. and U.S.S.R. education systems, focusing in part on the portrayal of girls in curriculum materials.

6. This post-Lacanian Marxist theory is often accused of being solely academic— that is, detached from political action and thus not "praxis" in that classical Marxist sense. However, teaching, writing, publishing, speaking, and social analyses are not only clearly practices, but this exclusion of theory from Marxist praxis is counter to Marx's own political involvement, and more generally the presumed role of the Marxist intellectual. The problem with this stream of Marxist academic thought is not any opposition to practice but its poststructuralist form that problematizes if not confounds the large structural distinctions upon which most preceding Marxist analysis relies.

7. The hysteric is nonmaternal, as the etiology of the term implies: "The womb is an animal which longs to generate children. When it remains barren too long after puberty, it is distressed and sorely disturbed, and straying about in the body and cutting off all passages of the breath, it impedes respiration and brings the sufferer into the extremest anguish and provokes all manner of diseases besides" (Plato quoted in Bernheimer 3). Anna O.'s phantom pregnancy, which eventually terminates her seminal therapy, is thus unsurprising and, rather than short-circuiting her cure, progresses in line with it (see Bowlby 76).

8. The women analysts who followed Freud made influential contributions to the field of psychoanalytic (and feminist) theory. Freud's work on femininity responded to these women, and even addressed them, sometimes ironically. Janine Chasseguet-Smirgel provides a useful overview of much of this work, emphasizing that some of these analysts were critical or at best ambivalent about a number of key psychoanalytic principles in both theory and practice.

9. Jung opposes Persephone's role as daughter to her role as bride: "the anima . . . is in the highest degree *femme à homme*, whereas Demeter-Kore exists in the plane of the mother-daughter experience, which is alien to man and shuts him out" (1982c:164).

10. Jung particularly claims mythical cyclic femininity as a truth about girls: "every mother contains her daughter in herself and every daughter her mother, and . . . every woman extends backwards into her mother and forwards into her daughter. This participation and mingling give rise to that peculiar uncertainty as regards *time*: a woman lives earlier as a mother, later as a daughter" (1982c:149).

11. Nancy Fraser objects to Kristeva's focus on the Mother as a "quasi-biologistic, essentializing identification of women's femininity with maternity. Maternity, for her, is how women, as opposed to men, touch base with the pre-Oedipal semiotic residue (men do it by writing avant-garde poetry; women do it by having babies)" (99).

12. From earlier concepts of dialogue and semiosis to widely appropriated work on abjection and the Symbolic Order, Kristeva emphasizes moments in which oppositional structures are breached. Exemplarily, the abject and the carnivalesque name the structural permeability of structure, the foundational failure of boundaries, but neither threaten the continuity of those structures.

13. The text thus presents this formation as of equal argumentative weight to "The Situation of Women" (the title of part 5) and as far more important than the aging of women in general—"From Maturity to Old Age" constitutes only one section of part 5. This structure also places sexual experience, heterosexual or homosexual, substantially in the girls' realm.

14. This is often referred to as "second wave" feminism in anglophone writing, marking the gap between suffragism and the feminist actions, primarily of the 1970s, often referred to as "women's liberation." Although this nomenclature is also appropriate to France, the concept of "second wave" should not be too easily globalized, even within Western cultures. Beauvoir's writing of *The Second Sex* in fact overlaps with debates around women's suffrage in France. Nevertheless, a generationalism is evident in 1990s writing on French feminism. See Sandrine Garcia (1994).

15. Rubin defines the "sex/gender system" as "the set of arrangements by which a society transforms biological sexuality into products of human activity, and in which these transformed sexual needs are satisfied" (534), but more recent feminist theory has also problematized the biological givenness of sex, so that sex and gender are supplementary rather than opposed.

16. Psychoanalysis, rather than existentialism, is the terrain in which Beauvoir understands the girl, and a psychoanalytic account of girlhood is the mode in which she addresses woman's secondary state. In the conclusion, Beauvoir writes: "Authorized to test her powers in work and sports, competing actively

with the boys, she would not find the absence of the penis—compensated by the promise of a child—enough to give rise to an inferiority complex" (735). However, the absence of the penis would remain a source of inferiority for the liberated woman were it not for the promise of the very maternity Beauvoir has seen as pinning her to her own submission.

17. De Lauretis identifies in feminism "a twofold pull in contrary directions—the critical negativity of its theory, and the affirmative positivity of its politics—[as] both the historical condition of existence of feminism and its theoretical condition of possibility" (26). Seyla Benhabib also discussed this doubled vision of feminist theory with reference to a reading of "the tradition," meaning the discourses of patriarchy: "one eye sees what the tradition has trained it to see, the other searches for what the tradition has told her was not even worth looking for" (130). Benhabib locates two different tendencies in approaching this problem—"the teaching of the good father" (a form of "liberal feminism") and "the cry of the rebellious daughter" (aligned with deconstruction and psychoanalysis (130).

18. These theories are explicitly indebted to Foucault, and some feminists have questioned recourse to male philosophers who do not foreground sex/gender to analyze the situation of women. Among these critics, Tania Modleski acknowledges that "since feminism has a great stake in the belief, first articulated by Simone de Beauvoir, that one is not *born* a woman, one *becomes* a woman (for if this were *not* the case it would be difficult to imagine social change), thinkers like Lacan and Foucault have provided the analytical tools by which we may begin the arduous task of unbecoming women" (15).

19. These are also evident in modernist panic over mass-cultural girls, and deployed again in citations of the Frankfurt school by various proponents of cultural criticism. In their alignment of girls with a threatening mass culture, then, I am suggesting that contemporary feminist practice often remains fundamentally modernist. See chapters 6 and 9.

20. Showalter describes the appearance in the 1920s of a fashionable new style of feminist who was "a good dresser, a good sport, and a pal; she resembles the gallant heroines of Fitzgerald's short stories," identifying with men rather than women and bound to marry in pursuit of her "fullest development" (16).

21. Sheila Jeffreys quotes this passage in her extension of O'Neill's thesis (Jeffreys 155). Jeffreys attributes this "decline" to the "Freudian" co-option of feminist practice under the name of "free love," the popular aesthetics of heterosexual union in Modernist art, and "the impact of consumerism and press hostility" (150)—thus outlining that decline as a snapshot of late modernity.

22. The opposition of old and new feminism on the grounds of sex continues, for example, in *Esquire's* 1994 article on "do-me feminism," constructing younger feminists as appealing to men by saying "look, feminists want sex too, and they want good sex" (Friend 1994). This article represents feminism as a lifestyle choice rather than a politics, but drew interested responses from influential feminists such as bell hooks.

23. Sabina Lovibond has argued incisively against the supposition that "radical" feminism avoids reliance on "the progressive identification and correction of defects in one's belief-set (or in the structures of representation within which one has been operating), but instead on the creation of something qualitatively new—a *'feminine* symbolic' " (1994:80) that opposes rationalist systems of value (86).

24. "The research of Chodorow and Gilligan, in particular, has suggested that men and women (growing up within a particular cultural framework, it must be emphasised), *do* appear to experience and conceptualize events differently, the key differences centering around different conceptions of the self/world, self/other relation: 'Girls emerge [. . .] with a basis for "empathy" built into their primary definition of self in a way that boys do not. Girls emerge with a stronger basis for experiencing another's needs or feelings as one's own (or thinking that one is experiencing another's needs or feelings) [. . .] girls come to experience themselves as less differentiated than boys, more continuous with and related to the external object-world and as differently oriented to their inner object-world as well' " (Bordo 1994:19, quoting Gilligan).

25. Along these lines De Lauretis wants "to conceive of the social subject and of the relations of subjectivity to sociality in another way: a subject constituted in gender, to be sure, though not by sexual difference alone, but rather across languages and cultural representations; a subject en-gendered in the experiencing of race and class, as well as sexual, relations; a subject, therefore, not unified but rather multiple, and not so much divided as contradicted" (De Lauretis 2).

26. These "new Victorians" are comprised of radical feminists, gender feminists, victim feminists, cultural feminists, wimp feminists, and ghetto feminists (Denfeld xi). Denfeld's argument is that contemporary radical/victim feminism has become conservative: "The leading causes in feminism today are all morally driven. The influential voices are entirely passive, speaking always in the language of victim mythology or inner transformation. And so the women's movement has come to duplicate Victorianism in all its repressive

glory: the woman revered on the pedestal, charged with keeping society's moral order yet politically powerless—and perpetually martyred" (16–17).

5. Sex and the Single Girl

1. I am not suggesting that single girls are more centered on sexual activity than other groups but, rather, noting that emphasis in studies of girls. Nor am I suggesting that single girls are actually not functional within a patriarchal economy—single girls, adolescent girls, may be mothers and wives and domestic workers and other crucial positions, but these roles are framed as exceptional in popular and public discourses.

2. The hymen is often undetectable in women regardless of sexual intercourse or other activities that "damage" the hymen as faithful indicator of virginity. Sissa argues that "as an organ of virginity, the hymen of imagination is a cover" (2).

3. Sissa points to the distinction between *parthenos* and *parthenios*. These words could be translated as "virgin"—"the peculiar status of the young [woman] who, though pubescent, was not yet married" (Claude Caleme quoted in Sissa 76)—and "virginity"—a term "not limited to any one period of a woman's life but . . . associated with a very definite attitude to sexuality" (77–8), where even this second term does not necessarily exclude sexual activity.

4. Despite the assertions in some patristic literature that virginity is an integrity of mind rather than a physical condition (Ambrose 13), the canonical insistence on Mary's physical purity—and thus her status as paradigmatic signifier of the Father's Word—masks her personal integrity and activity.

5. As the son of God was "incarnate by the Holy Ghost of the Virgin Mary" (*Catholic Missal* 633–34), Mary's Virginity involves a denial of sexual activity or pleasure and of her place as Mother of God—Mary is not mother but container. The succession of the Father thus explicitly relies on the establishment of girls' dedication to virginity and desire to incarnate the Father in a Son.

6. The self-regard proliferated through the virgin is evidenced by the popular power of the Virgin. A recent demonstration of virginity's ambivalence is the conservative and impassioned declaration of "reclaimed virginity" by some United States' Christian groups—these groups give out cards stating the bearer's virginity and intent to remain virgin till marriage, regardless of any prior sexual activity.

7. The popularity of girl-saints or gods in the early twentieth century is evinced by Joan of Arc's canonization in 1920 and her utilization in World War II as

"figurehead for both sides in occupied France" (Warner 1988:14). Popular texts on Saint Joan in the period surrounding her canonization emphasized that her vigilant and self-defining virginity was only justified by extraordinary circumstance. Moreover, Joan was not a Woman. Marina Warner quotes Michelet: "She had, body and soul, the divine gift of remaining childlike. She grew up, she became strong and beautiful, but she never ever knew the physical miseries of woman kind" (Warner 1988:19). Warner argues that such representations emphasize the ambiguities of Joan's position, but they are also more broadly suggestive for a consideration of virginity: "*Pucelle* means 'virgin,' but in a special way, with distinct shades connoting youth, innocence and, paradoxically, nubility. It is the equivalent of the Hebrew *'almah*, used of both the Virgin Mary and the cleaning girls in Solomon's harem in the bible. It denotes a time of passage, not a permanent condition. It is a word that looks forward to a change in state" (Warner 1988:22).

8. Although this proposition could be referred to much of the literary and semiotic theory circulating around the emergence of poststructuralism in the 1960s—1970s, I am citing Roland Barthes's deployment of semiotics in his theories of textuality, reading, and signification. See, in particular, his *Image—Music—Text* and *The Pleasure of the Text.*

9. Bat-Ami Bar On states that "until recently the history of philosophy has been understood to belong to an old-fashioned history of ideas according to which historians should attend only to the relationship between ideas themselves, because the social and political context in which ideas occur is irrelevant to their truth" (46). But Benhabib's argument is also a demand that philosophy be seen in context—that is, as a text.

10. One of the most cited forms of the excessive maternal principle is *écriture féminine*, a concept that entered anglophone literary criticism as a discourse on the mother's body as textuality. It was most influentially promulgated by Hélène Cixous, who figures the mother as an indefinable question concerning the flesh that grounds the Subject: "I am spacious singing Flesh: onto which is grafted no one knows which I—which masculine or feminine, more or less human but above all living, because changing I" (Cixous and Clément 88). Nevertheless, her work often focuses on transformations proper to feminine adolescence.

11. Foucault produced some specialized terms to account for the undecidability of historical cause and effect, including "episteme" (an historical period defined by dominant systems of knowledge), "archaeology" (the process of uncovering epistemological breaks or shifts in history), and "genealogy" (the process of an-

alyzing the transformative construction of discourses and their objects). The distinction between these terms is not as neat as many commentators on Foucault imply.

12. For an overview of some feminist responses to Foucault see de Lauretis (1987), Diamond and Quimby (1988), Butler (1990), Sawicki (1991), and Grosz (1994).

13. The Christian holy family is comprised of Father, Son, Holy Ghost, and the purified but corporeal humanity of the Virgin body. In this family in its various forms the most obscure position is the Virgin's role as daughter, an aspect of Mary's character excluded from the gospels but present in the Christian Apocrypha. Mary has a mortal daughterhood, a fact the apocryphal texts (in attempting to deny it) raise too clearly for orthodoxy.

14. See Hayden White (1987) and Michel De Certeau (1988). The narrative position of the historiographer makes the particularity of the position from which a story is told is as evident in history as in fiction.

15. Certeau interrogates Foucault's claims that everything is internal to discourse, while expanding on Lacan's interest in what appears (nominally) to be outside of discourse. This distinction does not necessarily describe a contradiction insofar as that outside can also be read as a discursive construct. Certeau suggests an important line of argument here, engaging with the discursive construction of the Other, for example in his analyses of colonial narratives of religious and political historiography. It is difficult, however, to locate any critique of Lacan in Certeau's work. See Driscoll (2000b).

16. This has been phrased as an opposition between synchronic and diachronic analysis important to debates over cultural studies analysis (see Frow and Morris, and chapter 6).

17. Foucault considers discourses on the great secret or mystery of sex as an injunction to speak about sex—to confess: "Is it not with the aim of inciting people to speak of sex that it is made to mirror, at the outer limit of every actual discourse, something akin to a secret whose discovery is imperative, a thing abusively reduced to silence and at the same time difficult and necessary, dangerous and precious to divulge?" (1984a:34–5).

18. For example, Mead, like other anthropologists, understands virginity as a relation to social evaluation rather than a representational structure. Mead emphasizes that virgins may only be offered in exchange for other virgins, "and a girl whose virginity is known to be lost can be exchanged only for one whose exchange value has been similarly damaged" (1939:217).

19. At the level of both sex/gender and minority girls are the principle of objects of legal discourses on consent. In the context of such debates, a notion of the

public good drawn in part from Rousseau instantiates a public sphere that will later be espoused as the goal of modernity by critics such as Habermas. Lynda Lange points out that "the common good is held by Rousseau to be an objective reality, whether or not the majority knows it or appreciates it. This good is most likely to be apprehended by citizens of a certain character and capacity. This in turn requires proper education, and above all equality, in the sense of freedom from dependence on others" (97). The unfathomable action of the general will on the public good that perplexed Rousseau is solved by Habermas as communicative action—which constitutes the processes by which the nineteenth century materialized age of consent legislation. But consent is not "communicative action" because it is not reciprocal and not even a set of reciprocal expectations.

20. Even the flapper movie was seen to be educational, as attested by an article in *Photoplay* magazine describing the visit of a senior judge with movie star Colleen Moore: "if it is opening the subject to all women, it may look wrong now, but it is to prove an eventful advantage" by introducing women to "the Art of Love" and "the sex question" ("Judge Ben Lindsay calls" 29).

21. Brumberg credits girls with ethical agency over their bodies, even if she sees this as necessarily authorized by adults: "adults and teens need to talk with one another about a code of sexual ethics for adolescent girls in a 'postvirginal' age. The goal of this code, Brumberg says, should be to help young girls understand both their emotions and the cultural forces at work around them so that their sexual behavior can be safe, reciprocal, and responsible" (Winter 16).

22. While it seems girls are increasingly successful at academic work, most educational success at higher levels and in more prestigious academic fields still accrues to men. Research on girls' education in the United Kingdom, the United States, and Australia indicates that at the end of the twentieth century they are still less likely than boys to take mathematics and science-based subjects and more likely to take language-rich and home-science subjects. References on this subject are very extensive and discussions of this change in the gender-profile of high-school education and undergraduate university education regularly appear in academic forums, popular publishing, and the mass media. See Orenstein (1994), Kenway (1995).

23. Observers of girls' lives often note that "teenage girls tend to drop interests once they started courting" (Cowie and Lees 28). Diana Leonard "found that they rejected earlier activities such as riding, judo, playing the piano, dancing (other than disco dancing) as childish and unfeminine" (quoted in Cowie and Lees 28).

24. The "disavowal" of homosexuality in the production of an unambiguously differentiated heterosexual ideal (Fuss 1992:732) remains unresolved in this context because the girl is constructed here as in need of education about heterosexuality and as such as not yet fully heterosexual—the exclusion of the woman-to-woman relation is projected for the future rather than produced here. I am not claiming that girls' passion for each other is always a sexual desire, or that the magazines claim that. I'm talking about the way these magazines represent girls' bodies to girls. The self and body images projected for this waiting to be born as a heterosexual woman coincide in the illustration of her desire.

25. Publishers and advertisers recognize a structured difference between the age of the largest audience for a particular girls' magazine and the age of the ideal girl posed by that magazine. The consistency with which girls read magazines describing/tracing the lives of a girl several years older than themselves indicates that this genre works to mediate and endorse a developmental schema.

26. In general the text endorses the heterosexual code with which the audience is expected to identify, while the visual images eroticize looking at girls and relations between girls. As McRobbie (1997) points out, there is some coverage of other sexual practices than heterosexual monogamous commitment in girls' magazines, but this is generally described as a variation on what girls are like.

27. Freud distinguishes between unorganized and organized groups according to whether group structures resemble a predetermined model of individuality: "if these conditions are fulfilled, the psychological disadvantages of the group formation are removed" (1922:31).

28. Phil Cohen's *Rethinking the Youth Question* insists that the "identification between researcher and informant" thought to enable such entry is not in fact desirable and that differences between researcher and research subjects allow analysis of "the differences—and the misunderstandings—which emerge in the context of an encounter which is inevitably structured by the very inequalities being studied" (17). With particular reference to girls, however, Cohen also recognizes this approach may produce an exclusion of rather than encounter with the other (148–9).

29. Like many guidance manuals it specializes in an address to the middle-class girl who lives at home with her parents. Carrington notes this tendency in girls' graffiti, finding "disproportionately more examples of 'advisory graffiti' in toilets with a middle-class clientele" (1989:98).

30. Mayhew conjures up childhood where it might otherwise not have been applied, indicating, for example, that the abuse suffered by an eight-year-old

"Watercress Girl" is the loss of her girlhood: "There was something cruelly pathetic in hearing this infant, so young that her features had scarcely formed themselves, talking of the bitterest struggles of life, with the calm earnestness of one who had endured them all. I did not know how to talk to her. At first I treated her as a child, speaking on childish subjects; so that I might, by being familiar with her, remove all shyness, and get her to narrate her life freely. I asked her about her toys and her games with her companions; but the look of amazement that answered me soon put an end to any attempt at fun on my part" (quoted in Tolson 123).

31. Mead interrogated the *sturm und drang* theory of adolescence propagated by Hall in her study of adolescence in Pacific Island cultures, and Freeman (1983) in turn critiques Mead's thesis for its presumptions concerning both adolescence and stress in Samoan culture.

32. Certeau considers this authorized place from which to speak: "in the relation maintained by the ethnographical tale with the 'other society' that it recounts and claims to make heard. With respect to the possessed woman, the primitive, and the patient, demonological discourse, ethnographical discourse, and medical discourse effectively assume identical positions: 'I know what you are saying better than you'; in other words, 'My knowledge can position itself in the place whence you speak' " (Certeau 1988:250). Certeau refers this to Lévi-Strauss's distinction between history and ethnology where "history organizes 'its data in relation to *conscious* expressions, while ethnology organizes its data in relation to *unconscious* conditions of social life" (210, quoting Lévi-Strauss).

33. Many of these criticisms have come from within anthropology, some of which appropriate to the interpretation of cultures techniques from literary analysis—reading a cultural object or event such as an image or a book. Clifford Geertz influentially described ethnographic analysis as "sorting out the structures of signification" and as a labor "like that of the literary critic" (241). For ethnography this means treating what people say about themselves as no more or less authentic than any other piece of language or set of signs, such as a novel or magazine advertisement.

34. See also Beverley Skeggs's discussion of ethics and representation in feminist ethnography (1995). Mica Nava's 1992 discussion of debates surrounding one of her ethnographic projects working with girl's groups is also relevant here.

35. This is particularly obvious in Sara Shandler's *Ophelia Speaks*, a collection of girls' life narratives published as a response to Pipher. Shandler's book is structured around the standard narrative of feminine adolescence, which begins with puberty and moves through the family, friends, and sex to independent

identity categories, concluding with feminism. Each solicited text is framed by a knowing girl-voice (framed by maturity and independence) as well as by the secondary authorization of Pipher's study.

36. McRobbie's subsequent work has increasingly referred to texts, blending analysis of magazines and girls' opinions of them, ballet novels and girls' readings of them, and later still focusing on those texts themselves as objects that can be read for what they say about girls. Across these methodological shifts McRobbie has continued to survey how girls place themselves in relation to normative expectations and to assess their forms and degree of resistance to such norms.

37. Cowie and Lees take many of the same questions and principles to their ethnography of British high-school girls as I did to a 1999 ethnography of Australian girls, where I experienced the same willingness to participate in research as a break from school—"Good it got me out of PE." Outside of schools, girls were far more concerned about the time required by the project. Given these questions about ethnographic practice, it is worth noting that these subject-girls voluntarily and capably reflect on discourses on girlhood and on the choices made available to them by researchers.

6. Becoming Bride: Girls and Cultural Studies

1. Cultural studies can be defined less rigorously, but it is the commitment to analyzing such constraints and pressures that draws cultural studies into controversies over changes to academic and intellectual practices. "Cultural studies" has become a term, sometimes interchangeable with "theory," to describe the move away from traditional humanities and social sciences. This criticism focuses on how but also and perhaps most visibly on what is studied in cultural studies, arguing that in changes to the focuses of arts or humanities disciplines in particular, with their responsibility for maintaining (high culture as) the idea of culture, some value has been lost.

2. This discussion will not foreground an historical analysis of bridal culture or interrogate its presumed audience or market. I am less concerned with who becomes a bride than with the idea of the bride and the pervasive patterns of the bride's constitution across a range of cultures.

3. The bride more generally encompasses every aspect of mass media, from the inevitable reference to romance novels to Internet shopping. In fact, bridal culture is particularly amenable to the Internet format of slowly unfurling images and information bites (lists, searches, guides, and pocket histories)

that is always the way bridal magazines work, as a stylistic and conceptual assemblage.

4. *Muriel's Wedding* is a quirky Australian character-based situation comedy. Quirky or eclectic film comprises an important genre of 1990s Australian film-making. The quirky film operates on borderlines between the mainstream and the avant-garde in film-making, sampling a range of genres and perspectives on culture, represented simultaneously through realism and exaggeration.

5. *Muriel's Wedding* focuses on what makes bridal culture so compelling. Muriel marries David to make a statement about her own transformation. Becoming a bride appears to counter everything else, including her father's power over her, and indeed the money she is paid for marrying David is the amount she has to pay her parents—it is a literal bid for freedom. But the film establishes layers of doubt concerning Muriel's desire to get married. The obvious reason that it is what girls in her position do has been taken from her by various changes she has undertaken, and her decision to marry David is represented as a regression emphasized by her return to Abba songs and the Porpoise Spit girls. It is not in fact the wedding that demands Mariel become a new Muriel, but the death of her mother, heralded in the way her mother's eviction from the mother-of-the-bride role punctuates a narrative of loss and betrayal.

6. Cultural studies is often opposed in this regard to established forms of anthropology. According to Frow and Morris, anthropology is "defined by its relation to an 'allochronic' Other—an Other defined as such by its sociocultural difference within a quite different structure of time, and especially by what's understood as a qualitative difference in social organisation." According to this opposition, "Cultural Studies takes as its object the ordinary culture [conceding the difficulty of those terms] . . . of its own society." (xxi)

7. For Certeau, the difference of everyday life from life that is "properly organised" to benefit the status quo corresponds to a distinction between the "tactical" and the "strategic," where the tactic "cannot count on a 'proper' (a spatial or institutional localization)" (Certeau 1984:xx).

8. Imitation or copying of such models among feminine adolescent audiences appears to manifest Irigaray's *masquerade*, what Diana Fuss describes as "the unconscious assumption of femininity" opposed to mimicry as "the deliberate and playful performance of femininity"—a difference marked by its "excess" (1993:22–23n). But the distinction between masquerade and mimicry again depends on recognition of resistance. Masquerade and mimicry also rely on a psychoanalytic understanding of a subject-object opposition, a process of constituting the desiring self that also seems inappropriate to considering bridal culture.

9. Bourdieu's sociology is designed to be "reflexive" (see Bourdieu and Wacquant), but also claims its techniques reflect its subject matter. It is thus significant that *Distinction* only secondarily refers to the impact of sex/gender on the reproduction of cultural capital.

10. Bourdieu groups his subjects according to their role in systems of economic production, and it is therefore probably not surprising that he finds cultural consumption to be distinguishable by class. Subdividing a subject group into class divisions in order to understand their data is as much a methodological decision as the decision to interview people or ask them to fill out questionnaires.

11. "The relation between habitus and the field through and for which it was created is an unmediated, infraconscious, practical relation of *illusio*, of investment, of interest in the game, which implies a sense of the game and a sense (with the twofold meaning of orientation, direction, and signification) of the history of the game; in short, a practical anticipation or inclination, not to be mistaken for a conscious project or a calculated scheme" (Bourdieu in Calhoun et al. 270).

12. The lesbian wedding is not a wedding, in this sense, though it can function as a commitment ceremony, because the symbolism does not determine the event's social and psychic force. Apart from anything else, a wedding cannot have two brides.

13. In 1963 Friedan writes of discovering "a strange thing, interviewing women of my own generation over the past ten years. When we were growing up, many of us could not see ourselves beyond the age of twenty-one. We had no image of our own future, of ourselves as women" (61).

14. For a survey of feminist cultural studies see Roman and Christian-Smith (1988), Franklin et al. (1991), Lovell (1995), and Skeggs (1995).

15. Žižek, however, also critiques Butler's deconstruction of identity politics: "the form of subjectivity which is produced by late capitalism is no longer patriarchal-identitarian. The predominant form of ideology today is precisely that of multiple identities, non-identity and cynical distance. . . . These Foucauldian practices of inventing new strategies, new identities, are ways of playing the late capitalist game of subjectivity" (1996:40).

16. Also called "female circumcision" or "female genital cutting." I am employing "mutilation" here to consider the positions of feminists and other activists who believe this practice must be stopped. The Fourth World Conference on Women that took place in Beijing, China, in 1995 endorsed a "Platform of Action" for ending discrimination against women and girls. This action not only distinguished girls from women (in international law) but included consultation with youth. At http://www.unicef.org/voy/meeting/girl/ the "girl child

interactive quiz" is especially directed against cultural tradition arguments for discrimination against girls.

17. Even when they are very similar—as with the practices of giving away the bride and the Hindu *kanyadaan*—or at least comparable—as with the status statements of Western weddings and non-Western dowry systems.

18. Sonia Shah's narrative about Indian-American parents who despair at their daughter's tight jeans but applaud her "display of flesh" in traditional Indian costume for girls (*chania chorri*) is one example of this normative process of deploying cultural traditions to define gender and sexuality through bridal cultures. Postcolonial feminist cultural studies has sometimes specifically addressed the place of girls in this idea of cultural specificity. See for example Gillespie (1995) and Dwyer (1998).

19. "*Muriel's Wedding* settles in the end for a kind of comedy that can do without the restoration of the old domestic order. . . . Muriel stops short of self-destruction; abandoning the maternal melodrama as well as fairy-tale romance, she takes Rhonda 'home' to Sydney to start a different kind of adventure, one with no set goal" (Morris 1996:402).

20. See also Driscoll (2000 and 1997).

21. Jardine argues that "for Deleuze, psychoanalysis is the last avatar of the anthropological representation of sexuality" (135), and Foucault also points to Deleuze's attack on "the poor technicians of desire—psychoanalysts and semiologists of every sign and symptom—who would subjugate the multiplicity of desire to the twofold law of structure and lack" (1977b:xii).

22. In *Cinema 2*, Deleuze argues that the minority is "still to come" (Deleuze 1989:196), while in *Kafka: Toward a Minor Literature* Deleuze and Guattari explicitly employ women as a metaphor for the minor. But even if becoming-woman or women as minority do continue to have a metaphoric function for Deleuze, women are not excluded from deploying the minor, which may be "still to come" in the same way that "becoming," for Deleuze, is never finalized, but always in process.

23. Deleuze rejects all predictable structures: his dualisms are not dichotomies but movements and effects. Morris notes that Deleuze and Guattari consistently deploy nonexclusive dualisms, a process for which "we can't assume that lines of flight are necessarily creative, that smooth spaces are always better than segmented or striated ones" (quoted in Morris 1996:24).

24. See Lacan (1977b and 1982a). For Deleuze, there is neither any lack in the body or in desire: "Desire does not lack anything; it does not lack its object. It is, rather, the subject that is missing in desire, or desire that lacks a fixed

subject; there is no fixed subject unless there is repression" (Deleuze and Guattari 1977:26).

25. Perhaps any doll might function as a body without organs in such ways, but the other kind of doll, the Babydoll, is a fetishized reference to the space of a lack.

26. Deleuze's *The Logic of Sense* deals erratically with the gender of this child despite reference to "the sexual object, the little girl" (1990:238). Both Carroll's Alice and Deleuze's "little girl" less connote "Woman" than displace her achievement. See Driscoll (1997).

7. Distraction: Girls and Mass Culture

1. Alex's age is not identified in Kubrick's film, but he is older than fifteen, his age in Anthony Burgess's novel on which it is based. While he is still a boy, Alex is thus positioned as making an informed choice to be violent that is not clearly undermined by his youth.

2. In 1972 Kubrick withdrew the film from Britain where it had been subject to heated calls for censorship, and it was rated *R* in the United States.

3. "In his classic essay on social generations, published in 1928–29, Karl Mannheim made the important distinction between'youth' and 'generation': while youth was a universal phenomenon—a 'mere collective fact' as he referred to it—a generation was created by specific historical circumstances, and consisted of people who shared not only age, but also a set of attitudes which placed them apart from society at large." (Ben-Amos 3)

4. Donna Gaines notes that "in the social order of the American high school, the athletes are always at the top of the heap and they are probably the most persistent of the cliques we have known" (91).

5. See Hebdige (1988). Carrington notes with reference to Australia that "youth has continuously appeared in . . . public discourse as a metaphor for trouble well before the post-war era" (1993:28), and David Oswell (1998) notes the regularity of rediscovering youth as a moral crisis to which girls have a special significance (see chapter 1).

6. Mark Davis's *Gangland: Cultural Elites and the New Generationalism* (2000) claims that at the end of the twentieth century this situation mythologized the youth of people who were now middle-aged and refuted any claims to resistance or rebellion on the part of youth today while also inspiring defensive attacks by baby-boomers in cultural industries including politics, media, art, and the academy.

7. These social projects continued the Enlightenment goals encoded in ideal maturity. They were especially opposed to popular culture designed for consumption by girls and women, particularly when it simplified and devalued important political and cultural issues. Despite extensive changes to relations between public and popular culture it remains common to claim that debates made amenable to a broad audience of immature (insufficiently discerning) consumers are trivialized.

8. Despite arguments about whether or not the film of *A Clockwork Orange* does justice to Burgess's book by leaving off the final chapter in which Alex realizes the error of his ways, it doesn't matter whether or not Kubrick knew about the twenty-first chapter, the chapter of Alex's burgeoning adulthood—it wouldn't have made a good ending to a youth film.

9. Film as youth culture has always tended to be retrospective on what youth used to be like, whether it was set in a past period such as *Quadraphenia* or *Hair* (both 1979), or *Grease* (1978)—and thus regardless of whether the retrospection refers to a past experienced by the audience (see Wyatt's commentary on the marketing of *Grease* [1–3]) or set in the present, such as the Beach Party films, *Saturday Night Fever* (1977), or *Clueless*. Teen films, however, tend to be precisely historically placed and to date quickly: *Grease* as opposed to *Saturday Night Fever* might be obvious, but *Clueless* and *Kids* also prove this point.

10. *Muriel's Wedding* is not a teen film for the simple reason that Muriel's imperfections are deployed in the film to distance her from the "any normal teenage girl" every teenage girl is assumed to want to be. That is, there are obvious blocks on identifying with Muriel. *Muriel's Wedding*, as its sound track demonstrates, is just as accessible if not more accessible to nostalgia for or critiques of youth culture, and it depends on a distance from an idea of youth culture as conformist and imprisoning even while it also sets up youth culture as the means to various escapes.

11. Often these are party films, such as *Porky's* (1982) or, in a different mode, *Ferris Bueller's Day Off* (1986) and conform to what Bernstein sees as a staple of the teen film, the revenge of a social underdog.

12. The series, by Jamie Hewlett and Alan Martin, appeared in *Deadline* magazine beginning in 1988.

13. Film magazines supported the image of the film audience as passive, malleable, imitative, and lacking individuation, as well as a public hierarchy of film production within which certain films became known as commercial films, women's films, or even "mainstream" films, and others were distinguished as films with variously higher purposes or degrees of artistic merit.

14. See Petro (1987), Hake (1987), and Hansen (1991) for insightful feminist approaches to distraction. Hake translates "*Zerstreuung*" as "diversion," which she argues better maintains the ambivalence of the German (147n): "The negative attribution of diversion to the feminine helps explain the concept's hidden ambivalences and obvious gray areas as an evasion of the issues behind it—most of all the social and political emancipation of women and the identification of the feminine as a threat to the bourgeoisie" (148).

15. Interested modernist authorities such as Adorno and D. H. Lawrence argue that works of art are ascetic and unashamed while the culture industry downgrades love not to sex but to (girlish) romance: "The mass production of the sexual automatically achieves its repression. Because of his ubiquity, the film star with whom one is meant to fall in love is from the outset a copy of himself. Every tenor voice comes to sound like a Caruso record, and the 'natural' faces of Texas girls are like the successful models by whom Hollywood has typecast them" (Adorno and Horkheimer 38–9). Adorno returns to the theme in *Aesthetic Theory*: "The most beautiful girl's face becomes ugly because of its striking resemblance to some movie queen, on whom it may well have been modelled in the first place" (1984:99). Jane Gaines notes that the early work of Kracauer, exemplified by the collection "The Little Shop Girls Go to the Movies," is also "disdainful of maids, salesclerks, and typists . . . saying that they 'love, choose their wardrobe and commit suicide' " (11).

16. Mary Ann Doane has argued that "the female spectator's infamous inability to distance herself from the image—her tendency to 'over identify' with events on the screen—suggests that the woman is constituted differently than the man in relation to the image and to structures of looking" (quoted in Petro 121).

17. See Deleuze's discussion of the camera as organization in *Cinema 1*, which he explicitly opposes to the organization of psychoanalytic versions of film theory. Deleuze argues that during the period in which cinema developed, "art and performing arts were abandoning figures and poses to release values which were not posed, not measured, which related movement to the any-instant-whatever. In this way, art, ballet and mime became actions capable of responding to accidents of the environment; that is, to the distribution of the points of a space, or of the moments of event. All this served the same end as the cinema" (1986b:6–7).

18. Bernstein frames the horror film as a film about puberty: "You're ugly and pustulent, You're oozing and repugnant. You're self obsessed but apt to fixate on others. You're moody and uncommunicative. You act like you're going to live forever, but you're eaten up by dread about death. You're . . . morbid and

miserable, paranoid and tragic, sick and scared. . . . You are in fact, the very audience that caused the horror movie to thrive in the eighties" (34).

19. Clover claims, "The popularity of the slasher began to tail off in the mideighties, and by the end of the decade the form was largely drained" (23). A similar contention is often made about teen films, but both genres resurfaced as dominant popular forms in the late 1990s.

20. Clover sees this as a structural relation between feminized childhood and masculinized adulthood, in which the assumption into power and individuality that the process of the "final girl" involves reinforces the structure by which it is explained and is thus coded as a process of becoming masculine (see Clover 49–50). What seems to me to be lost in this analysis is the degree to which the teen horror film takes place in the girls' domain in the first place—the home, family, sexual negotiation, and other individualized personal spaces.

21. Exceptions such as *Evil Dead* (1983) emphasize the rule by their exception from it but also imbue "the last boy" with the youthful and innocent/knowing connotations of the final girl.

22. In the prior film version, Buffy, as Martin notes, does "achieve a rite of passage in the course of the story—she transforms from materialistic shopping-mall bimbo to fearless vampire slayer in command of the world's destiny" (64).

23. For this point I am indebted to Sara Murphy. See also Meaghan Morris's 1997b commentary on the importance of Scully's continual failure to deploy her own knowledge.

8. In Visible Bodies

1. As Irigaray argues in *This Sex Which Is Not One*: "in order to reflect (oneself), to speculate (oneself), it is necessary to be a 'subject,' and that matter can serve as a support for speculation but cannot itself speculate in any way" (177). Thus the subject of the gaze is predicated on there being an object of the gaze in opposition to his subjectivity and his sight. Grosz writes: "The subject, to be a subject at all, internalizes otherness as its condition of possibility. It is thus radically *split*, unconscious of the processes of its own production, divided by lack and rupture" (1990:43).

2. Merleau-Ponty claims the subject "can nevertheless be seen by an external witness at the very place at which he feels himself to be with the same visual appearance that he has from the mirror" (Grosz 1990:37).

3. "With the onset of puberty the maturing of the female sexual organs, which up till then have been in a condition of latency, seems to bring about an in-

tensification of the original narcissism, and this is unfavourable to the development of a true object-choice with its accompanying sexual overvaluation. Women, especially if they grow up with good looks, develop a certain self-contentment which compensates them for social restrictions which are imposed on them in their choice of object. Strictly speaking it is only themselves that such women love with an intensity comparable to that of the man's love for them. Nor does their need lie in the direction of loving, but of being loved" (Freud 14:88–9).

4. In *Speculum,* Irigaray writes: "Now the little girl, the woman, supposedly has *nothing* you can see. . . . This nothing, which actually cannot well be mastered in the twinkling of an eye, might equally well have acted as an inducement to perform castration upon an age-old occulocentrism. It might have been interpreted as the intervention of a difference, of a deferent, as a challenge to an imaginary where functions are often improperly regulated in terms of sight" (1985a:47–8).

5. Andrew Ross defines subcultural dressing as "confrontational dressing that both resisted and affirmed the subordinate status of the subculture," recognizing some of the problems with "the subcultural premise that street style is created by reference to an alternative market economy" (1994:285).

6. The Internet seems to be an exception to this reliance on the girls' being seen in her cultural relations, although it is also defined as visual culture. See chapter 9.

7. These genres share not only the objectification of women's bodies, which they approach differently, but the interactive production of ideals of heterosexual activity projected onto an untouchable feminine body. Like Wolf, Adrienne Rich describes pornography as a "powerful economic interest" of "compulsory heterosexuality" (Rich 316), within which she includes "the most apparently innocuous advertising" (322). But what happens, in this account, to women's identifications with images of their own bodies among themselves? Definitions of pornography according to "*the popularity of sexually explicit representations*" (Ross 1993:223) in turn obscure power-relations in definitions of the "explicit" and "representation." Pornography relies on assumptions regarding the subject to whom pornography is addressed and the cultures with which they identify in order to consume it. A centerfold poster of Jodie Foster (legs apart, shirt open to the waist) becomes explicitly perverse in its reproduction in the gay press (*Brother/Sister* 1993), but means something entirely different in its prior publication in a girls' magazine as the "poster you've been *begging* for" (*Dolly* May 1993).

8. This is "a form of surveillance contrasting forms of direct violence present in other disciplinary institutions. This surveillance provokes states of docility in the prisoner, and produces actions of self-surveillance in those prisoners." This "state of conscious and permanent visibility . . . assures the automatic functioning of power" (Foucault 1977a:201), and supports Foucault's claim that power is not repressive, but productive.

9. Several writers refer this to an intersection of anorexia and saintliness. Warner notes that the qualities of feminine sainthood, "fear of food, nausea, horror of outside impurities entering the stronghold of the personal body—all are characteristics of anorexics" (1988:21). See also Brumberg 1988; Bell, *Holy Anorexia*; and Vandereycken and van Deth, *Fasting Saints*. The disagreements among these texts on whether fasting among young women prior to the late nineteenth century should be labeled anorexic rests on whether the anorexic is defined by a determination of identity through food refusal or by an obsessive goal of slimness. The latter emphasis excludes pious fasting, while representing the faster and the anorexic as similarly conformist.

10. This position distances Grosz from Bordo's otherwise similar argument that hysteria and anorexia are characterized by "the spectacle each presents of the *patient* (however unconsciously or self-destructively) creating and bestowing meaning on her own body in a form that is opaque and baffling to the Cartesian mind of the Scientist" (Bordo 1993:67).

11. This association is intrinsic to representations of young women since before Rousseau, who writes in *Emile* that "a girl 'has more hunger for finery than for food' " (quoted in Koffman 53).

12. In *Volatile Bodies* Grosz takes up Deleuze and Guattari's argument that the "body without organs" "is the body without an image," detaching the identificatory practices of body image from the "natural" body. The BwO is "a limit; a tendency; a becoming that resists the processes of overcoding and organization according to the three great strata or identities it opposes: the union of the *organism*, the unification of the *subject*, and the structure of *significance*." This perspective does not necessarily present the anorexic as an admirable force because deploying the body against powers which order it is not necessarily a good thing. Not all lines of flight are as good as one another. Deleuze and Guattari insist: "Mimic the strata. You don't reach the BwO, and its plane of consistency, by wildly destratifying" (Deleuze and Guattari 1987:160).

13. Despite the racialization of most dominant discourses on the Western body, the body marked by race (as racially different) is not excluded from mainstream beauty or sport cultures. However, they function as the exotic and the "natural," respectively, in these fields, as limit-discourses on the body's formation.

14. In women's gymnastics, for example, costume and body are aligned. Moreover, the display of sporting bodies is dramatically inflected as prepubescent in the emphasis on the smallness of the athletes, their youth in comparison to other athletes, and their bodies, which are in general articulated as unmarked by signs of womanhood.

15. Girls are also named in Western drug policies and educational programs, but in general as participating less in drug cultures. These tendencies were altered somewhat in the 1990s by increased emphasis on boys' need for dietary advice and increased reference to girls' drug use, especially of legal drugs such as alcohol and tobacco. However, girls also make excellent visuals for antidrug propaganda because of the highly recognizable signification of the happy healthy responsible girl to which such images can be opposed.

16. "McRobbie and Garber (1975) argue that girls are not marginal, but structurally different, pushed to the periphery of social activity because they are centered on a different set of activities. Girls spend more time at home, according to Barker (1972); Crichton et al. (1962); and McRobbie (1978)" (Brake 142).

9. The Girl Market and Girl Culture

1. Girl pop fandom is often seen to produce striking consistencies over time. The criteria of the girl pop video, for example, are one way of assembling the genre: the tableau poses arranging every shot as a potential poster, emphasized by multiple costume changes and centering every clip on circulation around a central girl or girls.

2. The themes of McRobbie's essay on "teenybop" with Simon Frith—that girl pop sells an image of male sexuality as unthreatening address to individual girls, but with continual reference to their place among a group of girls—are equally evident in the work of Ehrenreich, Hess, and Jacobs on Beatlemania or Sheryl Garratt's essay on the Bay City Rollers, although these see a powerful self-reference in that pop consumption. That seems an important development, but this self-reference is an explicitly transient phase, balanced between a recognized image of conformity and resistance. Garratt representatively argues that "falling in love with posters can be a way of excluding real males and of hanging on to that ideal of true love for just a little longer. It is a safe focus for all that newly discovered sexual energy, and a scream can often be its only release" (Garratt 401).

3. The Official Spice Girls' Web site is at http://c3.vmg.co.uk/spicegirls/. During the frenetic period for Spice Girls fans in which Geri Halliwell left the group and

two different Spice Girls announced engagements and one a pregnancy, I was subscribed to a number of Spice Girls (and related) mailing lists and news groups. On these lists, including, for example, SpiceZone@valleys.ndirect.co.uk, most fans were young girls, despite the perceived dominance of boys and men on Internet sites (on these Spice Girls lists the most frequent posters, as distinct from the largest number of posters, were men).

4. The leaflets in Spice Girls' compact discs, poster books and videos that invite consumers to respond directly to the Spice Girls leave open the possibility that boys buy these things, but the questions are mostly girl-oriented and their format is based on girls' magazines and music/television/star magazines marketed mainly to girls, all heady with similar calls for connection and identification. The liner notes ask who your favorite Spice Girl is, and show off the gold rings inscribed *Spice* on the outside and *Girls* on the inside. Their official Web site has featured a "which Spice Girl are you most like" quiz, the Spice Girls pencil case containing gossip, advice, pictures etc., and later a Spice Cadet club that similarly invokes a field of belonging. While these are conventional girl objects based on interactivity, they also invoke identification with and as a Spice Girl.

5. The early Spice Girls cassettes disseminated little of the Girl Power rhetoric outside a brief reference to the "Spice Girl Experience." The decision to elaborate on this experience came in response to the success of the group and their public use of feminist slogans.

6. There are a number of academic discussions of riot grrrl attesting to their relevance to feminist cultural studies. See, for example, Leonard (1997), Kearney (1997), and Duncombe (1997).

7. One letter of complaint states: "The web is not the universe. riot grrrl is still very much alive, not in your sorority girl circles, but in real life, grass roots, punk communites [*sic*]. alive in people who don't own computers or have email addresses. media conglomerates and webpages do not an organization make." In response, the editors write: "It's a case of mistaken identity, grrls look for information about the Riot Grrrl organization and are lead unwittingly to RiotGrrl webzine, a non-affiliated publication with the same name. Riot Grrrl resources on the web are scarce. There just isn't much out there about this 'organization.' When the grrls are directed to RiotGrrl, the webzine, they experience a mixture of confusion and anger. This webzine isn't the punk rock, Bikini Kill influenced world, filled with vitriole [*sic*] that they are looking for."

8. "Courtney Love=Riotgrrl" includes this quick eclectic history: "Cleopatra, Mary Magdalene, Joan of Arc, the Suffragettes, Carrie Nation, Suzi Quattro,

Cher, The Runaways, the Slits, Annie Sprinkle, Alternagrrls." And, of course, Courtney Love: "By definition, she is one of us" (Harpold).

9. Žižek claims something like this as "the ethical paradox of our age: the overlapping of the transgressive and the normal" (2000).

10. Rosie Cross notes that "*geekgirl* had to pursue people and companies in the USA who were using our trademark" (80), while simultaneously insisting that the "Internet is offering an alternative to commercialism, capitalism and profit for profit's sake" (84). There are anticapitalist tactics among cybergirls, such as the Guerilla Girls' counteradvertising projects, but a similar paradox operates in the girls' slogan ("reproduce our images today") being available only on the Internet.

11. References to VNS Matrix are common on cybergirl sites, often cited, along with Sadie Plant, as an older sister or mother figure. Indeed riot grrls, cyber girls, and the Spice Girls are all strongly invested in genealogies or histories of women's resistance—the Spice Girls cite figures such as Madonna and Neneh Cherry in pop music, although they also refer to their mothers and sisters in feminism (Golden's book on the Spice Girls phrases this as "hippie mother and academic big sister"). Some of their selections are less obvious—such as Margaret Thatcher, famously called "The Original Spice Girl."

12. See http://sysx.apana.org.au/artists/vns/themepark.html.

13. Discourses inevitably contain the negative as well as the positive of their structuring oppositions: "We cannot utter a single destructive proposition that has not already slipped into the form, the logic, and the implicit postulations of precisely what it seeks to contest" (Derrida 1978b:280–81).

14. Despite their own success in the field of global popular culture, the Spice Girls represent themselves as both global—every girl around the world (the Generation NexT to quote their US$4 million Pepsi ad)—and local. They refer repeatedly within and outside their lyrics and vocal styles to accents and local identities: they won't sell out and move to America; they're proud to be British.

15. It remains important to consider the girl market as subject to its historical contexts. During argues that "in the 1970s, new youth markets appeared for a variety of genres and combinations of genres, of which the most successful were teen, horror/slasher, sci-fi, and action movies. This segmentation of the market . . . fed into globalisation" (812). His proposition is that spectacular film, and the filmic representation of spectacular embodiment in particular, is a key example of globalization and a testing ground for ideas about globalization.

16. The global music audience does not describe what everyone in the world wants, has, or does. It is not homogenous—and not only because of "what

Sony calls 'global localisation' or 'glocalisation' " (Iwabuchi 1998a:168) or During defines as local products generated by globalized technologies and production (809). The global is an idea in relation to which particular markets for popular music operate.

17. If "the life of the nomad is in the intermezzo" (Deleuze and Guattari 1987:379) this does not foreclose on territorializing marks such as signatures, names, and brands: "If one is to free movement from the distortion of consciousness and conceive of it as it is in itself, one must adopt as a model 'a state of things which would ceaselessly change, a matter-flow in which no anchoring point or center or reference would be assignable' " (Deleuze 1986:85).

18. Education reformers such as Sumi Oe directed their efforts in general to preserving the virtue of girls in the face of modernization while simultaneously insisting on the necessity of their modernization as key to Japan's new social organization. These new modes of girls' education were thus principally organized around domestic science, as were the conservative educational reforms in Victorian England.

19. Thorn claims the genre's special "effects express the visceral, emotional responses of characters, as if the reader is given an electron-microscope-view of characters' synaptical activity." Thorn's Web site: http://www.ky.xaxon.ne.jp/matt/index.html provides a relevant overview of the genre.

20. "If genuine hybridity invokes the image of cyborg, it is because true hybridisation would be impossible without simultaneously transforming the subject of hybridization. In contrast, the selective hybridity of the Japanese merely dehistoricizes foreign cultures, and the identity and purity of the body as a receptor of foreign cultures are never questioned." (Yoshimoto quoted in Iwabuchi 1998b)

21. The recent popularity of *anime* in the West has mostly been identified with boys but does not exclude girls. The obsessive boy-fandom identified with the *otaku anime*-fan in fact resembles to a striking degree the absorption in fan culture considered more typical of girl-teen pop music fans. There are gendered formations in Japanese *anime* fandom (and in *seishun eiga* [youth film]), and specific forms of *anime* and *manga* addressed to girls, but Western commentary on these forms has been especially interested in conventions (often resembling the "pornographic") more usually associated with boys and men, and girl-directed *manga* and *anime* has thus seemed largely secondary.

22. Iwabuchi argues that Japanese animators may not intentionally erase racial markers from their work in order to sell it overseas, but that this is at least an important by-product of the generic characteristics of *mu-kokuseki* figures (1998a:167). Animation does produce some marked racialization, even within

terms Iwabuchi would recognize—Chineseness is signified in numerous video games in relation to a less specific Japaneseness, as is Westernness or even Americanness.

23. Beginning as *manga*, "Sailor Moon" became a prime-time Japanese television show. One reference cites an 11 percent rating, but it is unclear whether this is an average or peak figure. "Sailor Moon" has been translated into English, Chinese, French, and Spanish, at least, and distributed across a number of countries on television and video (Disney Buena Vista Home Video).

24. Sailor Moon is a superhuman teenage girl. To take one promotional paraphrase, the show tells the story of a fourteen-year-old girl "who struggles daily to maintain peace among the myriad evildoers threatening her word and who commits good deeds between homework and karate kicks." The evildoers are often centered on "the Dark Agency" (translated for Americans as "the Negaverse") or its evil queen, and Sailor Moon's girl drama mostly centers around her oppositions to feminized and adult threats. But Sailor Moon is not alone—she has a group of fellow high-school students come warrior princesses who are referred to collectively as the Senshi or, in English fan material, as the Sailor Scouts.

25. The link between girls as a group and consumption is made also in publications that more directly contest representation or construction of *shōjo*, such as the novels of Yoshimoto Banana that, to quote Treat, mark "a shift towards a fiction unapologetically and intimately targeted towards *anata*, 'you,' i.e., the teenage woman and her cohorts, an audience and point of view never too removed from the center arena of contemporary Japanese public culture" (280). Sailor Moon reflects this centrality in her defense of and representation of her society, and in such activity also questions the articulation of the *kawaii* girl as more or less passive object.

26. One of the exemplary figures of the Idol or *tarento* systems is Seiko. "Discovered" in a Miss Seventeen talent contest sponsored by Sony Music, Seiko had twenty-four consecutive number one songs in 1980 to 1988 and hosted her own television show. Her superstardom was confined to her teens, however, and in the 1990s she exemplified the idol singer in decline, although she is still a highly recognizable icon of J-Pop culture. This process continues in the "Komuro family" and in televised star searches and developments. While not specific to Japan, and currently a highly successful Western television formula, this has remarkably continuous success in Japan.

27. Imported popular culture, including music, is consumed in Japan, but "locally produced media products tend to be more popular than imported ones, even though they may entirely imitate the products of foreign origin" (Iwabuchi

1998a:178). Out of twenty-seven million-selling albums in Japan in 1997, only Mariah Carey's *Butterfly* was not Japanese (*Billboard* 28 February 1998:52). *Billboard* tracked a further decline in the first quarter of 1999 (16 January 1999:42), and in 2000 only transnational chains stocked more than a few current Western hits.

28. An example of this contradiction is the punk band Lolita No.18. The band name employs a loanword that might be loaded with public debate about the sexual fetishization of young girls among popular cultural forms directed to straight Japanese men. But in interview neither the band nor its producers claim significance for the label, and they disavow political content in their punk stylings, billing themselves as the punk-band-next-door and their stylistic citation of the Sex Pistols as "just fun" (Kimura 2000).

Bibliography

Adler, Patricia A. "The Past and Future of Ethnography." *Journal of Contemporary Ethnography* 16, no. 1 (April 1997): 4–25.

Adorno, Theodor W. *Prisms.* London: Spearman, 1967.

———. *Aesthetic Theory.* Trans. C. Lenhardt. London: Routledge and Kegan Paul, 1984.

———. "On Popular Music." In *Cultural Theory and Popular Culture: A Reader,* ed. John Storey. Hemel Hempstead, England: Harvester Wheatsheaf, 1994, pp. 202–14.

Adorno, Theodor W., and Max Horkheimer. "The Culture Industry: Enlightenment as Mass Deception." In *The Cultural Studies Reader,* ed. Simon During. London: Routledge, 1993, pp. 29–43.

Althusser, Louis. "Ideology and Ideological State Apparatuses." In *Cultural Theory and Popular Culture,* ed. John Storey, pp. 151–63. Hemel Hempstead, England: Harvester Wheatsheaf, 1994.

Ambrose, (Bishop of Milan). *On Virginity.* Trans. D. Callam. Peregrina, n.d.

Ang, Ien. *Watching Dallas: Soap Opera and the Melodramatic Imagination.* Trans. Della Couling. London: Routledge, 1989.

Angie. "Bikini Kill: Biography." In *Rebel Girl's Jigsaw Youth Bikini Kill Page.* Web site. http://rebelgirl.simplenet.com/bkbo.html. Accessed January 2001.

Appelbaum, Robert. " 'Standing to the Wall': The Pressures of Masculinity in Romeo and Juliet." *Shakespeare Quarterly* 48, no. 3 (fall 1997): 251–72.

Ariés, Phillipe. *Centuries of Childhood: A Social History of Family Life.* Trans. R. Baldrick. New York: Knopf, 1962.

Aristotle. *The Art of Rhetoric.* Vol. 2. London: Macmillan, 1986.

Asher, William, dir. *Beach Party.* AIP/Alta Vista. U.S., 1963.

Austen, Jane. *Pride and Prejudice.* London: Thomas Nelson, 1813.

———.*Emma.* 1815. Reprint, Basingstoke, England: Macmillan, 1992.

Backwell, Andrew, prod. *Popstars.* Channel 7. Australia, 2000.

Badham, John, dir. *Saturday Night Fever.* Paramount/Robert Stigwood. U.S., 1977.

Bail, Kathy, ed. *DIY Feminism.* St. Leonards, Australia: Allen and Unwin, 1996.

Barber, Ross. "The Criminal Law Amendment Act of 1891 and the 'Age of Consent' Issue in Queensland." *Australian and New Zealand Journal of Criminology,* 10 (June 1977): 95–113.

Barrett, Michelle. *The Politics of Truth: From Marx to Foucault.* Cambridge and Oxford: Polity Press, 1991.

Barthes, Roland. *Mythologies.* Trans. A. Lavers. London: J. Cape, 1972.

———. *Empire of the Signs.* Trans. Richard Howard. New York: Hill and Wang, 1982.

Battersby, Christine. "Feminist Interpretations of Soren Kierkegaard (Review)." *Hypatia* 14, no. 3 (summer 1999).

Beauvoir, Simone de. *The Second Sex.* Trans. H. M. Parshley. London: Picador, 1988.

Bell, Rudolph M. *Holy Anorexia.* Chicago: University of Chicago Press, 1985.

Ben-Amos, Ilana Krausman. *Adolescence and Youth in Early Modern England.* New Haven: Yale University Press, 1994.

Benhabib, Seyla. "On Hegel, Women, and Irony." *Feminist Interpretations and Political Theory,* ed. Mary Lyndon Shanley and Carole Pateman. London: Polity Press, 1991, pp. 129–45.

Bennett, T., M. Emmison, and J. Frow, *Accounting for Tastes: Australian Everyday Cultures.* Cambridge: Cambridge University Press, 1999.

Berger, John. *Ways of Seeing.* London: BBC/Penguin, 1972.

Bernheimer, C. "Introduction." In *In Dora's Case,* ed. C. Kahane and C. Bernheimer. London: Virago, 1985, pp. 1–18.

Bernstein, Jonathan. *Pretty in Pink: The Golden Age of Teenage Film.* New York: St. Martin's Griffin, 1997.

Biddulph, Steve. *Raising Boys: Why Boys Are Different, and How to Help Them Become Happy and Well-Balanced Men.* Sydney: Finch, 1997.

Bikini Kill. *Reject All American.* Olympia, Wash.: Kill Rock Stars, 1996.

Bird, S. Elizabeth. "Understanding the Ethnographic Encounter: The Need for Flexibility in Feminist Reception Studies." *Women and Language* 18, no. 2 (fall 1995): 22–7.

Bordo, Susan. *Unbearable Weight: Feminism, Western Culture, and the Body.* Berkeley: University of California Press, 1993.

———. "The Cartesian Masculinization of Thought and the Seventeenth-Century Flight from the Feminine." In *Modern Engendering: Critical Feminist Readings in Modern Western Philosophy*, ed. Bat-Ami Bar On. Albany: State University of New York Press, 1994, pp. 3–26.

———. "The Body and the Reproduction of Femininity." In *Writing on the Female Body: Female Embodiment and Feminist Theory*, ed. Katie Conboy, et al. New York: Columbia University Press, 1997, pp. 90–110.

Boufis, Christina. " 'Of Home Birth and Breeding': Eliza Lynn Linton and the Girl of the Period." *The Girl's Own: Cultural Histories of the Anglo-American Girl, 1830–1915*, ed. Claudia Nelson and Lynne Vallone. Athens: University of Georgia Press, 1994, pp. 98–123.

Boundas, Constantin. "Introduction." In *The Deleuze Reader*, ed. C. Boundas. New York: Columbia University Press, 1993.

Bourdieu, Pierre. *Distinction: A Social Critique of the Judgment of Taste*. Trans. R. Nice. Cambridge: Harvard University Press, 1986.

———. *In Other Words: Essays Toward a Reflexive Sociology*. Trans. Matthew Adamson. Stanford, Cal.: Stanford University Press, 1990.

———. *On Television and Journalism*. Trans. P. P. Ferguson. London: Pluto Press, 1998.

Bourdieu, Pierre, and Loic J. D. Wacquant. *An Invitation to Reflexive Sociology*. Chicago: University of Chicago Press, 1992.

Bowlby, Rachel. *Shopping With Freud*. London and New York: Routledge, 1993.

Boyle, Danny, dir. *Trainspotting*. Channel 4 Films. U.K., 1996.

Braidotti, Rosi. *Nomadic Subjects: Embodiment and Sexual Difference in Contemporary Feminist Theory*. New York: Columbia University Press, 1994.

Brake, Mike. *The Sociology of Youth Culture and Youth Subcultures: Sex and Drugs and Rock 'n Roll*. London: Routledge and Kegan Paul, 1980.

Bronfenbrenner, Urie. *Two Worlds of Childhood: U.S. and U.S.S.R.* Harmondsworth, England: Penguin Education, 1974.

Brook, Peter et al. "Shakespeare in the Cinema: A Film Directors' Symposium." *Cineaste* 24, no. 1 (winter 1998): 48–56.

Brooks, Richard, dir. *The Blackboard Jungle*. MGM. U.S., 1955.

Bruch, Hilde. *The Golden Cage: The Enigma of Anorexia Nervosa*. Cambridge: Harvard University Press, 1978.

Brumberg, Joan Jacobs. *Fasting Girls: The Emergence of Anorexia Nervosa as a Modern Disease*. Cambridge: Harvard University Press, 1988.

———. *The Body Project: An Intimate History of American Girls*. New York: Random House, 1997.

Buchanan, Ian. "The Problem of the Body in Deleuze and Guattari; or, What Can a Body Do?" *Body and Society* 3, no. 3 (September 1997): 73–91.

Burchell, Graeme, Colin Gordon, and Peter Miller, eds. *The Foucault Effect: Studies in Governmentality.* Chicago: University of Chicago Press, 1991.

Burgess, Anthony. *A Clockwork Orange.* London: Heinemann, 1962.

Butler, Judith. *Gender Trouble: Feminism and the Subversion of Identity.* New York: Routledge, 1990.

——. *Bodies That Matter: On the Discursive Limits of Sex.* New York: Routledge, 1993.

——. *The Psychic Life of Power: Essays in Subjection.* Los Angeles: Stanford University Press, 1997.

——. *Antigone's Claim: Kinship Between Life and Death.* New York: Columbia University Press, 2000.

Calhoun, Craig, Edward LiPuma, and Moishe Postone, eds. *Bourdieu: Critical Perspectives.* Cambridge, England: Polity, 1993.

Cantarella, Eve. "Dangling Virgins: Myth, Ritual, and the Place of Women in Ancient Greece." In *The Female Body in Western Culture: Contemporary Perspectives,* ed. S. R. Suleiman. Cambridge: Harvard University Press, 1986, pp. 57–67.

Carpenter, John, dir. *Halloween.* Falcon International. U.S., 1978.

Carrington, Kerry. "Girls and Graffiti." *Cultural Studies* 3 (January 1989): 89–100.

——. "Cultural Studies, Youth Culture and Delinquency." In *Youth Subcultures: Theory, History and the Australian Experience,* ed. Rob White. Hobart, Australia: National Clearinghouse for Youth Studies, 1993, pp. 27–32.

Carroll, Lewis. *Alice's Adventures in Wonderland and Through the Looking-Glass,* ed. M. Gardner. 1865/1887. Reprint, London: Penguin, 1970.

Carter, Chris, prod. *The X-Files.* Fox. U.S., 1996–2000.

Carter, S. "Real Simulacra Redux: Barbie and Jane Versus the Wooden Nutmegs of Connecticut." *Journal of Popular Culture* 27, no. 3 (1993): 41–59.

Caulfield, Sophia F. "Some Types of Girlhood; or, Our Juvenile Spinsters, Part 1." *The Girl's Own Annual* 562 (4 October 1890): 4–6.

Caulfield, Sue-Ann. "Getting into Trouble: Dishonest Women, Modern Girls, and Women-Men in the Conceptual Language of *Vida Policial,* 1925–1927." *Signs: Journal of Women in Culture and Society* 19 no. 1 (fall 1993): 146–65.

de Certeau, Michel. *The Practice of Everyday Life.* Trans. Steven Rendall. Berkeley: University of California Press, 1984.

——. *Heterologies: Discourse on the Other.* Trans. Brian Massumi. Minneapolis: University of Minnesota Press, 1986.

——. *Culture in the Plural.* Trans. Tom Conley. Minneapolis: University of Minnesota Press, 1997.

Chanter, Tina. "Tragic Dislocations: Antigone's Modern Theatrics." *differences: A Journal of Feminist Cultural Studies* 10, no. 1 (spring 1988): 75–77.

Chasseguet-Smirgel, Janine et al., eds. *Female Sexuality: New Psychoanalytic Views.* 1964. Reprint, London: Virago, 1970.

Chernik, Abra Fortune. "The Body Politic." In *Listen Up: Voices from the Next Feminist Generation,* ed. Barbara Findlen. Seattle, Wash.: Seal Press, 1995, pp. 75–84.

Chisholm, L. "A Sharper Lens or a New Camera? Youth Research, Young People and Social Change in Britain." In *Childhood, Youth and Social Change: A Comparative Perspective,* ed. L. Chisholm et al. London: Falmer, 1990, pp. 260–82.

Chodorow, Nancy. *The Reproduction of Mothering: Psychoanalysis and the Sociology of Gender.* Los Angeles: University of California Press, 1978.

Chow, Rey. *Writing Diaspora: Tactics of Intervention in Contemporary Cultural Studies.* Bloomington: Indiana University Press, 1993.

——. "Where Have All the Natives Gone?" In *Displacements: Cultural Identities in Question,* ed. Angelika Bammer. Bloomington: Indiana University Press, 1994, pp. 125–51.

Cixous, Hélène, and Catherine Clément. *The Newly Born Woman.* Trans. B. Wing. Minneapolis: University of Minnesota Press.

Clark, Bob, dir. *Porky's.* Porky's Productions. U.S., 1980.

Clark, Larry, dir. *Kids.* Excalibur. U.S., 1994.

Clarke, John, Stuart Hall, Tony Jefferson and Brian Roberts. *Resistance Through Rituals.* Birmingham, England: Center for Contemporary Cultural Studies, 1975.

Clavell, James, dir. *To Sir with Love.* Columbia. U.K., 1967.

Clover, Carol J. *Men, Women and Chainsaws: Gender in the Modern Horror Film.* London: B.F.I., 1992.

Cohen, Phil. *Rethinking the Youth Question: Education, Labour and Cultural Studies.* London: Macmillan, 1997.

Cohen, Morton N., and Roger Lancelyn Green, eds. *The Letters of Lewis Carroll.* London: Macmillan, 1979.

Cowie, Celia, and Sue Lees. "Slags or Drags." *Feminist Review* 9. Autumn 1981: 17–31.

Craik, Jennifer. *The Face of Fashion: Cultural Studies in Fashion.* London: Routledge, 1993.

Craven, Wes, dir. *Scream.* Miramax. U.S., 1996.

Creed, Barbara. *The Monstrous-Feminine: Film, Feminism, Psychoanalysis.* London: Routledge, 1993.

Cross, Rosie. "Geekgirl: Why Grrrls Need Modems." In *DIY Feminism*, ed. Kathy Bail. Sydney, Australia: Allen and Unwin, 1996, pp. 77–86.

Cunningham, Sean, dir. *Friday the Thirteenth*. Georgetown. U.S., 1980.

Dalsimer, Katherine. *Female Adolescence: Psychoanalytic Reflections on Works of Literature*. New Haven: Yale University Press, 1986.

Davis, Mark. *Gangland: Cultural Elites and the New Generationalism*. 2nd ed. St. Leonards, Australia: Allen and Unwin, 2000.

de Palma, Brian, dir. *Carrie*. UA/Red Bank. U.S., 1976.

De Lauretis, Teresa. *Alice Doesn't: Feminism, Semiotics, Cinema*. Bloomington: Indiana University Press, 1984.

——. *Technologies of Gender: Essays on Theory, Film, and Fiction*. Bloomington: Indiana University Press, 1987.

Deleuze, Gilles. *Cinema 1: The Movement-Image*. Trans. H. Tomlinson and B. Habberjam. London: Athlone Press, 1986.

——. *Foucault*. Trans. S. Hand. London: Athlone Press, 1988.

——. *Cinema 2: The Time-Image*. Trans. H. Tomlinson and R. Galeta. London: Athlone Press, 1989.

——. *The Logic of Sense*. Trans. M. Lester, ed. C. V. Boundas. New York: Columbia University Press, 1990.

Deleuze, Gilles, and Felix Guattari. *Anti-Oedipus*. Trans. R. Hurley, M. Seem, and H. R. Lane. Vol. 1 of *Capitalism and Schizophrenia*. Minneapolis: University of Minnesota Press, 1987.

——. *Kafka: Toward a Minor Literature*. Trans. Dana Polan. Minneapolis: University of Minnesota Press, 1986.

——. *A Thousand Plateaus*. Trans. B. Massumi. Vol. 2 of *Capitalism and Schizophrenia*. Minneapolis: University of Minnesota Press, 1977.

Denfeld, Rene. *The New Victorians: A Young Woman's Challenge to the Old Feminist Order*. St Leonards, Australia: Allen and Unwin, 1995.

Derrida, Jacques. *Spurs: Nietzsche's Styles*. Trans. B. Harlow. Chicago: University of Chicago Press, 1978a.

——. "Structure, Sign, and Play in the Discourse of the Human Sciences." Trans. Alan Bass. In *Writing and Difference*. Chicago: University of Chicago Press, 1978b.

——. *Glas*. Trans. John P. Leavey and Richard Rand. Lincoln: University of Nebraska Press, 1986.

des Ras, Marion, and Mieke Lunenberg, eds. *Girls, Girlhood, and Girls' Studies in Transition*. Amsterdam: Het Spinhuis, 1993.

Deutsch, Helene. *Psychology of Women: A Psychoanalytic Interpretation*. Vols. 1 and 2. New York: Grune and Stratton, 1971.

Diamond, Irene, and Lee Quimby, eds. *Feminism and Foucault: Reflections on Resistance.* Boston: Northeastern University Press, 1988.

Diprose, Roslyn. "In Excess: The Body and the Habit of Sexual Difference." *Hypatia: Feminism and the Body* 6, no. 3 (fall 1991): 156–71.

Douglas, Susan J. "Girl Power Puts a New Spice into Feminist Debate." *Nation*, 25 August/1 September 1997, 29.

"Dress, In Season and In Reason." *Girls Own Annual, 1890–1891* (26 September 1891): 824–5.

Driscoll, Catherine. "The Little Girl." *Antithesis* 8, no. 2 (special issue, *Time and Memory*) (1997): 79–100.

——. "Girls: Images and Ideas of Girlhood." Unpublished report. Adelaide: University of Adelaide, 1999.

——. "The Woman in Process: Deleuze, Kristeva and Feminism." In *Deleuze and Feminist Theory*, ed. Clare Colebrook and I. Buchanan. Edinburgh: Edinburgh University Press, 2000, pp. 80–94.

——. "The Moving Ground: Locating Everyday Life." *South Atlantic Quarterly* 99, no. 1 (winter 2000/summer 2001).

Ducille, Anne. "Dyes and Dolls: Multicultural Barbie and the Merchandising of Difference." *differences* 6, no. 1 (1994): 46–68.

Duncombe, Stephen. *Notes from Underground: Zines and the Politics of Alternative Culture.* New York: Verso, 1997.

During, Simon. "Popular Culture on a Global Scale: A Challenge for Cultural Studies." *Critical Inquiry* 23, no. 4 (summer 1997): 808–33.

Dwyer, Claire. "Contested Identities: Challenging Dominant Representations of Young British Muslim Women." In *Cool Places: Geographies of Youth Culture*, ed. Tracey Skelton and Gill Valentine. London: Routledge, 1998, pp. 50–65.

Dyhouse, Carol. *Girls Growing Up in Late Victorian and Edwardian England.* London: Routledge and Kegan Paul, 1981.

Edut, Tali, Dyann Logwood, and Ophira Edut. "*hues* Magazine: The Making of a Movement." In *Third Wave Agenda: Being Feminist, Doing Feminism*, ed. L. Heywood and J. Drake. Minneapolis: Minnesota University Press, 1997, pp. 83–98.

Ehrenreich, Barbara, Elizabeth Hess, and Gloria Jacobs. "Beatlemania: A Sexually Defiant Subculture?" In *The Subculture Reader*, ed. K. Gelder and S. Thornton. London: Routledge, 1997, pp. 523–36.

Ellis, Havelock. *Studies in the Psychology of Sex.* Vol. 3. Philadelphia: F. A. Davis, 1928.

——. *Man and Woman: A Study of Human Secondary Sexual Characters.* New York: Arno Press, 1974.

Elsaesser, Thomas. "Screen Violence: Emotional Structure and Ideological Function in *A Clockwork Orange.*" In *Approaches to Popular Film*, ed. C. W. E. Bigsby. London: Edward Arnold, 1976.

Engels, Frederick. *The Origin of the Family, Private Property, and the State.* New York: International Publishers, 1972.

Erikson, Erik. *Identity: Youth and Crisis.* 1968. Reprint, London: Faber and Faber, 1974.

———. "Reality and Actuality: An Address." In *In Dora's Case: Freud—Hysteria—Feminism*, ed. C. Bernheimer and C. Kahane. London: Virago, 1985, pp. 44–55.

Fein, Ellen, and Sherrie Schneider. *The Rules: Time Tested Secrets for Capturing the Heart of Mr. Right.* New York: Warner, 1996.

Ferguson, Marjorie. *Forever Feminine: Women's Magazines and the Cult of Femininity.* London: Heinemann, 1983.

Findlen, Barbara, ed. *Listen Up: Voices from the Next Feminist Generation.* Seattle, Wash.: Seal Press, 1995.

Fiske, John. *Understanding Popular Culture.* Boston: Unwin Hyman, 1989.

Fomin, Feodora, and Deborah Tyler. "Gender and Schooling Project." In *Cultural Politics.* Vol. 5, ed. Deborah Tyler and Lesley Johnson. Melbourne Working Papers. Brunswick, Australia: Department of Education, 1984, pp. 168–70.

Foucault, Michel. *Archaeology of Knowledge.* Trans. A. M. Sheridan. New York: Harper Colophon, 1972.

———. *The Birth of the Clinic: An Archaeology of Medical Deception.* London: Tavistock, 1973a.

———. *The Order of Things: An Archaeology of the Human Sciences.* New York: Vintage, 1973b.

———. *Discipline and Punish: The Birth of the Prison.* Trans. Alan Sheridan. London: Allen Lane, 1977a.

———. "Preface." Trans. Mark Seem. In Gilles Deleuze and Felix Guattari, *Anti-Oedipus.* Vol. 1 of *Capitalism and Schizophrenia.* London: Athlone Press, 1977b.

———. *Power/Knowledge: Selected Interviews and Other Writings 1972–1977.* Trans. C. Gordon et al. New York: Pantheon, 1980.

———. *The History of Sexuality: An Introduction.* Trans. R. Hurley. Vol. 1. Harmondsworth, England: Penguin, 1984a.

———. *Language, Counter-Memory, Practice: Selected Essays and Interviews*, ed. D. F. Bouchard. Ithaca, N.Y.: Cornell University Press, 1984b.

———. *The Care of the Self.* Trans. R. Hurley. Vol. 2 of *The History of Sexuality.* Harmondsworth, England: Penguin, 1986.

———. *Technologies of the Self: A Seminar with Michel Foucault,* ed. Luther H. Martin, Huck Gutman, and Patrick H. Hutton. Amherst: University of Massachusetts Press, 1988.

———. "Governmentality." In *The Foucault Effect: Studies in Governmentality,* ed. Graham Burchell et al. Chicago: University of Chicago Press, 1991, pp. 87–104.

Franklin, Sarah, Celia Lury, and Jackie Stacey, eds. *Off-Centre: Feminism and Cultural Studies.* London: HarperCollins Academic, 1991.

Franson, J. Karl. " 'Too soon marr'd': Juliet's Age as Symbol in 'Romeo and Juliet.' " *Papers on Language and Literature* 32, no. 3 (summer 1996): 244–63.

Fraser, Nancy. "The Uses and Abuses of French Discourse Theories for Feminist Politics." *Boundary 2* 17, no 2 (1990): 177–94.

Freeman, D. *Margaret Mead and Samoa: The Making and Unmaking of an Anthropological Myth.* Cambridge: Harvard University Press, 1983.

Freud, Sigmund. *Group Psychology and the Analysis of the Ego.* Trans. J. Strachey. Vol. 19. *The Standard Edition of the Complete Psychological Works of Sigmund Freud.* London: Hogarth Press, 1922.

———. "The Dissolution of the Oedipus Complex." Trans. J. Strachey. In *The Standard Edition of the Complete Psychological Works of Sigmund Freud.* Vol. 19. London: Hogarth Press, 1953, pp. 173–82.

———. "Femininity." Trans. J. Strachey. In *The Standard Edition of the Complete Psychological Works of Sigmund Freud.* Vol. 22. London: Hogarth Press, 1953, pp. 112–35.

———. "A Fragment of an Analysis of a Study in Hysteria." Trans. J. Strachey. In *The Standard Edition of the Complete Psychological Works of Sigmund Freud.* Vol. 7. London: Hogarth Press, 1953, pp. 31–164.

———. "Jokes and Their Relation to the Unconscious." Trans. J. Strachey. In *The Standard Edition of the Complete Psychological Works of Sigmund Freud.* Vol. 8. London: Hogarth Press, 1953.

———. "On Narcissism: An introduction." Trans. J. Strachey. In *The Standard Edition of the Complete Psychological Works of Sigmund Freud.* Vol. 14. London: Hogarth Press, 1953, pp. 73–102.

———. "Psychogenesis of a Case of Homosexuality in a Woman." Trans. J. Strachey. In *The Standard Edition of the Complete Psychological Works of Sigmund Freud.* Vol. 18. London: Hogarth Press, 1953, pp. 145–72.

———. "Some Psychical Consequences of the Anatomical Distinction Between the Sexes." Trans. J. Strachey. In *The Standard Edition of the Complete Psychological Works of Sigmund Freud.* Vol. 19. London: Hogarth Press, 1953, pp. 241–60.

——. "The Taboo of Virginity: Contributions to The Psychology of Love III." Trans. J. Strachey. In *The Standard Edition of the Complete Psychological Works of Sigmund Freud.* Vol. 11. London: Hogarth Press, 1953, pp. 191–208.

——. "Three Essays on the Theory of Sexuality." Trans. J. Strachey. In *The Standard Edition of the Complete Psychological Works of Sigmund Freud.* Vol. 7. London: Hogarth Press, 1953, pp. 123–243.

Friedan, Betty. *The Feminine Mystique.* Harmondsworth, England: Penguin, 1963.

Friedkin, William, dir. *The Exorcist.* Warner/Hoya. U.S., 1973.

Friend, Tad, et al. "The Rise of 'Do Me' Feminism." *Esquire,* February 1994.

Frith, Simon, and Angela McRobbie. "Rock and Sexuality." In *On Record: Rock, Pop, and the Written Word,* ed. S. Frith and A. Goodwin. New York: Pantheon Books, 1990, pp. 371–89.

Frow, John, and Meaghan Morris, eds. *Australian Cultural Studies.* St Leonards, Australia: Allen and Unwin, 1993.

Fuss, Diana. *Essentially Speaking.* New York: Routledge, 1989.

Fuss, Diana. "Fashion and the Homospectatorial Look." *Critical Inquiry* 18, no. 4 (1992): 713–37.

Fuss, Diana. "Freud's Fallen Women: Identification, Desire, and 'A Case of Homosexuality in a Woman.' " *Yale Journal of Criticism* 6, no. 1 (spring 1993): 1–23.

Gaines, Donna. *Teenage Wasteland: Suburbia's Dead End Kids.* New York: Pantheon, 1991.

Gaines, Jane. "Introduction: Fabricating the Female Body." In *Fabrications: Costume and the Female Body,* ed. J. Gaines and C. Herzog. New York and London: Routledge, 1990, pp. 1–27.

Garcia, Sandrine. "Project for a Symbolic Revolution: The Rise and Fall of the Women's Movement in France." *South Atlantic Quarterly* 93, no. 4 (1994): 825–70.

Garratt, Sheryl. "Teenage Dreams." (1984). In *On Record: Rock, Pop and the Written Word,* ed. A. Goodwin and S. Frith. London: Pantheon, 1990, pp. 395–411.

Gatens, Moira. "A Critique of the Sex-Gender Distinction." In *Imaginary Bodies: Ethics, Power and Corporeality.* London: Routledge, 1996, pp. 3–20.

Geertz, Clifford. "Thick Description: Toward an Interpretative Theory of Culture." *A Cultural Studies Reader: History, Theory, Practice,* ed. J. Munns, G. Rajan, and R. Bromley. London: Longman, 1996.

Gilbert, P., and S. Taylor. *Fashioning the Feminine: Girls, Popular Culture and Schooling.* Sydney, Australia: Allen and Unwin, 1991.

Giles, N. *Susan, be Smooth!: A Hand-Book of Good Grooming for Girls, Especially Girls Under Twenty, Who Want to Be Seen and Heard.* Boston: Hale, Cushman, and Flint, 1940.

Gillespie, Marie. *Television, Ethnicity and Cultural Change.* London: Routledge, 1995.

Gilligan, Carol. "In a Different Voice: Women's Conceptions of Self and of Morality." In *Women and Values: Readings in Recent Feminist Philosophy*, ed. M. Pearsall. Belmont, Cal.: Wadsworth, 1986.

Golden, Anna. *The Spice Girls: An Uncensored Account.* London: NewBooks Press, 1997.

Goodwin, Andrew. "Popular Music and Postmodern Theory." In *Cultural Theory and Popular Culture: A Reader*, ed. J. Storey. Hemel Hempstead, England: Harvester Wheatsheaf, 1994, pp. 414–27.

Gorham, Deborah. "The 'Maiden Tribute of Modern Babylon' Re-examined: Child Prostitution and the Idea of Childhood in Late-Victorian England." *Victorian Studies* 21, no. 3 (1978): 353–79.

———. *The Victorian Girl and the Feminine Ideal.* London: Croom Helm, 1982.

Green, R. L. "Alice." 1960. Reprinted in *Aspects of Alice: Lewis Carroll's Dreamchild as Seen Through the Critic's Looking Glasses 1865–1971*, ed. R. Phillips. Harmondsworth, England: Penguin, 1981, pp. 13–38.

Griffin, Christine. *Representations of Youth: The Study of Youth and Adolescence in Britain and America.* London: Polity Press, 1993.

Grossberg, Lawrence. "The Deconstruction of Youth." 1986. Reprinted in *Cultural Theory and Popular Culture: A Reader*, ed. J. Storey. Hemel Hempstead, England: Harvester Wheatsheaf, 1994, pp. 183–90.

Grosz, Elizabeth. *Jacques Lacan: A Feminist Introduction.* Sydney, Australia: Allen and Unwin, 1990.

———. "A Thousand Tiny Sexes." *Gilles Deleuze and the Theater of Philosophy*, ed. Constantin Boundas and Dorothea Olkowski. New York: Routledge, 1993, pp. 187–21.

———. *Volatile Bodies: Towards a Corporeal Feminism.* St. Leonards, Australia: Allen and Unwin, 1994.

Growth and Development at Puberty. Audiovisual presentation. Melbourne, Australia: Royal Melbourne Children's Hospital, 1988.

Grunberger, Bela. "Outline for a Study of Narcissism in Female Sexuality." In *Female Sexuality*, ed. Janine Chasseguet-Smirgel. 1964. Reprint, London: Virago, 1970, pp. 68–83.

Habermas, Jürgen. "Modernity: An Incomplete Project." In *The Anti-Aesthetic*, ed. H. Foster. Townsend, Wash.: Bay Press, 1983, pp. 3–15.

———. *The Theory of Communicative Action.* 2 vols. Trans. Thomas McCarthy. Boston: Beacon Press, 1984–1987.

Hake, Sabine. "Girls and Crisis: The Other Side of Diversion." *New German Critique* 40 (1987): 147–64.

Hall, A. G. *Womanhood: Causes of its Premature Decline.* Rochester, N.Y.: E. Shepherd, 1845.

Hall, G. Stanley. *Adolescence: Its Psychology and Its Relations to Physiology, Anthropology, Sociology, Sex, Crime, Religion, and Education.* 2 vols. New York: Appleton, 1904.

Hall, Stuart. "The Emergence of Cultural Studies and the Crisis in the Humanities." In *Cultural Studies*, ed. L. Grossberg, C. Nelson, and P. Triechler. New York: Routledge, 1992.

———. "Notes on Deconstructing the Popular." in *Cultural Theory and Popular Culture: A Reader*, ed. John Storey. Hemel Hempstead, England: Harvester Wheatsheaf, 1994, pp. 455–66.

Hall, Stuart, and Paddy Whannell. "The Young Audience." In *Popular Culture and Cultural Theory: A Reader*, ed. J. Storey. Hemel Hempstead, England: Harvester Wheatsheaf, 1994.

Hancock, Emily. *The Girl Within.* New York: E. P. Dutton, 1989.

Hansen, Miriam. "Pleasure, Ambivalence, Identification: Valentino and Female Spectatorship." In *Stardom: Industry of Desire*, ed. Christine Gledhill. London: Routledge, 1991, pp. 259–82.

———. "Mass Culture as Hieroglyphic Writing: Adorno, Derrida, Kracauer." *New German Critique* 56 (1992): 43–73.

Harper, J. F., and J. K. Collins. *The Adolescent Boy: An Australian Analysis.* Sydney: Cassell Australia, 1978a.

———. *The Adolescent Girl: An Australian Analysis.* Sydney, Australia: Cassell, 1978b.

Harpold, Leslie. "Courtney Love = Riot Grrl." *RiotGrrl* 1997. Web site. Accessed 12 December 1997.

Hartmann, Heidi. "The Unhappy Marriage of Marxism and Feminism: Towards a More Progressive Union." *Critical Theory: A Reader*, ed. Douglas Tallack. Hemel Hempstead, England: Harvester Wheatsheaf, 1995, pp. 183–91.

Haug, W. F. *Critique of Commodity Aesthetics: Appearances, Sexuality, and Advertising in Capitalist Society.* Trans. R. Bock. Minneapolis: University of Minnesota Press, 1986.

Heath, Stephen. *Questions of Cinema.* Bloomington: Indiana University Press, 1981.

Hebdige, Dick. *Subculture: The Meaning of Style.* London: Methuen, 1979.

———. *Hiding in the Light.* London: Routledge, 1988.

Heckerling, Amy, dir. *Clueless.* Universal. U.S., 1994.

Hegel, G. F. W. *Phenomenology of Spirit.* Trans. A. von Miller. Oxford: Oxford University Press, 1977.

Helsinger, E. K., et al. *The Woman Question: Defining Voices, 1837–1883.* Vol. 1, *The Woman Question: Society in Britain and America, 1837–1883.* 1868. Reprint, New York: Garland, 1983.

Heywood, Leslie, and Jennifer Drake. "We Learn America Like a Script: Activism in the Third Wave; or, Enough Phantoms of Nothing." In *Third Wave Agenda: Being Feminist, Doing Feminism,* ed. L. Heywood and J. Drake. Minneapolis: Minnesota University Press, 1997, pp. 40–54.

Hirsch, Marianne. *The Mother/Daughter Plot: Narrative, Psychoanalysis, Feminism.* Bloomington and Indianapolis: Indiana University Press, 1989.

Hogan, P. J., dir. *Muriel's Wedding.* House and Moorhouse Films. Australia, 1993.

Hole. "doll parts." *Live Through This.* Seattle: Geffen Records, 1994.

Hughes, John, dir. *The Breakfast Club.* AandM/Universal. U.S., 1985.

Hughes, John, dir. *Ferris Beuller's Day Off.* Paramount. U.S., 1986.

Humphreys, N. K. *American Women's Magazines: An Annotated Historical Guide.* New York and London: Garland, 1989.

Hurlock, Elizabeth. *The Psychology of Dress: An Analysis of Fashion and Its Motive.* New York: Ronald Press, 1929.

Huyssen, Andreas. *After the Great Divide: Modernism, Mass Culture, Postmodernism.* Bloomington: Indiana University Press, 1986.

Inness, Sherrie A. " 'It Is Pluck, But—Is It Sense?': Athletic Student Culture in Progressive-Era Girls' College Fiction." In *The Girl's Own: Cultural Histories of the Anglo-American Girl, 1830–1915,* ed. Claudia Nelson and Lynne Vallone. Athens: University of Georgia Press, 1994, pp. 216–42.

Irigaray, Luce. *An Ethics of Sexual Difference.* Trans. C. Burke and G. C. Gill. Ithaca, N.Y.: Cornell University Press, 1984.

——. *Speculum of the Other Woman.* Trans. G. C. Gill. Ithaca, N.Y.: Cornell University Press, 1985a.

——. *This Sex Which Is Not One.* Trans. C. Porter and C. Burke. Ithaca, N.Y.: Cornell University Press, 1985b.

——. "How to Define Sexuate Rights?" In *The Irigaray Reader,* ed. M. Whitford. Oxford: Basil Blackwell, 1991a, pp. 204–12.

——. "The Bodily Encounter with the Mother." Trans. D. Macey. In *The Irigaray Reader,* ed. Margaret Whitford. Oxford: Basil Blackwell, 1991b: 34–46.

——. *Sexes and Genealogies.* Trans. G. C. Gill. New York: University of Columbia Press, 1993.

Iwabuchi, Koichi. "Marketing 'Japan': Japanese Cultural Presence Under a Global Gaze." *Japanese Studies* 18, no. 2 (1998a): 165–80.

———. "Pure Impurity: Japan's Genius for Hybridity." *Communal/Plural* 6, no. 1 (1998b): 71–85.

Jardine, Alice A. *Gynesis: Configurations of Woman and Modernity.* Ithaca, N.Y.: Cornell University Press, 1985.

"Jodie Foster." Reprinted in *Brother/Sister* (May 1993).

Johnson, Lesley. *The Modern Girl: Girlhood and Growing Up.* Sydney, Australia: Allen and Unwin, 1993.

Jones, Ernest. "The Early Development of Female Sexuality." *International Journal of Psycho-Analysis* 8 (1927): 459–72.

Joseph, Gerhard. "The *Antigone* as Cultural Touchstone: Matthew Arnold, Hegel, George Eliot, Virginia Woolf, and Margaret Drabble." *PMLA* 96, no. 1 (1981): 22–35.

"Judge Ben Lindsay Calls upon Colleen Moore and Tells her the Flapper Type of Motion Picture Is Doing a Lot Towards Teaching America that Sex Isn't a Sin." *Photoplay,* November 1927, 29, 40.

Jung, Carl G. "The Theory of Psychoanalysis." In *Freud and Psychoanalysis.* Trans. R. F. C. Hull. In *The Collected Works of C. G. Jung.* Vol. 4, ed. H. Read et al. London: Routledge and Kegan Paul, 1970, pp. 83–228.

———. "The Love Problem of a Student." Trans. R. F. C. Hull. In *Aspects of the Feminine: From the Collected Works of C. G. Jung.* Princeton: Princeton University Press, 1982a: 27–40.

———. "The Psychological Aspects of the Kore." Trans. R. F. C. Hull. In *Aspects of the Feminine: From the Collected Works of C. G. Jung.* Princeton: Princeton University Press, 1982b: 143–64.

Kahn, Coppelia. "Coming of Age in Verona." In *The Woman's Part: Feminist Criticism of Shakespeare,* ed. C. Lenz et al. Urbana: University of Illinois Press, 1980.

Kazan, Elia, dir. *On the Waterfront.* Columbia. U.S., 1954.

Kearney, Mary Celeste. "The Missing Links: Riot grrrl—Feminism—Lesbian Culture." In *Sexing the Groove: Popular Music and Gender,* ed. S. Whitely. London: Routledge, 1997.

Kenway, Jane. *Critical Visions: Policy and Curriculum Rewriting the Future of Education, Gender and Work.* Canberra, Australia: Department of Employment, Education, and Training, 1995.

Kierkegaard, Soren. *Either/Or: Part 1.* Princeton: Princeton University Press, 1987.

Kile, Crystal. *The PopTart Home Page.* 1998. Web site. Available: <http://ernie.bgsu.edu/~ckile/ckile.html>. 16 November 1998.

Kimura, Shisaka. Interview with Catherine Driscoll. Tokyo, Japan, 24 February 2000.

Kimura, Audrey (Shisaka). *Sister Records and Benten On-Line.* 1999. Web site. Available: http://www.sister.co.jp/english/index.html. 2 February 1999.

Kleiser, Randal, dir. *Grease.* Paramount/Robert Stigwood, Allan Carr. U.S., 1978.

Koffman, Sarah. "Rousseau's Phallocratic Ends." Trans. M. Dukats. In *Revaluing French Feminism: Critical Essays on Difference, Agency, and Culture,* ed. N. Fraser and S. Bartky. Bloomington: Indiana University Press, 1992, pp. 45–56.

Kracauer, Siegfried. "Cult of Distraction: On Berlin's Picture Palaces." Trans. T. Y. Levin. *New German Critique* 40 (1987): 91–96.

Kristeva, Julia. *Powers of Horror: An Essay on Abjection.* Trans. L. S. Roudiez. New York: Columbia University Press, 1982.

——. *Revolution in Poetic Language.* Trans. M. Walter. New York: Columbia University Press, 1984.

——. "About Chinese Women." Trans. Sean Hand. In *The Kristeva Reader,* ed. T. Moi. Oxford: Basil Blackwell, 1986a: 139–59.

——. "Stabat Mater." Trans. Leon S. Roudiez. In *The Kristeva Reader,* ed. T. Moi. Oxford: Basil Blackwell, 1986b: 161–86.

——. "Women's Time." Trans. A. Jardine and H. Blake. In *The Kristeva Reader,* ed. T. Moi. Oxford: Basil Blackwell, 1986c: 188–213.

Kruse, Holly. "Subcultural Identity in Alternative Music Culture." *Popular Music* 12, no. 1 (1993): 29–41.

Kubrick, Stanley, dir. *A Clockwork Orange.* Warner/Polaris. U.K., 1971.

Kumble, Roger, dir. *Cruel Intentions.* Columbia TriStar. U.S., 1999.

Lacan, Jacques. "Desire and the Interpretation of Desire in *Hamlet.*" *Yale French Studies* 55/56 (1977a): 11–52.

——. *Ecrits: A Selection.* Trans. A. Sheridan. London: Tavistock, 1977b.

——. "God and the *Jouissance* of The Woman." In *Feminine Sexuality: Jacques Lacan and the Ecole Freudienne,* ed. J. Rose and J. Mitchell. London: Macmillan, 1982a, pp. 137–48.

——. "Intervention on Transference." In *Feminine Sexuality: Jacques Lacan and the Ecole Freudienne,* ed. J. Rose and J. Mitchell. London: Macmillan 1982b, pp. 61–73.

Laclau, Ernesto, and Chantal Mouffe. "From Hegemony and Socialist Strategy." In *Critical Theory: A Reader,* ed. Douglas Tallack. Hemel Hempstead, England: Harvester Wheatsheaf, 1995, pp. 340–53.

Lamm, Naomi. "It's a Big Fat Revolution." In *Listen Up: Voices from the Next Feminist Generation,* ed. Barbara Findlen. Seattle, Wash.: Seal Press, 1995, pp. 85–94.

Landers, O. R. *The Modern Hand Book for Girls.* New York: Garden City Publishing, 1933.

Lange, Lynda. "Women and Rousseau's Democratic Theory: Philosophical Mon-
sters and Authoritarian Equality." In *Modern Engendering: Critical Feminist
Readings in Modern Western Philosophy,* ed. Bat-Ami Bar On. Albany: State
University of New York Press, 1994, pp. 95–116.

Leavis, F. R. *Mass Civilisation and Minority Culture.* Philadelphia: R. West, 1930.

Leavis, F. R., and Denys Thompson. *Culture and Environment: The Training of
Critical Awareness.* 1933. Reprint, London: Chatto and Windus, 1964.

Leblanc, Lauraine. *Pretty in Punk: Girls' Gender Resistance in a Boys' Subculture.*
New Brunswick, N.J.: Rutgers University Press, 1999.

Lees, Sue. *Losing Out.* London: Hutchinson, 1986.

Leonard, Marion. " 'Rebel Girl, You Are the Queen of My World': Feminism,
'Subculture,' and grrrl power." In *Sexing the Groove: Popular Music and Gender,*
ed. S. Whitely. London: Routledge, 1997.

Lester, Richard, dir. *A Hard Day's Night.* UA/Proscenium. U.K., 1964.

Leys, Ruth. "The Real Miss Beauchamp: Gender and the Subject of Imitation."
In *Feminists Theorize the Political,* ed. J. Butler and J. W. Scott. New York:
Routledge, 1992, pp. 167–214.

Linton, Eliza Lyn. "The Girl of the Period." In *The Woman Question: Defining
Voices, 1837–1883,* ed. E. K.Helsinger et al. Vol. 1, *The Woman Question: Society
in Britain and America, 1837–1883.* 1868. Reprint, New York: Garland, 1983,
pp. 109–25.

Llewellyn-Jones, Derek, and Suzanne Abraham. *Everygirl.* Oxford: Oxford University Press, 1987.

Lovell, Terry, ed. *Feminist Cultural Studies.* 2 vols. London: E. Elgar, 1995.

Lovibond, Sabina. "Maternalist Ethics: A Feminist Assessment." *South Atlantic
Quarterly* 93, no. 4 (special issue, *Materialist Feminism*) (fall 1994): 779–802.

Luhrmann, Baz, dir. *William Shakespeare's Romeo + Juliet.* Twentieth-Century
Fox. U.S., 1994.

Lumby, Catharine. *Bad Girls: The Media, Sex and Feminism in the 90s.* Sydney,
Australia: Allen and Unwin, 1997.

Lund, Christian. *Anthony Burgess About A Clockwork Orange.* 1999. We site.
Available: http://www.geocities.com/Athens/Forum/3111/aco_ab.htm. Accessed
12 August 1999.

Lymn, Jessie. "The Ideal Menstruating Girl: Normalisation and the Menstrual
Taboo." Honours thesis, University of Adelaide, Australia, 1999.

Lynd, R. S., and Lynd, H. M. *Middletown: A Study in American Culture*. New York: Harcourt, Brace, 1929.

Lyons, Bridget Gellert. "The Iconography of Ophelia." *ELH* 44, no. 1 (spring 1977): 60–74.

Mackie, Vera. "Japayuki Cinderella Girl: Containing the Immigrant Other." *Japanese Studies* 18, no. 1 (May 1998): 45–64.

Malinowski, Bronislaw. *The Sexual Life of Savages*. London: Routledge, 1929.

Marchant, J. R. V., and J. F. Charles, eds. *Cassell's Latin Dictionary, Latin-English and English-Latin*. 28th. ed. London: Cassell, 1957.

Marcus, Stephen. "Freud and Dora: Story, History, Case History." In *In Dora's Case*, ed. C. Kahane and C. Bernheimer. London: Virago, 1985, pp. 56–92.

Martin, Adrian. "Teen Movies: The Forgetting of Wisdom." In *Phantasms*. Ringwood, Australia: McPhee Gribble, 1994.

Marx, Karl. *Economic and Philosophic Manuscripts of 1844*. Trans. Martin Milligan, ed. Dirk J. Struik. New York: International Publishers, 1964.

Mason, Bobbie-Ann. *The Girl Sleuth: A Feminist Guide*. New York: The Feminist Press, 1975.

Masson, Jeffrey. *The Assault on Truth: Freud and Child Sexual Assault*. London: Fontana, 1992.

Matthews, Jill Julius. "Building the Body Beautiful." *Australian Feminist Studies* 5 (1987): 17–34.

——. "Dancing Modernity." In *Transitions: New Australian Feminisms*, ed. B. Creed. St. Leonards, Australia: Allen and Unwin, 1995.

Mavor, Carol. "Dream-Rushes: Lewis Carroll's Photographs of the Little Girl." In *The Girl's Own: Cultural Histories of the Anglo-American Girl, 1830–1915*, ed. C. Nelson and L. Vallone. Athens: University of Georgia Press, 1994, pp. 156–93.

McCormick, R. W. "From *Caligari* to Dietrich: Sexual, Social, and Cinematic Discourses in Weimar Film." *Signs: Journal on Women in Culture and Society* 18, no. 3 (1993): 640–68.

McGrath, Douglas, dir. *Emma*. Miramax. U.S., 1998.

McRobbie, Angela. *Feminism and Youth Culture: From "Jackie" to "Just Seventeen"*. London: Unwin Hyman, 1991.

——. "Post-Marxism and Cultural Studies." In *Cultural Studies*, ed. L. Grossberg, C. Nelson, and P. Triechler. New York: Routledge, 1992, pp. 730.

——. "*More!*: New Sexualities in Girls' and Women's Magazines." In *Back to Reality?: Social Experience and Cultural Studies*, ed. A. McRobbie. Birmingham, England: Birmingham University Press, 1997, pp. 190–209.

McRobbie, Angela, and Jenny Garber. "Girls and Subcultures." In *Feminism and Youth Culture: From "Jackie" to "Just Seventeen"*, ed. A. McRobbie. 1975. Reprint, Boston: Unwin Hyman, 1991, pp. 1–33.

McRobbie, Angela, and Trisha McCabe, eds. *Feminism for Girls: An Adventure Story.* London: Routledge and Kegan Paul, 1981.

McRobbie, Angela, and Mica Nava, eds. *Gender and Generation.* London: Macmillan Education, 1984.

Mead, Margaret. "Sex And Temperament." In *From the South Seas.* New York: William Morrow, 1939.

———. *Coming of Age in Samoa: a Study of Adolescence and Sex in Primitive Societies.* 1928. Reprint, Harmondsworth, England: Penguin, 1963.

———. *Male and Female.* 1950. Reprint, New York: William Morrow and Company, 1967.

———. *Growing Up in New Guinea.* 1930. Reprint, Harmondsworth, England: Penguin, 1975.

Mitchell, Juliet, and Jacqueline Rose, eds. *Feminine Sexuality: Jacques Lacan and the École Freudienne.* London: Macmillan, 1982.

Mitchell, Sally. "Girl's Culture: At Work." In *The Girl's Own: Cultural Histories of the Anglo-American Girl, 1830–1915*, ed. Claudia Nelson and Lynne Vallone. Athens: University of Georgia Press, 1994, pp. 243–58.

———. *The New Girl: Girls' Culture in England 1880–1915.* New York: Columbia University Press, 1995.

Modleski, Tania. *Loving with a Vengeance: Mass-produced Fantasies for Women.* New York: Methuen, 1982.

———. *Feminism Without Women: Culture and Criticism in a Postfeminist Age.* New York: Routledge, 1991.

Moi, Toril. "Psychoanalysis, Feminism, and Politics: A Conversation with Juliet Mitchell." *South Atlantic Quarterly* 93, no. 4 (special issue, *Materialist Feminism)* (fall 1994): 925–50.

Morris, Meaghan. "Banality in Cultural Studies." In *The Logics of Television*, ed. P. Mellancamp. Bloomington: Indiana University Press, 1990, pp. 14–43.

———. "Crazy Talk is Not Enough." *Environment And Planning D: Society And Space* 14, no. 4 (1996): 390–412.

———. "A Question of Cultural Studies." In *Back to Reality?: Social Experience and Cultural Studies*, ed. Angela McRobbie. Manchester: Manchester University Press, 1997a: 36–57.

———. " 'The Truth Is Out There' . . . " *Cultural Studies* 11, no. 3 (October 1997b): 367–76.

Moxcey, Mary. *Girlhood and Character.* New York: Abingdon Press, 1916.

Mulvey, Laura. *Visual Pleasure and Narrative Cinema.* London: Macmillan, 1989.

Nava, Mica. *Changing Cultures: Feminism, Youth and Consumerism.* London: Sage, 1992.

Nelson, Carey, Patricia Treichler, and Lawrence Grossberg. "Introduction." *Cultural Studies.* New York: Routledge, 1992.

Nelson, Claudia, and Lynne Vallone, eds. *The Girl's Own: Cultural Histories of the Anglo-American Girl, 1830–1915.* Athens: University of Georgia Press, 1994.

Nelson, Claudia, and Lynne Vallone. "Introduction." In *The Girl's Own: Cultural Histories of the Anglo-American Girl, 1830–1915.* Athens: University of Georgia Press, 1994, pp. 1–10.

"The Nicene Creed." In *The Catholic Missal: Being a Translation of the New Missile Romanum: Arranged for Daily Use,* ed. C. J. McHugh and J. A. Callan. New York: P. J. Kennedy, 1934, pp. 633–4.

Nietzsche, Friedrich. *The Gay Science: With a Prelude in Rhymes and an Appendix of Songs.* Trans. W. Kaufmann. 2d ed. New York: Random House, 1974.

Nye, Andrea. "The Hidden Host: Irigaray and Diotima at Plato's Symposium." In *Revaluing French Feminism: Critical Essays on Difference, Agency, and Culture,* ed. S. Bartky and N. Fraser. Bloomington: Indiana University Press, 1992, pp. 77–93.

Oliver, Kelly. "Antigone's Ghost: Undoing Hegel's 'Phenomenology of Spirit.' " *Hypatia* 11, no. 1 (special issue, *The Family and Feminist Theory*) (winter 1996): 67–91.

Oppel, Frances. "Irigaray's Goddesses." In *Australian Feminist Studies* 20 (summer 1994): 77–90.

Orenstein, Peggy. *School Girls: Young Women, Self-Esteem, and the Confidence Gap.* New York: Anchor, 1994.

Oswell, David. "A Question of Belonging: Television, Youth, and Youth Cultures." In *Cool Places: Geographies of Youth Culture,* ed. T. Skelton and G. Valentine. London: Routledge, 1998, pp. 35–49.

Padel, Ruth. "With God Inside." In *Images of Women in Antiquity,* ed. A. Khurt and R. A. Cameron. London: Croom Helm, 1983, pp. 2–39.

Pallotta-Chiarolli, Maria, ed. *Girls Talk: Young Women Speak Their Hearts and Minds.* Sydney, Australia: Finch, 1998.

Parker, Dorothy. "The Lovely Woman and the Honest Labouring Man." *Vogue,* 15 July 1919, 69.

Pedersen, Joyce. "Life's Lessons: Liberal Feminist Ideals of Family, School, and Community in Victorian England." In *The Girl's Own: Cultural Histories of the*

Anglo-American Girl, 1830–1915, ed. C. Nelson and L. Vallone. Athens: University of Georgia Press, 1994, pp. 194–215.

Peirce, Kate. "Socialization of Teenage Girls Through Teen-Magazine Fiction: The Making of a New Woman or an Old Lady?" *Sex Roles: A Journal of Research* 29, no. 1/2 (July 1993): 59–68.

Peterson, Kaara. "Framing Ophelia: Representation and the Pictorial Tradition." *Mosaic* 31, no. 3 (September 1998): 1–25.

Petro, Patrice. "Modernity and Mass Culture in Weimar: Contours of a Discourse on Sexuality in Early Theories of Perception and Representation." *New German Critique* 40 (winter 1987): 115–46.

Pini, Maria. "Women and the Early British Rave Scene." In *Back to Reality?: Social Experience and Cultural Studies*, ed. A. McRobbie. Manchester: Manchester University Press, 1997, pp. 152–69.

Pipher, Mary. *Reviving Ophelia: Saving the Selves of Adolescent Girls.* New York: G. P. Putnam's Sons, 1994.

Polanski, Roman, dir. *Rosemary's Baby.* Paramount/William Castle. U.S., 1968.

Prince, Morton. *The Dissociation of a Personality: A Biographical Study in Abnormal Psychology.* 2d ed. New York: Longmans, Green, 1913.

Radway, Janice. *Reading the Romance: Women, Patriarchy, and Popular Literature.* Chapel Hill: University of North Carolina Press, 1984.

——."On the Gender of the Middlebrow Consumer and the Threat of the Culturally Fraudulent Female." *South Atlantic Quarterly (Materialist Feminism)* 93, no. 4. (fall 1994): 871–94.

Raimi, Sam. dir. *The Evil Dead.* Palace/Renaissance. U.S., 1983.

Rand, Erica. *Barbie's Queer Accessories.* Durham, N.C.: Duke University Press, 1995.

Ray, Nicholas, dir. *Rebel Without A Cause.* Warner (David Weisbart). U.S., 1955.

"Report of the Consultative Committee on the Differentiation of the Curriculum for Boys and Girls Respectively in Secondary Schools." London: Board of Education, HMSO, 1923.

Rich, Adrienne. "Afterword." In *Take Back the Night: Women on Pornography*, ed. L. Lederer. New York: Bantam, 1980.

Richards, Thomas. *The Commodity Culture of Victorian England: Advertising and Spectacle, 1851–1914.* Stanford, Cal.: Stanford University Press, 1990.

Robertson, Jennifer. *Takarazuka: Sexual Politics and Popular Culture in Modern Japan.* Berkeley: University of California Press, 1998.

Roddam, Franc, dir. *Quadrophenia.* Polytel. U.K., 1979.

Roman, L. G., and L. K. Christian-Smith, eds. *Becoming-Feminine: The Politics of Popular Culture*. London: Falmer Press, 1988.

Rose, Jacqueline. "*Hamlet*: 'the Mona Lisa of literature.' " In *Sexuality in the Field of Vision*. London: Verso, 1991, pp. 123–40.

Ross, Andrew. "The Popularity of Pornography." In *The Cultural Studies Reader*, ed. S. During. London: Routledge, 1993.

Ross, Andrew. "Tribalism in Effect." In *On Fashion*, ed. S. Benstock and S. Ferriss. New Brunswick, N.J.: Rutgers University Press, 1994, pp. 284–300.

Rousseau, Jean Jacques. *Emile*. Trans. B. Foxley. London: Dent, 1911.

Rowbotham, Julia. *Girls Make Good Wives: Guidance for Girls in Victorian fiction*. Oxford: Basil Blackwell, 1989.

Rubin, Gayle. "The Traffic in Women: Notes on the 'Political Economy' of Sex." In *Literary Theory: An Anthology*, ed. J. Rivkin and M. Ryan. Malden, Mass.: Blackwell, 1998, pp. 533–60.

Rutter, Michael. *Changing Youth in a Changing Society: Patterns of Adolescent Development and Disorder*. Cambridge: Harvard University Press, 1980.

Said, Edward. *Orientalism: Western Conceptions of the Orient*. London: Penguin, 1995.

Sass, Louis A. "Introspection, Schizophrenia, and the Fragmentation of Self." *Representations* 19 (summer 1987): 1–33.

Sawicki, Jana. *Disciplining Foucault: Feminism, Power, and the Body*. New York: Routledge, 1991.

Scott, Joan Wallach. "The Evidence of Experience." *Critical Inquiry* 17 (1991): 773–97.

Searles, P., and J. Mickish. " 'A Thoroughbred Girl': Images of Female Gender Role in Turn-of-the-Century Mass Media." *Women's Studies* 10 (1984): 261–81.

Sedgwick, Eve Kosofsky. *Epistemology of the Closet*. Berkeley: University of California Press, 1990.

——. "Jane Austen and The Masturbating Girl." *Critical Inquiry* 17, no. 4 (summer 1991): 818–37.

Seem, Mark. "Introduction." In Gilles Deleuze and Felix Guattari, *Anti-Oedipus*. Vol. 1. *Capitalism and Schizophrenia*, 1977, pp. xv–xxiv.

Shah, Sonia. "Tight Jeans and Chania Chorris." In *Listen Up: Voices from the Next Feminist Generation*, ed. B. Findlen. Seattle, Wash.: Seal Press, 1995, pp. 113–9.

Shakespeare, William. *Hamlet*, ed. E. Hubler. Harmondsworth, England: Penguin, 1960.

——. *Romeo and Juliet*, ed. T. J. B. Spencer. Harmondsworth, England: Penguin, 1981.

———. *King Lear*, ed. G. K. Hunter. Harmondsworth, England: Penguin, 1987a.

———. *The Merchant of Venice*, ed. M. M. Mahood. Cambridge: Cambridge University Press, 1987b.

Shandler, Sara. *Ophelia Speaks: Adolescent Girls Write About Their Search for Self.* New York: HarperCollins, 1999.

Shiach, Morag. "Feminism and Popular Culture." In *Cultural Theory and Popular Culture: A Reader*, ed. J. Storey. Hemel Hempstead, England: Harvester Wheatsheaf, 1994, pp. 331–39.

Showalter, Elaine. *The Female Malady: Women, Madness, and English Culture, 1830–1980*. New York: Pantheon, 1985.

Shuttle, Penelope. *The Wise Wound: Menstruation and Everywoman*. London: Paladin, 1986.

Siegel, Deborah L. "Reading Between the Waves: Feminist Historiography in a 'Postfeminist' Moment." In *Third Wave Agenda: Being Feminist, Doing Feminism*, ed. L. Heywood and J. Drake. Minneapolis: Minnesota University Press, 1997, pp. 55–82.

Simons, Margaret, ed. *Feminist Interpretations of Simone de Beauvoir*. University Park: Pennsylvania State University Press, 1995.

Simpson, A. E. "Vulnerability and the Age of Female Consent: Legal Innovation and its Effect on Prosecutions for Rape in 18th Century London." In *'Tis Nature's Fault: Unauthorized Sexuality During the Enlightenment*, ed. R. P. Maccubbin. Cambridge: Cambridge University Press, 1987, pp. 181–205.

Sissa, Giulia. *Greek Virginity*. Trans. A. Goldhammer. Cambridge: Harvard University Press, 1990.

Skeggs, Beverley. "Theorising, Ethics and Representation in Feminist Ethnography." In *Feminist Cultural Theory*, ed. B. Skeggs. Manchester: Manchester University Press, 1995, pp. 190–206.

Skelton, Tracey, and Gill Valentine, eds. *Cool Places: Geographies of Youth Cultures*. London: Routledge, 1998.

Smith, Lindsay. " 'Take Back Your Mink': Lewis Carroll, Child Masquerade, and the Age of Consent." *Art History* 16, no. 3 (September 1993): 369–85.

"A Society for the Protection of Cruelty to Mothers." *Girl's Own Paper*, 12 October 1889, 19–20.

Sophocles. *Antigone*. Trans. A. Brown. Warminster: Aris and Phillips, 1987.

Sorisio, Carolyn. "A Tale of Two Feminisms: Power and Victimization in Contemporary Feminist Debate." In *Third Wave Agenda: Being Feminist, Doing Feminism*, ed. L. Heywood and J. Drake. Minneapolis: Minnesota University Press, 1997, pp. 134–49.

Spacks, Patricia Meyer. *The Adolescent Idea: Myths of Youth and the Adult Imagination.* New York: Basic Books, 1981.

Spice Girls. "Wannabe." *SPICE.* London: Virgin Records, 1995.

Spivak, Gayatri C. "Displacement and the Discourse of Woman." In *Displacement and After,* ed. M. Krupnik. Bloomington: Indiana University Press, 1983, pp. 169–95.

Stacey, Judith. "Can There be a Feminist Ethnography?" *Women's Studies International Forum* 17, no. 4 (July/August 1994): 417–20.

Stack, Peter. "Avenue Of Escape: Holy Matrimony! Australian director P.J. Hogan's Muriel's Wedding." *San Francisco Chronicle,* 12 March 1995, 39.

Stern, Lesley. "Emma in Los Angeles: *Clueless* as a Remake of the Book and the City." *Australian Humanities Review* (1997). Web site. Available: http://www.lib.latrobe.edu.au/AHR/archive/Issue-August-1997/stern.html. Accessed 12 January 2000.

Stone, Lawrence. *The Family, Sex and Marriage: In England 1500–1800.* London: Penguin, 1979.

Stuart, Dorothy Margaret. *The Girl Through the Ages.* Philadelphia: J. B. Lipincott, 1933.

Tait, Gordon. "Re-assessing Street Kids: A Critique of Subculture Theory." In *Youth Subcultures: Theory, History, and the Australian Experience,* ed. R. White. Hobart, Australia: National Clearinghouse for Youth Studies, 1993, pp. 1–6.

Talalay, Rachel, dir. *Tank Girl.* MGM. U.S., 1995.

Taylor, Sandra. "Sub-versions: Feminist Perspectives on Youth Subcultures." In *Youth Subcultures: Theory, History, and the Australian Experience,* ed. R. White. Hobart, Australia: National Clearinghouse for Youth Studies, 1993, pp. 19–26.

Television, Spelling, prod. *Charmed.* Fox. U.S., 1999–2000.

Thalberg, Irving. "The Modern Photoplay." In *Film and Society,* ed. R. D. MacCann. New York: Scribners, 1964, pp. 44–46.

Thomas, Helen, ed. *Dance, Gender, and Culture.* New York: St. Martin's Press, 1993.

Thorn, Matt. *The Shoujo Manga Homepage: Japanese Girls' and Women's Comics.* 1996. Web site. Available: http://www.ky.xaxon.ne.jp/~matt/index.html. Accessed 12 February 2000.

Thornton, Sarah. *Club Cultures: Music, Media and Subcultural Capital.* Oxford: Polity Press, 1995.

——. "Introduction." In *The Subcultures Reader,* ed. S. Thornton and K. Gelder. London: Routledge, 1997.

Tolman, Deborah. "Doing Desire: Adolescent Girls": Struggles for/with Sexuality." *Gender and Society* 8, no. 3 (September 1994): 324–42.

Tolson, Andrew. "Social Surveillance and Subjectification: The Emergence of 'Subculture' in the Work of Henry Mayhew." *Cultural Studies* 4, no. 2 (May 1990): 113–27.

Treat, John W. "Yoshimoto Banana Writes Home." In *Contemporary Japan and Popular Culture*. Surrey, England: Curzon, 1996, pp. 275–308.

Vail, Tobi. "The First Two Albums: Liner Notes." Bikini Kill, in *The First Two Albums*. Olympia, Wash.: Kill Rock Stars. 1996.

Valentine, Gill, Tracey Skelton, and Deborah Chambers. "Introduction." In *Cool Places: Geographies of Youth Cultures*, ed. T. Skelton and G. Valentine. London: Routledge, 1998.

Vallone, Lynne. *Disciplines of Virtue: Girls' Culture in the Eighteenth and Nineteenth Centuries*. New Haven: Yale University Press, 1995.

Vandereycken, W., and R. van Deth. *From Fasting Saints to Anorexic Girls: The History of Self-Starvation*. New York: Athlone/New York University Press, 1994.

Van Wyck, Carolyn. "Hollywood Beauty Shop: Conducted by Carolyn Van Wyck." *Photoplay*, April 1932, 182–3.

VNS Matrix. *Theme Park*. 1997. Web site. Available: http://sysx.apana.org.au/artists/vns/themepark.html. 12 December 1997.

Walker, Rebecca, ed. *To Be Real: Telling the Truth and Changing the Face of Feminism*. New York: Anchor, 1995.

Walkowitz, Judith. *City of Dreadful Delight: Narratives of Sexual Danger in Late Victorian London*. London: Virago, 1993.

Walsh, Lisa. "Her Mother Her Self: The Ethics of the Antigone Family Romance." *Hypatia* 14, no. 3 (summer 1999): 96–126.

Warner, Marina. *Alone of All Her Sex: The Myth and the Cult of the Virgin Mary*. London: Picador, 1976.

——. *Joan of Arc: The Image of Female Heroism*. London: Vintage, 1988.

Watts, Rob. "Doing Ethnography with Young People: How and Why?" In *Youth Subcultures: Theory, History and the Australian Experience*, ed. R. White. Hobart, Australia: National Clearinghouse for Youth Studies, 1993, pp. 54–60.

Welsh, Irvine. *Trainspotting*. London: Minerva, 1996.

Whedon, Joss. *Buffy the Vampire Slayer*. Warner Bros. U.S., 1997–2000.

White, Cynthia L. *Women's Magazines from 1693–1965*. London: Michael Joseph, 1970.

White, Hayden. *The Content of the Form: Narrative Discourse and Historical Representation*. Baltimore, Md.: Johns Hopkins University Press, 1987.

Williams, Raymond. "Base and Superstructure in Marxist Critical Theory." In *Debating Texts*, ed. R. Rylance. London: Open University Press, 1987, pp. 214–16.

——. "The Analysis of Culture." In *Popular Culture and Cultural Theory: A Reader*, ed. J. Storey. Hemel Hempstead, England: Harvester Wheatsheaf, 1994, pp. 56–64.

Willis, Paul. *Learning to Labour: How Working Class Kids Get Working Class Jobs*. Hampshire, England: Gower, 1980.

Winter, Metta. "Teenage Girls in Jeopardy." *Human Ecology Forum* 25 no. 3 (1997): 12–7.

Wise, Robert, and Jerome Robbins, dirs. *West Side Story*. Producers (UA) Mirisch/Seven Arts. U.S., 1961.

Wolf, Naomi. *The Beauty Myth: How Images of Beauty Are Used Against Women*. London: Vintage, 1991.

——. *Promiscuities: A Secret History of Female Desire*. London: Chatto and Windus, 1997.

Wyatt, Justin. *High Concept*. Austin: University of Texas Press, 1994.

Zefirelli, Franco, dir. *Romeo and Juliet*. Paramount. U.S., 1968.

Žižek, Slavoj. *The Sublime Object of Ideology*. London: Verso, 1989.

——. "Postscript." In *A Critical Sense: Interviews with Intellectuals*, ed. P. Osborne. New York: Routledge, 1996, pp. 36–44.

——. "When Straight Means Weird and Psychosis is Normal." *Brittanica On-Line 2000*. Web site. Britannica.com. Available: <http://www.britannica.com/bcom/original/article/0,5744,5602,00.html>. Accessed 21 April 2000.

Index